Anonymous

A Grammar of the Arabic Language

Anonymous

A Grammar of the Arabic Language

ISBN/EAN: 9783744785617

Printed in Europe, USA, Canada, Australia, Japan

Cover: Foto ©Paul-Georg Meister /pixelio.de

More available books at **www.hansebooks.com**

A GRAMMAR OF THE ARABIC LANGUAGE, TRANSLATED FROM THE...

A GRAMMAR OF THE ARABIC LANGUAGE

BY

WILLIAM WRIGHT.

A GRAMMAR

OF THE

ARABIC LANGUAGE,

TRANSLATED

FROM THE GERMAN OF CASPARI,

AND EDITED,

WITH NUMEROUS ADDITIONS AND CORRECTIONS,

BY

WILLIAM WRIGHT,
Assistant in the Ms. Department, British Museum.

WILLIAMS AND NORGATE:
14, HENRIETTA STREET, COVENT GARDEN, LONDON;
AND
20, SOUTH FREDERICK STREET, EDINBURGH.
1862.

PRINTED BY FR. NIES (CARL B. LORCK), LEIPZIG.

TO

THE REV. ROBERT GWYNNE,

Assistant Curate of St. Thomas', Charterhouse, London,

THIS WORK IS DEDICATED

AS A SMALL MARK

OF THE EDITOR'S RESPECT, ESTEEM, AND AFFECTION,

...

A Gentleman, a Scholar, and a Friend.

PREFACE.

In editing this grammar, I feel conscious of having filled up a gap in the philological literature of England. The older works of Richardson (1st ed. Lond. 1786, 2nd ed. Lond. 1801) and Price (Lond. 1823) are almost worthless; that of Stewart (Lond. 1841) not much better; for, though the author had the advantage of the previous labours of De Sacy and Ewald, he does not appear to have been thoroughly qualified for the task that he undertook. Lumsden's unfinished work (Calcutta, 1813) is a magnificent one, but based entirely on the system of the Arab grammarians, a circumstance which renders it ill-adapted, apart from its bulk and rarity, for the use of the beginner. As for the smaller grammars of Fáris el-Shidiac (Lond. 1856), the Rev. Herman Philip (Edinb. 1855), and the Rev. W. J. Beamont (Lond. 1861), as well as the "Reading Lessons" published by the Messrs. Bagster, they are intended to facilitate the study of the modern spoken dialects, rather than that of the older literary language; and are better suited for the use of the traveller and the tourist, than of the student who desires to become conversant with the Arabic literature.

Such, however, is the general neglect of almost every branch of Oriental study in England at the present day, that this state of matters is not surprising. The nations of the Continent — even those whose cônnection with the East is small or absolutely none — are better off. France can point to De Sacy (whose immortal work has been the basis of all subsequent grammars) and to Bresnier; Germany to Ewald, Schier, and Caspari; Holland to Roorda. It is inconvenient, however, for a teacher to use a book written in a foreign language, particularly if that language be German, which is, I regret to say, as yet but little cultivated in our Universities; and it is this circumstance which has mainly induced me to undertake the present work.

As the basis of this Grammar, I have selected that of Professor Caspari of Christiania, the first edition of which (in Latin) appeared at Leipzig in 1848, and the second (in German) in 1859 This is, in my opinion, the best of the smaller Arabic grammars that have been published during the last twenty years, and forms a good introduction to the study of the larger works of De Sacy and Ewald, or of the native grammarians. The second (German) edition is, however, strange to say, not so accurate in many points as the first (Latin) one; whilst both admit of many improvements. The present work is not, therefore, a mere translation of Caspari's, but an enlarged and, as I trust, improved edition of it. Those who take the trouble of examining the two, will find, I think, that a great many sections have been altered for the better, either by giving them greater precision of expression, or by adding more and preferable examples. As instances, I may refer, in the first volume, to those sections that treat of the verba med. rad. و et ى (§§. 149—163), of the relative adjectives (§§. 251—267), the diminutives (§§. 269—284), and the broken plurals (§§. 304—5); and, in the second volume, to those that treat of the interjections (§. 38), and of كُلّ and similar words (§§. 82—85). Besides the entire fourth part (§§. 191—252), I have also added, here and there, sections of some importance, e. g. vol. I. §. 285 to §. 288, vol. II. §§. 184—186; and omitted others that I thought superfluous, such as vol. I. §§. 93—102 of the original. The grammars of De Sacy and Ewald, and the 'Alfiyya of 'Ibn Mâlik (ed. Dieterici, Leipzig, 1851), have, I need scarcely say, been always at my side.

A feature peculiar to this edition are the notes that touch upon the comparative grammar of the Shemitic languages, a subject little understood in this country, yet highly interesting to the student of Hebrew as well as of Arabic. Our deficiency in Hebrew scholarship is, in fact, to be traced in a great measure to our almost total neglect of the study of the cognate languages, Arabic, Aramaic, and Aethiopic. Many of us take the Hebrew Bible in one hand, and our Authorized Version in the other; read the former by the light of the latter; and call ourselves Hebraists. There is, however, no such royal road to a thorough knowledge of the Old Testament Scriptures. Hebrew is in itself a difficult language, especially to those who commence it fresh from the study of Greek and Latin; whilst the Biblical texts are few in number, and in many passages very obscure, not to say corrupt. In short, we have need of every ray of light that we can concentrate upon them. Manuscripts must be collated, ancient versions compared, and, above all, the cognate languages studied, so that we may become familiarised with the modes of thought and forms of expression of the Shemitic nations. The so-called Shemitic languages — Arabic, Aethiopic,

Hebrew, Phoenician, and Aramaic (Chaldee and Syriac) — are as closely connected with one another as the Romance languages — Italian, Spanish, Portuguese, Provençal, and French; they are all daughters of a deceased mother, standing to them in the relation of Latin to the other European languages just specified. The Hebrew, perhaps, resembles this parent tongue most in some points; but, on the whole, the Arabic (and next to it, the Aethiopic) has preserved the greatest degree of likeness to the primitive Shemitic speech. The Hebrew, even of the Pentateuch, has already attained pretty nearly the same degree of grammatical development (or decay) as the spoken Arabic of the present day. Of that the comparative notes interspersed throughout this grammar give ample proof.

In conclusion, I have to express my gratitude to the Provost and Senior Fellows of Trinity College, Dublin, for their very liberal contribution towards paying the expenses of printing this work; and to thank my friend and former pupil, the Rev. R. Gwynne, to whom I have the pleasure of dedicating it, for the assistance he has so kindly afforded me, not only by reading it over in manuscript and suggesting many useful alterations, but also by correcting a proof of every sheet, and thereby contributing greatly to its typographical accuracy,

LONDON.
March 1862.

Wm. Wright.

CONTENTS.

VOL. I.

Part I. Orthography and Orthoepy.

	Page.
I. THE LETTERS AS CONSONANTS	1
II. THE VOWELS AND DIPHTHONGS	6
III. OTHER ORTHOGRAPHIC SIGNS	11
1. Gézma or Sukūn	11
2. Tésdid or Sidda	12
3. Hémza or Nèbra	14
4. Wasla	16
5. Médda or Matta	22
IV. THE SYLLABLE	24
V. THE ACCENT	25
VI. THE NUMBERS	25

Part II. Etymology or the Parts of Speech.

I. THE VERB	27
A. General View.	
1. The Forms of the Triliteral Verb	27
The First Form	28
The Second Form	29
The Third Form	31

CONTENTS.

		Page
The Fourth Form		32
The Fifth Form		34
The Sixth Form		36
The Seventh Form		37
The Eighth Form		38
The Ninth and Eleventh Forms		39
The Tenth Form		40
The Twelfth, Thirteenth, Fourteenth and Fifteenth Forms		42
2. The Quadriliteral Verb and its Forms		43
3. The Voices		45
4. The States (Tenses) of the Verb		46
5. The Moods		46
6. The Numbers, Persons and Genders		47

B. The Strong Verb.

1. The Active Voice of the First Form 48
   a. The Inflexion by Persons 48
      The Separate Pronouns 49
      The Suffixed Pronouns, expressing the Nominative . . 50
      The Prefixed Pronouns 50
   b. Forms of the Tenses and Moods 56
      The Imperfect Indicative 56
      The Subjunctive and Jussive 58
      The Energetic 59
      The Imperative 60
2. The Passive Voice of the First Form 60
3. The Derived Forms of the Strong Verb 61
4. The Quadriliteral Verb 65
5. Verbs of which the Second and Third Radicals are Identical . 65

C. The Weak Verb.

1. Verba Hêmzata 69
2. Verbs which are more especially called Weak Verbs . . . 74
   Verba Primae Radicalis و et ى 74
   Verba Mediae Radicalis و et ى 78
   Verba Tertiae Radicalis و et ى 85

3. Verbs that are doubly and trebly weak	91
Doubly Weak Verbs	91
Trebly Weak Verbs	95

APPENDIX A.

1. The Verb لَيْسَ	96
2. The Verbs of Praise and Blame	97
3. The Forms expressive of Wonder	98

APPENDIX B.

The Verbal Suffixes, which express the Accusative	99

II. THE NOUN 106

A. The Nouns Substantive and Adjective.

1. The Derivation of Nouns Subst. & Adj., & their different Forms	106
a. The Deverbal Nouns.	
The Nomina Verbi	109
The Nomina Vicis	117
The Nomina Speciei	118
The Nomina Loci et Temporis	118
The Nomina Instrumenti	122
The Nomina Agentis et Patientis and other Verbal Adject.	123
b. The Denominative Nouns.	
The Nomina Unitatis	133
The Nomina Abundantiae vel Multitudinis	133
The Nomina Vasis	134
The Nomina Relativa or Relative Adjectives	134
Changes of the Auxiliary Consonants	135
Changes of the Final Radicals و and ى	139
Changes in the Vocalisation	141
The Abstract Nouns of Quality	145
The Diminutive	146
Some other Nominal Forms	152
2. The Gender of Nouns	153
Formation of the Feminine of Adjectives	157
Forms that are of both Genders	158
3. The Numbers of Nouns	160
The Dual	160

CONTENTS.

	Page.
The Pluralis Sanus	161
The Pluralis Fractus	166
4. The Declension of Nouns	190
The Declension of Undefined Nouns	190
The Declension of Defined Nouns	201
5. Appendix.	
The Pronominal Suffixes that denote the Genitive	205

B. The Numerals.
1. The Cardinal Numbers	206
2. The Ordinal Numbers	211
3. The remaining Classes of Numerals	212

C. The Nomina Demonstrativa and Conjunctiva.
1. The Demonstrative Pronouns and the Article	215
2. The Conjunctive (Relative) and Interrogative Pronouns	219
The Conjunctive Pronouns	219
The Interrogative Pronouns	222

III. THE PARTICLES ... 224

A. The Prepositions.
1. The Inseparable Prepositions	224
2. The Separable Prepositions	225

B. The Adverbs.
1. The Inseparable Adverbial Particles	227
2. The Separable Adverbial Particles	227
3. Adverbial Accusatives	230

C. The Conjunctions.
1. The Inseparable Conjunctions	231
2. The Separable Conjunctions	232

D. The Interjections ... 234

IV. APPENDIX:
Paradigms of the Verbs	238

VOL. II.

Part III. Syntax.

I. THE SEVERAL COMPONENT PARTS OF A SENTENCE.

A. The Verb.

	Page.
1. The States or Tenses	1
The Perfect	1
The Imperfect Indicative	11
The Imperfect Subjunctive	16
The Imperfect Jussive	16
The Imperfect Energetic	17
2. The Moods	18
The Subjunctive	19
The Jussive	24
The Energetic of the Imperfect	27
The Imperative and its Energetic	28
3. The Government of the Verb	29
a. The Accusative	30
The Objective Complement	30
The Adverbial Complement	71
b. The Prepositions	81
The Simple Prepositions	81
The Compound Prepositions	125

B. The Noun.

1. The Nomina Verbi, Agentis and Patientis	128
2. The Government of the Noun. The Status Constructus & the Genit.	133
3. The Numerals	161

II. THE SENTENCE AND ITS PARTS.

A. The Sentence in General.

1. The Parts of the Sentence: the Subject, the Predicate, and their Complements	176
2. Concord in Gender & Number between the Parts of a Sentence	205

B. The Different Kinds of Sentences.

Page.
1. Negative and Prohibitive Sentences 214
2. Interrogative Sentences ; 220
3. Relative Sentences 228
4. Copulative Sentences 235
5. Adversative, Restrictive and Exceptive Sentences 242
6. Conditional and Hypothetical Sentences 247

Part IV. Prosody.

I. THE FORM OF ARABIC POETRY.
   1. The Rhyme 250
   2. The Metres 258

II. THE FORMS OF WORDS IN PAUSE AND IN RHYME 270

III. POETIC LICENSES 274

PART THIRD.
Syntax.

I. The Several Component Parts of a Sentence.

A. The Verb.

1. The States or Tenses.

1. The *Perfect*, ٱلْمَاضِى (Vol. I. §. 77—9), indicates:

a) An act completed at some past time (the historic tense, the Greek aorist, German imperfect, and English past); as: ثُمَّ جَآءَ زَيْدٌ, *then came Zeid*; جَلَسُوا عَلَى ٱلْبَابِ, *they sat down at the door*.

b) An act which, at the moment of speaking, has been already completed and remains in a state of completion (the Greek, German and English perfect); as: ٱذْكُرُوا نِعْمَتِىَ ٱلَّتِى أَنْعَمْتُ عَلَيْكُمْ, *be mindful of my favours, which I have conferred upon you*.

c) A past act, of which it can be said that it often took place or still takes place — a use of the perfect which is common in proverbial expressions, and which the Greek aorist also has; as: رَوَتِ ٱلرُّوَاةُ, *historians say (have handed it down by oral tradition from one to another)*; ٱتَّفَقَ ٱلْمُفَسِّرُونَ, *commentators are agreed (have agreed and still agree)*.

d) An act which is just completed at the moment, and by the very act, of speaking; as: أَنْشَدْتُكَ ٱللّٰهَ, *I conjure you by God;* بِعْتُكَ هٰذَا, *I sell you this.*

Rem. On the similar uses of the perfect in Hebrew, see Gesenius' Gr. §. 124, 1 and 3.

e) An act, the occurrence of which is so certain, that it may be described as having already taken place. This use prevails in promises, treaties, bargains, &c., and after the particle لَا, *not*, especially in oaths or asseverations; as: تَأْعْطِنَا ٱلْأَمَانَ عَلَى خَلَّتَيْنِ إِمَّا أَنَّكَ قَبِلْتَ مَا أَتَيْنَاكَ بِهِ وَإِمَّا سَتَرْتَ وَأَمْسَكْتَ عَنْ أَذَانَا حَتَّى نَخْرُجَ مِنْ بِلَادِكَ, *grant us, therefore, quarter on one of two conditions, either that you will accept* (lit. *have accepted*) *what we have proposed to you, or that you will keep it secret and refrain* (lit. *have kept it secret and refrained*) *from doing us any injury, till we get out of your country;* وَٱللّٰهِ لَا أَقَمْتُ بِمَكَّةَ, *by God, I shall certainly not remain in Mekka;* آلَيْتُ لَا خَامَرَتْنِى ٱلْخَمْرُ مَا عَلِقَتْ رُوحِى بِجِسْمِى, *I swear that wine shall not make me intoxicated, as long as my soul remains in my body.*

Rem. *a.* Compare the Hebrew usage, Gesenius' Gr. §. 124, 4.

Rem. *b.* When a clause commencing with لَا is connected with a previous clause beginning with مَا followed by the perfect, or لَمْ followed by the jussive, in that case لَا does not give to the following verb in the perfect the sense of the future, because it merely supplies the place of these particles; as: بَلَوْتُ مِنَ ٱلْعَجَائِبِ مَا لَمْ يَرَهُ

1. The States or Tenses.

ٱلرَّآوُونَ وَلَا رَوَاهُ ٱلرَّاوُونَ, *I have experienced wonderful things, such as neither those who see have seen, nor those who narrate have narrated.*

f) Something which we hope may be done or may happen. Hence the perfect is constantly used in wishes, prayers, and curses; as: رَحِمَهُ ٱللّٰهُ تَعَالَى, *may God (be he exalted!) have mercy on him!* دَامَ مُلْكُهُ, *may his reign be long!* جُعِلْتُ فِدَاكَ, *may I be made thy ransom!* أَبَيْتَ ٱللَّعْنَ, *mayest thou avoid execration* (a formula used in addressing the ancient Arab kings)! لَعَنَكَ ٱللّٰهُ, *God curse thee!* The proper signification of the perfect in this case is: "if it be as I wish, God has already had mercy on him, &c." The perfect has this sense also after لَا; as: لَا لَقِيتُمْ مَا بَقِيتُمْ ضُرًّا, *may you never meet with injury, as long as you live!* لَا فُضَّ فُوكَ, *may thy teeth* (lit. *mouth*) *not be broken!* — When a conditional clause precedes the optative, the particle فَـ must be prefixed to the latter, in order that the influence of the conditional particle in the former may not extend to it; as: إِنْ كُنْتَ ٱبْنَ هَمَّامٍ فَحُيِّيتَ بِٱكْرَامٍ, *if thou art 'Ibn Hammâm* (lit. *the son of Hammâm), mayest thou be saluted with honour!*

Rem. On the optative use of the perfect in Hebrew, see Gesenius Gr. §. 124, 4, note *.

2. The perfect is often preceded by the particle قَدْ, *already* (Vol. I. §. 362, 16). When this is the case, if the perfect has either of the meanings mentioned in §. 1, *b* or *d*, it now implies that the act is really finished and completed

just at the moment of speaking. Its completeness may consist either a) in the removal of all doubt regarding it, — in its perfect certainty as opposed to uncertainty; or b) in its having taken place in agreement or disagreement with what preceded it, in accordance or non-accordance with what was, or might be, expected, — or just a little before the time of speaking. For example: قَدْ ذَكَرْنَا وِزَارَةَ جَدِّهِمْ خَالِدِ بْنِ بَرْمَكَ فِى أَيَّامِ ٱلْمَنْصُورِ وَنَذْكُرُ هَاهُنَا وِزَارَةَ ٱلْبَاقِينَ, we have already spoken of the vizirate of their ancestor Hâlid 'ibn Bërmëk in the reign of el-Mansûr, and we will now speak of the vizirates of the rest (in this example the just completed act is contrasted with the future one); إِنَّ ٱبْنَتَكَ قَدْ مَاتَتْ, thy daughter is, as was expected, dead, or thy daughter is just dead; أَمَّا ٱلْوِلَايَةُ فَقَدْ وَلَّيْتُ ٱبْنَكَ مِصْرَ, as regards the post of governor, I appoint thy son governor of Egypt (§. 1, d); قَالَ لَهُ وَعَدْتَ هٰذَا فَقَالَ قَدْ وَفَيْتُ ٱلْمَوْعُودَ, he said to him, You promised this, and he replied, I now really fulfil what I promised.

3. The *Pluperfect* is expressed:

a) By the *simple perfect*, in relative or conjunctive clauses*), that depend upon clauses in which the verbs are in the perfect; as: عَرَضَ عَلَيْهِمْ مَا أَمَرَ بِهِ ٱلْمَأْمُونُ, he laid before them what el-Mamûn had ordered; جَلَسَ حَيْثُ جَلَسَ أَبُوهُ, he sat where his father had sat; فَلَمَّا وَصَلَ ٱلثَّوْرُ إِلَى ٱلْمَوْضِعِ تَوَلَّى هَارِبًا, and after the ox had come to the place, he turn-

---

*) By a relative or conjunctive-clause we mean a clause that is joined to a preceding one by means of a relative pronoun or a connective particle.

1. The States or Tenses.

ed his back in flight; اِنْهَزَمَ لَمَّا قُتِلَ أَهْلُ بَيْتِهِ, he fled after his kinsmen had been killed.

Rem. Compare, as regards Hebrew, Gesenius' Gr. §. 124, 2.

b) By the *perfect* along with the particle قَدْ, preceded by وَ or without it, provided the preceding clause is one which has its verb in the perfect; as: أَخْرَجَهُ وَقَدْ عُمِّيَ, he led him out blinded (lit. *and he had been blinded*); بَكَرَ إِلَى الْفَضْلِ فَوَجَدَهُ قَدْ بَكَرَ إِلَى دَارِ ٱلرَّشِيدِ, he went early to el-Faḍl, and found that he had gone still earlier to the palace of ar-Rašīd (lit. *and found him, he had already gone early*). These clauses with قَدْ and وَقَدْ are clauses expressing a state or condition (حَالٌ).

c) By the verb كَانَ, *to be*, prefixed to the *perfect*; as: مَاتَ ٱلرَّشِيدُ بِطُوسَ وَكَانَ خَرَجَ إِلَى خُرَاسَانَ لِمُحَارَبَةِ رَافِعِ ابْنِ ٱللَّيْثِ, ar-Rašīd died at Ṭūs, after he had set out (lit. *and he had set out*) for Ḥorāsān to combat Rāfi' 'ibn el-Leit. These clauses also express the state (ٱلْحَالُ).

d) By كَانَ and the *perfect*, with the particle قَدْ interposed; as: كُنْتُ قَدْ رَبَّيْتُ جَارِيَةً وَعَلَّمْتُهَا ثُمَّ أَهْدَيْتُهَا إِلَى ٱلْفَضْلِ, I had brought up and educated a female slave; I then presented her to el-Faḍl. Sometimes the particle قَدْ is placed before both verbs, instead of between them; as: يُرْوَى أَنَّ رَسُولَ ٱللّٰهِ صلعم قَالَ لِعَائِشَةَ رَحِمَهَا وَقَدْ نَذَرَتْ أَنْ تُعْتِقَ قَوْمًا مِنْ وَلَدِ إِسْمٰعِيلَ الخ, there is a tradition that the apostle of God (God bless him and grant him peace!)

said to 'Áïṣa (God have mercy on her!), after she had vowed (lit. *and she already had vowed) to set free some persons of the children of Ishmael, &c.*

Rem. *a.* When one of two or more pluperfects is anterior to the rest in point of time, it is indicated by means of the particle قَدْ, the others having merely كَانَ; as: مَاتَ ٱلرَّشِيدُ بِطُوسَ وَكَانَ خَرَجَ إِلَى خُرَاسَانَ لِمُحَارَبَةِ رَافِعِ بنِ ٱللَّيْثِ وَكَانَ هٰذَا ٱلرَّافِعُ قَدْ خَرَجَ وَخَلَعَ ٱلطَّاعَةَ وَتَغَلَّبَ عَلَى سَمَرْقَنْدَ, *ar-Rasíd died at Tús, after he had set out for Ḫorásán to combat Ráfi' ibn el-Leit, who had rebelled* (lit. *and this Ráfi' had already rebelled), and cast off his allegiance, and taken forcible possession of Samarkand.*

Rem. *b.* A conjunctive clause may be introduced between كَانَ and the following perfect; as: كَانَ لَمَّا بَلَغَ صَلَاحَ ٱلدِّينِ خَبَرُ ٱلْعَدُوِّ وَتَقْصِدِهِ عَكَّا جَمَعَ ٱلْأُمَرَآءَ, *after the news of the enemy's making for Akká* (Acre) *had reached Saláhu 'd-dín* (Saladin), *he had assembled the commanders.*

4. *a)* If two *correlative* clauses follow the hypothetical particles لَوْ, *if,* لَوْ أَنْ, *if that,* and لَوْلَا, *if not* (vol. I. §. 367, 12),*) the verbs in both clauses have usually the signification of our pluperfect subjunctive or potential, though occasionally too of our imperfect subjunctive or potential. For instance: لَوْ شَآءَ رَبُّكَ لَجَعَلَ ٱلنَّاسَ أُمَّةً وَاحِدَةً, *if thy*

*) The protasis of the sentence, when introduced by لَوْلَا, although it has not a verb actually expressed, includes a verbal idea, viz. that of the verb كَانَ.

1. The States or Tenses. 7

Lord had chosen, he would have made (all) mankind one people; لَوْلَا عَلِيٌّ لَهَلَكَ عُمَرُ, *had it not been for 'Alī, 'Omar would have perished;* وَلَوْ أَنَّ أَهْلَ ٱلْقُرَى آمَنُوا وَٱتَّقَوْا لَفَتَحْنَا عَلَيْهِمْ بَرَكَاتٍ مِنَ ٱلسَّمَآءِ وَٱلْأَرْضِ, *and if the people of those towns had believed and feared (God), we would have bestowed upon them blessings from heaven and earth;* وَلْيَخْشَ ٱلَّذِينَ لَوْ تَرَكُوا مِنْ خَلْفِهِمْ ذُرِّيَّةً ضِعَافًا خَافُوا عَلَيْهِمْ, *and let those fear (God), who, if they should leave* (or *were to leave*) *behind them helpless children, would have fears for them* (or *would be afraid on their account*). — *b*) Occasionally كَانَ is placed between لَوْ and the perfect in the protasis of the sentence, and sometimes كَانَ is repeated before the perfect in the apodosis. If this be the case, the signification of the verb in both clauses is always and necessarily that of the pluperfect; as: لَوْ كُنْتُ عَلِمْتُ ذٰلِكَ لَضَرَبْتُكَ, *if I had known this, I would have beaten you;* لَوْ كَانُوا عَرَفُوهَا لَمَا كَانُوا صَلَبُوا رَبَّ ٱلْمَجْدِ, *if they had known this, they would not have crucified the Lord of glory.* — *c*) If the verb of the protasis be an imperfect, and that of the apodosis a perfect, both must be translated by the imperfect subjunctive or potential; as: لَوْ نَشَآءُ أَصَبْنَاهُمْ بِذُنُوبِهِمْ, *if we wished it, we would punish them for their sins.*

Rem. Compare the use of the Hebrew perfect, Gesenius' Gr. §. 124, 5, *a* and *b*.

5. After إِذَا, *when, as often as* (Vol. I. §. 367, 2), the perfect takes the meaning of the imperfect, the future act being

represented as having already taken place; e. g. اِسْتَجِيبُوا لِلَّهِ وَلِلرَّسُولِ إِذَا دَعَاكُمْ لِمَا يُحْيِيكُمْ, *respond to God and to the apostle, when he calls you to that which can give you life.* — Consequently, if the particle إِذَا be followed by two correlative clauses, the first of which extends its conversive influence to the verb of the second, the verbs have in both clauses either a present or a future signification. For example: إِذَا جَاءَ وَعْدُ ٱلْآخِرَةِ جِئْنَا بِكُمْ لَفِيفًا, *when the promised term of the future life comes* (or *is come*, or *shall have come*), *we will collect you together.* In such cases the Latin and German require the future-perfect in the first clause, and the future in the second. The imperfect is sometimes used instead of the perfect in the protasis; as: وَإِذَا تُتْلَى عَلَيْهِمْ آيَاتُنَا قَالُوا آلخ, *and when our verses are read to them, they say, &c.* — If a clause dependent on إِذَا is introduced by such a perfect as كَانَ or صَارَ, or stands in the middle of a narrative of past events, the verb governed in the perfect by إِذَا is likewise a historical perfect; e. g. كَانَ إِذَا تَكَلَّمَ أَبْلَغَ, *when he spoke, he spoke eloquently.*

Rem. *a.* What has been said of إِذَا, applies equally to إِذَا مَا, *as often as, when*; as: أَثُمَّ إِذَا مَا وَقَعَ آمَنْتُمْ بِهِ, *will you (only) then believe it, when it* (the punishment) *is come (upon you)?*

Rem. *b.* When إِذَا or إِذَا مَا is immediately preceded by the particle حَتَّى, *until*, and followed by two correlative clauses, the verbs of which are in the perfect, these perfects take the sense of historical past tenses, expressing a state that closes the action of a previous per-

I. The States or Tenses.

feet. For instance: فَتَحْنَا عَلَيْهِمْ أَبْوَابَ كُلِّ شَىْءٍ حَتَّى إِذَا فَرِحُوا بِمَا أُوتُوا أَخَذْنَاهُمْ بَغْتَةً, *we opened for them the doors to everything* (opened to them the road to everything, permitted them to obtain and enjoy everything), *until, when they rejoiced over what they had obtained, we swept them away suddenly.*

6. *a)* After the conditional particle إِنْ, *if* (Vol. I. §. 367, 5), and after many words which imply the conditional meaning of إِنْ (مَعْنَى ٱلشَّرْطِ, or مَعْنَى إِنْ), the perfect takes a future sense, the condition being represented as already fulfilled; but it may be rendered in English by the present. Such words, for instance, are: أَىّ and مَنْ, *who, whoever,* أَيْمَنْ *whosoever,* مَا *what,* أَيًّا *whatever,* مَهْمَا *whatever,* كُلَّمَا *as often as,* حَيْثُ *where,* حَيْثُمَا *wherever,* مَتَى *when,* مَتَامَا *whenever,* أَيْنَ *where,* أَيْنَمَا *wherever,* كَيْفَ *how,* كَيْفَمَا *however,* أَنَّى *in whatever way,* أَيَّانَ and مَا أَيَّانَ, *as often as, whenever,* إِذْمَا *whenever.* Examples: إِنِّى أَخَافُ إِنْ عَصَيْتُ رَبِّى عَذَابَ يَوْمٍ عَظِيمٍ, *I fear, if I rebel* (lit. *have rebelled*) *against my Lord, the punishment of a great* (i. e. *terrible*) *day;* ٱقْتُلُوهُمْ حَيْثُ ثَقِفْتُمُوهُمْ, *slay them wherever you find them* (lit. *have found them*); هُوَ مَعَكُمْ أَيْنَمَا كُنْتُمْ, *he is with you wherever you are.* The same remark applies to the perfects before and after أَوْ, *or,* in such phrases as: سَوَآءٌ غَابُوا أَوْ حَضَرُوا, *it is all the same whether they are absent or present;* أَكْرِمِ ٱلضَّيْفَ غَنِيًّا كَانَ أَوْ فَقِيرًا, *show honour to a guest, whether he be rich or poor.* —
b) If the words إِنْ, أَىْ, مَنْ, &c., be followed by two clauses,

the first of which expresses the condition, and the second the result depending upon it, then the verb in both clauses is put in the *perfect*, both the condition and the result being represented as having already taken place. For example: إِنْ فَعَلْتَ ذٰلِكَ هَلِكْتَ, *if you do this, you will perish*, lit. *if you shall have done this, you have perished* or *will perish* (§. 1, c); مَنْ كَتَمَ سِرَّهُ بَلَغَ مُرَادَهُ, *he who* (= *if one*) *keeps* (has kept) *his own secret, attains his object;* اَلْحِكْمَةُ ضَالَّةُ ٱلْمُؤْمِنِ أَيْنَمَا وَجَدَهَا أَخَذَهَا, *wisdom is the strayed camel of the believer; wherever he finds it* (= *if he shall have found it anywhere*), *he lays hold of it* (*will lay hold it*). — *c*) If the perfect after إِنْ, أَىْ, مَنْ, &c., is to retain its original meaning, then كَانَ or one of the أَخَوَاتُ كَانَ, *the sisters of the verb kāna* (such as صَارَ *to become,* ظَلَّ *to be by day,* بَاتَ *to be by night,* أَصْبَحَ *to be in the morning,* أَمْسَى *to be in the evening*), must be inserted between those words and the perfect in the protasis, and the apodosis must be indicated by the particle فَ. For example: إِنْ كَانَ قَمِيصُهُ قُدَّ مِنْ قُبُلٍ فَصَدَقَتْ, *if his shirt is* (*has been*) *torn in front, she has spoken the truth;* إِنْ كُنْتُمْ آمَنْتُمْ بِٱللّٰهِ فَعَلَيْهِ تَوَكَّلُوا, *if ye have believed in God, place your trust in him;* فَتَهَجَّدْ ٱلْعُذْرَ أَوْ فَسَامِحْ إِنْ كُنْتُ أَجْرَمْتُ أَوْ جَنَيْتُ, *accept my excuse or* (*at least*) *be indulgent, if I have committed a crime or a fault.* — *d*) But if the perfect after these words is to have the historical sense (English past tense, §. 1, *a*), the verb كَانَ, or one of its "sisters", must be prefixed to the correlative clauses; e. g. كَانُوا إِنْ بَالَغُوا بَلَغُوا, *if they*

1. The States or Tenses.

exerted themselves to attain an object, they attained it; though it is also sufficient that the correlative clauses should be dependent upon others that are historical; as: اِنَّمَا أَدْرَكْتُ ٱلْعِلْمَ بِٱلْحَمْدِ فَكُلَّمَا فَهِمْتُ قُلْتُ ٱلْحَمْدُ لِلّٰهِ *I attained knowledge only by praising (God), for, whenever I understood (anything), I said, Praise be to God!*

Rem. *a.* Where أَيُّ, مَنْ, and مَا are interrogatives or simple relatives, مَتَى, أَنَّى, أَيَانَ, أَيْنَ, and كَيْفَ, interrogatives, and حَيْثُ a simple relative adverb, without any admixture of the conditional signification of إِنْ, perfects dependent upon them retain their original sense.

Rem. *b.* On the Hebrew perfect after אִם and other conditional particles, see Gesenius' Gr. §. 124, 5, *c.*

7. After the particle مَا, *as long as, whilst* (Vol. I. §. 367, 13), the perfect takes the meaning of the imperfect (present or future); as: لَا لَقِيتُمْ مَا تَقِيتُمْ ضُرًّا, *may you never meet with injury* (§. 1, *f*) *as long as you live!* ٱلنَّاسُ مَا دَامُوا فِي ٱلْحَيوٰةِ ٱلدُّنْيَوِيَّةِ غَافِلُونَ, *men are careless, as long as they live in this world* (lit. *remain in the life of this world*). If this imperfect is to be historical, the rule laid down in §. 6, *d*, must be observed. The negative *as long as not* is always expressed by مَا لَمْ with the jussive (see §. 11).

8. The *Imperfect Indicative* (ٱلْمُضَارِعُ ٱلْمَرْفُوعُ) does not in itself express any idea of time; it merely indicates a *begun, incomplete, enduring* existence, either in *present, past* or *future time*. Hence it signifies:

a) An act that does not take place at any one particular time, to the exclusion of any other time, but that takes place at all times, or rather, in speaking of which no notice is taken of time, but only of duration (the *indefinite present*); as: اَلْإِنْسَانُ يُدَبِّرُ وَٱللّٰهُ يُقَدِّرُ, *man forms plans and God directs them (man proposes, God disposes)*; يُسْتَعْبَدُ ٱلْحُرُّ بِٱلْبِرِّ, *the free man is enslaved by benefits (conferred upon him).*

b) An act which, though commenced at the time of speaking, is not yet completed, — which continues during the present time (the *definite present*); as: ٱللّٰهُ يَعْلَمُ بِمَا تَعْمَلُونَ, *God knows what ye are doing.*

c) An act that is to take place hereafter (the *simple future*); as: كَذٰلِكَ يُحْيِى ٱللّٰهُ ٱلْمَوْتَى وَيُرِيكُمْ آيَاتِهِ, *thus will God bring to life the dead, and show you his miracles;* فَٱللّٰهُ يَحْكُمُ بَيْنَهُمْ يَوْمَ ٱلْقِيٰمَةِ, *but God will judge between them on the day of the resurrection.* — To render the futurity of the act still more distinct, the adverb سَوْفَ (Vol. I. §. 364, 4), or its abbreviated form سَ (Vol. I. §. 361, 2),* *in the end*, is prefixed to the verb; as: مَنْ يَفْعَلْ ذٰلِكَ عُدْوَانًا وَظُلْمًا فَسَوْفَ نُصْلِيهِ نَارًا, *if any one does this maliciously and wickedly, we will burn him with hell-fire;* سَنُبَيِّنُهُ فِى مَوْضِعِهِ, *we will explain it in its (proper) place;* سَتُكْفَى مِنْ عَدْوِكَ كُلَّ كَيْدٍ, *thou shalt be protected (through God's grace) from every machination of thy enemy.*

---

*) Very rare abbreviations are سَوْ and سَفْ.

1. The States or Tenses.

Rem. On corresponding uses of the Hebrew imperfect, see Gesenius' Gr. §. 125, 1, 2.

d) An act which was future in relation to the past time of which we speak. When this is the case, the imperfect is simply appended to the preceding perfect without the intervention of any particle, and forms, along with its complement,* a secondary, subordinate clause, expressing the state (اَلْحَالُ) in which the subject of the previous perfect found himself, when he completed the act expressed by that perfect; as: جَاءَ إِلَيْهِ يَعُودُهُ, *he came to him to visit him;* أَتَى إِلَى عَيْنِ مَاءٍ يَشْرَبُ, *he came to a spring of water to drink.*

e) An act which continues during the past time. When this is the case, the imperfect may be appended to the perfect without the interposition of any connective particle, or it may be joined to it by the particle وَ. In either case, it forms, along with its complement, a secondary, subordinate clause, indicating the state (اَلْحَالُ) in which the subject of the previous perfect found himself, when he did what that perfect expresses; as: جَاءَ زَيْدٌ يَضْحَكُ, *Zeid came laughing;* اِنْكَفَأَ يَحْمَدُ مَغْدَاهُ, *he returned, congratulating himself on* (lit. *praising*) *his morning-walk;* جَعَلَ يَلُومُهُ, *he began to scold him;* اِقْتَبَلَتِ ٱلْحَمَامَةُ تَحُومُ فِي طَلَبِ ٱلْمَاءِ, *the pigeon began to fly about in search of water;* إِنَّنَا نَرَاكَ مَا خَرَجْتَ ٱلْيَوْمَ

*) That is to say, any word or words governed by, or otherwise connected with, it.

تَدْرِى كَيْفَ ٱلطَّرِيقِ, *you seem to us to have come out to-day without exactly knowing how* (lit. *we think* or *see you, you have come out today without knowing how was the road*). As the above examples show, the imperfect is in this case generally expressed in English by the infinitive or the participle.

Rem. *a*. Compare, as regards Hebrew, Gesenius' Gr. §. 139, 3, *c*.

Rem. *b*. After the negative particle لَا, the imperfect retains its general idea of incompleteness and duration; as: كَانَ لَا يَفْعَلُ, *he was wont not to do* (lit. *he was not doing*, non faciebat); خَرَجَ لَا يَعْلَمُ أَيْنَ هُوَ, *he went out, not knowing*, or *without knowing, where he was*; لَا يُكْرِمُ ٱلسَّخِىُّ ٱلْبَخِيلَ, *the liberal (man) does not respect the stingy*. — After the negative particle مَا it takes the meaning of the present; as: مَا يَوَدُّ ٱلَّذِينَ كَفَرُوا مِنْ أَهْلِ ٱلْكِتَابِ وَلَا ٱلْمُشْرِكِينَ أَنْ يُنَزَّلَ عَلَيْكُمْ مِنْ خَيْرٍ مِنْ رَبِّكُمْ, *it is not the wish of those who are unbelievers, whether among those who possess a (revealed) book or among the polytheists, that any good should be sent down unto you from your Lord;* إِنَّ ٱلَّذِينَ يَكْتُمُونَ مَا أَنْزَلَ ٱللّٰهُ مِنَ ٱلْكِتَابِ وَيَشْتَرُونَ بِهِ ثَمَنًا قَلِيلًا أُولٰئِكَ مَا يَأْكُلُونَ فِي بُطُونِهِمْ إِلَّا ٱلنَّارَ وَلَا يُكَلِّمُهُمُ ٱللّٰهُ يَوْمَ ٱلْقِيٰمَةِ, *they who conceal the book that God has revealed, and buy with it something of small price, these swallow down into their bellies nothing but fire, and God will not speak to them on the day of judgment.*

9. To express the imperfect of the Greek and Latin languages, كَانَ is frequently prefixed to the imperfect; as:

1. The States or Tenses.

كَانَ يُحِبُّ ٱلشِّعْرَ وَٱلشُّعَرَآءَ, *he was fond of poetry and poets;* كَانَ يَرْكَبُ فِي كُلِّ يَوْمٍ عِدَّةَ مِرَارٍ, *he used to ride out every day several times.* If this signification is to be attached to several imperfects, it is sufficient to prefix كَانَ to the first alone. — If one or two perfects precede the imperfect, or if the context clearly shows that the verb in the imperfect has the sense of the Latin imperfect, كَانَ need not be prefixed to it; as: وَٱتَّبَعُوا مَا تَتْلُو ٱلشَّيَاطِينُ عَلَى مُلْكِ سُلَيْمَانَ, *and they followed the doctrines which* (lit. *that which*) *the evil spirits taught* (mankind) *in the reign of Solomon;* قُلْ فَلِمَ تَقْتُلُونَ أَنْبِيَآءَ ٱللَّهِ مِنْ قَبْلُ, *Say, Why then did ye kill the prophets of God before?* Here تَتْلُو and تَقْتُلُونَ stand for كَانَتْ تَتْلُو and كُنْتُمْ تَقْتُلُونَ.

Rem. In this sense the Hebrew uses the simple imperf.; Gesenius' Gr. §. 125, 4, b.

10. To express the future-perfect, the imperfect of كَانَ (يَكُونُ) is frequently prefixed to the perfect, the particle قَدْ being sometimes interposed. For example: وَسَأَسْتَأْجِرُ أَقْوَامًا يَحْمِلُونَهُ إِلَى مَنْزِلِي وَأَكُونُ أَنَا آخِرَهُمْ وَلَا يَكُونُ بَقِيَ وَرَآئِي شَىْءٌ يُشْغِلُ فِكْرِى بِفِعْلِهِ وَنَقْلِهِ وَأَكُونُ قَدِ ٱسْتَظْهَرْتُ لِنَفْسِى فِي إِرَاحَةِ بَدَنِى عَنِ ٱلْكَدِّ بِيَسِيرِ أُجْرَةٍ أُعْطِيهَا لَهُمْ, *and I shall hire some people to carry it to my house, and I shall be the last of them (to depart), and there shall not have been left (shall not be left) behind me anything to occupy my mind with the doing or removing of it, and by the trifling pay*

I give them, I shall have provided help for myself (so as) *to spare my own body all the labour.*

11. The *Subjunctive* of the imperfect (اَلْمُضَارِعُ ٱلْمَنْصُوبُ) has always a future sense after the adverb لَنْ, *not* (Vol. I. §. 362, 22), and the conjunctions أَنْ, *that*, أَنْ لَا or أَلَّا, *that not,* كَيْ and لِكَيْ, *that,* كَيْلَا and لِكَيْلَا, *that not,* حَتَّى, *till, until,* and لِ, *that;* as: لَنْ يَدْخُلَ ٱلْجَنَّةَ إِلَّا مَنْ كَانَ هُودًا أَوْ نَصَارَى, *none shall enter Paradise except those who are Jews or Christians;* أَمْ حَسِبْتُمْ أَنْ تَدْخُلُوا ٱلْجَنَّةَ, *do ye think that ye shall enter Paradise?* See §. 15.

12. The *Jussive* of the imperfect (اَلْمُضَارِعُ ٱلْمَجْزُومُ), when dependent upon the adverbs لَمْ, *not,* and لَمَّا, *not yet* (Vol. I. §. 362, 20—1), has invariably the meaning of the perfect; or, to speak more accurately, it has that meaning which the imperfect preceded by كَانَ would have (§. 9), if the proposition were an affirmative one. For example: أَلَمْ تَعْلَمْ أَنَّ ٱللَّهَ لَهُ مُلْكُ ٱلسَّمَوَاتِ وَٱلْأَرْضِ, *hast thou not learned* (or *dost thou not know*) *that God's is the sovereignty over the heavens and the earth?* أَمْ حَسِبْتُمْ أَنْ تَدْخُلُوا ٱلْجَنَّةَ وَلَمَّا يَأْتِكُمْ مَثَلُ ٱلَّذِينَ خَلَوْا مِنْ قَبْلِكُمْ, *do ye think that ye shall enter Paradise, before there shall have come* (lit. *and there has not yet come*) *upon you what came upon those who passed away before you?* أُزِفَ ٱلتَّرَحُّلُ غَيْرَ أَنَّ رِكَابَنَا لَمَّا تَزُلْ بِرِحَالِنَا, *our departure is close at hand, save that our camels have not yet moved off with our saddles* (i. e. we have all but started); إِنْ لَمْ تَفْعَلْ ذَلِكَ هَلَكْتَ, *if you do*

1. The States or Tenses.

لَمْ يَكُنْ يُحِبُّ ٱلشِّعْرَ *not do this, you will perish* (§. 6, b); وَٱلشُّعَرَآءَ, *he was not fond of poetry and poets.*

13. After إِنْ and the various words that have the sense of إِنْ, the jussive has the same meaning as the perfect (§. 6); as: إِنْ تُخْفُوا مَا فِي صُدُورِكُمْ أَوْ تُبْدُوهُ يَعْلَمْهُ ٱللّٰهُ, *whether you conceal what is in your breasts, or disclose it, God will know it;* إِنْ تَعْمَلْ فِي إِسْلَامِكَ عَمَلًا صَالِحًا تُثَبْ عَلَيْهِ, *if, now that you have become a Muslim, you do a good work, you will be rewarded for it;* إِنْ تُنْصِفُونَا يَا آلَ مَرْوَانَ نَقْتَرِبْ إِلَيْكُمْ, *if you do us justice, O family of Merwān, we will draw near to you;* مَا تَفْعَلُوا مِنْ خَيْرٍ يَعْلَمْهُ ٱللّٰهُ, *whatever good you do, God will know it;* أَيْنَمَا تَكُونُوا يُدْرِكْكُمُ ٱلْمَوْتُ, *wherever you are, death will overtake you;* مَتَى أَضَعِ ٱلْعِمَامَةَ تَعْرِفُونِي, *when I lay aside my turban, you recognise me.* — When the first of two correlative clauses contains a verb in the imperative, and the second in the jussive, then the jussive has the same meaning as if the first clause had contained a verb in the jussive preceded by إِنْ; as: قَالُوا كُونُوا هُودًا أَوْ نَصَارَى تَهْتَدُوا, *they said, Become Jews or Christians, (and) you will be guided aright.* Here كُونُوا is equivalent to إِنْ تَكُونُوا, *if you become Jews or Christians, you will be &c.*

14. The *Energetic* forms of the imperfect have always a future sense; as: لَئِنْ أَنْجَيْتَنَا مِنْ هَٰذِهِ لَنَكُونَنَّ مِنَ ٱلشَّاكِرِينَ, *if thou deliverest us from this (danger), verily we shall be of (the number of) the grateful;* وَٱللّٰهِ لَأَضْرِبَنَّ

عُنْقَلَ, *by God! I will cut thy head off* (lit. *strike thy neck*).

2. The Moods.

15. The *Subjunctive* mood occurs only in subordinate clauses. It indicates an act which is dependent upon that mentioned in the previous clause, and future to it in point of time; and hence it mostly corresponds to the Latin subjunctive after *ut*. It is governed by the following particles.

1) *a*. By أَنْ, *that*, after verbs which express inclination or disinclination, order or prohibition, duty, effect, effort, fear, necessity, permission, &c.; أَنْ لَا or أَلَّا, *that not;* and لَنْ (for لَا أَنْ, i. e. لَا يَكُونُ أَنْ, *it will not be* or *happen that*), *certainly not, not at all.* For example: أَرَدْتُ وَأَحْبَبْتُ أَنْ أُبَيِّنَ لَهُمْ طَرِيقَ ٱلتَّعَلُّمِ, *I wished and desired to make plain to them the path of learning;* لَا يَأْبَ كَاتِبٌ أَنْ يَكْتُبَ, *let no one who can write, refuse to write;* يَنْبَغِى أَنْ يَنْوِىَ ٱلْمُتَعَلِّمُ بِطَلَبِ ٱلْعِلْمِ رِضَا ٱللّٰهِ, *it behoves the learner to strive by his search for knowledge to please God;* يَجُوزُ أَنْ يَكُونَ ٱلنَّصْبَ, *it may be the accusative;* قَالَ فَٱهْبِطْ مِنْهَا فَمَا يَكُونُ لَكَ أَنْ تَتَكَبَّرَ فِيهَا, *He (God) said, Get thee down then from it (Paradise), for it is not allowed thee to behave with pride in it;* إِنِّى أَخَافُ أَلَّا يَتْرُكَنِى, *I am afraid he will not leave me,* or, in accordance with a particular idiom of the language, *I am afraid he will leave me;* مَا مَنَعَكَ أَلَّا تَسْجُدَ,

2. The Moods.

what has prevented thee from worshipping (him)? لَنْ تَمَسَّنَا ٱلنَّارُ إِلَّا أَيَّامًا مَعْدُودَةً, *the fire (of hell) will certainly not touch us save for (will certainly touch us only for) a certain number of days;* لَنْ يَدْخُلَ ٱلْجَنَّةَ إِلَّا مَنْ كَانَ هُودًا أَوْ نَصَارَى, *no one shall enter Paradise save those who are Jews or Christians.*

b) But if the verb to which أَنْ is subordinate, does not indicate any wish, effect, expectation, or the like; and the verb which is governed by أَنْ has the meaning of the perfect or present; in that case the indicative of the perfect or imperfect is used after أَنْ; as: أَعْلَمُ أَنْ قَالَ, *I know that he has said;* أَعْلَمُ أَنْ يَنَامُ, *I know that he is asleep.* As أَنَّ, *quod, ὅτι,* is more usual in such clauses, the native grammarians designate أَنْ, when it has the same meaning as أَنَّ and governs the indicative, by the name of أَنِ ٱلْمُخَفَّفَةُ مِنَ ٱلثَّقِيلَةِ *the* ان *that is lightened from the heavy form,* or, more shortly, أَنِ ٱلْمُخَفَّفَةُ, *the lightened* ان: but when it is equivalent to the Latin *ut,* they call it أَنِ ٱلنَّاصِبَةُ, *the* ان *that governs the subjunctive* (ٱلْمُضَارِعُ ٱلْمَنْصُوبُ). After verbs of thinking, supposing, and doubting, when they refer to the future, أَنْ may govern the indicative of the imperfect, as ظَنَنْتُ أَنْ يَقُومُ, ٱلْمُخَفَّفَةُ, or the subjunctive, as ٱلنَّاصِبَةُ; e. g. *I think he will get up.*

2) By لِ, *that, in order that* (originally a preposition, Vol. I. §. 356, 3); لِكَيْلَا, كَيْلَا, لِكَيْ, كَيْ, and لِأَنْ, *id.;* and لِئَلَّا, *that not, in order that not;* particles which indicate the

intention of the agent and the object of the act. For example:
يَنْبَغِي أَنْ يَسْأَلَ ٱلْمُسْلِمُ ٱللّٰهَ تَمَّ ٱلْعَافِيَةَ لِيَصُونَهُ عَنِ ٱلْبَلَايَا,
it behoves the Muslim to ask God (may he be exalted!) to keep him in health, that he preserve him from misfortunes;
إِذَا حَفِظْتَ شَيْئًا فَعَلِّقْهُ كَيْ تَعُودَ إِلَيْهِ عَلَى ٱلتَّأْبِيدِ, *when you have learned anything, write it down, so that you may constantly refer to it;* لَمْ نَشْتَغِلْ بِذِكْرِ ذٰلِكَ كَيْلَا يَطُولَ ٱلْكِتَابُ, *we have not occupied ourselves with giving an account of this, in order that the book might not become too long;* إِنَّمَا قَالَ ذٰلِكَ لِئَلَّا يُسْتَخَفَّ بِٱلْعِلْمِ, *he said this only in order that learning might not be disparaged.*

3) *a.* By حَتَّى (also originally a preposition, Vol. I. §. 358, 2), *until, until that, that, in order that,* when it expresses the intention of the agent and the object of the act, or the result of the act, as taking place not without the will of the agent or, at least, according to his expectation. For example: لَابُدَّ مِنَ ٱلتَّأَمُّلِ قَبْلَ ٱلْكَلَامِ حَتَّى يَكُونَ صَوَابًا, *we must meditate before we speak, in order that our words may be appropriate;* يَنْبَغِي أَنْ لَا يُضْعِفَ ٱلنَّفْسَ حَتَّى يَنْقَطِعَ عَنِ ٱلْعَمَلِ, *he must not weaken the spirit so that it is hindered from acting;* قُولُوا لَهُ إِنْ شَآءَ فَلْيَتَجَلِّسْ وَلْيُعْطِينِي يَدَهُ حَتَّى أُقِيمَهُ أَوْ يُقْعِدَنِي, *tell him, if he chooses, to sit down and give me his hand, that I may force him to rise or he force me to sit down.* — *b.* But if حَتَّى expresses only a simple temporal limit, or the mere effect or result of an act, without any implied design or expectation on the part of the agent, it is followed by the perfect or the indicative of the

2. The Moods.   21

imperfect. For example: سَارُوا حَتَّى طَلَعَتِ ٱلشَّمْسُ, *they journeyed till the sun was up*; يَهْرُبُ حَتَّى أَبْعَدَ, *and so he fled till he got a great way off*; مَرِضَ حَتَّى لَا يَرْجُونَهُ, *he is so ill that they have no hope of his living*; وَثِقُوا لِلْعِلْمِ وَٱلنَّشْرِ حَتَّى بَقِيَ ٱسْمُهُمْ إِلَى يَوْمِ ٱلْقِيَمَةِ, *and on this account they were enabled by God's help to acquire and diffuse knowledge to such an extent, that their name will maintain itself till the day of the resurrection.*

    R e m. With حَتَّى compare the Latin *donec*.

    4) By فَ, when this particle introduces a clause that expresses the result or effect of a preceding clause. The preceding clause must contain an imperative (affirmative or negative), or words equivalent in meaning to an imperative; or else it must express a wish or hope, or ask a question; or, finally, be a negative clause. The signification of فَ in all these cases is equivalent to that of حَتَّى. For example: اِغْفِرْ لِي يَا رَبِّ فَأَدْخُلَ ٱلْجَنَّةَ, *pardon me, O my Lord, so that I may enter Paradise*; لَا تُوَاخِذْنِي فَأَهْلِكَ, *do not punish me, so that (or lest) I perish*; ٱللَّهُمَّ لَا تَكِلْنَا إِلَى أَنْفُسِنَا فَنَعْجِزَ وَلَا إِلَى ٱلنَّاسِ فَنَضِيعَ, *O God, hand us not over to ourselves, lest we be too feeble (for the charge), nor to (other) men, lest we perish*; لَيْتَ لِي مَالًا فَأَتَصَدَّقَ مِنْهُ, *would that I had money, that I might give part of it away in alms*; هَلْ زَيْدٌ فِي ٱلدَّارِ فَأَمْضِيَ إِلَيْهِ, *is Zeid at home, that I can go to him (= tell me whether Z. is at home, so that*

يَا ٱبْنَ ٱلْكِرَامِ أَلَا تَدْنُو فَتُبْصِرَ مَا قَدْ حَدَّثُوكَ (؟.)&c., *O son of the noble, will thou not draw near, that thou mayest see what they have told thee?* لَا يُقْضَى عَلَيْهِمْ فَيَمُوتُوا, *sentence is not passed upon them, so that they die;* مَا تَأْتِينَا فَتُحَدِّثَنَا, *thou dost not come to us to tell us something;* تَقَدَّمْ إِلَيْهِ فَيَخِيطَهُ, *go up to him that he may sew it.*

5) By وَ, when the governed verb expresses an act subordinate to, but simultaneous with, the act expressed by the previous clause; as: لَا تَنْهَ عَنْ خُلُقٍ وَتَأْتِيَ مِثْلَهُ, *do not restrain (others) from any habit, whilst you yourself practise one like it;* هَلْ تَأْكُلُ ٱلسَّمَكَ وَتَشْرَبُ ٱللَّبَنَ, *do you eat fish and drink milk at the same time?* The Arab grammarians call وَ, thus used, وَاوُ ٱلْجَمْعِ or وَاوُ ٱلْمَعِيَّةِ, *the waw of simultaneousness,* and explain it by مَعَ أَنْ.

6) By أَوْ, when it is equivalent either to إِلَّا أَنْ, *unless that,* or to إِلَى أَنْ or حَتَّى, *until that;* as: لَأَقْتُلَنَّ ٱلْكَافِرَ أَوْ يُسْلِمَ, *I will certainly kill the unbeliever, unless he becomes a Muslim;* لَأَلْزَمَنَّكَ أَوْ تُعْطِيَنِي حَقِّي, *I will stick to you till you give me my due;* لَأَسْتَسْهِلَنَّ ٱلصَّعْبَ أَوْ أُدْرِكَ ٱلْمُنَى, *I will deem everything difficult easy, until I attain my wishes.* In the former case, the preceding act is to be conceived as taking place but once and as momentary; in the latter, as repeated and continued.

7) By إِذَنْ or إِذًا, *in that case, well then,* when this particle commences a clause expressing the result or effect of a previous statement, provided that the verb in the subordinate

clause refers to a really future time, and that it is in immediate juxtaposition to إِذَنْ, or, at least, separated from it only by the negative لَا or by an asseveration. For example, one may say: أَنَا آتِيكَ غَدًا, *I will come to you tomorrow*, and the reply may be: إِذَنْ أُكْرِمَكَ, *well then, I will treat you with respect*, or, إِذَنْ وَٱللّٰهِ أُكْرِمَكَ, *well then, by God, I will &c.*, or إِذَنْ لَا أُهِينَكَ, *well then, I will not insult you*. — If the particle وَ be prefixed to إِذَنْ, the verb may be put in the indicative as well as the subjunctive, e. g. وَإِذَنْ أُكْرِمَكَ; but if any of the other conditions specified above be violated, the indicative alone can be used: e. g. أُحِبُّكَ, *I am fond of you*, إِذَنْ أَظُنُّكَ صَادِقًا, *well, I think you speak the truth* (where the verb refers to present, and not to future, time); or أَزُورُ زَيْدًا, *I shall visit Zeid*, إِذَنْ زَيْدٌ يُكْرِمُكَ *well then, Zeid will treat you with respect* (where زَيْدٌ separates إِذَنْ from the verb).

> Rem. Owing to the Hebrew having lost the final vowels of the imperfect, the form which it employs after such particles as כִּי, אֲשֶׁר, פֶּן, יַעַן אֲשֶׁר, לְמַעַן, &c., can no longer be distinguished from that which expresses the indicative. See Gesenius' Gr. §. 125, 3, *a*. The same remark applies to the Syriac; but the Ethiopic makes a distinction, using, for example, the form ይነግር: *yĕnáger* (root ነገረ: *nagára*, to speak) for the indicative, and ይንግር: *yĕnger* for the subjunctive. See Dillmann's Gr. §. 90.

16. Since, in Arabic, the subjunctive is governed only by the conjunction أَنْ, *that*, and other conjunctions that have

the meaning of اَنْ, the indicative must be used in all other subordinate clauses, whether they be dependent upon a conjunctive or relative word, or simply annexed to an undefined substantive; as: أَعْطَانِى مَا آكُلُ, *he gave me what I was to eat;* لَا يَدْرِى أَيْنَ يَذْهَبُ, *he does not know where he is to go;* سَيُدْخِلُهُمْ جَنَّاتٍ يَخْلُدُونَ فِيهَا, *he will bring them into gardens, to dwell in them for ever.* In such sentences the Arabic language does not distinguish the *intention* from the *effect*. Hence the first example may also be translated: *he gave me what I ate (at that time),* or *what I am (now) eating,* or *what I shall (hereafter) eat;* the second: *where he is going* or *will go;* the third: *in which they shall dwell for ever.*

17. The *Jussive*, — connected with the imperative both in form and signification, — implies an *order*. It is used:

1) With the particle لِ prefixed (which is very rarely omitted, except perhaps in poetry), instead of the imperative; as: لِيُنْفِقْ ذُو سَعَةٍ, *let the possessor of wealth lay out (money);* لِيَقُمِ ٱلْمُتَّقُونَ, *let those that fear God, arise.* If the particle وَ or فَ be prefixed to لِ, as is often the case, then لِ loses its vowel; as: إِنْ حَدَثَ بِى حَادِثٌ فَلْتُبَعْ وَلْتُقْسَمْ عَلَى سَبِيلِ كَذَا, *if anything happens to me, let it be sold and (the proceeds) divided in such and such a way;* مَنْ أَرَادَ أَنْ يَتْرُكَ عِلْمَنَا هَذَا سَاعَةً فَلْيَتْرُكْهُ ٱلسَّاعَةَ, *whoever wishes to give up (the study of) this science of ours for a time,*

let him do so now. It is the *third* person of the jussive that is most used in this way.

2) After the particle لَا, *not*, in connection with which it expresses a prohibition or a wish that something may not be done; as: لَا تَحْزَنْ إِنَّ ٱللَّهَ مَعَنَا, *be not grieved, for God is with us;* لَا تَنْقُضْ مَا فَعَلَ سَعْدٌ, *do not break through what Sa'd has done.*

3) In the protasis and apodosis of correlative conditional clauses, that depend upon إِنْ or any particle having the sense of إِنْ (§. 6). It stands in the protasis, when the verb is neither a perfect, nor an imperfect preceded by كَانَ, but a simple imperfect; and in the apodosis, when the verb is likewise a simple imperfect, and not separated from the protasis by the conjunction فَ (for if this latter be the case, the indicative must be used). For example: إِنْ تُخْفُوا مَا فِى صُدُورِكُمْ أَوْ تُبْدُوهُ يَعْلَمْهُ ٱللَّهُ, *whether you conceal what is in your breasts, or disclose it, God will know it;* مَا تَفْعَلُوا مِنْ خَيْرٍ يَعْلَمْهُ ٱللَّهُ, *whatever good you do, God will know it;* أَيْنَمَا تَكُونُوا يُدْرِكْكُمُ ٱلْمَوْتُ, *wherever you are, death will overtake you;* إِنْ تَفْعَلُوا فَإِنَّهُ فُسُوقٌ بِكُمْ, *if ye do it, it is a trespass (against God's law) of which ye make yourselves guilty;* مَنْ كَانَ يُرِيدُ حَرْثَ ٱلْآخِرَةِ نَزِدْ لَهُ فِى حَرْثِهِ, *whosoever chooses the tillage of the life to come, to him will we give an ample increase in his tillage;* إِنْ يَسْرِقْ فَقَدْ سَرَقَ أَخٌ لَهُ مِنْ قَبْلُ, *if he steals, (why,) a brother of his has stolen before;* مَنْ يُؤْمِنْ بِرَبِّهِ فَلَا يَخَافُ بَخْسًا, *whosoever believes in his Lord, will dread no evil.* — The jussive also stands

in the apodosis, when the protasis contains a verb in the imperative; as: عِشْ قَنِعًا تَكُنْ مَلِكًا, *live contented and you will be a king*; أَوْفُوا بِعَهْدِكُمْ أُوفِ بِعَهْدِى, *be faithful to your engagement, and I will be faithful to mine.* — The jussive is used in a protasis that is dependent upon إِنْ, &c., because, when anything is supposed or assumed, an order is, as it were, made that it be given or take place. That this is the correct account of the matter, is evident from the fact of the jussive being employed in the apodosis as well of an imperative as of a conditional protasis. The use of the jussive in the apodosis, again, has for its reason, that, when a thing takes place or is assumed, whatever depends upon it takes place or is assumed at the same time; and, consequently, when the one thing is ordered, the other too seems to be ordered at the same time.

Rem. The Hebrew cannot, owing to the loss of the final vowels, distinguish in every case the jussive from the indicative and subjunctive; but the shortened form of the imperfect, wherever it exists, is the proper one to be used in all the above cases. See Gesenius' Gr. §. 126, 2. It has, however, no particle corresponding to لِ, and uses אַל in certain cases instead of לֹא (لا); see Gesenius' Gr. §. 125, 3, *c*. — The Ethiopic employs the shorter form of the imperfect, ይንገር: *yĕngĕ'r*, to express the jussive as well as the subjunctive (see §. 15, rem.), and often prefixes to it the particle ለ: *la* = لِ. See Dillmann's Gr. §. 90, §. 169, 7, and §. 197, *a* (the second paragraph).

18. The jussive is also used after the particles لَمْ, *not*, and لَمَّا, *not yet* (compounded of لَمْ and the مَا ٱلَّذِيْنُومَةِ,

2. The Moods.

§. 7); e. g. اَلَمْ تَعْلَمْ أَنَّ ٱللَّهَ لَهُ مُلْكُ ٱلسَّمٰوَاتِ وَٱلْأَرْضِ, *dost thou not know, that God's is the sovereignty over the heavens and the earth?* لَمَّا يَذُوقُوا عَذَابٍ, *they have not yet tasted my punishment;* أَهٰذَا وَلَمَّا تَمْضِ لِلْبَيْنِ سَاعَةً, *is this so, and we have not yet been* (or *ere we have been*) *parted an hour?* The verb after لَمْ and لَمَّا has, however, only the form, not the signification, of the jussive, and their effect upon the following imperfect seems to be similar to that which the Hebrew *waw consecutivum* (.וַ) exercises upon the imperfect annexed to it.

Rem. If the particle لَمْ be followed by two or more imperfects, of which the second depends upon the first, the third upon the second, and so on, then, of course, the first alone is put in the jussive; e. g. لَمْ يَكُنْ يَعْرِفْ يَسْبَحْ, *he did not know (how) to swim.* See §. 12 and §. 8, *c*.

19. The *Energetic* of the imperfect is used:

1) With the particle لَ, *truly, surely,* prefixed to it, both in simple asseverations and in those that are strengthened by an oath; as: اَلَّذِينَ جَاهَدُوا فِينَا لَنَهْدِيَنَّهُمْ سُبُلَنَا, *those who have fought in our (holy) cause, we will surely guide in our paths;* لَتَرَوُنَّ ٱلْجَحِيمَ, *they shall surely see hell-fire;* عَمَّا قَلِيلٍ لَيُصْبِحُنَّ نَادِمِينَ, *verily within a short time they shall repent it;* وَٱللَّهِ لَأُودِّبَنَّكُمْ غَيْرَ هٰذَا ٱلْأَدَبِ, *by God! I will teach you manners different from these;* فَبِعِزَّتِكَ لَأُغْوِيَنَّهُمْ أَجْمَعِينَ, *then, by thy glory, I will surely lead them all astray.*

2) In commands or prohibitions wishes and questions; as: لَا تَمُوتُنَّ إِلَّا وَأَنْتُمْ مُسْلِمُونَ, *do not die before you have become* (or *without having become*) *Muslims*; لَيْتَكَ تَرْجِعَنْ, *would that you would come back!* أَلَّا تَنْزِلَنْ, *why did you not come down?*

3) In the apodosis of correlative conditional clauses, in which case لَ is prefixed to the protasis as well as to the apodosis; as: وَلَئِنْ سَأَلْتَهُمْ مَنْ خَلَقَ السَّمٰوٰاتِ وَٱلْأَرْضَ وَسَخَّرَ ٱلشَّمْسَ وَٱلْقَمَرَ لَيَقُولُنَّ ٱللّٰهُ, *and if thou askest them, Who created the heavens and the earth and obliged the sun and moon to serve him? verily they will say, God;* لَئِنْ لَمْ يَنْتَهِ لَنَسْفَعًا بِٱلنَّاصِيَةِ, *verily, if he does not refrain, we will seize and drag him by the forelock.*

4) In the protasis of a sentence after إِمَّا (= إِنْ مَا); as: ٱهْبِطُوا مِنْهَا جَمِيعًا فَإِمَّا يَأْتِيَنَّكُمْ مِنِّى هُدًى فَمَنْ تَبِعَ هُدَايَ فَلَا خَوْفٌ عَلَيْهِمْ, *get ye down from it* (Paradise), *all of you; and if there shall (hereafter) come unto you a direction from me, then whosoever shall follow my direction, on them no fear shall come;* فَإِمَّا تَثْقَفَنَّهُمْ فِى ٱلْحَرْبِ فَشَرِّدْ بِهِمْ مَنْ خَلْفَهُمْ, *and if you capture them in battle, put to flight, by (making an example of) them, those who are behind them.*

Rem. On corresponding uses of the Hebrew energetic or cohortative, see Gesenius' Gr. §. 126.

20. No negative particle can be placed before the imperative, and, consequently, when a prohibition is uttered,

the jussive must be used; as: أَمْكُثْ شَهْرَيْنِ وَلَا تَعْجَلْ فِى الْآخِتِلَافِ إِلَى الْآئِمَّةِ, *remain two months, and be not in a haste to run from one 'imām to another.* — The energetic forms of the imperative serve to increase its force; as: تَعْلَمَنْ أَنَّ طُولَ ٱلْعَيْشِ تَعْذِيبٌ, بِٱللّٰهِ ٱضْرِبَنْ, *strike, by God! learn that length of life is a punishment or torment* ٱلْكِبْرِيَآءُ لِرَبِّنَا صِفَةٌ لَهُ مَخْصُوصَةٌ; (تَعْذِيبٌ in rhyme for تَعْذِيبٌ) فَتَجَنَّبْنَهَا وَٱتَّقِ, *glory belongs to God (alone), as an attribute peculiar to him; therefore keep thyself afar from it, and fear him*.

Rem. The same remarks apply to the imperative and its lengthened form in Hebrew.

---

3. The Government of the Verb.

21. The verb may govern either *a*) the *accusative* of a noun, or *b*) a *preposition with the genitive* of a noun, which takes the place of the accusative and gives greater precision and accuracy to the expression. — This government is not restricted to the finite tenses of the verb, but extends to the nomen verbi or actionis, the nomina agentis and patientis, and other verbal substantives and adjectives, whenever and in so far as these different kinds of nouns contain somewhat of the conception or nature of the verb. — The verb, too, need not necessarily be expressed; it may be understood, or it may lie concealed, as it were, in a particle that has a verbal force.

a. The Accusative.

22. The verb governs the *accusative* of the noun — which we may call the *determinative* case of the verb or the *adverbial* case (see Vol. I. §. 364) — either

1) as an *objective complement* (determinans), i. e. as that which, by assigning its object, limits and restricts the act; or

2) as an *adverbial complement* in a stricter sense, indicating various limitations of the verb, which are expressed in non-Shemitic languages by adverbs, prepositions with their respective cases, conjunctive clauses, or (as in the Slavonic languages) by the instrumental case.

23. Most *transitive* verbs take the objective complement in the accusative, though a considerable number of them are connected with the object by means of a preposition. Not a few are construed in both ways with a variety of signification, and different prepositions may sometimes be joined to the same verb with a difference of meaning; e. g. دَعَاهُ, *he called him;* دَعَا لَهُ بِكَذَا, *he prayed that he might receive something as a blessing;* دَعَا عَلَيْهِ, *he cursed him.* In other cases a transitive verb may be construed indifferently with the accusative or with a preposition and the genitive, the former being the older and more vigorous, the latter the younger and feebler construction; e. g. عَلِقَ, *to adhere to, to attach oneself to,* and لَحِقَ, *to adhere to, to overtake,* are construed indifferently with the accusative of the person or with بِ and the genitive. More rarely the converse is the case, the accusative being the later and less correct construction; e. g. فَرَغَ, *to have finished, to be done*

3. The Government of the Verb.

with, is construed with مِنْ, and اِحْتَاجَ, *to have need of, to be in want of*, with اِلَى, whereas in modern Arabic both take the accusative.

Rem. *a.* Transitive verbs are called by the Arab grammarians اَلْأَفْعَالُ ٱلْمُتَعَدِّيَةُ, and they designate by this name not only those verbs that govern their object in the accusative, but also those that connect themselves with it by means of a preposition. The former are distinguished as اَلْأَفْعَالُ ٱلْمُتَعَدِّيَةُ بِأَنْفُسِهَا, *the verbs that pass on (to an object) through themselves* (and not by help of a preposition), and the latter as اَلْأَفْعَالُ ٱلْمُتَعَدِّيَةُ بِغَيْرِهَا, *the verbs that pass on (to an object) through something else than themselves* (viz. يَحْرَفِ جَرٍّ, *through a preposition*). For example, بَلَغَ, *to reach, to arrive* (of a message, &c.), is a فِعْلٌ مُتَعَدٍّ بِنَفْسِهِ, because we say بَلَغَنِى ٱلْخَبَرُ, *the news reached me;* but قَدَرَ, *to have power, to be able*, is a فِعْلٌ مُتَعَدٍّ بِغَيْرِهِ, because it is construed with عَلَى, and we say قَدَرَ عَلَى شَىْءٍ, *he was able to do something*.

Rem. *b.* Only careful study and the use of the dictionary can teach the learner whether a verb is construed with the accusative, or with a preposition, or with both; and, if more than one construction be admissible, what are the different meanings that the verb assumes. Here we merely remark that verbs signifying *to come,* which are construed in Latin and English with prepositions, admit in Arabic also the accusative; as: جَاءَنَا عَامِرٌ, *Amir came to us;* إِنَّ ٱلْغُرَبَاءَ وَأَوْلَادَ ٱلْكُبَرَاءَ يَأْتُونَنِى مِنْ أَقْطَارِ ٱلْأَرْضِ, *strangers and the sons of noblemen come to me from (all) quarters of the earth* (compare in Hebrew בָּא with the accusative; e. g. Ps. 100, 4; Prov. 2, 19; Lament.

1, 10). Hence these verbs have in Arabic a *personal passive*, so that we may say اُتِىَ بِشَىْءٍ, lit. *he was come to with a thing*, i. e. it was brought to him, the active construction being اَتَاهُ بِشَىْءٍ, *he came to him with a thing*, i. e. he brought it to him.

24. Many verbs take *two objective complements in the accusative*, either both of the person, or both of the thing, or the one of the person and the other of the thing. — These verbs form *two classes*, according to the relation of their objects to one another; the first class consisting of those whose objects are different from, and in no way connected with, one another, the second of those whose objects stand to one another in the relation of subject and predicate. — *a*) To the *first* class belong all causatives of the second and fourth verbal forms (Vol. I. §. 41 and 45), whose ground-form is transitive and governs an accusative, as also verbs that signify *to fill* or *satisfy, give, deprive, forbid, ask, entreat,* and the like, the most of which have likewise a causative meaning. For example: اَعْلَمَنِى ٱلْاَمْرَ, *he informed me of the thing* (lit. *he made me know it*); عَلَّمَهُ عِلْمَ ٱلْهَيْئَةِ, *he taught him the science of astronomy;* زَوَّجْتُ زَيْدًا ٱبْنَةَ اَخِى, *I gave Zeid my brother's daughter in marriage;* مَلَأَ ٱلدَّلْوَ مَاءً, *he filled the bucket with water;* اَشْبَعَهُ خُبْزًا, *he let him eat as much bread as he could* (شَبِعَ خُبْزًا, *he ate as much bread as he could*); اَطْعَمَهُ ٱلسَّيْفَ, *he let him taste the sword* (ran him through with it); سَقَوْا زَيْدًا خَمْرًا مَسْمُومَةً, *they gave Zeid poisoned wine to drink;* اَعْطَاهُ ٱلْكِتَابَ, *he gave him the book;* رَزَقَهُ ٱللّٰهُ ٱلْعِلْمَ, *God gave*

3. The Government of the Verb.

him his life; وَقَاهُ ٱللَّبَنَ, he gave him milk in abundance; وَعَدَنَا ٱللّٰهُ ٱلْحَيْوَةَ ٱلْأَبَدِيَّةَ, he recited a poem to me; وَعَدَنَا ٱللّٰهُ ٱلْحَيْوَةَ ٱلْأَبَدِيَّةَ, God has promised us everlasting life; حَرَمَهُ ٱللّٰهُ بَرَكَةَ ٱلْعِلْمِ, God has deprived him of the blessing of learning; قِنَا عَذَابَ ٱلنَّارِ, preserve us from the punishment of hell-fire (in إِسْأَلِ ٱللّٰهَ ٱلْغَفْرَ ,(فِي imperative of وَقَى Vol. I. §. 178); ask pardon of God. — b) To the *second* class belong 1) verbs that mean *to make, appoint, call, name,* and the like; and 2) those verbs which are called by the Arab grammarians أَفْعَالُ ٱلْقَلْبِ, *verbs of the heart,* i. e. which signify an act that takes place in the mind, or أَفْعَالُ ٱلْيَقِينِ وَٱلشَّكِّ, *verbs of certainty and doubt* (such as رَأَى, *to think,* عَلِمَ, *to know,* وَجَدَ, *to find, to perceive,* دَرَى, *to know;* خَالَ, *to think, to imagine,* ظَنَّ, *to think, to believe,* حَسِبَ, *to think, to reckon,* زَعَمَ, *to think, to deem,* عَدَّ, *to count, to reckon,* and جَعَلَ, *to think, to imagine*). For example: جَعَلَ لَكُمُ ٱلْأَرْضَ فِرَاشًا, *he hath made the earth a bed for you;* صَيَّرْتُ ٱلطِّينَ إِبْرِيقًا, *I have made the clay into a jug;* ٱتَّخَذَ ٱللّٰهُ إِبْرَاهِيمَ خَلِيلًا, *God chose Abraham for a friend;* دَعَوْتُهُ مُحَمَّدًا, *I called him Mohammed;* سَمَّيْتُ كِتَابِي تَعْلِيمَ ٱلْمُتَعَلِّمِ طَرِيقَ ٱلتَّعَلُّمِ, *I named my book, The Instruction of the Learner in the Path of Learning;* عَلِمْتُ زَيْدًا جَاهِلًا, *I know Zeid is a fool;* رَأَيْتُ أَحَقَّ ٱلْحَقِّ حَقَّ ٱلْمُعَلِّمِ, *I think the duty we owe to a teacher the greatest of duties;* لَا تَحْسِبَنَّ ٱلَّذِينَ قُتِلُوا فِي سَبِيلِ ٱللّٰهِ أَمْوَاتًا, *do not deem those dead who have been slain in the path of God* (i. e. for the sake of their religion); وَجَدْتُهُ شَيْخًا حَلِيمًا, *I found him a mild (or gentle) old man;* مَا أَظُنُّ ٱلسَّاعَةَ قَآئِمَةً. *I do not think that the hour (of judgment) is at hand.*

Rem. *a*. Of the two objective complements, that which is the subject is called ٱلْمَفْعُولُ ٱلْأَوَّلُ, *the first object*, and the other, or predicate, ٱلْمَفْعُولُ ٱلثَّانِى, *the second object*.

Rem. *b*. When verbs like رَأَى and وَجَدَ are mere أَفْعَالُ ٱلْحِسِّ or *verbs of sense*, — i. e. express nothing but acts of the external organs of sense, — they may still be connected with two accusatives, but the second accusative is no longer a مَفْعُولٌ ثَانٍ or *second object*, but a حَالٌ or *circumstantial accusative*, i. e. an accusative expressing a state or condition of the object in actual connection with those acts; e. g. رَأَيْتُكَ نَآئِمًا, *I saw you sleeping;* وَجَدْتُهُ مَرِيضًا, *I found him sick* (in a state of sleep, of sickness). The learner will observe that, in these and similar phrases, رَأَى and وَجَدَ may often be translated by the very same words, whether they are أَفْعَالُ ٱلْحِسِّ or أَفْعَالُ ٱلْقَلْبِ; but, in the latter case, the object is merely the individual, apart from any predicate, whereas, in the former, it is the logical proposition *you were asleep*, *he was sick*, that is to say, the individual as the possessor of this quality.

Rem. *c*. The fourth form of the أَفْعَالُ ٱلْقَلْبِ governs three accusatives; e. g. يُرِيكُمْ أَعْمَالَكُمْ خَبِيثَةً, *he will*

3. The Government of the Verb.

make you think your actions bad, or *he will show you that your actions are bad.*

Rem. *d.* The اَفْعَالُ ٱلْقَلْبِ may also be construed so as to exercise no grammatical influence upon the clause that is immediately dependent upon them. This happens 1) when the verb is inserted parenthetically, as: زَيْدٌ ظَنَنْتُ جَاهِلٌ, *Zeid is, I think (or as I think), a fool;* 2) when it is placed at the beginning of the sentence, but the dependent clause is either negative, or interrogative, or else an affirmative clause introduced by the particle لَ, *truly;* e. g. عَلِمْتُمْ مَا جِئْنَا لِنُفْسِدَ فِي ٱلْأَرْضِ, *ye know we are not come to work evil on the earth;* مَا عَلِمْتَ أَيُّهُمْ جَآءَ, *do you not know which of them has come?* لَمْ أَدْرِ مَتَى يَجِيءُ, *I did not know when he would come;* ظَنَنْتُ لَزَيْدٌ قَآئِمٌ, *I think Zeid is standing up.* In the last example لَزَيْدٌ قَآئِمٌ is virtually in the accusative, for if another object be added, without the particle لَ being prefixed to it, it is put in the accusative; e. g. ظَنَنْتُ لَزَيْدٌ قَآئِمٌ وَعَمْرًا مُنْطَلِقًا, *I think Zeid is standing up and Amr going away.* In modern Arabic the particle أَنْ is interposed between the فِعْلُ ٱلْقَلْبِ and a dependent interrogative clause; as: لَمْ أَدْرِ أَنَّهُ مَتَى; مَا عَلِمْتَ أَنْ أَيُّهُمْ جَآءَ يَجِيءُ; لَا بُدَّ أَنْ يُبَيَّنَ أَوَّلًا أَنْ ٱلْاِسْمَ مَا هُوَ, *it must be first explained what the noun is.*

Rem. *e.* In reference to the first class of the verbs that govern two accusatives, see Gesenius' Heb. Gr. §. 136, 1, 2 (in connection with §. 135, in particular, paragraph 3); and in reference to the first division of the second class, §. 136, 2, the second paragraph.

25. If the verbs of the two classes mentioned in §. 24. are put in the *passive* voice, one of the two accusatives becomes the nominative. — In the case of the *first* class, it is the accusative of the person; e. g. عُلِّمَ عِلْمَ ٱلْهَيْئَةِ, *he was taught the science of astronomy;* أُطْعِمَ ٱلسَّيْفَ, *he was made to taste the sword* (was stabbed with it); سُقِيَ ٱلْوَزِيرُ مَآءً مَسْمُومًا, *poisoned water was given to the vizir to drink;* رُزِقَ ٱلْعُمْرَ, *life was granted him;* أُنْشِدتُ شِعْرًا لِغَيْرِهِ, *a poem by another (author) was recited to me;* حُرِمَ بَرَكَةَ ٱلْعِلْمِ, *he was deprived of the blessing of knowledge.* Should it happen that both accusatives are accusatives of the person, that which is next to the verb becomes the nominative; as: زُوِّجَ زَيْدٌ ٱبْنَةَ أَخِي, *my brother's daughter was given in marriage to Zeid.* If both are accusatives of the thing, that one becomes the nominative which designates the thing that is affected by, or receives or passes into the other, or the reverse; as: مُلِئَتِ ٱلدَّلْوُ مَآءً, *the bucket was filled with water.* — In the case of the *second* class, that accusative which is the subject of the other becomes the nominative; e. g. جُعِلَتْ لَكُمُ ٱلْأَرْضُ فِرَاشًا, *the earth has been made a bed for you;* صُيِّرَ ٱلطِّينُ إِبْرِيقًا, *the clay has been made into a jug;* حُسِبُوا أَمْوَاتًا, *they are deemed dead.*

Rem. *a.* As the verb أَتَى, *to come,* is construed with the accusative of the person (§. 23, rem. b), its fourth form (آتَى) becomes doubly transitive, and takes an accusative both of the person and of the thing; e. g. آتَى مُوسَى بَنِى إِسْرَآئِيلَ ٱلْكِتَابَ, *Moses brought the (holy) book to the children of Israel* (lit. *made it come to them*). Now, as this accusative of the thing is the nearer object of آتَى, we should expect it to become the nominative when the verb passes into the passive (أُوتِيَ); but the reverse is the case, because the person is of greater importance than the thing. We say therefore أُوتِيَ بَنُو إِسْرَآئِيلَ ٱلْكِتَابَ, *the (holy) book was brought to the children of Israel*, and not أُوتِيَ ٱلْكِتَابُ بَنِى إِسْرَآئِيلَ.

R e m. *b.* If the verb should happen to govern three accusatives in the active voice (§. 24, rem. *c*), that which is next to the verb becomes the nominative to the passive; e. g. نُبِّئْتُ لَيْلَى بِٱلْعِرَاقِ مَرِيضَةً, *I was informed (that) Leila is sick in el-'Irak*; إِذَا أُخْبِرْتَنِى دَنِفًا, *when thou art told (that) I am sick*.

R e m. *c.* On the Hebrew construction, see Gesenius' Gr. §. 140, 1.

26. All verbs, whether transitive or intransitive, active or passive, may take their own abstract nouns (nomina verbi, vol. I. §. 195), as also the deverbal nouns of the classes nomina vicis and nomina speciei (vol. I. §§. 193, 219, 220), as objective complements in the accusative. This may be the case either when they have no other objective complement or complements, or when they have

one or more; and the verbal noun may either stand alone, or it may be connected with an adjective or demonstrative pronoun, a noun in the genitive, or a descriptive or relative clause. For example: ضَرَبَ ضَرْبًا, lit. *he struck a striking*; نَامَ نَوْمًا, *he slept a sleep*; سَارَ سَيْرًا, *he journeyed a journey*; ضُرِبَ ضَرْبًا, lit. *he was struck (with) a striking*, or, impersonally, *there was struck a striking*; ضُرِبْتُ ضَرْبًا, lit. *I was struck (with) a striking*; سِيرَ سَيْرًا, lit. *there was journeyed a journey*; ضَرَبْتُهُ ضَرْبَةً وَضَرَبَنِي ضَرْبَتَيْنِ, *I struck him one stroke and he struck me two* (ضَرَبَنِي ضَرْبَتَيْنِ would mean *he struck me on two different occasions*, without specifying the number of blows he gave); ضَرَبْتُهُ ضِرْبَةً وَطَعَنَنِي طِعْنَةً, *I gave him a particular sort of stroke and he gave me a particular kind of thrust*; ضَرَبَ زَيْدًا رَأْسَهُ ضَرْبًا, lit. *he struck Zèid (as to) his head (with) a striking*; ضَرَبْتُهُ ضَرْبًا شَدِيدًا, or, omitting the nomen verbi, ضَرَبْتُهُ شَدِيدًا, *I gave him a violent beating*;* مَشَى مِشْيَةً حَسَنَةً, *he walked (with) a graceful gait*; ضَرَبَنِي هٰذَا الضَّرْبَ, *he beat me in this manner*, lit. *(with) this beating*; ضَرَبَهُ ضَرْبَ الْمَوْتِ, *he beat him to death*; ضَرَبَنِي خَافَ خَوْفَ الْجَبَانِ, *he feared as a coward fears*;

*) The undetermined object in such phrases as ضَرَبْتُهُ شَدِيدًا may, however, where the sense allows or requires it, assume a more definite meaning, and be viewed as an accusative of *time*; e.g. سَارُوا طَوِيلًا may be translated *they travelled a long time*, scil. زَمَانًا طَوِيلًا.

3. The Government of the Verb.

ضَرَبَنِي أَوْجَعَنِي, *he beat me so as to hurt me much*, lit. *he beat me a beating that pained me;* ضَرَبَنِي ٱلضَّرْبَ ٱلَّذِي لَا يَخْفَى عَلَيْكَ, *he gave me a good beating, as you know well,* lit. *he beat me the beating which is not concealed from you.*—This objective complement, which is called by the Arab grammarians ٱلْمَفْعُولُ ٱلْمُطْلَقُ, *the absolute object,** or ٱلْمَصْدَرُ (see Vol. I. §. 195, rem.), is used in the two following ways.

1) When it stands alone and undefined, it is used لِلتَّأْكِيدِ, *for strengthening,* or لِلتَّعْظِيمِ, *for magnifying,* i. e. to add greater force to the verb; e. g. إِذَا زُلْزِلَتِ ٱلْأَرْضُ زِلْزَالًا, *when the earth shall tremble a trembling* (but what a trembling!), i. e. *shall tremble violently;* إِذَا رُجَّتِ ٱلْأَرْضُ رَجًّا وَبُسَّتِ ٱلْجِبَالُ بَسًّا, *when the earth shall be shaken with a shaking* (i. e. *shaken violently*), *and the mountains shattered with a shattering* (i. e. *shattered to atoms*); رَضَّ عِظَامَهُ رَضًّا, *he crushed his bones with a crushing* (i. e. *crushed them to pieces*). This signification lies in the indefiniteness of the verbal noun, which leaves the verbal idea quite unlimited in its force and effect.

2) When it is connected with an adjective or demonstrative pronoun, a genitive, or a descriptive or relative clause (see the examples given above), it defines and limits the verbal idea by an addition which is expressed in our

---

*) Because it does not, like the object in a narrower sense, depend only upon a verb that governs one, two, or three accusatives in the active voice, or one or two accusatives in the passive.

family of languages by means of an adverb or a relative clause.

If the اَلْمَفْعُولُ ٱلْمُطْلَقُ be a nomen vicis, it is used لِلتَّعَدادٍ, *for enumeration;* and if it be a nomen speciei, or have an adjective, &c., connected with it, it is used لِلنَّوْعِ, *to indicate the kind, for specification,* or لِلتَّمْيِيزِ, *for distinction.*

Rem. *a.* Instead of the nomen verbi of the same finite verb, that of another verb of the same meaning, or else a concrete substantive, is sometimes employed; as: جَلَسَ قُعُودًا, lit. *he sat a sitting;* اِنْهَزَمُوا هَزِيمَةً شَنِيعَةً, *they fled a shameful flight.*

Rem. *b.* The accusative of the nomen verbi remains, as we have seen, unchanged, when the active voice, on which it depends, passes into the passive. It may, however, be changed into the nominative, when there is no other subject, as ضُرِبَ ضَرْبٌ, *a striking was struck,* a form of expression that corresponds to the impersonal passive of our languages. When the accusative is employed, the verb is impersonal; when the nominative, it is personal.

Rem. *c.* Compare the uses of the Hebrew infinitives קָטֹל and קָטֹל as explained in Gesenius' Gr. §§. 128, 129, and see also §. 135, 1, rem. 1.

27. It has been mentioned above (§. 21), that the nomina verbi derived from verbs that govern an objective complement in the accusative, may be construed in the same way as the finite verbs themselves. We shall here enter into some further details on this point.

3. The Government of the Verb.

1) If only the objective complement of the act, (and not likewise its subject,) be expressed, it is put after the nomen actionis in the genitive*; unless it be separated from the nomen actionis by one or more words, in which case it is put in the accusative, because the genitive can never be parted from the word that governs it. For example: لَا يَسْأَمِ ٱلْإِنْسَانُ مِنْ دُعَآءِ ٱللّٰهِ, *let a human being never get tired of calling upon* (or *praying to*) *God;* إِطْعَامٌ فِى يَوْمٍ ذِى مَسْغَبَةٍ يَتِيمًا, *to give an orphan food in time of famine;* بِضَرْبٍ بِٱلسُّيُوفِ رُءُوسَ قَوْمٍ, *by cutting off with swords the heads of some people.* In like manner, the object is put in the accusative, when the nomen actionis is defined by the article, because a noun, when so defined, cannot take a genitive after it; as: ضَعِيفُ ٱلنِّكَايَةِ أَعْدَآءَهُ, *feeble in harming his enemies;* لَمْ أَنْكُلْ عَنِ ٱلضَّرْبِ مِسْمَعًا, *I did not desist from striking Misma'*.

Rem. On the Hebrew construction, see Gesenius' Gr. §. 130, 1, along with the note †.

2) If both the subject and the objective complement of the act be expressed, three constructions are permitted. *a)* The subject may be put in the genitive, and the objective complement in the accusative; as: كَانَ قَتْلُ ٱلْخَلِيفَةِ جَعْفَرًا فِى هٰذِهِ ٱلسَّنَةِ, *in this year the chalif put Gafar to death* (lit. *the chalifs killing G. was in this year);* ٱذْكُرُوا ٱللّٰهَ كَذِكْرِكُمْ آبَآءَكُمْ, *think on God as ye think on your fathers. b)* The

---

*) This is called the objective genitive, to distinguish it from the subjective genitive or that which designates the subject of the act.

objective complement may be put in the genitive and the subject in the nominative; as: سَقَتْهُمْ رِيحُ ٱلْفَنَآءِ سَفْىَ ٱلرِّمَالِ يَدُ ٱلدَّبُورِ, *the wind of annihilation swept them away, as the hand of the west wind sweeps away the sands*; تَنْفِى يَدَاهَا ٱلْحَصَى فِى كُلِّ هَاجِرَةٍ نَفْىَ ٱلدَّرَاهِمِ تَنْقَادُ ٱلصَّيَارِيفِ, *her fore-feet scatter the gravel every midday, as the money-changers scatter the dirhems whilst selecting them*; مَنَعَ ٱلنَّاسَ كَآفَّةً مِنْ مُخَاطَبَتِهِ أَحَدٌ بِسَيِّدِنَا, *he gave orders to the entire people against any one's addressing him by the title of „our Lord"* (el nuestro Cid). *c)* The subject may be put in the nominative and the objective complement in the accusative; as: بَلَغَنِى تَطْلِيقُ ٱلْيَوْمَ زَيْدٌ هِنْدًا, *I have heard that Zeid has today divorced Hind*; بَلَغَنِى ٱلْقَتْلُ مَحْمُودٌ أَخَاهُ, *I have heard that Mahmūd has murdered his brother*; أَعْجَبَنِى ٱنْتِظَارُ يَوْمَ ٱلْجُمْعَةِ مُحَمَّدٌ عَمْرًا, *I am surprised at Mohammed's expecting 'Amr on Friday*. The first of these three constructions is the most usual. The second is pretty common, especially when the objective complement is a pronoun. The third, in which the nomen actionis may be accompanied by the article, or by a specification of the time or place of the act in the genitive, is of comparatively rare occurrence.

Rem. *a*. If both the subject and the objective complement be pronouns, they may both be suffixed to the nomen actionis; e. g. حُبِّيهِ عَلَّمَنِى ٱلتَّنَسُّكَ, *my love of him has taught me to be religious*. Here the suffix of the first person is the subject, and that of the third person the accusative.*

*) حُبٌّ *is, strictly speaking, an* اِسْمُ مَصْدَرٍ, *and not an actual*

Rem. b. Not only the nomina actionis, but also those nouns that are of similar force and signification, and which consequently can supply the place of the former, may be construed with the genitive of the subject and the accusative of the object. For example: بِعِشْرَتِكَ ٱلْكِرَامَ تُعَدُّ مِنْهُمْ, *through thy associating with the noble, thou art reckoned one of them* (مُعَاشَرَةٌ = عِشْرَةٌ); قُبْلَةِ ٱلرَّجُلِ زَوْجَتَهُ ٱلْوَضُوءُ, *ablution is (rendered necessary) by a man's kissing his wife* (تَقْبِيلٌ = قُبْلَةٌ); وَبَعْدَ عَطَائِكَ ٱلْمِائَةَ ٱلرِّتَاعَا, *and after thy giving the hundred grazing (camels)* (اَلرِّتَاعُ) ٱلرِّتَاعَا: إِعْطَاءً = عَطَاءً) in rhyme for).

Rem. c. What has been said of the nomina actionis of singly transitive verbs, applies equally to those of doubly transitive verbs. The only difference is, that the latter take an accusative after the objective genitive, or even add a second accusative to the first. For example: تَعْلِيمُ ٱلْمُتَعَلِّمِ طَرِيقَ ٱلتَّعَلُّمِ, *the instruction of the learner in the path of learning*; تَعْلِيمُ ٱلْمُعَلِّمِ ٱلْمُتَعَلِّمَ طَرِيقَ ٱلتَّعَلُّمِ &c., *the teacher's instructing the learner &c.*; إِنَّ ٱلنَّاسَ كَرِهُوا إِطْعَامَ مُحَمَّدٍ عَمْرًا خُبْزًا مَسْمُومًا, *the people have condemned Mohammed's giving Amr poisoned bread to eat.*

Rem. d. The complement in the genitive may also be expressed, when it represents the subject of the act, by مِنْ; when it represents the object, by لِ (see §. 29); and when it indicates time or place, by فِى; e. g. حُبَيْبٍ مِنْىَ لَهُ, in rem. *a*, by اَلْحُبُّ (ٱلْحَاصِلُ) مِنْىَ لَهُ (see §. 26); but it is used, instead of إِحْبَابٌ, as the masdar of أَحَبَّ (IV. of حَبَّ), *to love*. See rem. *b*.

the love (that accrues) from me to him; سَنَقَى ٱلْرِّمَالِ يَدُ ٱلدُّبُورِ,

in §. 27, 2, by ٱلسُّقْىَ مِنْ يَدِ ٱلدُّبُورِ لِلرِّمَالِ; and ٱنْتِظَارُ

ٱلْآنْتِظَارُ فِى يَوْمِ ٱلْجُمْعَةِ, ibid., by يَوْمَ ٱلْجُمْعَةِ.

R e m. *e*. On the corresponding constructions in Hebrew, see Gesenius' Gr. §. 130.

28. In the case of verbs that govern their objective complement by means of a preposition, the nomen actionis retains that preposition; e. g. مَا لِى قُدْرَةٌ عَلَى ذٰلِكَ, *I have no power to do this*, from قَدَرْتُ عَلَى شَىْءٍ.—The same thing holds good in the case of mixed government, the nearer object or accusative being converted into the genitive, and the more remote retaining its preposition; e. g. تَوْفِيقُ ٱلْإِنْسَانِ لِلطَّاعَةِ, *man's being helped (by God) to obey (him)*. Occasionally, however, the closer connection by means of the genitive is substituted for the looser construction with a preposition; e. g. مَيْلُ ٱلْإِسْلَامِ, *inclination (of the mind) towards el-'islām*, for ٱلْمَيْلُ إِلَى ٱلْإِسْلَامِ.

29. The nomen actionis often takes its objective complement not in the accusative but in the genitive with لِ, in which case this preposition is used as an outward exponent of the relation that subsists between the nomen verbi and its object. Hence the Arab grammarians rightly call it ٱللَّامُ لِتَقْوِيَةِ ٱلْعَامِلِ, *the lām that strengthens the regent* (the nomen actionis or the verbal power that it possesses); for, since the verbal force that dwells in the nomen actionis

3. The Government of the Verb. 45

is less than that in the finite verb, the language helps the former to exercise its influence upon its object by annexing to it a preposition expressing the direction of the action towards the object. This construction with لِ is used in the following cases.

a) When the nomen actionis immediately precedes the object and is undefined (see §. 27, 1); as: مِنْ غَيْرِ تَأَمُّلٍ لِخَطَآئِهِ وَصَوَابِهِ, *without considering what was false and what true in it*, instead of خَطَآءَهُ وَصَوَابَهُ. This is especially the case when the nomen actionis is in the adverbial accusative (see §. 44); as: أَقُومُ لَهُ تَعْظِيمًا لِأُسْتَاذِى, *I stand up in his presence to shew respect to my teacher*, instead of تَعْظِيمًا أُسْتَاذِى; إِنَّمَا قَالَ ذٰلِكَ إِكْرَامًا لَهُ, *he said this only to do him honour*, instead of إِكْرَامًا إِيَّاهُ.

b) When the nomen actionis immediately precedes the object, and is defined by the article (see §. 27, 1); as: تَرْكُ ٱلْمُطَالَبَةِ لِلنَّاسِ, *the giving up of persecuting the people*.

c) When the genitive of the subject is interposed between the nomen actionis and the object (see §. 27, 2); as: يَبْقَى أَنْ تَسْخِينَ ٱلشَّمْسِ لِلْأَرْضِ إِنَّمَا هُوَ عَلَى سَبِيلِ ٱلْإِضَآءَةِ, *it results, therefore, that the sun warms the earth in no other way than by his light* (lit. *that the sun's warming the earth is only by the way of his light*), for ٱلْأَرْضِ; لِمُطَالَبَةِ أَعْدَآئِى لِى, *because of my enemies' persecuting me*, for إِيَّايَ; رُؤْيَتُهُ لِلّٰهِ, *his seeing God*; تَبْلِيغِى لَكَ إِلَى مُنَاكَ, *my enabling you to attain your wishes*.

In such clauses the choice between the older and closer construction with the accusative, and the later and looser with the preposition, is left in most cases to the taste and judgment of the writer.

Rem. *a*. In more modern Arabic إِلَى is often used لِتَقْوِيَةِ ٱلْعَامِلِ instead of لِ; as: اِذِّكَارِي إِلَيْهِ, *my bearing him in mind;* رَدِّي إِلَى ٱلْجَوَابِ, *my returning an answer.*

Rem. *b*. This use of لِ to designate the objective complement of the verb is common in Chaldee and Syriac, rare in Hebrew (see Gesenius' Gr. §. 151, 3, *c*) and Aethiopic (see Dillmann's Gr. §. 179). See §. 31, rem.

30. The nomina agentis, which hold a middle position between the verb and the noun, and partake of the force of both, may, like the nomina verbi, follow the government either of the verb or the noun, or of both. The following rules are to be observed regarding them.

1) If the nomen agentis has but *one* objective complement, this may be put either in the accusative or in the genitive; as: سَارِعُوا إِلَى جَنَّةٍ أُعِدَّتْ لِلْكَاظِمِينَ ٱلْغَيْظَ, *hasten to a garden (Paradise) that is prepared for those who restrain (their) wrath;* كُلُّ نَفْسٍ ذَائِقَةُ ٱلْمَوْتِ, *every soul is a taster of death (tastes* or *shall taste death);* رَبَّنَا إِنَّكَ جَامِعُ ٱلنَّاسِ, *our Lord! thou shalt be an assembler of (shalt assemble) mankind;* ٱلَّذِينَ يَظُنُّونَ أَنَّهُمْ مُلَاقُو رَبِّهِمْ, *who think that they shall be meeters of (shall meet) their Lord.* — The no-

3. The Government of the Verb.

mina agentis of directly transitive verbs admit of being construed, in so far as they have verbal power, either with the accusative or with the genitive, provided they have the meaning of the اَلْمُضَارِعُ or *imperfect* (historical imperfect, present, future). As the genitive connexion is in this case غَيْرُ ٱلْحَقِيقِيَّةِ, improper or representative (see §. 75, rem.), the governing word may be defined by the article; as: اَلْقَاتِلُ ٱلنَّاسِ or قَاتِلُ ٱلنَّاسِ, *one who kills people;* اَلْقَاتِلُ ٱلنَّاسَ or ٱلْقَاتِلُ ٱلنَّاسَ, *he who kills people,* = اَلَّذِى يَقْتُلُ ٱلنَّاسَ. When, on the contrary, the nomina agentis of directly transitive verbs have the meaning of the *perfect* (perfect, pluperfect, aorist, and future perfect), they approach more nearly to the nature of the noun that originates from them (as كَاتِبٌ, *writing, a writer*), and hence are construed, like this latter, with the genitive only. Further, since this genitive connection is حَقِيقِيَّةٌ or proper (see §. 75, rem.), the governing word cannot be defined by the article; as: قَاتِلُ ٱلنَّاسِ (and not اَلْقَاتِلُ ٱلنَّاسَ or ٱلْقَاتِلُ ٱلنَّاسِ), *one who killed, has killed, had killed, or shall have killed people,* = اَلَّذِى قَتَلَ, or اَلَّذِى كَانَ قَتَلَ, or اَلَّذِى يَكُونُ قَتَلَ. The same remarks naturally apply, when the genitive is a pronominal suffix instead of a separate substantive; as: لَاْئِمِى = اَللَّائِمِى, أَحَدٌ يَلُومُنِى, *one who reproaches me,* and اَلَّذِى يَلُومُنِى, *he who reproaches me;* but *he who reproached* or *has reproached me,* is لَائِمِى, اَلَّذِى لَامَنِى, not اَللَّائِمِى. — If the nomen agentis be undefined, it go-

verns the accusative only in the following cases. *a)* When it is the attribute or the predicate of a (usually preceding) subject, or stands in the accusative to express a state or condition of that subject (see §. 40); e. g. زَيْدٌ ضَارِبٌ أَبُوهُ أَخًا لِي, *Zeid's father* (lit. *Zeid, his father) is beating* (or *will beat) a brother of mine;* مَرَرْتُ بِفَارِسٍ طَالِبٍ ثَأْرَ أَبِيهِ, *I passed by a horseman (who was) seeking revenge for the murder of his father;* جَآءَنِي عَمْرٌو طَالِبًا أَدَبًا, *'Amr came to me seeking instruction.* *b)* After an interrogative or negative particle, when it is the attribute of a preceding or (less usually) following subject; e. g. هَلْ مُكْرِمٌ أَنْتَ زَيْدًا, *will thou treat Zeid with respect?* مَا أَنْتَ بِتَابِعٍ قِبْلَتَهُمْ, *thou dost not follow their ḳibla;* مَا مُجِيرٌ أَحَدٌ عَدُوَّ أَحِبَّائِهِ *no one gives protection to the enemy of his friends.*
c) After the interjection يَا, as the predicate of a suppressed subject; e. g. يَا طَالِعًا جَبَلًا, *O thou that art climbing a hill!*

Rem. *a.* The nomen agentis in the singular number, when followed by a substantive in the genitive, can take the article only when that substantive is itself defined by the article or governs another substantive that is so defined; e. g. اَلضَّارِبُ الْعَبْدِ, *he who beats the slave;* اَلضَّارِبُ رَأْسِ الْعَبْدِ, *he who beats the slave on the head* (lit. *beats the head of the slave);* but we cannot say اَلضَّارِبُ عَبْدٍ, nor اَلضَّارِبُ عَبْدِهِ, nor even اَلضَّارِبُ عَبْدِ زَيْدٍ or اَلضَّارِبُ زَيْدٍ. The reason of this seems to be that a certain equipoise may be preserved between the اَلْمُضَافُ, or governing word, and the

3. The Government of the Verb.

ٱلْمُضَافُ إِلَيْهِ, or governed word. On the other hand, the article may be prefixed to the dual or to the pluralis sanus masc., even when the following genitive is not defined in either of the above ways; because, after the rejection of the terminations ن and نِ (vol. I. §. 315, 2, 3), the ٱلْمُضَافُ and the ٱلْمُضَافُ إِلَيْهِ become more closely connected, and grow, as it were, into one word, just like the nomen agentis when defined by the article and followed by a pronominal suffix. Hence we may say ٱلضَّارِبَا عَبْدِ, ٱلضَّارِبِى عَبْدِهِ, ٱلضَّارِبُو عَبْدِ زَيْدٍ, ٱلضَّارِبَىْ زَيْدٍ as well as ٱلضَّارِبِينَ, ٱلضَّارِبُونَ عَبْدَ زَيْدٍ, ٱلضَّارِبَيْنِ زَيْدًا, ٱلضَّارِبَانِ عَبْدًا عَبْدَهُ. There is even a third form of expression admissible, arising out of a combination of these two, viz. ٱلضَّارِبَىْ زَيْدٍ, ٱلضَّارِبَا عَبْدَهُ, ٱلضَّارِبِى عَبْدَهُ, ٱلضَّارِبُو عَبْدَ زَيْدٍ; in which examples the rejection of the terminations ن and نِ serves only to indicate the close logical connection, as in the phrase ٱلْأَمِيرُ ٱلْقَاتِلَا أَخَوَاهُ مُحَمَّدًا, the emir whose two brothers killed Mohammed, in which another noun (أَخَوَاهُ) is actually inserted between the nomen agentis in the dual (ٱلْقَاتِلَا) and its accusative (مُحَمَّدًا). — When a pronoun is annexed as object to the dual or pluralis sanus masc. of a nomen agentis that is defined by the article, three forms of expression are likewise admissible; viz. 1) ٱلضَّارِبَاهُ, ٱلضَّارِبُوهُ (2 ; ٱلضَّارِبَانِ إِيَّاهُ; and ; ٱلضَّارِبُونَ إِيَّاهُ or ٱلضَّارِبُونَ لَهُ, ٱلضَّارِبَانِ لَهُ or (3 ٱلضَّارِبُونَهُ, ٱلضَّارِبَانِهِ. In the last case the pronoun, though apparently a nominal suffix in the genitive, is in reality a verbal suffix in the accusative; and even in the first case, the Arabs regard the pronominal object as an accusative, and not as a genitive, using نِي instead of ـِي for the 1st pers. sing.; e. g. اَلْمُوَافِينِي, *he who comes to me*; لَيْسَ بِمُعْيِينِي, *he is not a too heavy burden for me*; ثُمَّ الْآمِرُونَ ٱلْخَيْرَ وَٱلْفَاعِلُونَهُ, *it is they who order what is right, and who do it themselves.*

Rem. *b*. When the nomen agentis is followed by two or more objects connected by وَ, it not rarely happens that the first alone is put in the genitive, and the others in the accusative, the nominal force of the nomen agentis being converted, because of the distance of the complements, into the verbal; as: مُبْتَغِي جَاهٍ وَمَالًا مَنْ نَهَضَ, *a seeker after rank and wealth is he who rises up (to travel)*; جَاعِلُ ٱللَّيْلِ سَكَنًا وَٱلشَّمْسَ وَٱلْقَمَرَ حُسْبَانًا, *he who appoints the night for rest, and the sun and moon for the reckoning (of time)*; اَلْوَاهِبِ ٱلْمِائَةِ ٱلْهِجَانِ وَعَبْدَهَا, *of him who gives a hundred fine white (camels) and their attendant* (either وَعَبْدَهَا or وَعَبْدِهَا).

Rem. *c*. On the government of the participle in Hebrew, see Gesenius' Gr. §. 132.

2) If the nomen agentis be derived from a verb that governs two objective complements (§. 24), it takes the second in the accusative, and the first either in the accusative (which is by far the more usual) or in the genitive; e. g. أَنَا كَاسٍ زَيْدًا ثَوْبًا فَاخِرًا, *I will dress Zeid in a splendid robe*; هَلْ أَنْتَ ظَانٌّ عَمْرًا عَاقِلًا, or ظَانُّ عَمْرٍو عَاقِلًا, *dost thou think 'Amr intelligent?*

Rem. *a*. If the objective complements of the nomen agentis of a doubly transitive verb be pronouns, both may be appended to it as suffixes; e. g. مُعْطِيكَهُ, *he who gives it to you*; مُطْعِمُنِيهَا, *he who gives me it to eat.*

3. The Government of the Verb. 51

Rem. *b.* The second of the two complements of a nomen agentis, or that which is in the accusative, is very rarely inserted between the nomen agentis and the first complement, or that in the genitive; e. g. وَرَسُولَاتٌ مَانِعٌ فَضْلَهُ ٱلْمُحْتَاجِ, *whilst others than you withhold their benefits from the needy;* لَا تَحْسِبَنَّ ٱللّٰهَ مُخْلِفَ وَعْدَهُ رُسُلَهُ, *do not think that God deceives his apostles by withholding what he has promised.* In the former of these examples, which is a half-verse of poetry, this construction has been followed in order to bring the word ٱلْمُحْتَاجِ into the rhyme; in the latter, which is taken from the Korân, ch. 14, v. 48, the preferable reading is مُخْلِفَ وَعْدِهِ رُسُلَهُ.

31. What has been said in §. 29 regarding the use of the preposition لِ after nomina verbi is equally applicable to nomina agentis. *a)* لِ is used when the nomen agentis immediately precedes the object and is undefined; as: مُحِبٌّ لَكَ, *making thee wonder;* وَهِيَ مُجَانِبَةٌ لَهُ, *whilst she avoided him* (in which example the undefined nomen agentis is the predicate of a جُمْلَةٌ حَالِيَّةٌ or circumstantial clause); وَٱلْحِيلَةُ لَا تَجُوزُ إِلَّا إِذَا كَانَ ٱلْخَصْمُ مُتَعَنِّتًا لَا طَالِبًا لِلْحَقِّ, *and artifice is not allowable* (in argument), *except when the opponent is a dogmatical sophist, and not one who seeks after the truth.* This is especially the case when the nomen agentis is in the adverbial accusative; as: نَزَلَ عَلَى ٱلْمَدِينَةِ مُحَاصِرًا لَهَا, *he halted before the city to besiege it;* وَكَفَى بِلَذَّةِ ٱلْعِلْمِ دَاعِيًا وَبَاعِثًا لِلْعَاقِلِ, *the sweetness of knowledge is a sufficient inducement and enticement to the intelligent.*

7*

b) لِ is also used when the nomen agentis immediately precedes the object, and is defined by the article; as: اَلْمُفَسِّرُونَ لِهٰذِهِ ٱلْأَبْيَاتِ, *the expounders of these verses;* أَقْوَى ٱلْأَسْبَابِ ٱلْجَالِبَةِ لِلرِّزْقِ إِقَامَةُ ٱلصَّلٰوةِ بِٱلتَّعْظِيمِ, *to perform one's devotions properly with reverence is the surest means of procuring one's daily bread;* وَبَقِيَ يَتَفَكَّرُ فِي ذٰلِكَ ٱلشَّيْءِ ٱلْمُصَرِّفِ لِلْجَسَدِ, *and he continued meditating about that thing which governs the body.* *c)* Finally, لِ is used when a genitive is interposed between the nomen agentis and the accusative; as: مُطْعِمُهَا لِي, *he who gave it to me to eat.*

Rem. لِ must be used instead of the accusative, when the object of the nomen agentis is rhetorically transposed and placed before it; as: مَا كُنَّا لَنَا عَابِدِينَ وَكَانُوا, *and they worshipped us;* إِنَّا لَهُ لَحَافِظُونَ, *we did not keep the secret;* لِلْغَيْبِ حَافِظِينَ, *verily we will take care of him;* ٱلْمَرْءُ مَا لَمْ تَرْزَأْ لَكَ مُكْرِمٌ, *a man, as long as you do not deprive him of any thing (by asking for it), treats you with respect.* So also with the finite verb: إِنْ كُنْتُمْ لِلرُّؤْيَا تَعْبُرُونَ, *if ye can explain the vision.* If the transposed object be a pronominal suffix, إِيَّا (vol. I. §. 188, 189) may be employed instead of لِ; as: إِيَّاكَ نَعْبُدُ وَإِيَّاكَ نَسْتَعِينُ, *thee we worship and to thee we cry for help* (compare §. 29, rem. *b*, and vol. I. §. 189, 2).

32. If the verb, from which a nomen patientis is derived, governs two accusatives in the active voice, its nomen patientis retains one of them, the other having passed into the nominative; as: زَيْدٌ مُعْطًى عَبْدُهُ دِرْهَمًا, *Zeid's*

3. The Government of the Verb. 53

servant (lit. *Zèid, his servant*) *is presented with a dirhèm.* See §. 25.

33. Verbal adjectives of those forms that differ in meaning from the nomina agentis only in being *intensive*, may govern, like the nomina agentis, either the accusative or the preposition لِ. Since, however, their verbal force is very slight, the latter construction is by far the more usual, the former being chiefly poetic. This rule applies principally to the forms فَعَّالٌ and فَعُولٌ (vol. I. §. 232 and rem. *c*, §. 233); more rarely to other forms, such as فَعِيلٌ (§. 232), فَعِلٌ (id.), and مِفْعَالٌ (§. 233, rem *c*). Examples with the accusative: أَخَا ٱلْحَرْبِ لَبَّاسًا إِلَيْهَا جِلَالَهَا, *inured to* (lit. *a brother of*) *warfare, constantly wearing the garments suited for it;* مُقْدِمًا إِلَى ٱلْمَوْتِ خَوَّاضًا إِلَيْهِ ٱلْكَتَائِبَا, *rushing upon death, wading in search of it through the ranks* (ٱلْكَتَائِبَا in rhyme for ٱلْكَتَائِبَ); ضَرُوبٍ بِنَصْلِ ٱلسَّيْفِ هَامَاتِ ٱلرِّجَالِ, *smiting with the edge of the sword the heads of men;* فَتَاتَانِ أَمَّا مِنْهُمَا نَشْبِيهَةٌ هِلَالٌ, *two maidens, (one) of them resembling a new moon* (in beauty); إِنَّ ٱللّٰهَ سَمِيعٌ دُعَآءَ مَنْ دَعَاهُ, *God hears the prayer of him who calls upon him;* حَذِرٌ أُمُورًا لَا تَضِيرُ, *taking precautions against things that cannot injure (him);* مَزِّقُونَ عِرْضِي, *defaming* (lit. *tearing in pieces*) *my character;* إِنَّهُ لَنَحَّارٌ بَوَآئِكَهَا, *he is a slaughterer of the fat ones among them* (the she-camels). Examples with لِ: سَمَّاعُونَ لِلْكَذِبِ أَكَّالُونَ لِلسُّحْتِ, *hearers of falsehood, eaters of what is unlawful;* مَنَّاعٍ لِلْخَيْرِ,

constantly striving to hinder good; جَمَاعَةٌ لِلْكُتُبِ, *a great collector of books;* &c.

34. Verbal adjectives of the form أَفْعَلُ, corresponding to our comparative and superlative (vol. I. §. 234), when derived from *transitive* verbs, generally take their object in the genitive with لِ, very rarely in the accusative; e. g. هُوَ أَطْلَبُ لِلْعِلْمِ مِنْكُمْ, *he seeks after knowledge more than you do;* اَلْمُؤْمِنُ أَحَبُّ لِلّٰهِ مِنْ نَفْسِهِ, *the believer loves God more than himself;* أَجْهَلُ ٱلنَّاسِ وَأَعْدَاهُمْ لِلْعِلْمِ وَأَمْقَتُهُمْ لِلشَّرْعِ, *the most ignorant of men, and the most opposed among them to learning, and the most inimical among them to the law.*

Rem. *a.* Verbal adjectives of the form أَفْعَلُ, derived from verbs signifying *love* or *hatred*, take the object with لِ when they are used in an *active* sense, as in the second and third of the above examples; but when they have a *passive* sense*, they take the subject with إِلَى, as: اَلْمُؤْمِنُ أَحَبُّ إِلَى ٱللّٰهِ مِنْ غَيْرِهِ, *the believer is more loved of God than any one else;* هُوَ أَبْغَضُ إِلَيَّ مِنْهَا, *he is more hateful to me than she.*

Rem. *b.* Verbal adjectives of the form أَفْعَلُ, derived from *intransitive* verbs, require the same preposition after them as the verbs

*) As there is *only one* form for the comparative and superlative, it may be derived from verbal adjectives of either active or passive signification; e. g. أَحَبُّ from يُحِبُّ, *loving*, or from حَبِيبٌ, *beloved, dear.*

3. The Government of the Verb.

from which they are derived. For example: هُوَ أَزْهَدُ فِي ٱلدُّنْيَا, وَأَسْرَعُ إِلَى ٱلْخَيْرِ وَأَبْعَدُ مِنَ ٱلْإِثْمِ وَأَحْرَصُ عَلَى ٱلْحَمْدِ, *he abstains more from worldly pleasures, and is more zealous for good, and keeps farther from (clearer of) crime, and is more eager after the praise (of God)*. They often, however, take their signification from one of the derived forms of the verb (generally the second or fourth); e. g. ذٰلِكُمْ أَقْوَمُ لِلشَّهَادَةِ, *this confirms the evidence more* (from أَقَامَ, IV. of قَامَ, *to stand*); خُمُولُ ٱلْمَرْءِ لِلدِّينِ أَسْلَمُ, *humility on the part of a man preserves his religion more (than pride)* (from سَلِمَ or سَلَّمَ, أَسْلَمَ, II. and IV. of سَلِمَ, *to be safe*); غَيْرُ ٱلدَّجَّالِ أَخْوَفُنِي عَلَيْكُمْ, *there is another besides the anti-Christ that fills me with still greater fear on your account than he does* (from أَخَافُ, II. and IV. of خَافَ, *to be afraid*); هُوَ أَحْوَجُ or خَوَّفَ إِلَيَّ مِنِّى إِلَيْهِ, *he has more need of me than I have of him* (from إِحْتَاجَ, VIII. of the radical حوج, *to be in need of*).

35. The accusative not unfrequently depends upon a verb that is understood. This happens:

1) In forms of praise, salutation, and the like, in which we must supply the verb from which the noun in the accusative is derived, and to which it serves as the اَلْمَفْعُولُ ٱلْمُطْلَقُ (§. 26). For example: سُبْحَانَ ٱللّٰهِ, *the glory of God!* or سُبْحَانَهُ, *His glory!* scil. أُسَبِّحُ, *I praise* (which is an إِخْبَارٌ or *statement of fact*), or سَبِّحِى, سَبِّحْ, &c., *praise thou,* &c. (which is an إِنْشَاءٌ, *a command* or *wish,* lit. *a production* or *creation*); سَمْعًا وَطَاعَةً, *hearing and*

obeying, to hear is to obey, i. e. أَسْمَعُ سَمْعًا وَأُطِيعُ طَاعَةً; مَعَاذَ ٱللّٰهِ, *God forbid!* i. e. أَعُوذُ مَعَاذَ ٱللّٰهِ, *I seek refuge with God.*

2) In various other cases, in all of which the verb to be supplied is not that from which the noun in the accusative is derived, but may be easily guessed from the manner in which that noun is uttered and the circumstances of the speaker. Such are:

a) Forms of salutation and the like; as: مَرْحَبًا وَأَهْلًا وَسَهْلًا, scil. أَتَيْتَ, *thou art come (O guest) to a roomy (convenient) place, and to friendly people, and to a smooth (comfortable) place;* مَرْحَبًا بِكَ, i. e. أَتَيْتَ مَكَانًا يَرْحُبُ بِكَ, *thou art come to a place where there is plenty of room for thee, to a comfortable place;* مَرْحَبًا بِكَ ٱللّٰهُ وَمَسْهَلًا, scil. جَعَلَ or some similar word, *God has given thee a roomy and smooth place;* all phrases equivalent to *welcome!* هَنِيئًا مَرِيئًا, scil. كُلْ, كُلِى, &c., *(eat) with easy digestion, may it agree with you,* Germ. *wohl bekomm' es.*

b) Phrases in which an individual is called upon to guard himself, or a part of his person, against some one or some thing (ٱلتَّحْذِيرُ); or in which one or more individuals are urged to begin something or attack some object (ٱلْإِغْرَاءُ). In the former case the speaker may mention α) either the person who is to be on his guard, or β) the person or thing he is to guard against, repeating the word or not, at his pleasure, or lastly γ) both together, connecting them by the conjunction وَ. In the latter case he mentions only the

3. The Government of the Verb.

object to be attacked, repeating the word or not, as he pleases. Examples: بَعْدُ, scil. ,&c. إِيَّاكَ إِيَّاكَ or ,.&c ,إِيَّاكُمْ ,إِيَّاكَ keep off! or اِحْذَرْ, guard thyself! take care! رَأْسَكَ رَأْسَكَ or رَأْسَكَ رَأْسَكَ, thy head! scil. نَحِّ, bend aside; أَمَامَكَ, before thee! scil. اُنْظُرْ, look; ٱلْأَسَدَ or ٱلْأَسَدَ ٱلْأَسَدَ, the lion! scil. اِحْذَرْ, guard against, take care of; إِيَّاكَ وَٱلْمُعَادَاةَ, guard thyself against enmity; إِيَّاكَ وَٱلْمُحْدَثَاتِ, keep clear of innovations; إِيَّاكَ وَأَنْ تَشْتَغِلَ بِهٰذَا ٱلْجَدَلِ, take care not to meddle with this sort of contention (where أَنْ, followed by the imperfect subjunctive, is put instead of the accusative of a noun); رَأْسَكَ وَٱلْحَائِطَ, thy head and the wall! scil. ٱلْعَدُوَّ ٱلْعَدُوَّ; نَحِّ رَأْسَكَ وَٱحْذَرِ ٱلْحَائِطَ, the foe! the foe! scil. خُذُوا, seize, attack; أَخَاكَ وَٱلْإِحْسَانَ إِلَيْهِ, be always kind to your brother, scil. اِلْزَمْ, adhere to; شَأْنَكَ بِإِبِلِكَ, do as you like with your camels, scil. اِفْعَلْ, do.*)

c) Phrases in which a pronoun — generally of the first, rarely of the second person — is followed by the noun to which it refers in the accusative, without any verb intervening. The object of this construction — named by the Arab grammarians ٱلْإِخْتِصَاصُ, the special relation (of the pronoun to some person or thing) — is to show that

---

*) If a single accusative be uttered only once, the verb may be added; but if the accusative be repeated, or if there be two accusatives connected by وَ, the verb is never expressed.

this accusative is the noun which the pronoun represents and to which the statement made refers. Being especially used in forms of praise and blame, it is also called نَصْبُ ٱلْمَدْحِ وَٱلذَّمِّ, *the accusative of praise and blame.* It is to be explained by an ellipsis of أَعْنِي, *I mean,* or أَخُصُّ, *I specify.* Examples: نَحْنُ ٱلْعَرَبَ أَتْقَى مَنْ بَذَلَ, *we Arabs* — lit. *we, (I mean) the Arabs,* — *are the most liberal among the generous;* نَحْنُ ٱلصَّعَالِيكَ لَا طَاقَةَ بِنَا عَلَى ٱلْمُرُوءَةِ, *we, the miserably poor, have not the ability to be generous as becomes men;* نَحْنُ مَعَاشِرَ ٱلْأَنْبِيَآءِ لَا نُوَرَّثُ, *we, the band of prophets, have no heirs (among men);* إِنَّا بَنِى مِنْقَرٍ قَوْمٌ ذَوُو حَسَبٍ, *we, the Benū Minkar, are a people of high worth;* أَلَمْ تَرَ أَنَّا بَنِى دَارِمٍ زُرَارَةُ مِنَّا أَبُو مَعْبَدِ, *seest thou not that Zurāra, the father of Má bed, is one of us, the Benū Dārim?* (مَعْبَدِ in rhyme for مَعْبَدٍ).

Rem. In such phrases as هَاكَ يَدِى, *there it is for you!* إِلَيْكَهَا, *there's my hand for you!* the accusative is used, because هَاكَ and إِلَيْكَ (vol. I. §. 368, rem. c) are in point of sense equivalent to خُذْ, *take* (خُذْ). Similarly, in the phrases خُذْ يَدِى, خُذْهَا إِلَيْكَ or خُذْهَا, دُونَكَ زَيْدًا, *seize Zeid!* دُونَكَ زَيْدًا, عِنْدَكَ زَيْدًا, عَلَيْكَ زَيْدًا, أَنْ تَأْخُذَ, دُونَكُمُوهُ, *seize him!* the accusative does not depend upon (*that thou shouldest seize*), to be supplied after the preposition, but upon an imperative, such as خُذْ or اِلْزَمْ, implied in the preposition itself. The literal meaning is: *seize Zeid, who is in front of, beside* or *close by you.* So also in رُوَيْدَ زَيْدًا, or, with the genitive, رُوَيْدَ زَيْدٍ, *treat Zeid gently!* where رُوَيْدَ is explained by

3. The Government of the Verb.

the grammarians as equivalent to أَمْهِلْ, *grant him respite.* In the first case, the fĕtha of رُوَيْدَ is a بِنَاءٌ or indeclinable ending (as in أَيْنَ, *where?*); in the second, it is the termination of the construct accusative of رُوَيْدَ, the diminutive of رُودٌ, *slow and gentle motion*. We may also say رُوَيْدَكَ زَيْدًا, *softly!* and رُوَيْدَكَ زَيْدًا, *gently with Zeid!*, رُوَيْدَكَنِى, *gently with me!* the agent (كَ) being in the genitive.

36. The adverb إِنَّ, *truly, certainly*, and the conjunction أَنَّ, *that*, as likewise the conjunctions compounded with these two words, such as لٰكِنَّ or وَلٰكِنَّ, *but, yet*, كَأَنَّ, *as if, as though*, and لِأَنَّ, *because* (see vol. I. §. 362, 6, and §. 367, 6, 10), take a following substantive or pronoun (which, according to our idiom, ought to be in the nominative, as the subject of a nominal or verbal proposition) in the accusative, because the force of the verb *to see* (رَأَى) is embodied in these particles.*) This takes place both when the subject immediately follows إِنَّ, &c., and when it is separated from them by a portion of the predicate of إِنَّ, &c., consisting of an adverb of time or place, or a preposition with its complement. In the former case, the affirmative particle لَ may be prefixed to the predicate of إِنَّ; in the latter to its subject. If, however, the predicate be negative, or consist of a verb in the perfect, not preceded by قَدْ, the particle لَ ought not to be prefixed to it. Examples: إِنَّ ٱللّٰهَ عَلَىٰ كُلِّ شَىْءٍ قَدِيرٌ, *God*

---

*) Compare *en* and *ecce* in Latin, as *en eum, ecce eum* or *eccum*.

is mighty over all (lit. see God, he is mighty over all); إِنَّ ٱلْحَدَائِقَ لَا تَدُومُ, youth does not last (lit. see youth, it does not last); وَإِنْ فَرِيقًا مِنَ ٱلْمُؤْمِنِينَ لَكَارِهُونَ, whilst a part of the believers were reluctant; أَئِنَّكُمْ لَتَشْهَدُونَ أَنْ مَعَ ٱللّٰهِ آلِهَةً أُخْرَى, do ye testify that there are other gods along with the (true) God? إِنَّ بِٱلشِّعْبِ ٱلَّذِى دُونَ سَلْعٍ لَقَتِيلًا, in the ravine that is below Selaʿ (there lies) a murdered man; إِنَّ فِى ذٰلِكَ لَعِبْرَةً لِأُولِى ٱلْأَبْصَارِ, in this there is an example (or warning) to those possessed of insight; إِنَّ فِى تَقْتِلِكَ أَيُّهَا ٱلشَّيْخُ لَصَلَاحًا لِلْمُسْلِمِينَ, in putting thee to death, old man, there is a benefit to the Muslims; حُكِيَ أَنَّ مَلِكًا مِنْ مُلُوكِ ٱلْهِنْدِ كَانَ لَهُ زَوْجَةٌ, it is narrated that one of the kings of India had a wife; وَفِى ٱلْحَدِيثِ أَنَّ رَجُلًا قَالَ يَرَسُولَ ٱللّٰهِ إِنَّ أُمِّى ٱنْفَلَتَتْ فُجَاءَةً, and in the hadît — or collection of traditions — (we read) that a man said, O apostle of God! my mother has died suddenly; كَأَنَّ زَيْدًا أَسَدٌ, as if Zeid were a lion; وَهٰذَا لِأَنَّ ٱلْعِلْمَ نُورٌ وَٱلْوَضُوءَ نُورٌ, and (he did) this because knowledge is a light and the ablution (before prayer) is a light; زَيْدٌ قَآئِمٌ وَلٰكِنَّ مُحَمَّدًا جَالِسٌ, Zeid is standing up, but Mohammed is sitting; وَلٰكِنَّ ٱلْمُنَافِقِينَ لَا يَفْقَهُونَ, but the hypocrites do not understand.

Rem. a. These particles, along with those mentioned in rem. d, are named by the grammarians إِنَّ وَأَخَوَاتُهَا, 'inna and its sisters. The word governed by إِنَّ and أَنَّ is called the اِسْمُ أَنَّ, the noun of 'inna and 'anna, and the predicate is called the خَبَرُ أَنَّ, the predicate of 'inna and 'anna.

3. The Government of the Verb.

Rem. *b.* If the predicate is placed between إِنَّ or أَنَّ and its noun, the logical accent lies upon the noun; whereas, if the predicate stands after the noun, it receives the logical accent itself. For example; إِنَّ مَعَكَ صَاحِبَكَ means: *your friend is with you*; but إِنَّ صَاحِبَكَ مَعَكَ, *your friend is with you*.

Rem. *c.* When مَا is appended to إِنَّ, كَأَنَّ, and لٰكِنَّ, their governing power does not extend beyond it, and consequently their اِسْم or noun is no longer put in the accusative, but in the nominative. Hence the word مَا is called in this case مَا ٱلْكَافَّة, *the hindering mâ*, because it hinders the government of these particles.

Rem. *d.* The words لَيْتَ, *utinam*, *would that —!* and عَلَّ or لَعَلَّ, *perhaps*, are construed in the same way as إِنَّ, &c.; e. g. يَا لَيْتَ بَيْنَكَ وَبَيْنِى بُعْدَ ٱلْمَشْرِقَيْنِ, *O that there were between thee and me as great a distance as there is between east and west!* وَمَا يُدْرِيكَ لَعَلَّ ٱلسَّاعَةَ قَرِيبٌ, *and what lets thee know (whether) perchance the hour (of the resurrection) is near?* If مَا be added (see rem. *c*), the government of عَلَّ or لَعَلَّ is hindered; but the noun of لَيْتَمَا may be put either in the nominative or in the accusative. These words seem, as has been already remarked in vol. I. §. 364, rem. *b*, to be verbs; and if so, they govern the accusative by their own force and not by that of an omitted or implied verb.

Rem. *e.* The corresponding Hebrew particle to إِنَّ, viz. הִנֵּה, also governs the accusative, as appears from the forms הִנְנִי and הִנֶּנִּי, *ecce me*.

37. If the conjunction وَ connects two nouns in such a way that the second is subordinate to, and not coordinate with, the first, it governs the second in the accusative; as: مَا شَأْنُكَ وَزَيْدًا, or مَا لَكَ وَزَيْدًا, *what have you to do with Zèid?* سِرْتُ وَزَيْدًا, *I went along with Zèid;* مَا لَكَ وَالتَّلَدُّدَ حَوْلَ نَجْدٍ, *what have you to do with loitering about Nèjd?* فَأَجْمِعُوا أَمْرَكُمْ وَشُرَكَاءَكُمْ, *agree on what you are to do along with your associates.* This وَ is called by the grammarians وَاوُ ٱلْمُصَاحَبَةِ, *the waw of association* or *concomitance*, and also, like the وَ that governs the subjunctive (§. 15, 5), وَاوُ ٱلْجَمْعِ or وَاوُ ٱلْمَعِيَّةِ, *the waw of simultaneousness.**)

Rem. This use of וְ also occurs, though but rarely, in Hebrew; e. g. Esther, IV. 16, גַּם־אֲנִי וְנַעֲרֹתַי אָצוּם כֵּן, *I too, along with my maidens, will fast so.*

38. The person or thing called, اَلْمُنَادَى, is generally preceded by one or other of the حُرُوفُ ٱلنِّدَآءِ, or حُرُوفُ ٱلْمُنَادَاةِ, *interjections.* The principal of these are: أَ, يَا, أَيَا, أَيْ, آ; أَيُّهَا (fem. أَيَّتُهَا), to which يَا mayalso be prefixed; and هَيَا.

1) Of the first five of these particles the most common are أَ, يَا, and أَيَا. They require after them a noun not defined by the article, which is put sometimes in the nominative, sometimes in the accusative.

a) The *nominative* — in the singular always with-

---

*) Quite correctly too, for the subjunctive of the verb corresponds both in signification and in form to the accusative of the noun. The one shows that a person or thing depends upon an act, the other that one act depends upon, or is affected or governed by, another act.

3. The Government of the Verb.

out the tenwin — is used when the person or thing called is present, or imagined to be present, to the speaker, and no explanatory term of any description is appended to it; as: يَا مُحَمَّدُ, O Mohammed (nom. مُحَمَّدٌ); أَعَمَّارُ, O 'Ammár (nom. عَمَّارٌ); يَا عَمْرُو, O 'Amr (nom. عَمْرٌو, vol. I. §. 8, rem. b); يَا ضَبِّيُّ, O man of the tribe of Dabba (ضَبَّةٌ); يَا سَيِّدُ, O sir; يَا عَيْنُ, O eye; يَا جَارِيَةُ مَا ٱسْمُكِ, what is your name, girl? يَا رَجُلَانِ, ho you two men; يَا هٰؤُلَاءِ, يَا هٰذِهِ, يَا هٰذَا, you there! يَا نَبِيُّونَ, O prophets;

b) The *accusative* is used α) when the person or thing called is absent; β) when it is present to the speaker, but has an explanatory term appended to it, namely, either a genitive, or an objective complement, or a preposition with its complement, or a determinative or limiting term. Examples: يَا رَاجِلًا يَبْغِي, أَيَا رَاكِبًا, O rider; يَا زَائِرَةً طَيْبَةَ, O traveller that wishest to visit Taiba (el-Medina); يَا سَيِّدَ ٱلْوُحُوشِ, O; يَا عَبْدَ ٱللّٰهِ, O 'Abdu-'lláh; يَا سَيِّدَ ٱلْوُحُوشِ, O lord of the wild beasts; يَا أَبَا ٱلْحُصَيْنِ, O father of the little fortress (an epithet of the fox); أَلْإِخْوَانَنَا, O brethren of ours; يَا طَالِعًا ٱلْجَبَلَ, O thou that art ascending the hill; يَا مُعْطًى كُلَّ خَيْرٍ, O thou that art gifted with every good thing; يَا خَيْرًا, يَا رَفِيقًا بِٱلْعِبَادِ, O thou that art kind towards men; يَا حَسَنًا وَجْهُهُ, مِن زَيْدٍ, O thou that art better than Zèid; O thou that art handsome in face; يَا صَاحِبَيَّ, O ye two companions of mine; يَا بَنِي إِسْرَآئِيلَ, O children of Israel.

The simple ٱلْمُنَادَى, when the accusative is used,

is properly an exclamation of joy, sorrow, astonishment, &c., regarding one who is absent (which may be expressed in German, for example, by *O über den und den!*); but when the nominative is used, it is a real address, خِطَابٌ, to one who is present or supposed to be so. In the compound اَلْمُنَادَى no such distinction is made, and even in a real address the accusative is used, as being the case that depends on a verb, and to which, therefore, other nominal and verbal dependencies can be more readily attached; in contradistinction to the nominative, which is independent and closes the construction. The reason of the omission of the tenwin in the nominative singular seems to lie in the energy with which the word is uttered, whereby its termination is shortened, as in the imperative and jussive of the verb (see also rem. *a*).

Rem. *a*. When no interjection is expressed, the same rules apply as above; e.g. عِثْبَانُ, *O Itbân*; أَحْبَابَ أَنْفُسِنَا, *beloved of our souls!* أَحِبَّتَنَا, *O friends of ours!* With pronouns this omission is very rare; as: ذَا أَرْعِوَآءِ, *you there, refrain (from folly)*, for مَنْ لَا يَمُوتُ ٱرْحَمْ مَنْ يَمُوتُ; يَاهَذَا or يَاذَا, *O thou that diest not, have mercy on him who is dying*.

Rem. *b*. The suffix of the first person singular ـِي, is generally shortened in the vocative into *kesra*, ـِ (see above, at the end of the section); as: رَبِّ or يَا رَبِّ, *O my lord;* يَا نَفْسِ, *O my soul;* أَخِلَّاءِ, *my friends!* يَا بُنَيِّ, *O my dear son*. Other forms, however, are admissible, such as, from عَبْدُ, *a slave*, عَبْدِيَ, عَبْدَاهُ or عَبْدَا, عَبْدَ, عَبْدِيَ, and in pause عَبْدِيَهْ or عَبْدَاهْ.

3. The Government of the Verb. 65

Accordingly we read اِبْنَ أُمَّ in the Ḳor'ân, ch. 7, v. 149, and يَاْبْنَ عَمِّ, يَا بُنَىَّ in ch. 25, v. 30, and find in Mss. يَا وَيْلَتَى instead of بُنَيَّ and عَمِّ. — The words أَبٌ, *father*, and أُمٌّ, *mother*, admit of the peculiar forms يَا أُمَّتِ and يَا أَبَتِ, with either fetḥa or kesra.

Rem. *c*. On the principle alluded to at the end of the section, as well as in rem. *a*, several classes of words admit of being shortened in the vocative by the rejection of one or more of their final letters. Namely: 1) All substantives, whether proper or common, masculine or feminine, that end in ةـ; as: أَجَارِىَ for أَجَارِيَةُ, يَا مُعْوِىَ for أَسْمَىَ (names of men); أُمَيْمَ for الْأُمَيْمَةُ, أَسْمَىَ for أَسْمِيَةُ (names of women); أَعَاذِلَ for أَعَاذِلَةُ, *O thou (woman) that reproachest (me)*; يَا مُسْلِمَ for يَا مُسْلِمَةَ, *O Muslim woman*; يَا شَا for يَا شَاةُ أَدْنِى, *stand still, sheep!* 2) Simple proper names, not ending in ةـ, that contain at least *four* letters; as: أَعَامِرُ for أَعَامِرُ, أَمَالِكُ for أَمَالِكَ, يَا سُعَا for يَا سُعَادُ (name of a woman). If the word consists of more than four letters, and the penult is servile and quiescent, it disappears along with the last letter; as: يَا عُثْمَ, يَا مَنْصُ, يَا مِسْكِ for عُثْمَانُ, مَنْصُورُ, مِسْكِينُ. Words not ending in ةـ may also be inflected without regard to the portion dropped; as: يَا حَارُ, يَا جَعْفُ, يَا ثَمِى, instead of (تَمُودُ, حَارِثُ, جَعْفَرُ and ثَمُو (for حَارِ, جَعْفَ, and the same thing is admissible when the termination ةـ is not of the fem. gender, as: يَا مَسْلَمُ, instead of مَسْلَمَ for مَسْلَمَةُ (a man's name). Proper names compounded with a genitive (as عَبْدُ شَمْسٍ), or forming a complete proposition (as تَأَبَّطَ شَرًّا), do not admit of any abbreviation; but if they belong to the class called مُرَكَّبٌ مَزْجِىٌّ (vol. I. §. 264), they are shortened by the rejection of the second word; as: مَعْدِى for يَا مَعْدِى كَرِبَ. 3) To these two classes may be added the common noun صَاحِبٌ, يَا صَاحِ, *O companion*, for, and the pronoun فُلُ, for فُلَانُ, *un tel*, as in يَا فُلُ = يَا رَجُلُ. — This abbreviation is called by the grammarians اَلتَّرْخِيمُ, *the softening* of the voice (compare vol. I. §. 283).

Rem. *d*. We have said above that the noun which follows these interjections does not admit the article. One exception is the name of *God*, اَللّٰهُ, from which we may say يَا اَللّٰهُ or, irregularly retaining the hémza, يَا أَللّٰهُ.*) Another is produced by the insertion of the pronoun هٰذَا between the interjection and the vocative; as: يَا هٰذَا اَلرَّجُلُ, instead of يَا رَجُلُ.

Rem. *e*. A noun in apposition to a vocative expressed by the nominative, may be put either in the nominative or the accusative; as: يَا مُحَمَّدُ اَلنَّبِىُّ or اَلنَّبِىَّ, *O Mohammed the prophet*; unless it has a genitive after it, when it must be in the accusative; as: يَا إِبْرٰهِيمُ خَلِيلَ اَللّٰهِ, *O Abraham, the friend of God;* يَا زَيْدُ ذَا أَخِى, *O Zéid, the crafty;* يَا زَيْدُ ابْنَ ذَا الْخَيلِ, *O Zéid, my brother's son*. — If the word ابْنُ stands between the names of son and father, it loses its prosthetic ا (vol. I. §. 21, 2), and the person addressed may be put either in the nominative or the

---

*) The more usual form, however, is اَللّٰهُمَّ, without any interjection prefixed, though we find occasionally in verse يَا اَللّٰهُمَّ. The origin of the termination مَّ is uncertain.

3. The Government of the Verb.

O يَا زَيْدَ بْنَ عَمْرٍو or يَا زَيْدُ بْنُ عَمْرٍو :accusative; as: Zéid, son of 'Amr.

Rem. *f.* An adjective in connection with a vocative expressed by the nominative, may likewise be put either in the nominative or the accusative; as: يَا زَيْدُ ٱلْعَاقِلُ or يَا زَيْدَ ٱلْعَاقِلَ, *O Zéid, the intelligent;* يَا زَيْدُ ٱلْكَرِيمُ ٱلْأَبِ or يَا زَيْدَ ٱلْكَرِيمَ ٱلْأَبِ, *O Zéid, whose father is noble.*

Rem. *g.* In Hebrew, we must look upon the governing noun in such phrases as הוֹי חֹשְׁבֵי אָוֶן וּפֹעֲלֵי רָע (Micha, ch. 2, v. 1), or אַשְׁרֵי הָאִישׁ (Ps. 1, v. 1), as being in the construct accusative; whilst הוֹי בֹּנֶה עִיר בְּדָמִים (Habak., ch. 2, v. 12) is in the simple accusative, governing עִיר as its objective complement. See above, *b, β.* In שְׁמַע־נָא יְהוֹשֻׁעַ הַכֹּהֵן הַגָּדוֹל (Zachar., 3, 8), the construction is the same as in rem. *e.*

2) يَا أَيُّهَا and أَيُّهَا (or يَأَيُّهَا) require after them a noun defined by the article in the nominative case; as: يَا أَيُّهَا ٱلنَّاسُ, *O people;* يَا أَيُّهَا ٱلْمَلِكُ, *O king;* يَا أَيُّهَا ٱلَّذِى تَعَلَ كَذَا, *O thou that hast done so and so.* The demonstrative ذَا is also admissible; as: يَا أَيُّهَا ذَا أَقْبِلْ, *you there, come forward!*

3) وَا, which is used to express sorrow or pain, and hence called حَرْفُ ٱلنُّدْبَةِ, *the particle of lamentation,* follows the same rules as يَا; e. g. وَا مُحَمَّدُ, *alas Mohammed!* وَا عَبْدَ ٱللّٰهِ, *alas 'Abdu-llāh!* More generally, however, the termination ـَا, in pause ـَاهْ, is added, which effaces the final vowels; as: وَا زَيْدَاهْ or وَا زَيْدَا, *alas Zéid!*

If a genitive follows, this termination is annexed to it, and not to the governing word; as: يَا أَمِيرَ ٱلْمُؤْمِنِينَاهْ, *alas for the commander of the faithful!*

Rem. *a*. Words ending in the élif maksūra (ىـَ) usually reject that termination before adding اهْ; as: يَا مُوسَاهْ, from مُوسَى, *Moses*. — The suffix pronoun of the first person singular may be either retained or rejected; as: يَا عَبْدَاهْ or يَا عَبْدِيَا, from عَبْدِى, *my servant*.

Rem. *b*. In verse, the form ـَاهْ is occasionally used; as: يَا هَنَاهْ, *you fellow!**)

39. 1) When the negative لَا is immediately followed by an indefinite object, of which it absolutely denies the existence, it governs that object in the accusative; and as the whole weight of the sentence falls upon the negative particle, the substantive is abbreviated, when possible, by the loss of the tenwīn. If there be a predicate expressed, it must be likewise indefinite, but in the nominative case. For example: لَا رَجُلَ فِى ٱلدَّارِ, *there is no man in the house*; لَا إِلٰهَ إِلَّا ٱللّٰهُ, *there is no god but God*; لَا رَجُلَ قَآئِمٌ, *there is no man standing*; لَا إِلٰهَيْنِ, *there are not two Gods*; لَا رِجَالَ هُنَا, *there are no men here*; لَا مُسْلِمِينَ فِى ٱلْمَدِينَةِ, *there are no Muslims in the city*; لَا مُسْلِمَاتٍ عِنْدَنَا, *there are no Muslim women in our possession*. But if the negative

---

*) See the Dīwān of Imru'u 'l-Kais, ed. de Slane, p. ۴۳, l. 11 (where the word is misprinted هُنَاهْ).

3. The Government of the Verb. 69

be separated from its object, it is put in the nominative; as: لَا فِيهَا غَوْلٌ, *in which* (viz. *the wine*) *there is no injurious force.*

2) If a genitive be attached to the substantive after لَا the accusative must of course be used in its construct form, as: لَا غُلَامَ رَجُلٍ حَاضِرٌ, *there is no slave of any man present;* but if the substantive be followed by an explanatory term of the nature of an objective complement, a preposition with its complement, or a determinative or limiting term, the tenwin must be retained (compare §. 38, 1, *b*, β); as: لَا طَالِعًا جَبَلًا ظَاهِرٌ, *there is no one ascending a hill visible;* لَا خَيْرًا مِنْ زَيْدٍ عِنْدَنَا, *there is no better (man) than Zeid in our opinion;* لَا حَسَنًا فِعْلُهُ مَذْمُومٌ, *no one whose deeds are good is blame-worthy.*

3) If an adjective be immediately annexed to the accusative after لَا, it may either take the same form without the tenwin, or it may retain the tenwin, or, lastly, it may be put in the nominative with the tenwin; as: لَا رَجُلَ ظَرِيفَ or لَا رَجُلَ ظَرِيفًا, or لَا رَجُلَ ظَرِيفٌ, *there is no witty man.* But if the adjective be separated in any way from the substantive, the first of these three constructions is no longer admissible; as: لَا رَجُلَ فِيهَا ظَرِيفٌ or ظَرِيفًا, *there is no witty man in it (the house),* but not ظَرِيفَ.

4) If another substantive be connected with this accusative by the conjunction وَ, the particle لَا may be repeated or not. *a*) If لَا be repeated, the first substantive may

be put in the accusative without the tĕnwîn, and the second either in the accusative, with or without the tĕnwîn, or in the nominative; as: لَا حَوْلَ وَلَا قُوَّةَ (قُوَّةً) إِلَّا بِٱللّٰهِ, *there is no power and no strength save in God;* or the first substantive may be put in the nominative, and the second either in the accusative without the tĕnwîn or in the nominative; as: لَا رَجُلٌ وَلَا ٱمْرَأَةَ (ٱمْرَأَةٌ) فِى ٱلدَّارِ, *there is neither man nor woman in the house.* b) If لَا be not repeated, the first substantive is put in the accusative without the tĕnwîn, and the second either in the nominative or in the accusative with the tĕnwîn; as: لَا رَجُلَ وَٱمْرَأَةٌ (وَٱمْرَأَةً) فِى ٱلدَّارِ.

Rem. a. The particle لَا, when thus used, is called by the grammarians لَا لِنَفْىِ ٱلْجِنْسِ, or لَا نَافِيَةُ ٱلْجِنْسِ, *the lā that denies the whole genus.* The substantive in the accusative is called ٱسْمُ لَا, *the noun of lā*, and the predicate, خَبَرُ لَا, *the predicate of lā*.

Rem b. The rule regarding the retention of the terminations نِ and نَ in the dual and plural may seem to be contradicted by such examples as: لَا يَدَىْ لَكَ بِٱلظُّلْمِ, *thou canst do no wrong* (lit. *thou hast not two hands for wrong);* لَا أُذُنَىْ لَهَا, *she has no ears;* لَا عَبْدَىْ لَكَ, *you have not got two slaves;* لَا عَبْدَىْ لَكَ, *you have not got two slaves;* قَمِيصٌ لَا كُمَّىْ لَهُ, *a shirt without sleeves;* but in these cases the Arab grammarians say that the preposition لِ is مُقْحَمَةٌ, *inserted without necessity,* and that the preceding noun is in reality in the construct state. In the same way too they explain the phrase لَا أَبَا لَكَ, lit. *thou*

3. The Government of the Verb.   71

hast no father, which is generally used instead of the regular لَا أَبَان.

40. Having thus treated of the accusative as the objective complement, we now proceed to speak of it as the *adverbial* complement in a stricter sense (see §. 22, 2). This depends

I. On the idea of *being* or *existence*, when expressed a) by the substantive verb كَانَ, or b) by other verbs, the signification of which includes that of كَانَ. The general idea of existence is in this case limited and determined by the accusative.

41. The verb كَانَ, *to be*, *to exist*, when it supplies the place of the logical copula, requires the predicate, to which the being or existence of the subject refers, to be put in the accusative; as: كُونُوا هُودًا أَوْ نَصَارَى, *be* (lit. *exist as*) *Jews or Christians*; إِنْ كَانَ الْبَلَاءَ مُقَدَّرًا يُصِيبُهُ لَا مَحَالَةَ *if the calamity is decreed* (or *fated*), *it will befal him without doubt*; مَنْ أَرَادَ أَنْ يَكُونَ ابْنُهُ عَالِمًا يَنْبَغِى أَنْ يُرَاعِىَ الْفُقَرَآءَ مِنَ الْفُقَهَآءِ, *whoever wishes his son to be learned, must provide for the poor among the learned*; كَانَ هُوَ وَأَخُوهُ مُعَلِّمَيْنِ بِالطَّآئِفِ, *he and his brother were teachers in et-Ṭā'if*. But if كَانَ has only a subject connected with it, to which the idea of existence inherent in the verb is attributed, that subject is put, like every other, in the nominative; as: كَانَ تَاجِرٌ وَكَانَ لَهُ بَنُونَ ثَلْثَةٌ, *there was* (or *lived*) *a merchant, and he had* (lit. *there were to him*) *three sons*

(كَانَ تَاجِرًا) would mean *he was a merchant*); فَمَنْ كَانَ لَهُ مَالٌ كَثِيرٌ, *but he who has* (lit. *to whom there is*) *much property*. In the former case, the substantive verb is called by the grammarians كَانَ ٱلنَّاقِصَةُ, *the incomplete* or *defective, relative kāna*, because it requires an attribute to complete the sense; in the latter, كَانَ ٱلتَّامَّةُ, *the complete, absolute kāna*, because it contains the attribute in itself and does not require any other.

Rem. The verb كَانَ, Aethiop. ኮነ: *kōna*, does not occur in Hebrew in the sense of *to be, exist, happen*, though it is so used in Syriac (rare) and Phoenician. The construction of the Aethiopic verb is the same as that of the Arabic; in the other Shemitic languages, which have lost the final flexional vowels, the case of the predicate cannot be observed, but doubtless it was the accusative. — In Hebrew the radical כון retains its original signification of *to stand* (compare Fr. *être*, older form *estre*, and Span. *estar*, from Lat. *stare*), and the place of كَانَ is supplied by הָיָה or הָוָה, Aram. הֲוָא, ווֹםּ, *to fall* (هَوَى), *happen, be* (compare وَقَعَ, *to fall, happen*, Lat. *accidit*, Eng. *it fell out*), of which the predicate must also be looked upon as in the accusative.

42. The same construction appertains to certain verbs, called by the grammarians أَخَوَاتُ كَانَ, *the sisters of kāna*. These are either 1) similar in signification to كَانَ, as صَارَ, *to become;* or 2) they add some circumstantial or modifying idea to the simple one of existence. This may be: *a)* the idea of *duration* or *continuity*, as in دَامَ, *to continue, to*

3. The Government of the Verb.

last, construed with the مَا ٱلدَّيْمُومَةِ (vol. I. §. 367, 13), اِنْفَكَّ, فَتِئَ, بَرِحَ, زَالَ, *to cease*, construed with a negative particle; or *b*) the idea of *repetition*, as in عَادَ and آضَ, *to return, do again, take place again;* or *c*) the idea of *time*, as in ظَلَّ, *to be* or *do during the whole day*, بَاتَ, *during the whole night*, أَسْفَرَ, *at daybreak*, أَصْبَحَ, *in the morning*, أَضْحَى, *in the forenoon*, أَمْسَى, *in the evening*, all of which verbs are often used as simple synonyms of كَانَ and صَارَ, without any regard to the secondary idea of time; or, lastly, *d*) the idea of *negation*, by which that of existence itself is absolutely denied, as in لَيْسَ, *not to be*. Examples: وَكَانَ يَرَى ٱلْمَآءَ يَصِيرُ بُخَارًا وَٱلْبُخَارَ يَصِيرُ مَآءً, *and he was beholding the water becoming vapour, and the vapour becoming water;* لَا تَعُدَّ نَفْسَكَ مِنَ ٱلنَّاسِ مَا دَامَ ٱلْغَضَبُ غَالِبًا عَلَيْكَ, *do not count thyself among men, as long as anger has the mastery over thee;* لَا يَزَالُ ٱللّٰهُ مُحْسِنًا إِلَيْكَ, *may God never cease being beneficent to you;* لَا تَنْزَلْ ذَاكِرَ ٱلْمَوْتِ, *never cease bearing death in mind;* إِنَّكَ قَدْ شُرِيتَ فَقَعَدْتَ عَبْدًا بِمَكَّةَ, *thou hast been sold and hast become a slave in Mekka;* أَصْبَحْتُمْ بِنِعْمَةِ ٱللّٰهِ إِخْوَانًا, *through the grace of God ye have become brethren;* تَمَنَّيْتَ أَنْ تُمْسِىَ فَقِيهَهَا مُنَاظِرًا, *you wish to become a scholar skilled in controversy;* لَا تَقُولُوا لِمَنْ أَلْقَى إِلَيْكُمُ ٱلسَّلَامَ لَسْتَ مُؤْمِنًا, *do not say to any one who gives you a salutation, Thou art not a believer*.

Rem. *a*. The verbs زَالَ, بَرِحَ, فَتِئَ, اِنْفَكَّ, and the like, must always be accompanied by a negative, expressed (as in the above examples with زَالَ) or implied, as: وَأَبْرَحُ مَا أَدَامَ ٱللّٰهُ قَوْمِي بِحَمْدِ ٱللّٰهِ مُنْتَطِقًا مُجِيدًا, *and I shall not cease, as long as God preserves my tribe, through God's grace to wear a girdle and ride a noble steed* (مُجِيدًا for لَا أَبْرَحُ, and مُجِيدًا in rhyme for أَبْرَحُ).

Rem. *b*. The verb وُجِدَ, *to be found, be extant, exist*, is often reckoned one of the أَخَوَاتُ كَانَ, but erroneously; for it is either = كَانَ ٱلتَّامَّةُ, and has no predicate, or it is the passive of وَجَدَ, which governs two accusatives, and so naturally retains the second object (ٱلْمَفْعُولُ ٱلثَّانِى); as: لَا يُوجَدُ مِنْهَا شَىْءٌ صِرْفًا, *not one of them is found pure (in a pure state)*, where صِرْفًا is a حَالٌ or circumstantial accusative, or *we* (Fr. *on*, Germ. *man*) *find that not one of them is pure*, where صِرْفًا is the second object.

Rem. *c*. The negative particles مَا and لَا, when used, as the grammarians say, بِمَعْنَى لَيْسَ, *in the signification of* léisa, are also construed with the accusative of the predicate, provided 1) that the predicate is placed after the subject, 2) that the exceptive particle إِلَّا is not interposed between them, 3) that the corroborative particle إِنْ is not added to مَا, and 4) that the subject of لَا is an undefined common noun; e. g. مَا هٰذَا بَشَرًا, *this is not a human being*, مَا هُنَّ أُمَّهَاتِهِمْ, *they are not their mothers*; لَا شَىْءَ عَلَى ٱلْأَرْضِ بَاقِيًا, *there is nothing on earth enduring*; نَصَرْتُكَ إِذْ لَا صَاحِبَ غَيْرَ خَاذِلٍ, *I aided you when you had no companion that was not faithless*. If مَا has a second predicate, connected with the first by an adversative particle, such as بَلْ or لٰكِنْ, then the second must be put in the nominative; but, in any other case, the accusative is preferable to the nominative; as: مَا زَيْدٌ قَآئِمًا بَلْ قَاعِدٌ, *Zeid is not standing, but sitting*, i. e. بَلْ هُوَ قَاعِدٌ. This government of مَا and لَا is peculiar to the dialect of el-Ḥiǵâz, and hence they are called مَا الْحِجَازِيَّة and لَا الْحِجَازِيَّة. — The same construction is also extended to لَاتَ (vol. I. §. 182, rem. b) and to إِنِ النَّافِيَة or *the negative 'in*; as: إِنْ هُوَ مُسْتَوْلِيًا عَلَى أَحَدٍ, *he rules over nobody*; لَاتَ حِينَ مَنَاصٍ, *there was no time for escape*; لَاتَ سَاعَةَ مَنْدَمٍ, *it is not an hour for repentance*. The government of لَاتَ seems to be restricted to nouns denoting *time*, and either its subject or predicate must be omitted, usually the former (لَاتَ الْحِينُ حِينَ مَنَاصٍ = لَاتَ حِينَ مَنَاصٍ).

43. The adverbial accusative depends

II. On any verbal idea that determines or limits in any way the subject, verb, or predicate of a sentence, or the whole sentence. In this case it supplies the place of a preposition with the genitive, or of a conjunctive clause, and amply makes up for the want of adverbs in Arabic.

44. By the adverbial accusative is designated:

1. The *time in* or *during which* an act takes place; as: رَآهُ الْخَلِيفَةُ يَوْمًا يَتَوَضَّأُ رِجْلَيْهِ, *the chalif saw him one day washing his feet*; لَا يَدْرِي كَيْفَ يَمُوتُ يَوْمَ الْهَلَاكِ, *he knows not how he shall die on his dying day*; لَمْ أَدْرِ الْأَمْسَ جَاءَ إِلَى هَهُنَا أَمِ الْيَوْمَ, *I did not know whether he came here yes-*

سَكَنَ فِى بَعْضِ ٱلْقُرَى أَيَّامًا *terday or today;* , *he stopped a few days in a village;* اِسْتَعِذْ بِٱللَّهِ مِنْهُ لَيْلًا وَنَهَارًا, *implore God night and day to protect you from it;* سَيُعْطِيكَ ٱلْكِتَابَ غَدًا, *he will give you the book tomorrow;* تَأَمَّلْ شَهْرَيْنِ فِى ٱخْتِيَارِ ٱلْأُسْتَاذِ, *reflect two months upon the choice of a teacher;* لَمْ يَبِتْ عَلَى ٱلْفِرَاشِ أَرْبَعِينَ سَنَةً, *he did not pass the night on a bed for forty years;* قَتَلْتُهُ ٱلسَّنَةَ ٱلْمَاضِيَةَ, *I killed him last year;* قَالَ حِينَ لَقِيَهُ, *he said at the time of his meeting him (or when he met him);* عَصْرَ حَانَ مَشِيبٌ, *at the time when old age is drawing near;* قَامَ فِى خِلَالِ ٱلدَّرْسِ أَحْيَانًا, *he stood up at times whilst lecturing;* وَكُنْتُ بُرْهَةً مِنَ ٱلزَّمَانِ أَتَفَكَّرُ, *and I continued reflecting for a considerable time.*

Rem. On the same construction in Hebrew, see Gesenius' Gr. §. 116, 2.

2. The *local extension* of an act, and, if general and indefinite, the *place in which* it is performed; as: نَظَرَ يَمِينًا سَارُوا أَرْبَعَةَ أَمْيَالٍ, *they travelled four miles;* إِنْتَصَرَ عَلَى ٱلْعَدُوِّ بَرًّا (وَشِمَالًا) وَيَسَارًا, *he looked right and left;* وَبَحْرًا, *he conquered the enemy by land and sea;* أَمَامَ, قُدَّامَ, *before;* وَرَاءَ, خَلْفَ, *behind;* وَسْطَ, *in the middle;* حَوْلَ, *around;* فَوْقَ, *above;* تَحْتَ, *under;* &c.

Rem. *a.* When the place of the act is definitely specified, the nomen loci (vol. I. § 221) is used with the preposition فِى; as:

3. The Government of the Verb.

صَلَّيْتُ فِي مَسْجِدِ ٱلنَّبِيِّ, *I prayed in the mosque of the prophet;* أَقَمْتُ فِي مَقْتَلِ حُسَيْنٍ, *I stopped at the place where Hosein was killed;* not أَقَمْتُ مَقْتَلَ and صَلَّيْتُ مَسْجِدَ. Excepted is the case when a general noun of place, such as مَكَانٌ or مَقَامٌ, is construed with a verb conveying the idea of stopping or remaining, as: جَلَسْتُ مَكَانَ زَيْدٍ, *I sat down in Zeid's place;* and also the case when a noun of place is construed with the verb from which it is derived, as: تَعَدَّتُ مَقْعَدَ زَيْدٍ, *I sat down in Zeid's seat.* — The nouns جَانِبٌ, *side,* خَارِجٌ, *outside,* دَاخِلٌ, *inside,* جَوْفٌ, وَجْهٌ, جِهَةٌ require فِي, as: نِمْتُ فِي خَارِجِ ٱلدَّارِ, *I slept outside the house;* but in later Arabic we often find the accusatives خَارِجَ, جَانِبَ, and دَاخِلَ, as also قُرْبَ, *near,* for فِي قُرْبِ, and the like.

Rem. *b.* On the corresponding accusative of place in Hebrew, see Gesenius' Gr. §. 116, 1.

Rem. *c.* The accusative of time and place is called by the grammarians ٱلظَّرْفُ, *the vessel* (see vol. I, §. 221, rem *a*), or ٱلْمَفْعُولُ فِيهِ, *that in which the act is done.*

3. The *state or condition* of the subject or object of an act, whilst the act is taking place; as: وَقَفَ عَلَى بَابِ ٱلْمَغَارَةِ مُسَلِّمًا عَلَيْهِ قَائِلًا لَهُ, *he stood at the entrance of the cave, saluting him (and) saying to him:* ٱدْخُلُوا ٱلْبَابَ سُجَّدًا, *enter the gateway prostrating yourselves;* ٱلَّذِينَ يَذْكُرُونَ ٱللَّهَ قِيَامًا وَقُعُودًا, *who call God to mind standing up and sitting down:* لَقِيتُ ٱلسُّلْطَانَ بَاكِيًا عِنْدَهُ, *I found the sul-*

tan weeping in his house; بِيَةً رُمَّ بِٱلثِّقَافِ ٱلْعُودُ لَدْنًا, *a piece of wood can be made straight with the plane while it is soft;* خُلُقٌ نَشَأْتُ بِهِ غُلَامًا, *a habit with which I grew up as a young man;* كُنْتُ فِي ٱلْبُسْتَانِ زَاهِرًا, *I was in the garden whilst it was in bloom.*

Rem. The same construction is found in Hebrew; e.g. Gen. 33, 18. וַיָּבֹא יַעֲקֹב שָׁלֵם עִיר שְׁכֶם, *and Jacob came safe (or in safety) to the city of Shechem;* Amos 2. 16. עָרוֹם יָנוּס בַּיּוֹם־הַהוּא, *naked shall he flee on that day;* Job 31, 26. יָרֵחַ יָקָר הֹלֵךְ, *and the moon walking in splendour;* where the adjectives שָׁלֵם, עָרוֹם and יָקָר are to be regarded as in the accus.

4. The *cause or motive and object* of the act; as: ضَرَبْتُ ٱبْنِي تَأْدِيبًا, *I beat my son for correction's sake;* إِذَا رَأَيْتُهُ أَقُومُ لَهُ تَعْظِيمًا لِأُسْتَاذِي, *when I see him, I stand up before him to show respect to my teacher;* وَمِنَ ٱلنَّاسِ مَنْ يَشْرِي نَفْسَهُ ٱبْتِغَاءَ مَرْضَاتِ ٱللّٰهِ, *and among men there are some who sell their souls (give up their lives) to win the favour of God;* بِئْسَمَا ٱشْتَرَوْا بِهِ أَنْفُسَهُمْ أَنْ يَكْفُرُوا بِمَا أَنْزَلَ ٱللّٰهُ بَغْيًا, *vile is the price for which they have sold their souls, that they should not believe in what God has sent down (revealed) out of envy;* يَجْعَلُونَ أَصَابِعَهُمْ فِي آذَانِهِمْ مِنَ ٱلصَّوَاعِقِ حَذَرَ ٱلْمَوْتِ, *they put their fingers in their ears on account of the claps of thunder, through fear of death.*

Rem. a. This accusative, which must always be a مَصْدَرٌ or *nomen verbi*, is called by the grammarians ٱلْمَفْعُولُ لَهُ or ٱلْمَفْعُولُ لِأَجْلِهِ, *that on account of which something is done.*

3. The Government of the Verb. 79

Rem, *b.* Similarly in Hebrew, Isaiah 7, 25. לֹא־תָבוֹא שָׁמָּה יִרְאַת שָׁמִיר וָשָׁיִת, *thou wilt not go thither for fear of thorns and thistles.*

5. Various other determinations and limitations of the predicate; as: اَللّٰهُ عَظِيمٌ قُدْرَةً, *God is great in might*; نَهَى كَالْحِجَارَةِ أَوْ أَشَدُّ قَسْوَةً, *but they (your hearts) are like stones or even harder* (lit. *stronger as to hardness*); طَابَ ٱلْوَرْدُ لَوْنًا, *the rose is charming in colour*; تَصَبَّبَ زَيْدٌ عَرَقًا, *Zeid streamed with perspiration*; وَفَجَّرْنَا ٱلْأَرْضَ عُيُونًا, *and we made the earth break forth into springs*; أَنْتَ أَعْلَى مَنْزِلًا وَأَكْثَرُ مَالًا, *thou art higher in station and richer in wealth*; أَكْرِمْ بِأَبِي بَكْرٍ أَبًا, *how noble is 'Abū Bekr as a father!*

Rem. *a.* This sort of adverbial accusative, which is always undefined, is called by the grammarians اَلتَّمْيِيزُ, *the specification.* It is equally common in Hebrew; e. g. Gen. 41, 40. רַק הַכִּסֵּא אֶגְדַּל מִמֶּךָּ, *in respect of the throne alone will I be greater than thou*; 1 Kings, 15, 23. חָלָה אֶת־רַגְלָיו, *he was diseased in his feet.* See Gesenius' Gr. §. 116, 3, and §. 136, rem.

Rem. *b.* The accusative after the cardinal numbers from 11 to 99, after the interrogative nouns of number كَمْ and كَأَيِّ (كَأَيِّنْ), كَأَيٍّ, كَآءٍ, كَأَيِّنْ), *how much? how many?* after the indefinite كَذَا or كَذَا وَكَذَا, *so and so much or many,* and after nouns that denote measure, belongs also to this class; as: أَحَدٌ وَعِشْرُونَ عَامًا, *one and twenty years*; اِبْنُ ثَمَانِينَ سَنَةً, *eighty years old* (lit. *a son of 80 years*); كَمْ دِرْهَمًا قَبَضْتَ, *how many dirhems have you got?* كَأَيِّنْ رَجُلًا قُتِلُوا, *how many men were killed!* مَلَكْتُ

قَفِيزٌ بُرًّا وَكَذَا وَكَذَا دِرْهَمًا, *I have got so and so many dirhems;* ذِرَاعَانِ زَيْتًا, *a bushel of wheat;* رِطْلَانِ زَيْتًا, *two pounds of olive oil;* جُوخًا, *two ells of cloth.* Compare Gesenius' Hebrew Gr., §. 118 (particularly 2, rem., and 4, rem. 2) and §. 116, 3.

6. An act expressed by a nomen verbi, with which another act, expressed by a finite tense, is compared; as: قَتَلُوهُ قَتْلَ ٱبْنِهِ أَخَاهُمْ عَمْرًا, *they killed him in the same way as his son had killed their brother Amr;* عَذَّبَ زَيْدًا تَعْذِيبَ اسْمعِيلَ أَبُو زَيْدٍ, *he tortured Zeid just as 'Ismā'il, Zeid's father, had tortured him;* لَوْ يُعَجِّلُ ٱللهُ لِلنَّاسِ ٱلشَّرَّ ٱسْتِعْجَالَهُمْ بِٱلْخَيْرِ, *if God should cause evil to come with haste upon men, as they wish good to come with haste unto them.* For this accusative may be substituted كَ with the genitive of the nomen verbi, or كَمَا with a finite tense of the verb; e. g., in the first example, كَمَا قَتَلَ ٱبْنَهُ or كَقَتْلِ ٱبْنِهِ.

45. If an entire clause, consisting of a subject and a predicate, be annexed to another clause, to define or limit either the subject or object of the latter, then the predicate of the former is placed before its subject and put in the accusative, the subject being left in the nominative. For example: وَلَّى تِيمُرْلَنْكُ مَكْسُورًا أَوَائِلُهُ وَمَذْعُورًا أَوَاخِرُهُ, *Timur-lēnk (Tamerlane) turned his back, after his van had been broken and his rear struck with panic;* هُوَ ٱلَّذِي أَنْشَأَ جَنَّاتٍ مَعْرُوشَاتٍ وَغَيْرَ مَعْرُوشَاتٍ وَٱلنَّخْلَ وَٱلزَّرْعَ مُخْتَلِفًا أُكُلُهُ, *he it is who has produced gardens with trellises for vines and without them, and the palmtrees and the grain, with*

3. The Government of the Verb. — The Prepositions.

their various edible fruits (كَآتِنَا أُكْلُهُ مُخْتَلِفًا=مُخْتَلِفًا أُكْلُهُ);

سَأَغْسِلُ عَنِّى ٱلْعَارَ بِٱلسَّيْفِ جَالِبًا عَلَىَّ قَضَآءُ ٱللّٰهِ مَا كَانَ جَالِبَا.

I will wipe away my disgrace with the sword, let God's decree bring upon me what it may (وَإِنْ جَلَبْ = جَالِبًا عَلَىَّ قَضَآءُ ٱللّٰهِ

جَالِبَا ; عَلَىَّ قَضَآءُ ٱللّٰهِ in rhyme for جَالِيًا).

B. The Prepositions.

46. The prepositions all originally designate relations of *place* (*local* relations), but are transferred, first, to relations of *time* (*temporal* relations), and next, to various sorts of *ideal* relations, conceived under the figure of the local relations to which they correspond.

47. The prepositions are divided into *simple* and *compound*. — The simple prepositions are again divisible into three classes, indicating respectively motion proceeding from or away from a place, motion to or towards it, and rest in it.

48. The prepositions that indicate motion proceeding from or away from a place are two in number; viz. مِنْ, *ex*, *out of*, *from*, and عَنْ, *ab*, *away from*.

Rem. In Hebrew, the simple preposition מִן supplies the place both of مِنْ and عَنْ. Compare, in general, Gesenius' Gr. §. 151, 3, c.

49. مِنْ (with pronominal suffixes مِنِّى, مِنْكَ, مِنَّا) designates:

1) The *local point of departure*, departure from a place; as: سَقَطَ مِنْ يَدِهَا ,خَرَجَ مِنْ مَكَّةَ, *he went forth from Mekka*; *it fell from her hand.* Hence it is connected with verbs that convey the idea of separation, departure, holding oneself or another aloof from any person or thing, liberating, preserving, fleeing, frightening away, forbidding, and the like; as: هُوَ ٱلْحِصْنُ يُنْجِى مِنْ جَمِيعِ ٱلشَّدَآئِدِ, *this* (learning) *is the fortress that preserves* (us) *from all calamities;* أَعُوذُ بِٱللّٰهِ مِنَ ٱلطَّمَعِ, *I take refuge with God (pray God to preserve me) from covetousness;* ٱلدُّنْيَا تَمْنَعُ مِنَ ٱلْخَيْرِ, *the world holds us back from good.*

2) The *temporal point of departure*, the point at which an act or state has commenced; as: عَبَدَ ٱللّٰهَ مِنْ شَبَابِهِ, *he served God from his youth;* وَقْتُ ٱلتَّعَلُّمِ مِنَ ٱلْمَهْدِ إِلَى ٱللَّحْدِ, *the time of learning extends from the cradle to the grave;* تُخُيِّرْنَ مِنْ أَزْمَانِ يَوْمِ حَلِيمَةَ, *they were chosen from the times of the battle* (lit. *day*) *of Halima.*

Rem. The Arab grammarians say that مِنْ, when used in the above significations, is employed لِٱبْتِدَآءِ ٱلْغَايَةِ فِى ٱلْمَكَانِ وَٱلزَّمَانِ, *to denote the commencement of the limit attained in place and time,* or simply لِلِٱبْتِدَآءِ, *to denote the commencement.*

3) The *causal point of departure*, the *origin* and *source* of a thing; as: ذٰلِكَ مِنْ نَبَإٍ جَآءَنِى, *this is in consequence of information that reached me;* تَوَقَّفَ يَتَعَجَّبُ مِنْهَا, *and he stood admiring it* (or *wondering at it,* his wonder proceeding from, or being caused by, it); مِمَّا خَطِيئَاتِهِمْ أُغْرِقُوا,

3. The Government of the Verb. — The Prepositions. 83

they were drowned because of their sins (the particle مَا is merely expletive and does not interfere with the government of مِن).

Rem. *a.* The grammarians say that مِن is used in this case لِلتَّعْلِيلِ, *to assign the reason*.

Rem. *b.* In speaking of persons مِنْ أَجْلِ, *on account of*, is always used instead of مِن, and often too in other cases; as: فَعَارٌ ثُمَّ عَارٌ ثُمَّ عَارٌ شَقَآءُ ٱلْمَرْءِ مِنْ أَجْلِ ٱلطَّعَامِ, *it is a threefold disgrace for a man to be in misery on account of (for want of) food*; مِنْ أَجْلِ كَلَامِهِ, *because of what he said*.

4) The *distance from* a place, person, or thing, particularly after words that signify proximity, such as قَرُبَ or دَنَا, *to be near*, قَرِيبٌ, *near*, &c. (compare: prope ab eo, Fr. près de lui, rapproché de lui); e. g. قَرُبَ ٱلْجَيْشُ مِنْهُمْ, *the army was near them*; دَنَا مِنِّي, *he was not far from me* (دَنَا إِلَىَّ would mean: *he came up close to me*); يَنْبَغِى لِطَالِبِ ٱلْعِلْمِ أَنْ لَا يَجْلِسَ قَرِيبًا مِنَ ٱلْأُسْتَاذِ, *it becomes the student not to sit too near the teacher*. Similarly in the phrases: خَرَجَ مِنَ ٱلْبَابِ, دَخَلَ مِنَ ٱلْبَابِ, *he went in*, or *came out*, *through the door*; أَبْرَاجُهَا ٱلَّتِى يَتَرَقَّى ٱلْمَآءُ مِنْهَا, *its towers through which the water ascended*. — Compare in Heb., Job 17, 12. אוֹר קָרוֹב מִפְּנֵי־חֹשֶׁךְ, *the light is drawing near the darkness*.

5) The *difference between* two persons or things that are compared with one another; as: أَيْنَ أَنْتَ مِنْ نُوحٍ وَطُولِ

11*

عُمْرِي, *what a difference there is between thee and Noah in length of life* (lit. *where art thou from Noah and his length of life?*)! Hence the use of مِنْ after comparative adjectives; as: هُوَ أَفْضَلُ مِنِّى, *he is more excellent than I.*

Rem. *a.* If any object be compared with itself in a different respect, the appropriate pronominal suffix must be attached to the preposition مِنْ; as: ٱلنَّاسُ أَشْبَهُ بِزَمَانِهِمْ مِنْهُمْ بِآبَائِهِمْ, *people are more like the time in which they are born than they are like their fathers;* هُمْ لِلْكُفْرِ يَوْمَئِذٍ أَقْرَبُ مِنْهُمْ لِلْإِيمَانِ, *they are nearer unbelief on that day than belief;* أَنَا مِنْكُمْ عَلَى ٱلْعَرَبِ أَخْوَفُ مِنِّى مِنَ ٱلْعَرَبِ عَلَيْكُمْ, *I have more fears of injury to the Arabs by you than I have of injury to you by the Arabs.* — Sometimes, in a less careful style of speaking or writing, the preposition مِنْ is annexed to the latter of the two objects, instead of to the person or thing which is compared with him or itself in respect of these two objects; as: صَارَ يُقَاتِلُهُمْ بِٱلْعَصَا أَقْوَى مِنَ ٱلسِّلَاحِ, *he fought against them with the stick more sturdily than with the weapons* (for أَقْوَى مِنْهُ بِٱلسِّلَاحِ); عَلَى أَنَّ ٱلظُّلْمَ مِنْكُمْ أَقْبَحُ مِنْ غَيْرِكُمْ, *because wrong proceeding from you is worse than from others* (for أَقْبَحُ مِنْهُ مِنْ غَيْرِكُمْ).

Rem. *b.* In the other Shemitic languages, which do not possess a peculiar comparative form of the adjective, the comparison is likewise expressed by means of the same preposition; Heb. מִן, Aram. מִן, Aeth. እም: or እምነ:: See Gesenius' Heb. Gr. §. 117.

6) The relation which subsists between the part and the whole, the species and the genus, the material and the

3. The Government of the Verb. — The Prepositions.

article made of it; as: عِلْمُ ٱلطِّبِّ سَبَبٌ مِنَ ٱلْأَسْبَابِ, *the science of medicine is one of the professions*; وَمِنْ تَعْظِيمِ ٱلْعِلْمِ تَعْظِيمُ ٱلْكِتَابِ, *and respect for the book is a part of the respect due to science*; ٱلْإِنْسَانُ مُرَكَّبٌ مِنْ نَفْسٍ وَجَسَدٍ, *man is compounded of soul and body*; وَرَأَى أَنَّ ٱلْحَيَوَانَ وَٱلنَّبَاتَ لَا تَلْتَئِمُ حَقَائِقُهَا إِلَّا مِنْ مَعَانٍ كَثِيرَةٍ, *and he saw that the natures of animals and plants are compounded of numerous elements*; فَصَعُبَ عَلَيْهِ لِعَدَمِ ٱلْآلَاتِ وَلِأَنَّهَا لَمْ تَكُنْ إِلَّا مِنَ ٱلْحِجَارَةِ وَٱلْقَصَبِ, *and it was difficult for him, because of the want of instruments, and because those (that he had) were made only of stones and reeds*; خَلَقَكُمُ ٱللَّهُ مِنْ نَفْسٍ وَاحِدَةٍ, *God has created you out of one soul*.

Rem. *a*. When it precedes a definite plural, the preposition مِنْ often indicates an indefinite number, *some*; as: أَخَذَ مِنَ ٱلدَّنَانِيرِ, *he took some of the dinars*; قَدْ أَرَاكُمْ مِنْ آيَاتِهِ, *he has already shown you some of his signs*. Compare, in French, *de* with the article, as *du lait*, „some milk"; and see Gesenius' Heb. Gr. §. 151, 3. *c*.

Rem. *b*. After negative particles, and after interrogatives put in a negative sense, مِنْ prefixed to an indefinite noun means *no*, *none at all*, *not one*; as: مِنْ أَحَدٍ, or مَا جَاءَنِي مِنْ رَجُلٍ, *no one came to me*; مَا لَكُمْ مِنْ إِلَٰهٍ غَيْرُهُ, *you have no god but Him*; مَا لَهُمْ مِنْ نَاصِرِينَ (=لَا نَاصِرِينَ لَهُمْ), *they have no helpers*; لَا فِي ٱلدَّارِ مِنْ رَجُلٍ (=لَا رَجُلَ فِي ٱلدَّارِ), *there is no man in the house*;

هَلْ تَحَسُّ مِنْهُمْ مِنْ رَجُلٍ, *do you perceive any one of them at all?* هَلْ لَنَا مِنَ ٱلْأَمْرِ مِنْ شَىْءٍ, *have we any portion at all of that thing?* With مِنْ أَحَدٍ compare the Hebrew מֵאֶחָד, Levit. 4, 2, Deuter. 15, 7.

Rem. c. When مِنْ indicates a part of a whole, it is said to be used لِلتَّبْعِيضِ, *to indicate a division into parts*; when it indicates the parts of which a whole is composed, لِلتَّرْكِيبِ, *to indicate composition*.

7) The definition or explanation of a general or universal by a special or particular, the latter being one of several objects that go to make up the former; as: وَكَذٰلِكَ يُفْتَرَضُ عِلْمُ أَحْوَالِ ٱلْقَلْبِ مِنَ ٱلتَّوَكُّلِ وَٱلْإِنَابَةِ وَٱلْخَشْيَةِ, *and in the same way we are enjoined to take cognizance of the different states of the heart, such as trust (in God), and repentance, and fear (of Him)*; فَتَصَفَّحَ جَمِيعَ ٱلْأَجْسَامِ ٱلَّتِى فِى عَالَمِ ٱلْكَوْنِ وَٱلْفَسَادِ مِنَ ٱلْحَيَوَانَاتِ وَٱلنَّبَاتِ وَٱلْمَعَادِنِ, *and he examined all the bodies that there are in this world of existence and decay, both animals, plants, and minerals;* كُلٌّ مِنْ هَابِيلَ وَقَابِيلَ, *both (of them), Abel as well as Cain;* إِخْوَانُنَا هٰؤُلَاءِ مِنَ ٱلْأَنْصَارِ, *these brethren of ours, the Ansár (or Helpers of the Prophet)*; لَا يَحْصُلُ مَقْصُودُهُمْ مِنَ ٱلْعِلْمِ, *their object, namely learning, is not attained;* فَٱجْتَنِبُوا ٱلرِّجْسَ مِنَ ٱلْأَوْثَانِ, *therefore avoid the abomination of idols;* وَٱلْعَرَبُ لَاتَيْتُ مِنْهُ ٱلْأَسَدَ, *I encountered in him a lion;*

3. The Government of the Verb. — The Prepositions. 87

تَحْذِفُ هٰذَا ٱلْفِعْلَ مِنْ قَالَ وَيَقُولُ, and the Arabs omit this verb ḳála yaḳúlu. In this way مِنْ is constantly used after the indefinite pronoun مَا, *what, whatever*, which cannot be construed with a genitive; as: مَا ذَهَبَ مِنَ ٱلْمَالِ, *the money that has been spent;* مَا تُنْفِقُوا مِنْ خَيْرٍ يُوَفَّ إِلَيْكُمْ, *whatever you lay out in charity, will be amply made up to you.*

Rem. In the language of the grammarians, مِنْ is here used لِلْبَيَانِ or لِلتَّبْيِينِ, *to make clear or explain.*

50. عَنْ (with pronominal suffixes عَنِّي, عَنْكَ, عَنَّا) designates motion away from, departure from a place or from beside a person; as: سَايِرْ عَنِ ٱلْبَلَدِ, *take your departure from the town;* حَتَّى لَا تَحْتَاجَ إِلَى تَرْكِهِ وَٱلْإِعْرَاضِ عَنْهُ, *that you may not be compelled to leave him and turn away from him.* Hence it is used:

1) After verbs denoting flight, avoidance, caution, abstinence, self-defence, guarding and setting free, forbidding and hindering, and, in general, to express the doing of something (e. g. fighting or paying) for or in behalf of another. For example: ٱلْهَرَبُ عَنْ قَضَآءِ ٱللّٰهِ تَعَ غَيْرُ مُمْكِنٍ, *it is impossible to flee from the decree of God Almighty;* يَنْبَغِي أَنْ يَجْتَنِبَ، تَنَحَّ عَنِ ٱلْقَبِيحِ, *avoid what is disgraceful;* عَمَّا يَضُرُّهُ, *it is necessary that he should avoid what injures him;* يَنْبَغِي أَنْ يَصْبِرَ عَمَّا تُرِيدُهُ نَفْسُهُ, *it is necessary that he should patiently abstain from what his soul desires*

(his passions desire): تَبَرَّأْتُ عَنْ وَلَآيِهِمْ, *I am free from all connexion with them* (as client): يَتَخَلَّصُ عَنْ عَذابِ ٱلْآخِرَةِ, *he is saved from punishment in the next world*; ٱلنَّهْىُ عَنِ ٱلْمُنْكَرِ, *the prohibition of what is abominable*; يَنُوبُ عَنِّى, *he acts as my deputy*; يُقَاتِلُ عَنْهُ, *he fights for him*; لَا تُجَادِلْ عَنِ ٱلَّذِينَ يَخْتَانُونَ أَنْفُسَهُمْ, *do not contend for those who betray themselves* (lit. *do not by contending try to keep off punishment from those &c.*); لَا تَجْزِى نَفْسٌ عَنْ نَفْسٍ شَيْئًا, *one soul shall not make satisfaction for another in any point*; حَمَلَ عَنْهُ كَذَا وَكَذَا دِرْهَمًا, *he paid so and so many dirhems in his stead.*

2) After verbs denoting uncovering, laying bare, opening, revealing, informing, asking and answering; for in these verbs there lies the idea of the removal of a covering, real or figurative. For example: لَوْ كُشِفَ عَنِّى سُتُورُ ٱلدُّنْيَا, *if the veils of this world were removed from me (from before my eyes)*; إِنْ كُنْتَ تَبْغِى شَاهِدًا يُخْبِرُ عَنْ غَائِبٍ, *if you want a witness who can inform you regarding what is hidden*; سَأُنْبِيكَ عَنْ تَجْمُوعِهَا, *I will tell you about all of them*; هٰذَا سُؤَالٌ سُئِلَ عَنْهُ رَسُولُ ٱللّٰهِ صلعم فَأَجَابَ عَنْهُ, *this is a question about which the apostle of God was questioned, and he gave an answer to it*; كَأَنَّمَا تَبْسِمُ عَنْ لُؤْلُؤٍ مُنَضَّدٍ أَوْ بَرَدٍ, *she laughs so as to show* (teeth like) *strung pearls or hailstones* (in whiteness).

3) After verbs denoting abandonment or neglect, and the ability to dispense with (عَنْ) one thing because of the

3. The Government of the Verb. — The Prepositions.

possession of another (بِ); because in them is implied the notion of turning away (أَعْرَضَ). For example: يَنْبَغِي لِلْإِنْسَانِ أَنْ لَا يَغْفُلَ عَنْ نَفْسِهِ, *a man must not be neglectful of himself*; وَهُوَ غَنِيٌّ عَنْهَا, *he does not require it*; لِي فِي طِلَابِ ٱلْعِلْمِ غِنًى عَنْ غِنَاءِ ٱلْقَائِنِيَاتِ, *I find in the study of science that which contents me so that I can dispense with the singing of women*; أَغْنِنِي بِحَلَالِكَ عَنْ حَرَامِكَ وَٱكْفِنِي بِفَضْلِكَ عَنْ سِوَاكَ, *satisfy me with what thou allowest, so that I may be able to dispense with what thou forbiddest, and suffice me through thy goodness, so that I may not have occasion for any other but thee.* Similarly: شَغَلَهُ ذٰلِكَ عَنِ ٱلْفِكْرَةِ فِي كُلِّ شَيْءٍ إِلَّا فِيهِ, *this circumstance occupied him so that he could not think of anything but it*; بِي حَصْرٌ عَنْ ذِكْرِ كُلِّ ٱلْمَنَاقِبِ, *there is in me inability to mention all the virtues*; إِنِّي أَحْبَبْتُ حُبَّ ٱلْخَيْرِ عَنْ ذِكْرِ رَبِّي, *I loved the good (of this world) so as to neglect all thought of my Lord*; يَبْخَلُ عَنْ نَفْسِهِ, *he is so stingy as to deny himself every thing.*

4) After verbs signifying to leave one behind or to surpass one; as: لَا أَفْضَلْتَ عَنِّي, *you do not surpass me in anything.* Hence the expression فَضْلًا عَنْ, *not to mention, much more* or *much less* (according to the context); as: تَتَبَيَّنُ لَهُ فِي أَقَلِّ ٱلْأَشْيَاءِ ٱلْمَوْجُودَةِ فَضْلًا عَنْ أَكْبَرِهَا مِنْ آثَارِ ٱلْحِكْمَةِ مَا تَقْضِي مِنْهُ كُلَّ ٱلْعَجَبِ, *and he clearly saw in the smallest of existing things, not to mention (and much more in) the largest of them, such traces of wisdom*

as set him in the greatest astonishment; لَا يُوجَدُ فِي ٱلشَّامِ بِأَسْرِهَا فَضْلًا عَنْ صَفَدَ, it is not found in the entire of Syria, not to mention (much less in) Ṣafèd. Hence too the use of عَنْ in comparisons (like مِنْ, § 49, 5); as: أَيْنَ أَنْتَ عَنِ ٱلْبَيْتِ ٱلنَّادِرِ ٱلْجَامِعِ لِمُشَبَّهَاتِ ٱلثَّغْرِ, where art thou (where are thy verses) in comparison with this rare verse, that contains all the things with which the mouth can be compared?

5) عَنْ also indicates the source from which something proceeds; as: رَضِيَ عَنْهُ, he was satisfied with him, was gracious to him; لَا نَفْعَلُ هٰذَا عَنْ قَوْلِكَ, we will not do this at your word, as it were, setting out from your word, moved by your authority. Hence it shows a) the authority for any statement, tradition, or the like; as: حُكِيَ عَنِ ٱلشَّافِعِيِّ, it is related on the authority of es-Sâfi'i; وَكَانَ أُسْتَاذُنَا يَحْكِي عَنْ شَيْخٍ مِنَ ٱلْمَشَايِخِ, and our teacher used to narrate on the authority of a certain sheikh; حَدِيثٌ صَحِيحٌ عَنْ رَسُولِ ٱللّٰهِ, an authentic tradition of the Apostle of God; وَعَنِ ٱلنَّبِيِّ أَنَّهُ قَالَ, it is told of the prophet that he said; and b) the cause from which an effect proceeds as its source; as: مَا هَلَكَ, ٱلَّلَازِمُ عَنْهُ, that which necessarily follows from it; ٱمْرُؤٌ عَنْ مَشْوَرَةٍ, no one ever perished through asking advice (of others).

6) Lastly, عَنْ is used of time as equivalent to بَعْدَ, after; as: عَنْ قَرِيبٍ يَكُونُ كَثِيرًا, in a short time it will be

3. The Government of the Verb. — The Prepositions.

much; عَمَّا قَلِيلٍ, *after a little while* (where مَا is redundant, as in §. 49, 3, last example).

Rem. *a.* Observe the phrases: مَاتَ عَنْ ثَمَانِينَ سَنَةً, *he died aged eighty;* مَاتَ عَنْ وَلَدٍ صَغِيرٍ, *he died leaving a young child.*

Rem. *b.* Because of their being related in meaning, مِنْ and عَنْ are sometimes used indifferently; for example, after مَنَعَ, *to hinder,* اِجْتَنَبَ, *to avoid,* بَرِئَ, *free from, clear of,* and the like. Compare §. 49, 5, with §. 50, 4; as also the use of the Heb. מִן, Gesenius' Thesaur., p. 804, second column, a.

Rem. *c.* عَنْ is sometimes used as an indeclinable noun, signifying *side,* which is its original meaning; e. g. مِنْ عَنْ يَمِينِهِ وَشِمَالِهِ, *on his right and his left.*

51. The prepositions that indicate motion to or towards a place, are إِلَى, *to;* حَتَّى, *up to;* لِ, *to;* نَحْوَ, *towards.*

52. إِلَى (with pronominal suffixes إِلَيْهِ, إِلَيْكَ, إِلَيَّ) is opposed to مِنْ and عَنْ; as: مِنَ ٱلْمَهْدِ إِلَى ٱللَّحْدِ, *from the cradle to the grave;* اِنْقَطَعَ عَنْهُ, *he severed himself from him, abandoned his cause,* but اِنْقَطَعَ إِلَيْهِ, *he was devoted to his cause;* إِلَيْكَ عَنِّى, *stand off* (see the end of the section)! It signifies:

1) Motion to or towards a place; as: جَاءَ إِلَى ٱلْمَدِينَةِ, *he came to the city.*

2). Transferred to time, the point up to which something lasts or continues; as: لَا تَزَالُ طَآئِفَةٌ مِنْ أُمَّتِى ظَاهِرِينَ عَلَى ٱلْحَقِّ إِلَى يَوْمِ ٱلْقِيٰمَةِ, *a part of my people shall not cease to hold fast the truth till the day of the resurrection.* It occurs in a somewhat different sense in the phrase: لَيَجْمَعَنَّكُمْ إِلَى يَوْمِ ٱلْقِيٰمَةِ, *he will assemble you to the day of the resurrection (for it).*

3) إِلَى also shows that one thing is added to another, and hence we find it construed with زَادَ, *to increase, augment;* as: لَا تَأْكُلُوا أَمْوَالَهُمْ إِلَى أَمْوَالِكُمْ, *do not devour their substance in addition to your own;* زَادُوا حِكْمَةً إِلَى حِكْمَتِهِمْ, *they have added a knowledge to the knowledge they possessed.*— It is also construed with adjectives of the form أَفْعَلُ and others, derived from verbs signifying love or hatred and used in a passive sense, to indicate the subject of the feeling (see §. 34, rem. *a*); for example: مَحْبُوبٌ, حَبِيبٌ, *dear;* أَحَبُّ, *dearer;* بَغِيضٌ, *hated, hateful;* أَبْغَضُ, *more hateful.* It is used too with قَرِيبٌ, *near,* and similar words, in so far as they convey the idea of approach or approximation, opposed to بَعِيدٌ عَنْ, *far from;* e. g. فَإِنَّهُ أَقْرَبُ إِلَى ٱلتَّعْظِيمِ, *for this comes nearer to reverence;* whereas in so far as they convey the idea of the measurement of the distance of one place from another, they are construed with مِنْ, §. 49, 4. — Finally, notice the phrases: إِلَى آخِرِهِ, إِلَى غَيْرِ ذٰلِكَ, lit. *on to others of this (kind),* and (contracted إلخ), *to the end of it,* i. e. *et caetera;* إِلَيْكَ, lit. *to thyself!* and إِلَيْكَ عَنِّى, *to thyself from me!* i. e.

3 The Government of the Verb. — The Prepositions.

stand off! let me alone! הָדָא إِلَيْهِ, scil. مُسَلَّم or مَفْرُوْض, *this is committed* or *entrusted to him*.

Rem. Compare, in general, the significations of the Heb. preposition אֶל- or אֱלֵי, as exhibited in Gesenius' Thesaurus. Examples of the third sense given above are Levit. 18, 18. וְאִשָּׁה אֶל־אֲחֹתָהּ לֹא גִשָּׂא לִכְבֵּנוּ אֶל־כַּפַּיִם אֶל־אֵל בַּשָּׁמָיִם תִּקָּח, Lament. 3, 41. The Hebrew uses לְ in several cases in which the Arabic employs إِلَى.

53. حَتَّى differs from إِلَى in indicating the motion towards and at the same time the arrival at an object, whether this object be actually touched and included or not; whereas إِلَى merely implies the motion towards an object, whether this be arrived at or not; as: حَتَّى مَطْلَعِ الْفَجْرِ, *till the dawn of morning.* However, when مِنْ and إِلَى are used in opposition to one another to designate the terminus a quo and terminus ad quem, إِلَى necessarily includes the idea of reaching the object. Further, when the reaching of the object is distinctly expressed by the governing verb or verbal noun itself, the meaning of إِلَى is naturally modified thereby; as: اِنْتَهَيْتُ إِلَيْهِ, *I came up to him;* الْاِنْتِهَاءِ إِلَيْهِ, *the attaining of it.* That حَتَّى does not necessarily include the object reached or attained is evident from its being used to indicate *exceptions*, like the German *bis auf.*

Rem. *a.* حَتَّى is scarcely ever used with pronominal suffixes.

Rem. *b.* The grammarians, when they wish to make a distinction, say that إلَى is used لِلْإِنْتِهَآءِ, *to designate the limit of the act*, whilst حَتَّى is employed لِآنْتِهَآءِ ٱلْغَايَةِ, *to designate the attainment of the extremity or utmost limit.*

Rem. *c.* When حَتَّى is a simple copulative particle (حَرْفُ عَطْفٍ, or عَاطِفَةٌ, or لِلْعَطْفِ), in the sense of *even*, it exercises, like the other copulatives, such as وَ, فَ, and ثُمَّ, no independent influence upon the following noun, which remains under the same government as the preceding one; as: قَدِمَ ٱلْحُجَّاجُ حَتَّى ٱلْمُشَاةُ, *the pilgrims have arrived, even those travelling on foot;* أَكَلْتُ ٱلْسَّمَكَةَ حَتَّى رَأْسَهَا, *I have eaten the fish, even the head of it* (وَكَانَ يُشَاوِرُ إِلَى رَأْسِهَا *would mean exclusive of the head*); رَسُولُ ٱللّٰهِ صلعم مَعَ أَصْحَابِهِ فِى جَمِيعِ ٱلْأُمُورِ حَتَّى حَوَآئِجِ ٱلْبَيْتِ, *and the Apostle of God used to consult his companions on all matters, even household affairs.*

Rem. *d.* The corresponding word to حَتَّى in Hebrew (and probably etymologically connected with it) is עַד; in Æthiopic እስከ: on which see Dillmann's Gr. §. 165, 5, and §. 203, 2, *b*, α.

54. لِ (with pronominal suffixes لَهُ, لَكَ, لِى) is connected in its derivation with إِلَى, and differs from it only in this, that إِلَى mostly expresses concrete relations, local or temporal, whilst لِ generally indicates abstract or ideal relations. The principal use of لِ is to show the passing on of the action to a *more distant* object, and hence it corresponds to the Latin or German *dative;* but it may also express the relation of the action to a *nearer* object,

3. The Government of the Verb. — The Prepositions.

and so stand in place of the *accusative* (compare §§. 29—34). Hence لِ indicates:

1) The simple relation of an act to the more distant object; as: وَهَبَهُ لَهُ, *he gave it to him;* قَالَ لَهَا, *he said to her.*

Rem. *a.* After the middle forms of the verb, لِ often expresses the yielding oneself up to the action of another or to the effect of a thing; as: جُرُّوا لَهُ ٱلْخَطِيرَ مَا ٱنْجَرَّ لَكُمْ, *pull his* (the camel's) *leading-string as long as you can pull it;* مَنْ خَدَعَنَا بِٱللّٰهِ ٱنْخَدَعْنَا لَهُ, *if any one deceives us with God* (i. e. *with a pretence of devoutness), we let ourselves be deceived by him.*

Rem. *b.* The grammarians say that the لَامُ ٱلْجَرِّ, or preposition لِ, is used in this case لِلتَّعْدِيَةِ, *to express the passing on of the action.*

2) The dative *a*) of possession; as: ٱلرَّجُلُ مَنْ لَهُ رَأْيٌ صَائِبٌ, *the man is he who has a correct judgment;* ٱلْحَمْدُ لِلّٰهِ, *praise belongs to God;* إِنَّا لِلّٰهِ, *we are God's;* whence it is used to indicate the author of a proverb, poem, &c.; as: كَمَا قِيلَ لِمُحَمَّدِ بْنِ ٱلْحَسَنِ, *as has been said by Mohammed ibn el-Ḥasan;* أَنْشَدَ لِبَعْضِهِمْ, *he recited (a poem) by one of them* (the poets); أُنْشِدْتُ وَقِيلَ أَنَّهُ لِعَلِيٍّ, *a poem was recited to me, and I was told it was by 'Ali;*
b) of permission; as: فَلَهُ ذٰلِكَ, *then this is allowed him* (lit. *is to him); c*) of advantage, as opposed to عَلَى, which indicates injury; as: ٱلْفِقْهُ مَعْرِفَةُ ٱلنَّفْسِ مَا لَهَا وَمَا عَلَيْهَا,

learning is the soul's cognizance of what is for its good and for its hurt.

Rem. *a.* The grammarians say that لِ, when it indicates possession, is used لِلْمِلْكِ, *to indicate the right of property*, or لِلِاخْتِصَاصِ, *to show that something is ascribed to one as his own.* — Compare the Hebrew usage, מִזְמוֹר לְדָוִד, *a psalm composed by David, &c.*

Rem. *b.* As the Arabs have no verb corresponding to our *have*, they are obliged to express it by the preposition لِ with the genitive of the possessor; as: كَانَ لِلْمَلِكِ زُهَيْرٍ مِائَتَا عَبْدٍ, *king Zuhair had two hundred slaves;* لَهُ بِبَغْدَادَ سِتُّمِائَةِ صَاحِبِ خَبَرٍ *he had in Bagdád six hundred secret police;* مَا لِي أَبٌ وَلَا ابْنٌ, *I have neither father nor son.* — So in Hebrew, Gen. 31, 1. אֵין לִי, *I have*, יֵשׁ לִי or הָיָה לִי, as also אֵת כָּל־אֲשֶׁר לְאָבִינוּ *I have not.*

Rem. *c.* لِ is often used, instead of a simple pronominal suffix, in order to avoid rendering a noun definite; e. g. مَاتَ لِي أَخٌ, *a brother of mine is dead;* whereas مَاتَ أَخِي would mean *my* (it may be, *only*) *brother is dead.* — So in Hebrew, Gen. 14, 18. כֹּהֵן לְאֵל עֶלְיוֹן, *a priest of the most high God*, not *the priest.*

Rem. *d.* In pecuniary transactions لِ is used to indicate the creditor, whilst عَلَى expresses the debtor; as: لِي عَلَيْكَ أَلْفُ دِرْهَمٍ, *you owe me* (lit. *there are to me upon you*) *a thousand dirhèms.*

Rem. *e.* Observe the expressions of admiration: لِلَّهِ دَرُّهُ,

3. The Government of the Verb. — The Prepositions.

what a man he is! لِلّٰهِ دَرُّكَ مِنْ رَجُلٍ, *what a man you are!*
(lit. *such a man can emanate only from God.* Compare Jonah 3, 3.
וְנִינְוֵה הָיְתָה עִיר גְּדוֹלָה לֵאלֹהִים, *Nineveh was a very large city*).
Remark also such phrases as: هَلْ لَكَ فِي ٱلشَّرَابِ, *would you
like some wine?* هَلْ لَكُمْ فِي أَنْ تَفْعَلُوا هَذَا, *have you a wish
to do this?* where we must supply the substantive رَغْبَةٌ,
desire, wish.

3) The purpose for which, and the reason why,
any thing is done (relation of the action to its purpose
and cause); as: قَامَ لِيُعَاوِنَتِهِ, *he arose to help him;*
مَا ٱلْعِلْمُ إِلَّا لِلْعَمَلِ, *science* (or *theory*) *is only for the purpose
of being applied in practice;* طَلَبَ ٱلْجَاهَ لِلْأَمْرِ بِٱلْمَعْرُوفِ,
he sought the dignity (or *office*) *for the purpose of or-
dering good;* وَلِهَذَا قِيلَ, *and for this reason it is said;*
لِأَنَّهُ يَضُرُّ, *because it does harm;* عَجِبْتُ لِقَوْلِهِ, *I wondered
at (because of) what he said.*

Rem. In this case ل *is said to be used* لِلْعِلَّةِ, or لِلتَّعْلِيلِ,
to indicate the cause. Compare in Hebrew Gen. 4, 23. כִּי אִישׁ
הָרַגְתִּי לְפִצְעִי, *for I have slain a man because of a wound given me.*

4) After the verb قَالَ, it often indicates the object in
reference to which something is said; as: وَلَا تَقُولُوا لِمَنْ يُقْتَلْ
فِي سَبِيلِ ٱللّٰهِ أَمْوَاتٌ, *do not say in regard to those who are
killed in the path of God, they are dead* (*do not call those
who are killed fighting for God's cause, dead*); أَتَقُولُونَ
لِلْحَقِّ لَمَّا جَاءَكُمْ أَسِحْرٌ هَذَا, *do ye say of the truth, after
it has come to you, Is this magic?* Similarly: قَالَ مَسْلَمَةُ

ٱبْنُ عَبْدِ ٱلْمَلِكِ يَوْمًا لِنَصِيبٍ أَمْتَدَحْتَ فُلَانًا لِرَجُلٍ مِنْ أَهْلِهِ قَالَ قَدْ فَعَلْتُ, *Mèslèma, the son of 'Abdu'l-mèlik, said one day to Noṣaib, Did you compose a poem in praise of so and so? meaning one of his family; he said, I did.*

Rem. *a*. Both אֶל and לְ are so used in Hebrew. See Gesenius' Thesaurus, p. 104, first col., 11, b, and p. 731, second col. 11.

Rem. *b*. After the interjection يَا, the preposition لِ is frequently prefixed to the name of a person called to aid, as well as to the name of him against whom help is implored, in which case it is said to be used لِلِٱسْتِغَاثَةِ, *to ask help.* If there be only one مُسْتَغَاثٌ or مُسْتَغَاثٌ بِهِ, i. e. person called to aid, the preposition takes the vowel fétha (just as with the pronominal suffixes, vol. I. §. 356, rem. *b*); as: يَا لَزَيْدٍ, *help, Zèid!* But if there be several, لِ is used with the first alone, and لِ with the rest, unless the interjection be repeated before each name, when لِ is retained throughout; as: يَا لَلْكُهُولِ وَلِلشُّبَّانِ, *help, old and young!* يَا لَزَيْدٍ وَلِعَمْرٍو or يَا لَزَيْدٍ وَيَا لِعَمْرٍو, *help, Zèid and 'Amr!* يَا لَقَوْمِي وَيَا لَأَمْثَالِ قَوْمِي, *help, O my family and ye who are like my family!* If the name of the person against whom aid is required, ٱلْمُسْتَغَاثُ لَهُ or ٱلْمُسْتَغَاثُ مِنْ أَجْلِهِ, be expressed, it takes لِ (with kèsra) before it, as يَا لَلنَّاسِ لِلْكَاذِبِ, *help, people, against this liar!* In the case of the ٱلْمُسْتَغَاثُ بِهِ, the vocative termination ـًا (see §. 38, 3) is sometimes used instead of لِ with the genitive; as: يَا زَيْدًا لِعَمْرٍو, *help, Zèid, against 'Amr!* — These expressions are also employed لِلتَّعَجُّبِ, *to express surprise,* in which case the ٱلْمُتَعَجَّبُ مِنْهُ, or object that causes surprise, is treated in the same

3. The Government of the Verb. — The Prepositions.

way as the بِ e. g. ;اَلْمُسْتَغَاثُ بِهِ, يَا لَلْمُتَعَجَّبِ, *O the wonder!* يَبَا لَخُسْرَانِ طَالِبِيهِ لِنَيْلِ فَضْلٍ مِنَ ٱلْعِبَادِ, *but O the disgrace of those who seek it* (learning) *in order to obtain benefits from men!* — In all these cases لِ seems to point out the person or thing, in reference to which the exclamation is uttered, as being the origin and cause of it.

55. نَحْوُ (accusative of نَحْوٌ, the nomen verbi of نَحَا, *to turn towards*) indicates 1) *towards* a place; as: ثُمَّ يَسِيرُونَ نَحْوَ بَيْتِ ٱلْمُقَدَّسِ, *then they will set out towards Jerusalem*; 2) *according to*; as: نَحْوَ قَوْلِهِ, *according to his saying, as he says* (compare the use of لِ in §. 54, 3). — نَحْوُ is also used in all its cases, with a following genitive, as a substantive or adjective, to signify *such as, like*; e. g. رَجُلٌ نَحْوُ زَيْدٍ, *a man such as Zeid*; وَكَذَلِكَ فِي سَائِرِ ٱلْأَخْلَاقِ نَحْوَ ٱلْجُودِ وَٱلْبُخْلِ, *and just so in regard to the other moral characteristics, such as liberality and niggardliness*; تَكَلَّمَ نَحْوَ زَيْدٍ (i. e. تَكَلَّمَ تَكَلُّمًا نَحْوَ تَكَلُّمِ زَيْدٍ), *he spoke like Zeid*. As a substantive it likewise means *about* (*circa*), in which case it may be followed either by the genitive or by مِنْ; as: طُولُهُ نَحْوُ مِائَةِ ذِرَاعٍ, *its length is about one hundred cubits*; عَلَى نَحْوِ سِتِّ مَرَاحِلَ, *at (a distance of) about six marches*; هِيَ فِي ٱلْكِبَرِ نَحْوٌ مِنْ فَيْدَ, *it is about the size of Feid*.

56. The preposition فِي (with pronominal suffixes فِيَّ, فِيكَ, فِيهِ), on the difference between which and بِ see §. 57, indicates:

1) Both rest in a place or during a time and motion into a place, in which latter case it corresponds to the Greek εἰς or the Latin *in* with the accusative; as: فِي ٱلْبَيْتِ, *in the house;* وَقَعَ فِي ٱلْبِئْرِ, *in this year;* فِي تِلْكَ ٱلسَّنَةِ, *he fell into the well;* وَقَعَ فِي ظَهْرِ ٱلْكِتَابِ, *he wrote on the back of the letter;* يُوقِعُهُ ٱللّٰهُ فِي ٱلرَّسَاتِيقِ, *God will cast him into* (make him dwell in) *the villages.* This signification is then transferred to the relation subsisting between any two things, the one of which is regarded as the place in which the other is, or happens, or into which it goes or is put; as: يَنْبَغِي فِي حَالِ ٱلتَّعَلُّمِ, *in the state of pupilage;* أَنْ يَمْتَثِلَ أَمْرَهُ فِي غَيْرِ مَعْصِيَةِ ٱللّٰهِ وَلَا طَاعَةِ ٱلْمَخْلُوقِ فِي مَعْصِيَةِ ٱلْخَالِقِ, *he must obey his* (the teacher's) *orders in all that is not contrary to the will of God, but not in those things which, whilst they are in accordance with the will of the creature, are against the will of the Creator;* مَا فِيهِ مِنَ ٱلْخَيْرِ, *whatever good there is in it;* دَخَلَ فِي ٱلتَّعَلُّمِ, *he commenced studying;* يُدْخِلُهُمُ ٱللّٰهُ فِي رَحْمَتِهِ, *God will let them enter into his mercy.*

2) فِي is sometimes equivalent in meaning to مَعَ, *with,* or بَيْنَ, *among;* as: تَوَجَّهَ فِي خَمْسِينَ أَلْفًا, *he set out with* (lit. *in the midst of*) 50,000 *men.*

3) It indicates the subject of thought or conversation, that in which these move; as: تَأَمَّلْ شَهْرَيْنِ فِي ٱخْتِيَارِ ٱلْأُسْتَاذِ, *reflect two months upon the choice of a teacher;* يَنْبَغِي أَنْ

3. The Government of the Verb. — The Prepositions.

تَكَلَّمَ فِى ذٰلِكَ, *he must meditate upon this*; يَتَفَكَّرَ فِى ذٰلِكَ, *he spoke about this* (whereas تَكَلَّمَ بِذٰلِكَ would mean *he spoke this out, he gave utterance to this opinion*). Hence it is used in stating the subject of a book or chapter; as: صَنَّفَ كِتَابًا فِى ٱلْأَخْلَاقِ, *he composed a book on morals;* فَصْلٌ فِى مَاهِيَّةِ ٱلْعِلْمِ, *a chapter treating of the nature of science;* كِتَابُ ٱلنُّجُومِ ٱلزَّاهِرَةِ فِى مُلُوكِ مِصْرَ وَٱلْقَاهِرَةِ, *the book of the shining stars, treating of the kings of Miṣr and el-Ḳâhira.*

4) فِى is used after verbs signifying desire, like طَمِعَ and رَغِبَ, in connection with the object desired; as: مَنْ وَجَدَ لَذَّةَ ٱلْعِلْمِ وَٱلْعَمَلِ بِهِ فَلِمَ يَرْغَبُ فِيمَا عِنْدَ ٱلنَّاسِ, *why should he, who has experienced the sweetness of knowledge and of the application of it in practice, desire anything that men possess?* يَنْبَغِى أَنْ لَا يَطْمَعَ فِى أَمْوَالِ ٱلنَّاسِ, *he must not covet people's property.*

5) It is employed in the comparison of two objects, governing the thing with which the other is compared; as: مَا ٱلْحَيٰوةُ ٱلدُّنْيَا فِى ٱلْآخِرَةِ إِلَّا مَتَاعٌ, *this life is merely a temporary usufruct, compared with the life to come;* lit. *when put into it*, the smaller object being, as it were, placed within the larger one for the purpose of comparing the two.

6) Lastly فِى is used to express *proportion* (e. g. length and breadth) and *multiplication*; as: طُولُهُ خَمْسُونَ ذِرَاعًا فِى ٱثْنَىْ عَشَرَ ذِرَاعًا عَرْضًا, *its length is fifty cubits, by twelve*.

cubits in breadth (Germ. bei or auf, Fr. sur); قَلْتَةٌ فِي خَمْسَةٍ,
three into five or three times five, according to the phrase
ضَرَبَ عَدَدًا فِي عَدَدٍ, he multiplied one number by another
(lit. struck the one into the other).

Rem. a. فِي is said by the grammarians to be used لِلظَّرْفِيَّةِ,
to indicate time and place (see vol. I. §. 221, rem. a).

Rem. b. The Hebrew uses בְּ in most of the above significations;
e. g. וִיפֹּל בְּשַׁחַת יִפְעָל, בְּשָׁנָה הַהִיא, בַּבַּיִת (Ps. 7, 16);
אֲחִיתֹפֶל בַּקֹּשְׁרִים עִם־אַבְשָׁלוֹם, Ahitophel is among those who are
conspiring with Absalom (2 Sam. 15, 31); דָּבַר בְּ, חָפֵץ בְּ,
רָצָה בְּ; &c.

57. بِ (with pronominal suffixes بِي, بِكَ, بِهِ) differs
from فِي in this, that فِي, like the Latin and German in,
shows that one thing is actually in the midst of another,
surrounded by it on all sides; whereas بِ merely indicates that the one is close by the other or in contact with
it, and corresponds therefore to the Latin prepositions prope,
juxta, apud, ad, and the German an or bei. For example:
قَرْيَةٌ بِبَابِ ٱلْقَاهِرَةِ, a village close to (or hard by) the gate
of El-Kâhira; مَرَرْتُ بِرَجُلٍ, I passed by a man; جَلَسَ بِهِ,
he sat beside (or by) him; نَصَرَكُمُ ٱللّٰهُ بِبَدْرٍ, God helped
you at Bedr; كَانَ بِٱلْمَدِينَةِ تَاجِرٌ, there was at (or in,
Germ. zu, Fr. à) El-Medina a merchant; قَرْيَةٌ بِمِصْرَ, a town
in (belonging to) Egypt; وَبِيَدِهِ سَيْفٌ, with a sword in his
hand; اِجْتَنِبْ دَارَنَا بِٱلنَّهَارِ, avoid our house by day (= نَهَارًا).—

3. The Government of the Verb. — The Prepositions.

Hence it is construed with verbs signifying to adhere, attach, or connect (e. g. لَفَّ, لَصِقَ, عَلِقَ) seize, take, or begin (e. g. بَدَأَ, أَخَذَ), flee for refuge to, believe in, and swear by (e. g. عَاذَ, آمَنَ, أَقْسَمَ). For example: رُءُوسُهُمْ لَاصِقَةٌ بِأَكْتَافِهِمْ لَا أَعْنَاقَ لَهُمْ, their heads adhere to their shoulders and they have no necks; لِأَنَّ الدُّودَ يَتَعَلَّقُ بِالثِّمَارِ, because the worms stick to the fruit; بَدَأَ بِالسَّبَقِ, he began to study; نَعُوذُ بِاللّٰهِ مِنْ تَخْطِهِ, we take refuge with God from his wrath; آمَنْتُ بِاللّٰهِ الْوَاحِدِ, I believe in the one God; أَقْسَمْتُ بِاللّٰهِ, I swear by God; بِرَأْسِكَ, by thy head! — Hence, too, it is used after إِذَا, lo! see! introducing a person or thing that comes suddenly into view (إِذَا الْمُفَاجَأَةِ or إِذَا الْفُجَائِيَّةِ); as: بَيْنَا هُوَ يَسِيرُ وَإِذَا بِرَهَجٍ, whilst he was going along, he suddenly perceived a cloud of dust; فَلَمَّا تَوَسَّطْتُ الدَّرْبَ وَإِذَا أَنَا بِصَوْتٍ عَظِيمٍ, and after I had got to the middle of the passage, I all at once heard a great noise; وَنَحْنُ فِي الْحَدِيثِ وَإِذَا بِضَجَّةٍ عَظِيمَةٍ عَلَى الْبَابِ, and whilst we were talking, a great clamour suddenly arose at the door; إِذَا بِرَجُلٍ يُقَالُ لَهُ السَّيِّدُ بَرَكَةُ قَدْ أَقْبَلَ, behold there came forward a man called the seiyid Bèraka. Here we must supply the participle of the verb أَحَسَّ, to perceive, which is construed with بِ, as, for instance, in the first of the above examples, وَإِذَا أَنَا مُحِسٌّ بِصَوْتٍ عَظِيمٍ. The same remark applies to كَأَنَّ in such phrases as: كَأَنِّي بِكَ تُخَادِعُنِي, it seems to me that you are trying to deceive me; كَأَنِّي بِكَ تَتِيلًا, methinks I see you *slain;* i. e. كَأَنِّى مُحِسٌّ بِكَ. — From the idea of contact there arises, in the case of a superior and inferior or primary and secondary object, that of companionship and connection; as: سَارَ بِأَهْلِهِ, *he set out with his household;* اِشْتَرَى ٱلْحِمَارَ بِلِجَامِهِ, *he bought the ass along with its bridle.* Under this idea are figuratively represented the following relations.

1) The relation between subject and predicate, especially in negative propositions; as: أَوَلَمْ يَرَوْا أَنَّ ٱللَّهَ بِقَادِرٍ عَلَى أَنْ يُحْيِىَ ٱلْمَوْتَى, *do they not see that God is powerful (enough) to bring the dead to life?* لَسْتُ بِعَالِمٍ, *I do not know;* لَسْتُ بِقَارِئٍ, *I cannot read;* مَا هُمْ بِمُؤْمِنِينَ, *they are not believers.*

2) The relation between the act and its object. *a*) This is always the case after *intransitive* verbs, especially such as indicate *motion*, e. g. ذَهَبَ, *to go,* أَتَى, جَآءَ, *to come,* نَهَضَ, قَامَ, سَارَ, رَاحَ, *to depart, set out,* نَهَضَ, *to get up, rise,* سَمَا, *to be high,* &c. These verbs are construed with بِ and the genitive of the thing, accompanied by, or in connection with, which one performs the act they denote. They must therefore be translated into English by transitive verbs. For example: فَأْتُوا بِسُورَةٍ مِنْ مِثْلِهِ, *then bring* (lit. *come with*) *a sūra* (*chapter*) *like it;* ذَهَبَ ٱللَّهُ بِنُورِهِمْ, *God took away* (lit. *went away with*) *their light;* قَامَ بِٱلْحَقِّ, *he upheld the truth;* نَهَضَ بِأَعْبَاءِ ٱلْمَمْلَكَةِ, *he took upon him the burden of the government;* سَمَا بِهِ, *he lifted it up on high. b*) The same construction is also employed

3. The Government of the Verb. — The Prepositions.

with *transitive* verbs, not only when they signify motion, but in other cases too, and the verbs must then be used absolutely; as: بَعَثْتُ إِلَيَّ بِهِمْ, *he sent them to me* (lit. *he performed the act of sending to me in connection with*, or *by means of, them*, using them as the objects through which he realized that act). This happens in particular when the transitive verb is used in a *figurative* sense, and the preposition is then called بَاءُ ٱلْمَجَازِ, *the figurative bi;* as: كَسَرَ ٱلْعَصَا, *he has broken the stick*, but كَسَرَ بِقَلْبِي, *he has broken my heart;* جَبَرَ ٱلْعَظْمَ, *he has set the bone*, but جَبَرَ بِقَلْبِي, *he has comforted my heart;* لَا مَحَالَةَ أَنْ ٱلْاِغْتِذَآءَ بِهَذِهِ ٱلنَّبَاتَاتِ مِمَّا يَقْطَعُ بِهَا عَنْ كَمَالِهَا, *and there is no doubt that the using of these plants for food is one of the reasons that prevents them* (lit. *cuts them off*) *from attaining their full growth*. In this case بِ indicates the adhesion of the action to its object. The relation of the acts of breaking, cutting, &c., to their objects in an improper spiritual sense, requires a prepositional exponent, as being a less immediate relation than when they are used in their proper material sense.

3) The relation between the act and the instrument with which, the means by which, or the reason why, it is performed; as: قَتَلَهُ بِٱلسَّيْفِ, *he slew him with the sword;* يَرْزُقُهُ ٱللَّهُ ٱلصَّبْرَ بِبَرَكَةِ دُعَائِهِ, *God will grant him patience through the salutary power of prayer to Him;* فَبِمَا نَقْضِهِمْ مِيثَاقَهُمْ لَعَنَّاهُمْ, *wherefore, because of their breaking their covenant, we have cursed them* (مَا redundant, see § 49, 3,

and § 50, 6). — Connected herewith is the use of بِ with surnames, &c., after عُرِفَ, *to be known;* as also after كَفَى, *to be enough, to suffice,* with the person or thing that suffices or is enough for one; e. g. حَسَنْ بْنْ عَلِيّ ٱلْمَعْرُوفْ بِٱلْمَرْغِينَانِي, *Hasan bin 'Ali, known by the name of el-Marginàní;* قَرْيَةٌ تُعْرَفُ بِبَقْرَى, *a village known by the name of Bakwà;* كَفَى بِٱللّٰهِ شَهِيدًا, *God sufficeth as a witness;* كَفَى بِلَذَّةِ ٱلْعِلْمِ دَاعِيًا وَبَاعِثًا لِلْعَاقِلِ, *the delight of learning is a sufficient motive and incentive to the sensible man.* — The *price* of any article is also expressed by the preposition بِ after verbs signifying to buy, pay, &c., as being the instrumental means with which the act is performed; as: اِشْتَرَى قَلَمًا بِدِينَارٍ, *he bought a reed-pen for a dinàr;* اِشْتَرَوُا ٱلضَّلَالَةَ بِٱلْهُدَى, *they have purchased error at the price of truth;* لَهُمْ عَذَابٌ أَلِيمٌ بِمَا كَانُوا يَكْذِبُونَ, *they shall suffer a painful punishment for having charged (others) with being liars* (بِمَا كَانُوا— لِكَوْنِهِمْ).

Rem. a. The preposition *without* is expressed in Arabic by بِلَا; بِدُونِ and مِنْ غَيْرِ and more rarely بِغَيْرِ, بِلَا can be used only with an indefinite substantive, بِغَيْرِ with one that is either definite or indefinite; as: سُلْطَانٌ بِلَا عَدْلٍ كَنَهْرٍ بِلَا مَاءٍ, *a ruler without justice is like a river without water;* بِغَيْرِ ضَرُورَةٍ, *without necessity;* بِغَيْرِ حَقٍّ, *unjustly;* مِنْ غَيْرِ خِلَافٍ, *without controversy;* بِدُونِ ثَمَنٍ, *without (paying any) price.* — Compare in Hebrew בְּלֹא, בְּבְלִי, בְּאֵין.

3. The Government of the Verb. — The Prepositions.

Rem. b. In formulas such as بِأَبِي أَنْتَ وَأُمِّي, *thou art as dear to me as father and mother*, the preposition depends upon the word مَفْدِيّ, *ransomed*, which is understood, and the literal meaning is: *thou art to be ransomed for my father and mother*. It is called by the grammarians بَآءُ ٱلتَّفْدِيَةِ, *the bi that expresses ransom*, but is in reality the بَآءُ ٱلثَّمَنِ, *or bi of price*, as used after بَاعَ, ٱشْتَرَى &c. (see above, no. 3, at the end). In the same way as بِأَبِي وَأُمِّي, are used بِنَفْسِي and بِرُوحِي.

Rem. c. In phrases like مَاتَ قَبْلَ ٱلنَّبِيِّ بِقَلِيلٍ (بِيَسِيرٍ), *he died a little before the Prophet*, قَدِمَ بَعْدَ ذٰلِكَ بِشَهْرَيْنِ وَأَيَّامٍ, *he arrived two months and some days after this*, ب is the *bi of measure*, and quite different in meaning from the accusative of time how long; سَافَرَ قَبْلِي يَوْمَيْنِ means *he travelled for two days before me*, profectus est biduum ante me, Germ. *er reiste zwei Tage lang vor mir*, but سَافَرَ قَبْلِي بِيَوْمَيْنِ, *he started two days before me*, profectus est biduo ante me, Germ. *er reiste zwei Tage vor mir ab*. Observe that ب with its genitive must in this case always be placed after قَبْلَ, بَعْدَ, &c.

Rem. d. The grammarians denote the various uses of ب by saying that it is used لِلْقَسَمِ, *to express adhesion*; لِلْإِلْصَاقِ, *swearing*; لِلْمُلَابَسَةِ or لِلْمُصَاحَبَةِ, *companionship and connection*; لِلتَّعْدِيَةِ, *to render an (intransitive) verb transitive*; لِلْإِسْتِعَانَةِ, *to indicate the instrument of whose aid we avail ourselves*; لِلتَّعْلِيلِ, *to express the reason or cause*; and لِلتَّعْوِيضِ or لِلثَّمَنِ, *to state the price given for anything*.

14*

Rem. e. בְּ is used in Hebrew in nearly all the above significations, as well as in those of فِي, (§. 56, rem. b). For example: 1 Sam. 29, 1. חָנָה בְּ, פָּגַע בְּ, נָגַע בְּ, דָּבַק בְּ, חֹנִים בָּעַיִן, *encamping by the well*; וַיֵּצֵא אֲרוֹם לִקְרָאתוֹ בְּעַם כָּבֵד; Num. 20, 20. נִשְׁבַּע בֵּאלֹהִים, הֶאֱמִין בְּ Jerem. 11, 19. עֵץ בְּלַחְמוֹ; the so-called *beth essentiae*, Exod. 6, 3. הִנֵּה אֲדֹנָי יְהוִה, וָאֵרָא אֶל־אַבְרָהָם... בְּאֵל שַׁדַּי Isaiah 40, 10. לֹא קְדָמוֹ בְּחָזָק יָבוֹא; Eccles. 5. 2. בָּא הַחֲלוֹם בְּרֹב עִנְיָן, Deut. 23, 5, סָקַל בָּאֲבָנִים, הָרַג בַּחֶרֶב; אֲחָכָם בַּלֶּחֶם וּבַמַּיִם; 2 Sam. 24, 24. וַיִּקֶן דָּוִד אֶת־הַגֹּרֶן וְאֶת־הַבָּקָר בְּכֶסֶף שְׁקָלִים חֲמִשִּׁים.

Rem. f. In the above section, under no. 3, as well as in §. 49, 3, and § 60, 6, we have examples of the redundant use of مَا after the prepositions مِنْ, عَنْ, and بِ. The same thing occurs in Hebrew, in which case מָה takes the form of מוֹ; as Job 27, 14. לְמוֹ־חָרֶב, Ps. 11, 2. בְּמוֹ־אֹפֶל, Exod. 15, 5. כְּמוֹ־אָבֶן.

58. مَعَ (rarely مَعْ) *with, along with*, indicates companionship and connection (مُصَاحَبَةٌ); as: سَارَ مَعِى, *he travelled along with me*; شَاوَرَ مَعِى, *he took counsel with me*; لَا يَصِحُّ الزُّهْدُ مَعَ ٱلْجَهْلِ, *sanctity cannot exist along with (is incompatible with) ignorance;* مَعَ تَكْرَارِ مَا تَقَدَّمَ مِنْهُ, *with the repetition of that portion of it which had gone before* (repeating at the same time what had been done before). Hence it is used to show that a person possesses something or has got it along with him; as: هَلْ مَعَكَ مِحْبَرَةٌ, *have you got an inkbottle with you?* مَا مَعِى دِينَارٌ وَلَا دِرْهَمٌ, *I have neither dīnār nor dirhem* (*neither gold nor silver*) *by me*. — Sometimes it signifies *in addition to, besides;* as: مَعَ كَوْنِهِ غَرِيبًا, *in addition to his being* (*besides his being*) *a*

3. The Government of the Verb. — The Prepositions.

stranger. — More frequently it means *notwithstanding, despite, although*; as: قُتِلَ مَعَ شَجَاعَتِهِ, *despite his bravery he was killed*; لَمْ يَكُنْ أَحَدٌ أَنْطَنَ مِنَ ٱلرَّسُولِ وَمَعَ ذٰلِكَ أُمِرَ بِٱلْمُشَاوَرَةِ, *no one was more clear-sighted than the Apostle (Moḥammèd), and notwithstanding this, he was ordered to consult others*; عَجَزَ عَنْ هَدْمِ ٱلْأَهْرَامِ مَعَ أَنَّ ٱلْهَدْمَ أَسْهَلُ مِنَ ٱلْبِنَآءِ, *he was unable to destroy the pyramids, although it is easier to destroy than to build* (compare in English *withal*; in Heb. בְּ, e. g. Job 1, 22. בְּכָל־זֹאת, Deut. 1, 32. וּבַדָּבָר הַזֶּה, Num. 14, 11. בְּכֹל הָאתוֹת; and in Persian بَا and بَا وُجُودِ). — Lastly مَعَ is used in comparisons, and must then be translated into English by *compared to, in comparison with*; as: ٱلْخَضِرُ مَعَهُ وَتِدٌ, *compared with him el-Ḥaḍir* (Elias, the wandering Jew of the Moḥammèdans) *is a tent-peg*, i. e. fixed and motionless, an expression used of one who leads an unsettled vagabond life.

Rem. *a.* مَعَ is, as the Arab grammarians remark, properly the accusative of a noun, signifying *association, connexion*. See vol. I. § 359.

Rem. *b.* To مَعَ corresponds in Hebrew עִם; e. g. Gen. 13, 1. וְלוֹט עִמּוֹ, *and Lot along with him*; אֱלֹהִים עִמָּךְ, דִּבֶּר עִם, נִלְחַם עִם; שָׁכַב עִם; Nehem. 5, 18. וְעִם־זֶה, *and notwithstanding this*.

59. عِنْدَ, properly the accusative of a noun عِنْدٌ, *a side*, signifies *beside, near, by*; as: وَكَانَ يَضَعُ عِنْدَهُ دَفَاتِرَ, *and he used to lay notebooks beside him*; وَيَنْبَغِي أَنْ لَا يَبْتَدِئَ ٱلْكَلَامَ عِنْدَهُ إِلَّا بِإِذْنِهِ, *and he must not commence*

to speak before him unless with his permission. Used of *time*, it shows that something is closely connected with what took place at a particular time, by happening either simultaneously or immediately after; as: عِنْدَ ذٰلِكَ, *whilst this took place* or *immediately after this took place, hereupon;* عِنْدَ مَا, *whilst, during,* or *immediately after.* — Further, عِنْدَ, like مَعَ, implies *possession* and *comparison;* as: مَا كَانَ عِنْدِى إِلَّا دِينَارٌ وَاحِدٌ, *I had only a single dinar by me;* مَا عِنْدَ ٱلنَّاسِ مُلُوكُ ٱلْأَرْضِ, *what the people have or possess;* عِنْدَ ٱللّٰهِ تُرَابٌ, *the kings of the earth are dust compared with* (lit. *at the side of*) *God.* — Lastly عِنْدَ (like the Latin *apud,* Fr. *chez,* and Persian نَزْدِيكِ) implies *in one's mind, in his opinion;* as: ٱلصَّوَابُ عِنْدِى مَا فَعَلَهُ مَشَايِخُنَا, *the right thing in my opinion is what our sheikhs have done;* كَانَ عِنْدَهُ أَنَّ ٱلْقُرْآنَ مَخْلُوقٌ, *the Korʾān was in his opinion created;* عِنْدَكُمْ يَسْتَحِيلُ أَنْ يَفْعَلَهُ, *according to you it is impossible that he (God) should do it.*

Rem. *a.* On the phrase خُذْ زَيْدًا - عِنْدَكَ زَيْدًا, see §. 35, rem.

Rem. *b.* عِنْدَ is sometimes (in modern Arabic generally) pronounced عَنْدَ, rarely عُنْدَ.

Rem. *c.* To عِنْدَ correspond in Hebrew עֵ֫מֶד and עִם; e. g. Gen. 25, 1. הָאֵלֶּה אֲשֶׁר עִם־שֵׁם, 35, 4. וַיֵּשֶׁב יִצְחָק עִם־בְּאֵר לַחַי רֹאִי. 24, 25. עִמָּ֫נוּ, *apud nos, in domo nostrâ;* Job 9, 2. וּמַה־יִּצְדַּק אֱנוֹשׁ עִם־אֵל, *and how can a man be just in God's sight* (judice Deo).

3. The Government of the Verb. — The Prepositions.

60. لَدَى or لَدَا (لَدُنَّا, لَدُنِّى with suffixes) لَدُنْ (with suffixes لَدَىَّ, لَدَيْكَ, لَدَيْهِ), is a comparatively rare word, equivalent in meaning to عِنْدَ (see §. 59); as: اِعْتَقَدَ أَنَّ ٱلنَّارَ أَفْضَلُ ٱلْأَشْيَاءِ ٱلَّتِى لَدَيْهِ, *he believed that fire was the most excellent of the things which were in his possession*; وَأَلْفَيَا سَيِّدَهَا لَدَا ٱلْبَابِ, *and they found her lord at the door.*

Rem. The lexicographers enumerate several other forms of this word; viz. لُدْ, لَدْ, لَدُ, لُدْنْ, لَدْنْ, لُدْنِ, لَدِنْ, لَدَنْ.

61. بَيْنَ, *between, among*, is properly the accusative of the substantive بَيْنٌ, signifying *intervening space*, which may be regarded either as *uniting* or as *separating* two or more objects, whence بَيْنَ may be construed with verbs of either meaning; as: جَمَعَ بَيْنَنَا, *he united us,* فَرَّقَ بَيْنَنَا, *he parted us*, lit. *he united our separation* and *parted our connection;* أَلَّفَ ٱللّٰهُ بَيْنَ قُلُوبِكُمْ, *God has united your hearts.* — If two genitives follow بَيْنَ, and either or each of them is a pronominal suffix, the preposition must be repeated before the second, and the conjunction وَ inserted; as: بَيْنِى وَبَيْنَهُ, *between me and him*; بَيْنَكُمْ وَبَيْنَ أَخِيكُمْ, *between you and your brother*. But if both are substantives, this is not done; as: بَيْنَ زَيْدٍ وَعَمْرٍو, *between Zeid and 'Amr.* — Instead of the simple بَيْنَ, we often meet with مَا بَيْنَ, *what is between*, and فِيمَا بَيْنَ, *in what is between*. Both بَيْنَ and مَا بَيْنَ are often used in the sense of *both — and*, and of *partly* — *partly* (tam — quam, partim — partim); as: مَا بَيْنَ مَعْرُوفٍ وَمَجْهُولٍ, *partly known and partly unknown;* جَآءَنِى مَا بَيْنَ فَقِيرٍ وَغَنِيٍّ, *there came to me both rich and poor;* ٱلْقَوْمُ بَيْنَ قَتِيلٍ وَأَسِيرٍ, *the tribe were partly slain, and partly taken prisoners.* In such cases بَيْنَ or مَا بَيْنَ holds the place of a substantive expressing that which unites both objects as parts of one whole. — If we wish to indicate the entire interval between two places or two points of time, إِلَى is used before the second substantive; as: بَيْنَ ٱلْبَصْرَةِ إِلَى مَكَّةَ, *between el-Baṣra and Mekka.* — Observe the phrase بَيْنَ يَدَىْ فُلَانٍ, *before any one, in his presence,* lit. *between his hands;* as: اِنْهِزَامُ ٱلذِّئْبِ بَيْنَ يَدَيْهِ, *the fleeing of the wolf before him* (the dog).

Rem. *a.* From بَيْنَ are formed the conjunctive adverbs of time بَيْنَمَا and بَيْنَا, *whilst*, which naturally exercise no influence upon the following clause; as: بَيْنَا نَحْنُ نَرْقُبُهُ, *whilst we are awaiting him;* بَيْنَا نَسُوسُ ٱلنَّاسَ, *whilst we govern the people;* بَيْنَا زَيْدٌ مَضْرُوبٌ, *whilst Zeid is being beaten.*

Rem. *b.* With the uses of بَيْنَ compare those of בֵּין; in particular בֵּין ... לְ and בֵּין ... וּבֵין, both *between* one thing *and* another, and also *whether — or.* See Gesenius' Thesaurus, p. 203, second column.

62. عَلَى (with pronominal suffixes عَلَىَّ, عَلَيْكَ, عَلَيْهِ), *over, above, upon,* is used:

1) In its original *local* sense (لِلَّاِسْتِعْلَآءِ), *to denote*

3. The Government of the Verb. — The Prepositions.

higher elevation); as: فَأَقْبَلَتْ تَحُومُ عَلَى حَائِطٍ, *and it* (the pigeon) *began to hover over a wall;* وَجَدَ إِنْسَانًا عَلَى ٱلطَّرِيقِ, *he found a person upon the road;* نَظَرَ عَلَى ٱلْحَائِطِ صُورَةَ رَجُلٍ, *he saw on the wall the figure of a man;* عَلَيَّ ثِيَابُ قُطْنٍ, *I had on cotton clothes.* The same sense is farther exemplified in: جَلَسَ عَلَى ٱلْمَائِدَةِ, *he sat at table* (because a person sitting at table rises *above* the level of it); وَقَفَ عَلَى ٱلنَّهْرِ, *he stood by the river;* قَعَدَ عَلَى بَابِ دَارِهِ, *he sat at the door of his house;* وَقَفَ عَلَى رَأْسِ فُلَانٍ, *he stood by the head of so and so;* فِي وَقْتِ شَهْوَتِهِ فِي ٱلْوُقُوفِ عَلَى خَصَائِصِ أَعْضَاءِ ٱلْحَيَوَانِ, *at the time when he was very eager to investigate the peculiarities of the limbs of animals;* طَالَعَ عَلَى شَيْءٍ, *he contemplated* or *examined something;* اِطَّلَعَ عَلَى شَيْءٍ, *he became acquainted with* or *acquired a knowledge of something;* قَرَأَ عَلَيْهِ, either *he* (the pupil) *read (a book) before him* (the teacher), studied under him, or *he* (the teacher) *read (a book) to him* (the pupil); بَدَأَ بِكِتَابٍ, تَلَا ٱلرِّسَالَةَ عَلَيْهِمْ, *he read the letter to them;* ٱلصَّلَوٰةِ عَلَى مُحَمَّدٍ, *he began the book of (canonical) prayer before Mohammed,* began to read it under him as his instructor. Similarly in the phrases: غُشِيَ عَلَيْهِ (عَلَيْهَا), *he (she) fainted* (lit. *there was a covering of darkness over him or her);* مَغْشِيٌّ عَلَيْهِ (عَلَيْهَا), *do.;* أُغْمِيَ عَلَيْهِ, *in a faint;* ٱلسَّلَامُ عَلَيْكُمْ, *peace be upon you!* رَحْمَةُ ٱللّٰهِ عَلَيْهِ, *God's mercy be upon him, may God have mercy on him.*

2) In a *hostile* sense, in which case it can generally be rendered by *against* or *upon;* as: خَرَجَ عَلَيْهِ, *he went out against him* (with an army), *he rebelled against him;* هَجَمَ عَلَيْهِ, *he rushed upon him;* فَأَعِنْ عَلَيْهِ, *therefore give aid against him;* يَنْبَغِي أَنْ يَصْبِرَ عَلَى ٱلْمِحَنِ, *he must bear his troubles patiently* (lit. *must exercise patience against them);* كَيْلَا يَكُونَ عَقْلُهُ وَعِلْمُهُ حُجَّةً عَلَيْهِ, *that his intelligence and his knowledge may not become an argument against him;* ٱلْفِقْهُ مَعْرِفَةُ ٱلنَّفْسِ مَا لَهَا وَمَا عَلَيْهَا, *learning is the soul's cognizance of what is for its good and for its hurt* (see §. 54, 2, c). Similarly in the phrases: صَعْبٌ (عَسِيرٌ) عَلَيَّ, *difficult for me,* opposed to سَهْلٌ (يَسِيرٌ) عَلَيَّ, *easy for me;* عَزِيزٌ عَلَيَّ, *difficult for me,* but also *dear to me,* opposed in both senses to خَفِيٌّ عَلَيَّ; هَيِّنٌ عَلَيَّ, *hidden from me, obscure to me,* opposed to جَلِيٌّ عَلَيَّ, *clear to me.* It is therefore construed with verbs signifying *to be angry with* and *to incite* or *instigate;* as: عَتَبَ عَلَيْهِ, *he was angry with him;* لَمْ يُكَلِّمْهُ سَخَطًا عَلَيْهِ, *he did not speak to him out of anger with him;* أَغْرَى ٱلْكَلْبَ عَلَيْهِ, *he urged on the dog against him, set the dog at* or *upon him* (بِهِ would mean *he made the dog attach itself to him).* Frequently, however, when construed with these verbs, it does not imply a hostile movement against an object, but merely motion towards it to get possession of it or do it; e. g. ٱلْحَثُّ عَلَى ٱلْفِعْلِ, *urging* or *encouraging to action;* خَاطَبُوهُ مُحَرِّضِينَ إِيَّاهُ عَلَى تَصْنِيفِ كِتَابٍ, *they talked to him, urging him to*

3. The Government of the Verb. — The Prepositions.

write a book; هَمُّ ٱلْآخِرَةِ يَحْمِلُ ٱلْإِنْسَانَ عَلَى ٱلْخَيْرِ, concern for the life to come induces man to do well (lit. carries him towards good); مَا حَمَلَكَ عَلَى هٰذِهِ ٱلدَّعْوَى ٱلْبَاطِلَةِ, what induced you to set up this empty claim? Hence too حَرَصَ, to be greedy or covetous, and its derivatives حِرْصٌ, greed, and حَرِيصٌ, greedy, are construed with عَلَى and the genitive of the thing coveted. — The phrase دَخَلَ عَلَى فُلَانٍ, to go in to one, is used when the person sought is in his house or room, so that we actually find him; دَخَلَ إِلَى فُلَانٍ merely means *to go into one's house* or *room*.

3) Of a debt that one owes, and a duty that is incumbent *upon* one; as: لِي عَلَيْكَ دِينَارَانِ, *you owe me two dinārs* (see §. 54, 2, rem. d.); طَلَبُ ٱلْعِلْمِ فَرِيضَةٌ عَلَى كُلِّ مُسْلِمٍ, *the search after knowledge is an ordinance for every Muslim (every Muslim is bound by divine command to seek after knowledge)*; عَلَيْكَ أَنْ تَفْعَلَ هٰذَا, *it is incumbent upon you to do this, you must do this*; عَلَيْكَ أَنْ تَتَحَرَّزَ عَنِ ٱلْغِيبَةِ, *you must refrain from slander or backbiting*.

4) Of the advantage, superiority or distinction that one person or thing enjoys *over* another; as: فَضْلُ آدَمَ عَلَى ٱلْمَلَائِكَةِ, *Adam's superiority over the angels*; ٱلَّذِينَ يَسْتَحِبُّونَ ٱلْحَيٰوةَ ٱلدُّنْيَا عَلَى ٱلْآخِرَةِ, *who love the present life more than the life to come*; آثَرَهُ (ٱخْتَارَهُ) عَلَى غَيْرِهِ, *he preferred it to the rest, selected it in preference to the others*.

5) Of the condition in which any one is in respect to

religion, trade or profession, health, fortune, mental or bodily gifts, &c. (properly, the ground or basis *on* which he stands in these respects). For example: اَلنَّاسُ عَلَىٰ دِينِ مُلُوكِهِمْ, *people follow, or conform to, the religion of their kings;* قَالَتِ ٱلْيَهُودُ لَيْسَتِ ٱلنَّصَارَىٰ عَلَىٰ شَىْءٍ, *the Jews say, The Christians are not (grounded) upon anything, have nothing to stand upon;* لَمْ يَجِدْ أَمْرًا عَلَىٰ خِلَافِ مَا كَانَ يَعْتَقِدُهُ, *he found nothing in opposition to what he believed;* سَوَآءٌ كَانَتْ عَلَىٰ صُورَةِ إِنْسَانٍ أَمْ لَمْ تَكُنْ, *no matter whether they be endowed with human form or not;* عَشِقَ قَيْنَةً عَلَىٰ أَوْفَرِ مَا يَكُونُ مِنَ ٱلْجَمَالِ وَٱلْمَعْرِفَةِ بِٱلْغِنَآءِ وَٱلضَّرْبِ, *he loved a slave-girl, endowed with the highest degree both of beauty and of knowledge of singing and instrumental music;* كُنْتُ عَلَىٰ أَنْ أُجِيبَ, *the state in which I am;* مَا أَنَا عَلَيْهِ دَاعِىَ ٱلْأَمِيرِ, *I was going to comply with (the orders of) the emir's messenger;* وَكَأْسٍ شَرِبْتُ عَلَىٰ لَذَّةٍ, *many a cup have I quaffed with delight.*

6) Of the ground on which, the cause or reason why, one does a thing; as: أَخَذَهُ عَلَيْهَا مَا لَا يَمْلِكُهُ, *he was seized with a passion for her which he could not restrain* (lit. *there seized him on her account something which he could not master);* اَلْحَمْدُ لِلّٰهِ عَلَىٰ مَا صَنَعَ, *praise be to God for what he has done;* يُعَاتِبُهُ عَلَىٰ تَرْكِ ٱلْمُهَادَاةِ, *he reproached him for having neglected to send him a present in return;* وَلِتُكَبِّرُوا ٱللّٰهَ عَلَىٰ مَا هَدَىٰكُمْ, *and that ye should glorify God for having guided you;* عَلَىٰ أَىِّ شَىْءٍ أُعْطِيكَ مَالِى, *why am I to give you my*

3. The Government of the Verb. — The Prepositions.

مَالٌ؟, جَآءَ عَلَى أَنَّهُ مَلِكٌ, *he came, on the ground of his being a king;* أَتَى بَابَ ٱلْمَلِكِ عَلَى أَنَّهُ أُخْتُهُ, *he came to the king's gate, pretending to be his sister;* لَا أَسْأَلُكُمْ عَلَيْهِ مَالًا, *I do not ask you for money on that account* (scil. بِنَآءً عَلَيْهِ, *building upon it,* or مُعْتَمِدًا عَلَيْهِ, *relying on it)*: particularly in the common phrase بِنَآءً عَلَى أَنْ, *building upon, reckoning* or *relying upon, such and such a thing.*

7) Of the terms or conditions, as the ground or basis, on which anything is done; as: أَجَابَهُمْ إِلَى ذَلِكَ عَلَى أَنْ يُزَوِّدُوهُ بِٱلسِّلَاحِ, *he consented to this proposal of theirs, on condition that they should provide him with weapons;* صَالَحَهُ عَلَى أَلْفِ دِرْهَمٍ, *he made peace with him on (the condition that he should pay him)* 1000 *dirhems.*

8) In saying that one thing happens in spite of or notwithstanding another thing, that might have prevented it; as: أُعَذِّبُكَ عَلَى كِبَرِ سِنِّكَ, *I will punish you notwithstanding your great age* (lit. *in your state of great age,* see no. 5); ٱلْخَيْلُ تَجْرِي عَلَى مَسَاوِيهَا, *the horses run notwithstanding their defects.*

9) Of the rule or standard according to which something is done; as: عَلَى هَذِهِ ٱلطَّرِيقَةِ, *after this manner;* عَلَى نِسْبَةٍ مَحْفُوظَةٍ, *according to a duly observed proportion;* عَلَى مَا رَأَيْتُ فِي ٱلْكُتُبِ, *according to what I have seen (stated) in books;* عَلَى مَا حَكَاهُ, *according to what he related.*

10) Of the thing of which we speak, which forms, as

it were, the basis of our conversation (compare *super*, Germ. *über*); as: قَالَ عَلَى ذٰلِكَ, *he said concerning this, on this matter*.

Rem. *a*. Observe the following phrases: عَلَىَّ بِهِ, *fetch him to me*, scil. اُدْخُلُوا or some similar word (see no. 2, at the end); عَلَى ٱلرَّأْسِ وَٱلْعَيْنِ, *(it is) upon the head and eye*, i. e. *it shall be done most willingly and promptly*; عَلَى ٱلرِّيقِ, *on an empty stomach, fasting* (lit. *on the spittle*); عَلَى حِينِ (عَهْدِ), *in the time or reign of so and so*; عَلَى يَدَيْ (يَدِ) فُلَانٍ, or simply عَلَيْهِ, *by his means, through him*, as: وَآتِنَا مَا وَعَدْتَنَا عَلَى رُسُلِكَ, *and grant us what thou hast promised by thy apostles*, قَالَهُ عَلَى لِسَانِ رَسُولِهِ, *he said it by the mouth* (lit. *tongue of his apostle*; and the adjurations بِٱللّٰهِ عَلَيْكَ, بِحَيَاتِى عَلَيْكَ, *I implore you by God, by my life* (to do so and so), which are usually followed by the particle إِلَّا, lit. this oath with all its consequences be upon you, if you do not do so and so. — The phrase عَلَيْكَ زَيْدًا, *seize Zeid*, has already been mentioned in §. 35, rem. In this sense عَلَيْكَ عَلَيْكُمْ is also construed with the preposition بِ, as: عَلَيْكُمْ بِٱلْيَمَامَةِ, *attack those men*, بِٱلرِّجَالِ, *invade el-Yemâma*.

Rem. *b*. The Hebrew preposition עֲלֵי, עַל, is used in all these various significations: e. g. עַל־בְּאֵר, עֲלֵי־נָתִיב, אֶת־בְּתֻלַת הַפְּחָדִים אֲשֶׁר, הָשֵׁב עַל, חָנָה עַל, קָם עַל (Ps, 103, 13); רִחַם עַל, עָלָיו (Gen. 37, 23), וְאֶהְיֶה עָלַי לְמַשָּׂא, כָּבֵד עַל (Job, 7, 20), פָּעֲרוּ עָלַי בְּפִיהֶם (Job, 16. 10), וְעָלַי לָתֶת לְךָ עֲשָׂרָה כָסֶף, הָלַךְ, בָּא עַל (2 Sam. 18, 11),

3. The Government of the Verb. — The Prepositions.

נִּבְרוּ (Ps. 89, 8), נוֹרָא עַל־כָּל־סְבִיבָיו (Prov. 7, 14); וְזִבְחֵי שְׁלָמִים עָלַי
כִּי־עָלֶיךָ הוֹרַגְנוּ כָל־, *on account of what?* (Gen. 49, 26); עַל
הַיּוֹם, *for thy sake* (Ps. 44, 23); עַל־דַּעְתְּךָ כִּי־לֹא־אֶרְשָׁע, *although*
or *notwithstanding thou knowest* (Job, 10, 7), עַל לֹא־חָמָס בְּכַפָּי,
though there is no wrong in my hands (Job, 16, 17); וַיְדַבֵּר עַל־
הָעֵצִים, *he spoke (wrote) about the trees* (1 K. 5, 13); שָׁמַעְתִּי עָלֶיךָ
דָּבָר דָּבֻר, *I have heard say concerning thee* (Gen. 41, 15); לֵאמֹר
עַל־אָפְנָיו, *a word spoken in season* (Prov. 25, 11).

63. دُونَ (properly the accusative of دُونٌ, a nomen actionis from دَانَ, *to be beneath, less, inferior*, related to دَنَا, *to come near*, and دَنَأَ, *to be less* or *worse*) and مِن دُونِ, in which combination مِن has a partitive force, signify *under, below, beneath*. They indicate:

1) That a person or thing dwells or is situated, or that an action takes place, *below* some place; as: إِنَّ بِالشِّعْبِ ٱلَّذِي ٱلْتَقَوْا دُونَ صَنْعَآءَ, *they met below San'a*; دُونَ سَلْعٍ لَقَتِيلًا, *in the ravine that is below Sèla* (there lies) *a murdered man*.

2) That one person or thing comes *near* or approximates to another, especially a higher one (properly, stands under it, does not reach it); as: قَامَ دُونَ ٱلْبَكْرَةِ, *he stood close by the young she-camel*; أُدْنُ دُونَكَ, *come nearer (to me)!* lit. approach not far from yourself (towards me); دُونَكَ زَيْدًا, *seize Zèid* (who stands not far from you, see §. 35, rem.)

3) That one space, distance or number does not equal

or complete another; as: وَبَيْنَهُمَا دُونَ رَمْيَةٍ حَجَرٍ, *and between them there was less than a stone's throw.*

4) That one thing is smaller or worse than another; as: مِنْ دُونِ ٱلْعِلْمِ عِزُّ ٱلْعُلَى فِى ٱلْمَوَاكِبِ, *magnificent splendour in the retinue of princes is less (glorious) than learning.*

5) That a quality which belongs to one person or thing is not possessed by another, and that the latter is therefore in this respect opposed to the other; as: مِنْهُمْ ٱلصَّالِحُونَ وَمِنْهُمْ دُونَ ذٰلِكَ, *some of them are upright, some not* (lit. *and some of them remain under uprightness, do not attain to that quality*). In this sense دُونَ is equivalent to غَيْرُ.

6) That a person or thing is excluded or excepted, neglected or postponed (properly, that the action affects it to a less degree than it does another); as: يَدْعُو مِنْ دُونِ ٱللّٰهِ مَا لَا يَضُرُّهُ وَمَا لَا يَنْفَعُهُ, *he invokes, to the exclusion of God, what can neither injure nor benefit him,* he invokes what can neither &c., but not God; أَهْلُ هٰذِهِ ٱلْمَدِينَةِ يَعْبُدُونَ ٱلْأَصْنَامَ مِنْ دُونِ ٱللّٰهِ, *the people of this city worship idols and not God;* مَا لَكُمْ مِنْ دُونِ ٱللّٰهِ مِنْ وَلِىٍّ وَلَا نَصِيرٍ, *ye have no patron and no helper except God;* عَمِلْتُمْ بِأَحَدِهِمَا دُونَ ٱلْآخَرِ, *you act according to one of these (two rules), but not the other;* يَنْبَغِى أَنْ يَخْتَارَ ٱلْعَتِيقَ دُونَ ٱلْمُحْدَثَاتِ, *he ought to choose the old in preference to the new;* وَأَمَّكُمْ دُونَ ٱلْأَنَامِ طُرًّا, *and he sought you*

3. The Government of the Verb. — The Prepositions.

out in preference to all other men. — Here must also be mentioned دُونَ, and the rarer بِدُونِ, in the sense of *without*; as: لَيْسَ ٱكْتِسَابُ ٱلْمَالِ دُونَ مَشَقَّةٍ, *wealth cannot be acquired without trouble*; دُونَ ذَا يَنْفِقُ ٱلْحِمَارُ, *the ass will be sold without this*; يَأْخُذُهَا تُجَّارُ بِلَادِ ٱلْمَعْبَرِ بِدُونِ ثَمَنٍ, *the merchants of the country of Malabar take them without (paying any) price (for them).*

Rem. دُونَكَ and دُونَكُمْ, as interjections, are equivalent to أَمَامَكَ, أَمَامَكُمْ (see §. 35, 2, b), *look out! take care!* as: دُونَكُمْ لَا تُقِيلُوهُمْ, *take care and give them no quarter.* — On the phrases دُونَكَ زَيْدًا, دُونَكُمُوهُ, &c., see §. 35, rem.

7) That one object is placed before another, either *a)* as a hindrance or obstacle to prevent a person from getting at it, or *b)* as a protection to defend it from some one; as: دُونَ ذَلِكَ جَمْرُ ٱلْغَضَا وَخَرْطُ ٱلْقَتَادِ, *before this there are the coals of the ğaḍā and the stripping of the ḳatād,* that is to say, before you can obtain this, you have many serious obstacles to surmount (the wood of the ğaḍā being noted for its long retention of fire, and the ḳatād for the number and size of its thorns); لَيْسَ دُونَهُمْ حِجَابٌ, *there is no barrier in front of them*; وَكَانَ مِجَنِّي دُونَ مَنْ كُنْتُ أَتَّقِي ثَلَثَ شُخُوصٍ, *my shield (protection) against those whom I feared was three persons*; إِنَّ ٱمْرَأَ ٱلْقَيْسِ جَرَى إِلَى مَدًى وَٱعْتَنَاقَهُ حِمَامُهُ دُونَ ٱلْمَدَى, *'Imru'u 'l-Ḳais ran for a goal, but death intercepted him before he reached that goal*; دُونَ ٱلنَّهْرِ جَمَاعَةٌ, *before*

(you reach) the river, there is a number of men (to be encountered), = قَبْلَ أَنْ تَصِلَ إِلَى ٱلنَّهْرِ. Hence verbs signifying *to shut a door against one, to fight for one*, and the like, are construed with دُون (compare §. 50, 1); e. g. قَاتَلَ دُونَهُمْ سَاعَةً, *he fought for them for some time;* إِنَّ ٱلْمُحِبَّ ٱلصَّادِقَ يَبْذِلُ نَفْسَهُ دُونَ حَبُوبِهِ, *a true friend gives up his life for his friend.* In this case دُون is synonymous with أَمَامَ, *in front of, before.* — Hence too it often denotes *on this side of (cis, citra);* as: دُونَ جَيْحُونَ, *on this side of the Oxus;* in which case it is opposed to وَرَاءَ, *behind, beyond,* as وَرَاءَ ٱلنَّهْرِ, *Transoxania* (lit. *what is beyond the river* Oxus).

Rem. دُون forms a diminutive دُوَيْنَ.

64. مُنْذُ is derived, by assimilation of the first vowel, from مِنْ and ذُو, which latter word is used in the dialect of the Benû Temîm in the sense of the demonstrative pronoun *this* (see vol. I. §. 340, with rem. *b*, and §. 347, with rem. *c* and *e*, and compare يَعُودَ مِنْ ذِى قَبْلُ, *that he may return to his former condition).* It is contracted into مُذْ, which becomes in the waṣl مُذُ (see vol. I. §. 20, 4). These particles signify *from such and such a time,* and may be construed with the *nominative* as well as the *genitive,* the latter being more particularly used when a yet unexpired period of time is spoken of. For example: مَا رَأَيْتُهُ مُنْذُ يَوْمِ ٱلْجُمْعَةِ, *I have not seen him since last Friday* (lit. *the terminus a quo is Friday);* مَا رَأَيْتُهُ مُذْ عَامٍ أَوَّلُ, *I have not*

3. The Government of the Verb. — The Prepositions.

seen him since last year; أَنَا أَعْلَمُ أَنَّهُ جَائِعٌ مُنْذُ خَمْسَةِ أَيَّامٍ, I know that he has been starving for the last five days; مَا كَلَّمْتُهُ مُذْ شَهْرِنَا هَذَا, I have not spoken to him since (the beginning of) this month.

Rem. a. The lexicographers mention the forms مُنْذُ and مِذْ. — مُذْ may also take in the wasl the form مُذِ.

Rem. b. The Bédawîn use مِنْ instead of مُنْذُ, as مُنْذُ سَنَةٍ = مِنْ سَنَةٍ. Compare in the Kor'ân, ch. 9, v. 109, أُسِّسَ عَلَى التَّقْوَى مِنْ أَوَّلِ يَوْمٍ, it was founded upon the fear of God from the first day. This is also the Hebrew construction.

65. The particle وَ, which is frequently used in swearing, is construed with the genitive of the object sworn by; as: وَٱللّٰهِ, by God! وَرَبِّ ٱلْكَعْبَةِ, by the Lord of the Ka'ba (the mosque of Mekka)! This وَ is used, however, only when a substantive follows, and the verb of swearing is omitted; before a pronominal suffix, as well as when the verb is expressed, the preposition بِ is used (see §. 57). Sometimes the particle فَ is prefixed to وَ, as فَوَٱللّٰهِ, by God then! — The particle تَ (the origin of which is very obscure) also takes the genitive, but is seldom used except in the oath تَٱللّٰهِ, by God!

66. Among the prepositions is usually reckoned كَ, as, like. This is, however, not a preposition, but a substantive, synonymous with مِثْلُ, likeness. It is formally undeveloped (like ذُو), but may stand in any case as مُضَافٌ, or

governing word, to a following noun in the genitive (see §. 75); as: وَعَلَى رَأْسِهِ كَٱلْقَلَنْسُوَةِ, *and on the top of it* (the pillar) *is (something) like a pointed cap*, = مِثْلُ ٱلْقَلَنْسُوَةِ; بِكَالسُّوذَانِقِ, *with (a horse) like a falcon (in speed)*, = بِمِثْلِ ٱلسُّوذَانِقِ; فَحِكَ عَنْ كَٱلْبَرَدِ, *he laughed so as to show (teeth) like hailstones* (as white as hailstones). The name of *preposition* can be applied to it, at the most, only when it virtually stands in the *accusative*, as a صِفَةٌ, *adjective* or *relative adjectival clause*, to an infinitive that is understood; as: جِئْتَ كَزَيْدٍ, *you are come like Zeid*, i. e. جِئْتَ مَجِيئًا كَمَجِيءٍ (مِثْلَ مَجِيءِ) زَيْدٍ, *you have come a coming like the coming of Zeid*. Or we might regard it as being a حَالٌ, or conditional expression, dependent upon the pronominal suffix of the second pers. sing. masc. in جِئْتَ, جِئْتَ كَآتِنَا كَزَيْدٍ (مِثْلَ زَيْدٍ), *you are come as one who is like Zeid*.

Rem. *a.* كَ is very rarely joined to a pronominal suffix; and equally rare is the use of the redundant مَا after it (compare §. 57, 3); as: وَنَعْلَمُ أَنَّهُ كَمَا ٱلنَّاسِ مَجْرُومٌ عَلَيْهِ وَجَارِمٌ, *and we know that he is, like (other) men, sinned against and sinning* (جَارِمٌ in rhyme for جَارِمْ). In Hebrew כָּהֵם and כָּהֶם, or כָּהֶם, are used; but with the other pronominal suffixes כְּמוֹ=כְּמוֹ is always employed, as also occasionally before substantives.

Rem. *b.* كَ is sometimes used redundantly along with the synonymous مِثْلُ; as: لَيْسَ كَمِثْلِهِ شَيْءٌ, *there is nothing like Him.*

Rem. c. كَ is said by the grammarians to be used لِلتَّشْبِيهِ, *to compare one object with another.*

67. Compound prepositions are rare in ancient Arabic, but more common in the modern language. The first part of the compound is almost invariably مِنْ, and the second part another so-called preposition, now however no longer in the accusative, but in the *genitive*. Such are:

1) مِنْ بَيْنِ (Heb. מִבֵּין); as: مِنْ الْمَخْصُوصُ هُوَ مُحَمَّدٌ بَيْنِ كَافَّةِ الْخَلْقِ بِالْفَضْلِ وَالْكَمَالِ, *Mohammed is the one preeminently distinguished among all mankind for excellence and perfection* (lit. *from among all mankind*); مِنْ بَيْنِ يَدَيْهِ, *from his presence* (lit. *from between his hands*); فِي آذَانِنَا وَقْرٌ وَمِنْ بَيْنِنَا وَبَيْنِكَ حِجَابٌ, *in our ears is hardness of hearing, and between us and thee there is a partition-wall.* In this last example مِنْ is partitive, the literal meaning being: *and in a part of the space between us and thee &c.*

2) مِنْ فَوْقِ, *above*, and مِنْ تَحْتِ, *from* تَحْتَ, *under, beneath*; as: جَعَلَ فِيهَا رَوَاسِيَ مِنْ فَوْقِهَا, *he placed immovable* (*mountains*) *upon it* (the earth); طَلَعَ مِنْ فَوْقِ الْجَبَلِ وَنَزَلَ مِنْ خَلْفِهِ, *he ascended the hill and descended by the other side* (from خَلْفَ, *behind*); جَنَّاتٌ تَجْرِي مِنْ تَحْتِهَا الْأَنْهَارُ, *gardens under* (*the trees of*) *which streams flow.* In all these examples مِنْ is partitive; the mountains form a part of what is raised above the earth; the man ascends a part of the summit and descends by a part of

the other side; the streams occupy a part of the space under the trees.

3) مِنْ قَبْلِ, مِنْ قَبْلِ, from قَبْلَ, *before* (of time), and مِنْ بَعْدِ, from بَعْدَ, *after* (of time); as: ٱلَّذِينَ مِنْ قَبْلِكُمْ, *those who were before you;* ثُمَّ بَعَثْنَاكُمْ مِنْ بَعْدِ مَوْتِكُمْ, *then we brought you again to life after your death;* مِنْ خَلَفَ بَعْدِهِمْ خَلْفٌ, *then there came after them an evil generation.* Here again مِنْ is partitive, *in a portion of the space of time before* or *after.*

4) مِنْ عَلَى (Heb. מֵעַל), *from off* (lit. *from upon*); as: قَفَزَ نَزَلَ مِنْ عَلَى فَرَسِهِ, *he dismounted from his horse;* مِنْ عَلَى ظَهْرِهِ, *he sprang from off its back.*

5) مِنْ عِنْدِ (Heb. מֵעִם) and مِنْ لَدُنْ; as: هَذَا مِنْ عِنْدِ ٱللهِ, *this is from* (lit. *from the side of, from beside*) *God;* هَبْ لَنَا مِنْ لَدُنْكَ رَحْمَةً, *grant us thy mercy* (lit. *mercy from beside thee*),

6) مِنْ قِبَلِ, from قِبَلَ, *beside, in the power or possession of* (penes, apud); as: كَانَ أَمِيرًا بِٱلشَّامِ مِنْ قِبَلِ عُثْمَانَ, *he was governor of Syria for 'Othmān* (lit. *from beside 'Othmān,* with whom lay the option of sending him as such); قَدِمَ عَلَيْهِ جَوَابُ كِتَابِهِ مِنْ قِبَلِ أَبِى بَكْرٍ, *there came to him an answer to his letter from* (Fr. *de la part de*) *Abū Bekr;* سَلَامٌ مِنْ قِبَلِى عَلَى مَنْ تَجَّتَنِى بِطَرْفِهَا, *peace be from me* (Fr. *de ma part*) *upon her who has enslaved me by her pleasing address.*

3. The Government of the Verb. — The Prepositions.

Rem. *a*. Of بِدُونِ and مِنْ دُونِ we have already spoken in § 63. — إِلَى is sometimes found in connection with other prepositions, but the compounds إِلَى نَحْوِ, إِلَى فَوْقِ, إِلَى عِنْدِ (and لِعِنْدِ), and إِلَى لَدُنْ are condemned by the grammarians.

Rem. *b*. The preposition is occasionally, though very rarely, omitted by a poet, and the genitive notwithstanding retained; as: إِذَا قِيلَ أَيُّ ٱلنَّاسِ شَرُّ قَبِيلَةً أَشَارَتْ كُلَيْبٍ بِٱلْأَكُفِّ ٱلْأَصَابِعُ, *when the question is asked, Who of mankind are worst as a tribe? the fingers point with the hands to K̈uléib* (for أَشَارَتْ إِلَى كُلَيْبٍ); حَتَّى تَبَذَّخَ فَٱرْتَقَى ٱلْأَعْلَامَ, *until he became haughty, and ascended the heights (of pride)*, for فَٱرْتَقَى إِلَى ٱلْأَعْلَامِ.

Rem. *c*. Sometimes by a more concise and bolder construction, the accusative is used instead of a preposition with the genitive (especially لِ); as: وَإِذَا كَالُوهُمْ أَوْ وَزَنُوهُمْ يُخْسِرُونَ, *and when they measure unto them or weigh unto them, they give less (than is due)*, for كَالُوا لَهُمْ أَوْ وَزَنُوا لَهُمْ; وَلَقَدْ جَنَيْتُكَ أَكْمُؤًا وَعَسَاقِلًا, *and I have gathered for you mushrooms and truffles*, for وَلٰكِنْ رَحَلْنَاهَا; عَسَاقِلًا in rhyme for عَسَاقِلَ; جَنَيْتُ لَكَ نُفُوسًا كَرِيمَةً, *but we made ready noble spirits to encounter these (calamities)*, for رَحَلْنَا لَهَا; أَمَرْتُكَ ٱلْخَيْرَ فَٱفْعَلْ مَا أُمِرْتَ بِهِ, *I bade you do good, do therefore as you were bidden*, for أَمَرْتُكَ بِٱلْخَيْرِ; كَمَا عَسَلَ ٱلطَّرِيقَ ٱلثَّعْلَبُ, *as the fox trots along the path*, for فِي ٱلطَّرِيقِ (see § 44, 2, rem. *a*).

B. The Noun.

1. The Nomina Verbi, Agentis and Patientis.

68. As we have already spoken of the idea of the *nomen verbi* or abstract verbal noun (vol. I. §. 195), of its use as the ٱلْمَفْعُولُ ٱلْمُطْلَقُ or objective complement of the verb (§. 26), and of its rection, in so far as it possesses verbal power (§§. 27—29), we have now only to remark that it is not (as might at first sight appear) rendered definite by the very nature of its idea, and, in consequence, able to dispense with the article in order to become definite; but, on] the contrary, is, like other nouns, indefinite, where it stands without the article. For example: قِتَالٌ فِيهِ كَبِيرٌ وَصَدٌّ عَنْ سَبِيلِ ٱللّٰهِ وَكُفْرٌ بِهِ وَٱلْمَسْجِدِ ٱلْحَرَامِ وَإِخْرَاجُ أَهْلِهِ مِنْهُ أَكْبَرُ عِنْدَ ٱللّٰهِ, *to fight in it* (one of the sacred months) *is a great sin, but to turn (others) away from the path of God, and not to believe in Him and (to prevent access to) the sacred mosque, and to turn his people out of it, is a yet greater sin in the sight of God* (قِتَالٌ is here *a fighting*, and not *the fighting*, and so with the other nomina verbi); ٱلطَّلَاقُ مَرَّتَانِ فَإِمْسَاكٌ بِمَعْرُوفٍ أَوْ تَسْرِيحٌ بِإِحْسَانٍ, *the divorce may take place twice* (and the woman be taken back after each occasion), *but after that ye must either retain (your wives) with kindness or dismiss (them) with benefits* (ٱلطَّلَاقُ, *the divorce*, إِمْسَاكٌ،. فَٱلْوَاجِبُ (هُوَ) إِمْسَاكٌ or فَإِمْسَاكٌ وَاجِبٌ).¹ Viz.

a retaining, تَسْرِيحٌ, *a dismissing*); لَا يَسْتَطِيعُونَ نَصْرًا, *they cannot give any help* (نَصْرًا = مَا نَصْرًا or مِنْ نَصْرٍ, whereas اَلنَّصْرَ would mean: *they cannot give the help* necessary in the particular case).

69. Of the rection of the nomina agentis and patientis or concrete verbal nouns, in so far as they possess verbal power, we have already treated in §§. 30—32. They designate the person or thing to which the verbal idea attaches itself as descriptive of it; e. g. اَلْبَاعِثُ, *the exciting cause, the motive;* اَلْمَانِعُ, *the hindering object, the hindrance.* Now, as both the person or thing and the verbal idea are something firm and abiding, it necessarily follows that the concrete verbal noun indicates a lasting and continuous action on the part of an agent or passion on that of a patient. This idea it possesses in common with the Imperfect (see §. 8), to which too it is often related in outward form (see Vol. I. §. 236, with rem. *a*). The difference between them is, that the concrete verbal noun designates a person or thing, to which the verbal idea closely attaches itself and consequently remains immovable; whilst the Imperfect, as verbum finitum, expresses the verbal idea as movable and indeed in constant motion.*) The employment of the concrete verbal noun as a perfect results from its use as a fixed immovable substantive.

*) The Arab grammarians ascribe to the finite verb, in general, the idea of اَلْحُدُوثِ, *the becoming new, the coming into existence of the act;* to the imperfect, in particular, that of اَلتَّجَدُّدُ, *constant renewal or repetition* (see §. 8); to the verbal noun, that of اَلثَّبَاتُ, *fixedness, immobility.*

130 Part Third. Syntax.

70. To what *point of time* this lasting and continuous state of the agent or patient, as designated by the nomen verbale concretum, is to be referred, can be deduced only from some other word in the sentence that points to a specific time, from the nature of the thing or the character of the thought, or from the connection of the context. The nomen agentis or patientis itself does not include the idea of any fixed time.

71. In a clause that is not circumstantial, whether it be absolute or dependent upon another clause, the concrete verbal noun shows that the verbal idea contained in it refers either to the present, the proximate future, or the future in general. For example: زَيْدٌ نَاكِحٌ ٱبْنُهُ غَدًا زُبَيْدَةَ, *Zeid's son is to be married tomorrow to Zubeida* (the reference of نَاكِحٌ to the proximate future is shown by غَدًا); أَنَا قَاتِلُهُ, *I am going to kill him;* أَنَا قَاتِلُكَ, *I will kill you* (ego te interficiam); هٰذَا مَقْتُولٌ, *this man must be killed* (in these three examples the context fixes the meaning); وَٱعْلَمُوا أَنَّكُمْ غَيْرُ مُعْجِزِى ٱللّٰهِ وَأَنَّ ٱللّٰهَ مُخْزِى ٱلْكَافِرِينَ, *and know that ye shall not find God feeble, and that God will put the unbelievers to shame;* ٱلَّذِينَ يَظُنُّونَ أَنَّهُمْ مُلَاقُو رَبِّهِمْ, *who think that they shall meet their Lord;* قَدْ أَطْرَقَ يَنْظُرَ مَا هُمْ صَانِعُونَ, *he kept silence, in order to see what they would do* (the reference of صَانِعُونَ to the future results from يَنْظُرُ).

Rem. *a*. When the perfect كَانَ is prefixed to a concrete verbal noun that refers to the future, the idea of futurity is transferred to a past time; as: اَمْرٌ كَانَ مَفْعُولاً, *a thing that should have been done* (equivalent to مَا كَانَ كَائِنًا لَوْ آلخ; اَمْرٌ كَانَ حَقِيقًا أَنْ يُفْعَلَ, *quid futurum esset si* etc. Compare the composition of the imperfect with كَانَ, §. 9.

Rem. b. On the corresponding Hebrew usage, see Gesenius' Gr. §. 131, 2, *a*, *b*, and rem. 1; and with the following sections compare §. 131, 2, *c*.

72. But if the concrete verbal noun stands in a *circumstantial* clause, the state that it describes belongs to the same period of time as the verb in the leading clause. For example: أَنْشَدَ وَهُوَ مَحْبُوسٌ بِمَكَّةَ, *he recited, whilst he was in prison at Mèkka, (the following verses)*; جَدَّ ٱلْمَهْدِىُّ فِى ٱلْهَرَبِ وَقَدِمَ طَرَابُلُسَ ٱلْغَرْبِ وَزِيَادَةُ ٱللّٰهِ مُتَوَقِّعٌ عَلَيْهِ, *el-Mahdi fled with all speed and reached Tarábulu (Tripolis) in North Africa, whilst Ziyádètu'lláh kept constantly pursuing him*; مَنْ يُسْلِمْ وَجْهَهُ إِلَى ٱللّٰهِ وَهُوَ مُحْسِنٌ, *who turns himself wholly towards God, whilst he does a good action*. In such subordinate clauses the imperfect is used in almost the same way as the concrete verbal noun (see §. 8, *c*).

73. In like manner, the concrete verbal noun refers to the same period of time as the verb with which it is connected, when it is annexed to the verb as an adverbial accusative. This may happen even when the subjects are different (§. 44, 3). For example: فَوَلَّى ٱلثَّوْرُ هَارِبًا, *the ox*

17*

turned his back fleeing; سَافَرَ بَارِيَا أَخُوهُ ٱلْقَوْسَ, he set off whilst his brother was cutting the bow; خَرَجَ قَاعِدًا أَبُوهُ, he went out whilst his father was seated; لَقِيتُ ٱلسُّلْطَانَ بَاكِيًا عِنْدَهُ, I found the sultan weeping in his house; كُنْتُ فِي ٱلْبُسْتَانِ زَاهِرًا, I was in the garden whilst it was in bloom; مَنْ يَعْصِ ٱللّٰهَ وَرَسُولَهُ وَيَتَعَدَّ حُدُودَهُ يُدْخِلْهُ نَارًا خَالِدًا فِيهَا, whosoever disobeys God and his Apostle, and transgresses his statutes, He will cast him into hell-fire to abide in it for ever (here the حَالْ or circumstantial term, خَالِدًا فِيهَا, is not ٱلْحَالُ ٱلْمُقَارِنُ, or the *ḥāl* that indicates a state present at a past time, but ٱلْحَالُ ٱلْمُقَدَّرُ, or the *ḥāl* that indicates a future state). The same is the case after بَقِيَ, to remain, دَامَ, to last, continue, لَا يَزَالُ, he will not cease, and the like (see §. 42, 2, a); as لَمْ يَزَلْ قَاعِدًا, لَا تَزَالُ طَائِفَةٌ مِنْ أُمَّتِي ظَاهِرِينَ he did not cease sitting; عَلَى ٱلْحَقِّ إِلَى يَوْمِ ٱلْقِيٰمَةِ, a part of my people shall not cease openly to hold fast the truth till the day of the resurrection; مَا دَامَ ٱلرُّوحُ سَاكِنًا فِي ٱلْجَسَدِ, as long as the spirit continues to dwell in the body; فَبَقِيَ مُتَحَيِّرًا, he remained in amazement; ذُو ٱلْعِلْمِ يَبْقَى عِزُّهُ مُتَضَاعِفًا, the reputation of the learned shall continue multiplied (after his death). The Imperfect is also used after these verbs, in many cases with this difference, that the Imperfect designates the constantly repeated action, the concrete verbal noun the lasting condition of the agent; as: مَا زَالَ يَقْتَصِرُ عَلَى ٱلسُّكُونِ

فِي قَعْرِ مَغَارَتِهِ, *he did not cease to restrict himself to sitting quietly at the bottom of his cave;* وَلَمْ يَزَلْ يُنْعِمُ ٱلنَّظَرَ فِيهَا, *and he did not desist from investigating it carefully* (يُنْعِنُ = يُنْعِمُ). Compare §. 8, *e*.

74. The concrete verbal noun is also sometimes annexed, like the Imperfect (§. 9), to the verb كَانَ, to express the praesens praeteriti or Greek and Latin imperfect; as: كَانَ نَازِلًا, *he was dwelling;* كَانَتْ مَرْكُوزَةً, *they (the spears) were sticking in the ground* (كَانَتْ تُرْكَزُ would mean *they were stuck into the ground*).

Rem. Similarly, in Hebrew, הָיָה with the participles; Gesenius' Gr. §. 131, 2.

2. The Government of the Noun.
The Status Constructus and the Genitive.

75. The idea of one noun is very often more nearly determined or defined by that of another. When this is the case, the noun so defined is shortened in its pronunciation by the omission of the tenwîn or the terminations بِ and نِ (vol: I. §. 315), on account of the speaker's passing on rapidly to the determining word, which is put in the genitive. The determined noun is called by the Arab grammarians ٱلْمُضَافُ, *the annexed;* the determining noun, ٱلْمُضَافُ إِلَيْهِ, *that to which annexation is made* or *to which another word is annexed;* and the relation subsisting between them is known as ٱلْإِضَافَةُ, *the annexation.* European grammarians are accustomed to say that the determined or governing word is in the *status constructus*.

Rem. *a*. The Arab grammarians speak of two kinds of annexation; the one called اَلْإِضَافَةُ ٱلْحَقِيقِيَّةُ, *the proper* or *real annexation*, اَلْخَفْضُ, *the pure annexation*, or اَلْمَعْنَوِيَّةُ, *the logical annexation*; the other, اَلْإِضَافَةُ غَيْرُ ٱلْحَقِيقِيَّةِ, *the improper annexation*, غَيْرُ ٱلْخَفْضِ, *the impure annexation*, or اَللَّفْظِيَّةُ, *the merely verbal* or *grammatical annexation*. The latter consists in this, that an adjective, a participle active intransitive, or a participle passive, takes a definite noun in the genitive instead of an indefinite *temyīz*-accusative (see §. 44, 5); or that the participle active of a directly transitive verb, being used with the meaning of the اَلْمُضَارِعُ or Imperfect (see §. 30, 1), takes the object in the genitive instead of the accusative. In both cases the genitive is only a looser, representative construction, instead of the stricter accusative, and consequently exercises no defining or limiting power upon the preceding governing word (see §. 88). We have here to deal almost exclusively with the real annexation.

Rem. *b*. The remarks contained in the following sections (as far as §. 79, inclusive) mostly apply to the other Shemitic languages as well as to Arabic.

76. By the genitive is indicated: *a*) the person to whom the quality designated by the governing word belongs, as حِكْمَةُ ٱللّٰهِ, *the wisdom of God*; *b*) the material of the form and the form of the material, as بَيْضَةُ فِضَّةٍ, *an egg of silver*, فِضَّةُ ٱلدَّرَاهِمِ, *the silver of the dirhems* (in the former case the annexation is *explicative*, إِضَافَةٌ بَيَانِيَّةٌ, the original expression being

The Government of the Noun.

بَيْضَةٌ فِضَّةٌ, i. e. بَيْضَةٌ هِيَ فِضَّةٌ, see §. 93); c) the cause of the effect and the effect of the cause, as خَالِقُ ٱلْأَرْضِ, the creator of the earth, حَرُّ ٱلشَّمْسِ, the heat of the sun; d) the part of the whole (*partitive* annexation, إِضَافَةٌ تَبْعِيضِيَّةٌ) and the whole as embracing the parts (explicative annexation), as رَأْسُ ٱلْحِكْمَةِ, the beginning of wisdom, كُلُّ ٱلْمَخْلُوقَاتِ, the totality of created things; e) the thing possessed by a possessor and the possessor of a thing possessed, as خَزِينَةُ ٱلسُّلْطَانِ, the treasury of the sultan, سُلْطَانُ ٱلْبَرِّ وَٱلْبَحْرِ, the lord of land and sea; and f) the object of the action and of the agent, as خَلْقُ ٱلسَّمَاءِ, the creation of heaven, كَاتِبُ ٱلرِّسَالَةِ, the writer of the letter.

77. The Arab grammarians say that in the real annexation is implied the force of a preposition, which is either لِ (that also represents the accusative, §§. 29—34), or فِي. For example: غُلَامُ زَيْدٍ, Zeid's slave, = ٱلْغُلَامُ ٱلَّذِي لِزَيْدٍ, the slave who (belongs) to Zeid; كَأْسُ فِضَّةٍ, a silver cup, = كَأْسٌ مِنْ فِضَّةٍ, a cup (made) of silver (see §. 49, 6); صَوْمُ ٱلْيَوْمِ, today's fast, = ٱلصَّوْمُ فِي ٱلْيَوْمِ, the fast (held) today (see §. 56, 1).

78. The *determining* noun is, in the real annexation, always either a substantive or a word regarded as such, a pronoun, or an entire clause. For example: رَسُولُ ٱللَّهِ, the Apostle of God; كَلِمَةُ إِنْ, the word 'in'; مَعْنَى قَتَلَ, the meaning of (the verb) katala; تَنْكِيرُ إِنْسَانٍ,

the indefiniteness of (*the substantive*) *'insān* (not كَلِمَةُ الْإِنْ،
&c., because words, regarded as substantives, are by their very nature definite, just like proper names, and therefore do not require the article); مَعْنَاهُ, *its meaning;* هٰذَا يَوْمٌ يَنْفَعُ الصَّادِقِينَ صِدْقُهُمْ, *this is the day* (*when*) *their truthfulness shall benefit the truthful;* إِلَى يَوْمِ يُبْعَثُونَ, *till the day* (*when*) *they* (the dead) *shall be raised;* وَقْتَ أَنِ اسْتَتَرَ, *at the time* (*when*) *he hid himself,* = وَقْتَ اسْتِتَارِهِ, *at the time of his hiding himself;* خَوْفَ (مَخَافَةَ) أَنْ يَفْعَلَ كَذَا, *for fear of his doing so and so;* عَصْرَ حَانَ مَشِيبٌ, *at the time* (*when*) *old age is coming on;* يَوْمَ تَوَلَّتِ الْأَظْعَانُ عَنَّا, *the day* (*that*) *the women* (*setting out on their journey*) *turned away from us;* حَتَّى سَقَتْهُ الْمَنِيَّةُ كَأْسَ مَاءٍ حَمِيمًا, *till death made him drink the cup of "and they were given boiling water to drink"* (èl-Ḳor'ān, ch. 47, v. 17). — The determined noun, on the contrary, can be only a substantive; for the numerals and prepositions (خَمْسَةُ رِجَالٍ, *five men,* بَعْدَ سَنَةٍ, *after the lapse of a year*) are in reality substantives; and adjectives, standing in the position of defined nouns, have the force of substantives, as خَيْرُ الْبَرِيَّةِ, *the best of* (*God's*) *creatures* (see §. 86), عَاجِلَ طَعْنَةٍ, *a hurried thrust.*

Rem. *a.* In later writers we find such phrases as سَيْفُ وَرُمْحُ زَيْدٍ, *Zèid's sword and spear,* for which the classical expression would be سَيْفُ زَيْدٍ وَرُمْحُهُ. See §. 176, *f.*

Rem. *b.* Examples of a clause supplying the place of a genitive in Hebrew, are given by Gesenius, Gr. §. 114, 3.

79. Not only common nouns, but also proper names, may be determined by a genitive; as: اِيلِيَاءُ فِلَسْطِين, *Iliya* (Aelia Capitolina, Jerusalem) *of* (i. e. *in*) *Palestine;* طَرَابُلُس ٱلشَّامِ, *Tripolis in Syria;* جِيرَةُ ٱلنُّعْمٰنِ, *Hira*, (*the capital of the kingdom*) *of en-No'mān;* تَغْلِبُ وَآئِلٍ, *Taglib*, (*son*) *of Wā'il*, for تَغْلِبُ بْنُ وَآئِلٍ; حَاتِمُ طَيِّءٍ, *Hātim of* (*the tribe of*) *Tayyi;* عَمْرُو ٱلْكَلْبِ, *'Amr of the dog*, so called because he was always accompanied by a hound.

Rem. Compare, in Hebrew, נַח פְּלִשְׁתִּים, בֵּית לֶחֶם יְהוּדָה, and the like. See Gesenius' Gr. §. 112, 3, rem. 2.

80. As the Arabic language possesses, comparatively speaking, but a small number of adjectives, it often happens that a noun is qualified by the genitive of another noun, where in other languages an adjective would be employed; as: رَجُلُ سَوْءٍ, *a bad man;* حِمَارُ وَحْشٍ, *a wild ass*. This is particularly the case in specifying the material of which a thing is made; as: بَيْضَةُ فِضَّةٍ, *ovum argenteum, a silver egg;* ثَوْبُ حَرِيرٍ, *vestis serica, a silk dress* (see §. 76—77). In the same way a genitive is attached to the name of a person, to express something peculiar to and descriptive of him; as: زَيْدُ ٱلضَّلَالِ, *the erring* (*apostate*) *Zeid*, = سَعْدُ ذُو ٱلْخَيْرِ ;زَيْدٌ ذُو ٱلضَّلَالِ, *the good Sa'd*, = سَعْدُ ٱلشَّرِّ, or سَعْدُ ٱلسَّوْءِ, to which would be opposed *the wicked Sa'd*, = سَعْدُ ذُو ٱلسَّوْءِ or ذُو ٱلشَّرِّ.

Rem. Compare, as regards Hebrew, Gesenius' Gr. §. 104, 1.

81. For the same reason, the Arabs use several nouns, which convey, at least secondarily, the ideas of possession, companionship, origination, &c., in combination with a following substantive (usually expressing a quality) in the genitive, as a substitute for adjectives. These quasi-adjectives are placed after the noun which they qualify, and in apposition to it. They are principally the following: ذُو, *the (man) of* such and such a thing, its *owner* or *possessor* (vol. I. §. 340, rem. *b*); صَاحِبٌ, *companion, possessor*; أَبٌ, *father*, and أُمٌّ, *mother*, i. e. originator, cause, origin, or principle of a thing; اِبْنٌ, *son*, and اِبْنَةٌ or بِنْتٌ, *daughter*, i. e. originating from, caused by, dependent upon or related to something; أَخٌ, *brother*, i. e. connected with or related to something. The nouns ذُو and صَاحِبٌ are constantly used in this way in common prose; the others, being metaphorical, belong almost exclusively to poetry and poetical diction. For example: ذُو ٱلْخَيْرِ, *the good*; ذُو ٱلشَّرِّ, *the bad*; ذُو ٱلْعِلْمِ, *the learned*; ذُو ٱلْجَهْلِ, *the ignorant*; أَرْضٌ ذَاتُ شَوْكٍ, *a piece of land covered with thorns*; أُولُو ٱلْأَلْبَابِ, *intelligent persons*; صَاحِبُ ٱلطَّبْعِ ٱلْمُسْتَقِيمِ, *one with good natural parts*; أَبُو ٱلْحَيَاةِ, *the father (supporter) of life*, i. e. *the rain*; أَبُو ٱلْحُصَيْنِ, *the father (constructor) of the little fortress*, i. e. *the fox*; أُمُّ ٱلْخَبَائِثِ, *the mother (cause) of disgraceful acts*, i. e. *wine*; اِبْنُ ٱلسَّبِيلِ, *the son of the way*, i. e. *the traveller*; اِبْنُ آوَى, *the son of howling*, i. e. *the jackal*; بِنْتُ ٱلْجَبَلِ, *the daughter of the mountain*, i. e. *the echo*;

أَخُو تَمِيم, *a brother of Temim, one of the tribe of Temim*;
أَخُو ٱلْعِلْمِ, *the brother of learning,* i. e. *the learned.*

Rem. Compare the use of such Hebrew words as אִישׁ, בַּעַל, בֶּן and בַּר; Gesenius' Gr. §. 104, 2.

82. Further, some secondary ideas, such as those of the whole, the part, the like, and the different, which we usually designate by adjectives, prepositions, or compound words, are expressed in Arabic by substantives, taking the primary substantives, to which they are attached, in the genitive. These substantives are:

1) كُلّ, *the totality, the whole* (lit. *what is rolled and gathered together*; compare גלל, *to roll,* مجد, إِكْلِيل, *a crown,* כל, *to finish,* כָּלִיל, *perfect, the whole*). If the leading substantive is definite, and signifies something single and indivisible, كُلّ means *whole*, as: كُلُّ ٱلْبَيْتِ, *the whole house,* كُلُّ ٱلْيَوْمِ, *the whole day;* if it is definite, but a plural or a collective, كُلّ means *all,* as: كُلُّ ٱلْحَيَوَانَاتِ, *all the animals,* كُلُّ ٱلنَّاسِ, *all mankind;* if it is indefinite, كُلّ means *each, every,* as: كُلُّ كَيْدٍ, *every stratagem,* كُلُّ يَوْمٍ, *every day,* كُلُّ وَاحِدٍ (أَحَدٍ), *each single one,* كُلُّ مَنْ, *every one who* (in which case the annexation is explicative, إِضَافَةُ ٱلتَّفْسِيرِ وَٱلْبَيَانِ; *each, viz. stratagem,* &c.). — Frequently, however, the definite primary substantive is put first, and كُلّ is placed after it, in annexation to a pronominal suffix agreeing with the primary substantive, which is, as

18*

it were, repeated in the suffix; as: اَلْبَيْتُ كُلُّهُ, *the whole house;* اَلْأَرْضُ كُلُّهَا, *the whole earth;* اَلنَّاسُ كُلُّهُمْ, *all mankind.* Instead of this construction, we sometimes find اَلْكُلُّ, τὸ πᾶν, and even كُلٌّ, which is definite, notwithstanding the tenwîn, and stands, according to circumstances, for كُلُّكُمْ, &c.; as: وَقَدْ تَجَمَّعَتِ الصَّعَالِيكُ وَآلْأَرَامِلُ وَآلْأَيْتَامُ وَآلْكُلُّ كُنَّا قَدْ أَتَرًا لِيَسْقُوا جِمَالَهُمْ وَآلْأَغْنَامَ وَبَقُوا الْكُلَّ عِنْدَ آلْمَآءِ قِيَامًا, *and the poor and widows and orphans had assembled, and had all come to water their camels and flocks, and they all remained standing near the water* (اَلْكُلُّ = كُلُّهُمْ); وَعَادٌ وَفِرْعَوْنُ وَإِخْوَانُ لُوطٍ وَأَصْحَابُ ٱلْأَيْكَةِ وَقَوْمُ تُبَّعٍ كُلٌّ كَذَّبَ ٱلرُّسُلَ, *and Ad, and Pharaoh, and the brethren of Lot, and the inhabitants of the grove and the people of Tubba, all accused the apostles of imposture* (كُلٌّ = كُلُّهُمْ).

Rem. *a.* This last remark applies also to غَدٌ, *tomorrow,* = غَدُ ذٰلِكَ ٱلْيَوْمِ, and to قَابِلٌ, *next year,* = قَابِلُ ذٰلِكَ ٱلْعَامِ and قَابِلُ هٰذَا ٱلْعَامِ.

Rem. *b.* On the similar construction of כֹּל in Hebrew, see Gesenius' Gr. §. 109, 1.

2) With the use of كُلٌّ coincides in most points that of جَمِيعٌ, *the totality, the whole* (lit. *what is collected,* from جَمَعَ, connected with جَمٌّ); as: جَمِيعُ ٱلنَّاسِ or اَلنَّاسُ جَمِيعُهُمْ, *all mankind* (but also اَلنَّاسُ جَمِيعًا, whereas اَلنَّاسُ كُلًّا is inadmissible); اَلْمَدِينَةُ جَمِيعُهَا, *the whole city;* فَلَمَّا وَلِيَ ٱلْمُلْكَ تَنَلَ ٱلْجَمِيعَ, *and after he obtained the sove-*

.reignty, he put them all to death (اَلْجَمِيعَ, τὸ ὅλον, equivalent in this case to جَمِيعُهُمْ).

Rem. The word سَائِرٌ, the rest, the remainder (properly the nomen agentis of سَئِرَ, to be over, to be left, Heb. שָׂאַר), is incorrectly used by later writers in the sense of all; as: قَدِمَ اِسْتَوْفَى سَائِرَ ٱلْخَرَاجِ , سَائِرُ ٱلْحَاجِّ, all the pilgrims have arrived; he has received the whole of the property-tax.

3) بَعْضٌ, a part, a portion, is used with the genitive of a plural or a collective to signify a certain one, some; as: خَاطَبَ بَعْضُ ٱلتَّلَامِيذِ مُحَمَّدَ بْنَ ٱلْحَسَنِ, some of the pupils addressed Mohammed the son of el-Hasan; فِي بَعْضِ ٱلْمَغَايِرِ, in a certain cave; فِي بَعْضِ ٱلْأَيَّامِ, one day; أَنْشَدَ لِبَعْضِهِمْ, he recited (the following verses) composed by one of them (one of the poets, by a certain poet); وَٱحْذَرْهُمْ أَنْ يَفْتِنُوكَ عَنْ بَعْضِ مَا أَنْزَلَ ٱللَّهُ إِلَيْكَ, and beware of them, lest they lead thee astray from part of what (from some of the precepts which) God has sent down (revealed) unto thee. — If بَعْضٌ be repeated as a correlative, no pronominal suffix is added to it in the second place; as: وَلَوْ كَانَ بَعْضُهُمْ لِبَعْضٍ ظَهِيرًا, even though they should aid one another; إِنْ يَعِدُ ٱلظَّالِمُونَ بَعْضُهُمْ بَعْضًا إِلَّا غُرُورًا, the wicked make to one another only vain (or deceitful) promises. In modern Arabic the second بَعْضٌ is omitted. — Lastly, ٱلْبَعْضُ is sometimes used instead of بَعْضٌ with the genitive; as: إِذَا قَامَ بِهِ ٱلْبَعْضُ فِي بَلْدَةٍ

سَقَطَ عَنِ ٱلْبَاقِينَ, *when some (people) in a town observe
it, it is not required of* (lit. *it falls off from) the rest*;
وَقَدْ خَالَفَهُمُ ٱلْبَعْضُ فِى ذٰلِكَ, *some opposed them in
this matter.*

4) غَيْرٌ, *alteration, difference,* as a concrete, *something
different,* is used with a following genitive to designate
one or more objects *other* than, *differing* from, or the *opposite* of the object or objects expressed by the genitive. In
the last case, it corresponds to our negative prefix *un* or
in; in the others, it may be rendered by *another, other, et
caetera,* and the like. For example: ٱلْمُلُوكُ وَغَيْرُهُمْ, *kings and
others;* ٱلشَّجَاعَةُ وَٱلْقُوَّةُ وَٱلشَّفَقَةُ وَغَيْرُهَا, *bravery, strength,
clemency, and other qualities;* جَآءَ ٱلْوُزَرَآءُ وَٱلْقُضَاةُ وَغَيْرُهُمْ,
there came the vizirs, judges, &c.; أَفَغَيْرَ دِينِ ٱللّٰهِ يَبْغُونَ,
do they then seek another religion than that of God;
غَيْرُ مَخْلُوقٍ, *uncreated;* غَيْرُ ٱلْمَخْلُوقِ, *the uncreated;*
وَجْهُهُ إِلَى غَيْرِ مِصْرَ, *his face was not turned towards Egypt.* — ٱلْغَيْرُ is
very rarely used instead of غَيْرٌ with the genitive; as:
تُصَافِحُهَا أَكُفُّ ٱلْغَيْرِ, *the hands of others clasp them* (=
غَيْرِهِمْ). — When put in the accusative, غَيْرَ, which always remains a substantive, often requires to be translated
by a preposition or conjunction, such as *except, but;* as:
قَامَ ٱلْقَوْمُ غَيْرَ أَبِى بَكْرٍ, *the people stood up, except Abû Bekr;*
لَا تُرَى غَيْرَ جَاهِلٍ, *you will never seem (or be thought) but
a fool.* — On بِغَيْرِ and مِنْ غَيْرِ, *without,* see §. 57, rem. *a.*

The Government of the Noun. 143

Rem. a. When the sense demands a repetition of غَيْر, the particle لَا is used instead, likewise followed by the genitive; as: غَيْرِ ٱلْمَغْضُوبِ مِنْ غَيْرِ أَبٍ وَلَا أُمٍّ, *without father and mother*; عَلَيْهِمْ وَلَا ٱلضَّالِّينَ, *of those with whom thou art not angry, and who do not go astray.*

Rem. b. Instead of غَيْرُ in the nom., genit. or accus., followed by the genit. of an adjective, we sometimes find لَا with the corresponding case of the adjective; as: نَاقَةٌ لَا ذَلُولٌ, *an unbroken she-camel*, = غَيْرُ ذَلُولٍ.

5) سِوَى (rarely سُوًى and سَوَاءٌ), *another (besides so and so)*, runs through all the cases; as: وَسِوَاكَ مَانِعٌ فَضْلَهُ ٱلْمُحْتَاجَ, *whilst others than you withhold their benefits from the needy* (see §. 30, 2, rem. b); فَسِوَاكَ بَائِعُهَا وَأَنْتَ ٱلْمُشْتَرِي, *then another than you is the seller and you are the buyer;* وَٱكْفِنِي بِفَضْلِكَ عَنْ سِوَاكَ, *and give me a sufficiency through thy goodness, so that I can dispense with any other but thee;* دَعَوْتُ رَبِّي أَنْ لَا يُسَلِّطَ عَلَى أُمَّتِي عَدُوًّا مِنْ سِوَى أَنْفُسِهَا, *I have prayed to my Lord that he would let no enemy conquer my people, that belonged to another race than themselves;* وَإِنْ سِوَاكَ مَنْ يُؤَمِّلُهُ يَشْقَى, *and he who places hope in any other than you, is wretched.* — When put in the accusative, it must often be translated by *besides* (compare غَيْرَ in no. 4); as: سِوَى ٱلْعِلْمِ, *besides science*; سِوَى كَوْنِهِ رَوْنَقَ ٱلْمَجْلِسِ, *besides its being an ornament to society.*

6) مِثْلٌ, plur. أَمْثَالٌ, *likeness*, as an adjective, *like*, also runs through all the cases; as: رَجُلٌ مِثْلُ زَيْدٍ, *a man like*

144 Part Third. Syntax.

مِثْلُهُ (*one*) *Zeïd,* genit. مِثْلِ زَيْدٍ, accus. رَجُلاً مِثْلَ زَيْدٍ; رَجُلٍ; *like him* or *it*; لَيْسَ كَمِثْلِهِ شَيْ‌ءٌ, *there is nothing like him;* وَبِهَا قُرُودٌ بِيضٌ كَأَمْثَالِ ٱلْكِبَاشِ ٱلْكِبَارِ, *and in it are white apes, like* (as big as) *large rams.*

Rem. Similar is the use of قَدْرُ, *measure, quantity;* as: صَنَمٌ قَدْرُ ٱلرَّجُلِ ٱلْمُعْتَدِلِ ٱلْخِلْقَةِ, *a statue as tall as* (lit. *the size of*) *a well-proportioned man;* وَخُضْرٌ طَوَاوِيسُ رُقْطٌ قَدْرُ ٱلنَّعَامِ ٱلْكِبَارِ, *peacocks speckled and green, as big as large ostriches.*

7) نَحْوُ, which properly signifies *direction, road,* and is used in the accusative as a preposition (§. 55), is construed exactly like مِثْلُ. It is generally to be translated by *the like, et caetera,* and *about.* See the examples in §. 55; to which add: كَٱلصَّلٰوةِ وَٱلصَّوْمِ وَنَحْوِهِمَا, *such as prayer, fasting, and the like;* وَهُمْ نَحْوُ مِنْ أَرْبَعِ مِائَةِ رَجُلٍ, *and they are* (in number) *about* 400 *men* (on this مِنْ see §. 77).

83. كِلَانِ, fem. كِلْتَانِ, *both, a pair* (compare Heb. כִּלְאַיִם, *two things of different kinds,* Aeth. ክልኤ፡ *k'lē,* fem. ክልኤቱ፡ *k'lētu, two*), is always construed with the genitive dual of a definite noun or pronoun, or, it may be, with the genitive singular of a pronoun, when it is to be taken in the sense of the dual; as: كِلَا ٱلرَّجُلَيْنِ, *both the men;* كِلْتَا ٱلْجَنَّتَيْنِ, *both the gardens;* أَحَدُهُمَا أَوْ كِلَاهُمَا,

The Government of the Noun.

one of the two or both of them; إِنَّ لِلْخَيْرِ وَلِلشَّرِّ مَدًى وَكِلَا ذٰلِكَ وَجْهٌ وَقَبَلْ, both good and evil have their limit, and both are plain and clear (قَبَلْ for قَبَلْ) in rhyme for (قَبَلْ). This word is not inflected except when it is connected with a pronominal suffix; as: رَأَيْتُ كِلَا أَخَوَيْكَ, I have seen your two brothers (not كِلَىْ); مَرَرْتُ بِكِلْتَا أُخْتَيْكَ, I passed by your two sisters (not بِكِلْتَىْ); but إِنَّ ٱلْمُعَلِّمَ وَٱلطَّبِيبَ كِلَيْهِمَا, the teacher and the physician, both of them; مَرَرْتُ بِزَيْنَبَ وَفَاطِمَةَ كِلْتَيْهِمَا, I passed by Zeineb and Fâtima, both of them. Although dual in form, it takes the predicate in the singular; as: كِلَانَا غَنِيٌّ عَنْ أَخِيهِ حَيْوَتَهُ, each of us can dispense with his brother, all his life long; كِلَانَا إِذَا مَا نَالَ شَيْئًا أَفَاتَهُ, when either of us obtains anything, he lets it slip; كِلْتَا ٱلْجَنَّتَيْنِ آتَتْ أُكُلَهَا, each of the gardens produced its fruit; هٰهُنَا رَجُلَانِ كِلَاهُمَا إِلَيْكَ بَغِيضٌ, here are two men, both of whom are hateful to you. — In poetry it is sometimes joined to two singular genitives; as: كِلَا أَخِى وَخَلِيلِى وَاجِدِى عَضُدًا فِى ٱلنَّائِبَاتِ, my brother and my friend both find me a help in misfortunes; but in prose we cannot say كِلَا زَيْدٍ وَعَمْرٍو, both Zeid and 'Amr; it must be كِلَاهُمَا مِنْ زَيْدٍ وَعَمْرٍو or زَيْدٌ وَعَمْرٌو كِلَاهُمَا.

Rem. a. When كِلَانِ necessarily denotes *both together*, not *each of the two separately*, it naturally takes the predicate in the dual, as: وَكِلَاهُمَا يَعْمَّانِ كُلَّ ضَارٍّ وَنَافِعٍ, *and these two to-*

gether comprise everything hurtful and useful; or even in the plural, as: كِلَانَا نَعَلْنَا ذٰلِكَ, *we two have done this together*.

Rem. b. كِلْتَا is also written كِلْتَى, and in poetry the shorter form كِلْتَ sometimes occurs.

84. رُبَّ, *many a* . . . . . , Germ. *manch*, Fr. *maint*, is construed with an indefinite substantive in the genitive, followed by an indefinite adjective in the same case, or by a nominal or verbal clause standing in place of such an adjective; as: رُبَّ رَجُلٍ عَالِمٍ لَقِيتُ, *many a learned man have I met*; رُبَّ رَجُلٍ رَأَيْتُهُ جَاهِلًا, *many a man have I seen to be foolish*. — Sometimes the pronominal suffix هُ is appended to رُبَّ, and the indefinite substantive put in the accusative, the verb أَعْنِي, *I mean*, being understood; as: وَرُبَّهُ عَطِبًا مِنْ عَطَبِهْ, *and many a perishing (man) have I saved from destruction* (عَطَبِهْ in rhyme for عَطَبِهِ). When the substantive is feminine, some grammarians allow the use of the feminine pronoun; as: رُبَّهَا آمْرَأَةً or رُبَّهُ آمْرَأَةً, *many a woman*.

Rem. a. Other forms of this word are: رَبَّ, رَبْ, رُبْ; أُمَيْمَ; of which the most common are رُبَّ and رُبَتَ; as: رُبَّتْ, رُبَتَ . هَلْ تَذْكُرِينَ أَنْ رُبَّ صَاحِبٍ فَارَقْتُ يَوْمَ حُشَاشٍ غَيْرِ ضَعِيفِ. *Umeima, dost thou know that I parted on the day* (i. e *at the battle*) *of Hos'âs from many a sturdy friend* (ضَعِيفِ in rhyme for ضَعِيفٍ); رُبَّ خُطْبَةٍ مُتْحَنْفِرَةٍ, *many a long oration* (in rhyme for مُتْحَنْفِرَةٍ). — The redundant مَا is sometimes added without destroying the influence of رُبَّ (see §. 57, 3); as: رُبَّتَمَا غَارَةٍ, *many a sudden foray.*

Rem. *b.* From رُبَّ and مَا is formed the adverb رُبَّمَا, *many a time, sometimes, perhaps;* as: رُبَّمَا يَوَدُّ ٱلَّذِينَ كَفَرُوا لَوْ كَانُوا مُسْلِمِينَ, *many a time shall those, who did not believe, wish that they had been believers;* رُبَّمَا يَقُولُ مَا لَا تَقْبَلُهُ ٱلْعُقُولُ, *perhaps he may say something that our understandings cannot receive (that we cannot admit).*

Rem. *c.* رُبَّ is the accusative of the substantive رُبٌّ, Heb. רֹב, *multitude, quantity,* dependent upon the interjection يَا (§. 38, 1, *b*), which is generally understood, though sometimes expressed; as: يَا رُبَّ خَالٍ لِي أَغَرَّ أَبْلَجَا, *many a maternal uncle have I, noble and illustrious* (أَبْلَجَا in rhyme for أَبْلَجَ); مَـاوِىَ يَا رُبَّتَمَا غَارَةٍ شَعْوَاءَ كَاللَّذْعَةِ بِالْمِيسَمِ, *Māwiya, many a far extending raid is like a burn with the branding iron.* Together with its genitive it has the value of a whole clause, to the indefinite noun in which there is added a صِفَة, that is to say, an adjective or a clause taking the place of an adjective. This صِفَة the grammarians call جَوَابُ رُبَّ, *the answer to rubba, what corresponds to rubba.* —It is curious to note that رُبَّ has passed, like the German *manch,* Fr. *maint,* and Eng. *many a....,* from its original signification of *multitude,* into one that is almost the opposite, viz. *not a great many.* The same remark applies to رُبَّمَا and the Germ. *vielleicht, perhaps.*

83. In consequence of the elision of رُبَّ, we frequently find the indefinite genitive alone after the conjunction

َزْ (وَاوُ رُبَّ), *the wāw of rubba, equivalent in meaning to rubba*); as: وَكَأْسٍ شَرِبْتُ, *many a cup have I quaffed*; وَأَرَاكَةٍ ضَرَبَتْ سَمَاءً فَوْقَنَا, *many an arāka-tree formed a roof over us.* — The same is the case, though rarely, after قَ, and still more rarely after بَلْ; as: كَمِثْلِكِ حُبْلَى قَدْ طَرَقْتُ وَمُرْضِعٍ, *many a one like thee have I visited by night, pregnant and nursing a child;* قَتَمَهْ بَلْ بَلَدٍ مِلْءُ ٱلْفِجَاجِ, *nay, there is many a town, the dust of which fills the wide roads* (قَتَمَهْ in rhyme for قَتَمُهُ). Occasionally even these particles are omitted, and the genitive alone appears; as: رَسْمِ دَارٍ وَقَفْتُ فِي طَلَلِهْ, *many a deserted abode, amid the ruins of which I have stood* (طَلَلِهْ in rhyme for طَلَلِهِ).

86. With the genitive are also construed verbal adjectives expressing the superlative, whether of the common form أَفْعَلُ (vol. I. §. 234), or of any other form, such as فَعْلٌ (e. g. خَيْرٌ, شَرٌّ); as: أَعْلَمُ ٱلْفَلَاسِفَةِ, *the most learned of the philosophers;* خَيْرُ ٱلْبَرِيَّةِ, *the best of created things.* Here the genitive designates the whole, out of which some one or something is brought conspicuously forward as its most remarkable part. As أَفْعَلُ and فَعْلٌ are in this construction definite substantives, and not adjectives (see §. 75, rem.), they do not conform in gender and number to the object or objects referred to; so that خَيْرُ ٱلْبَرِيَّةِ or أَفْضَلُ ٱلْقَوْمِ may be said of a single man or woman, or of two or more persons of either sex. — To indicate that an object is the greatest or most distinguished of its kind, the

substantive is often repeated in the form of the definite genitive plural; as: أَمِيرُ ٱلْأُمَرَآءِ, *the emir of the emirs*, i. e. *the chief emir;* قَاضِى ٱلْقُضَاةِ, *the chief judge;* طَلْحَةُ ٱلطَّلَحَاتِ, *the noblest of those who bear the name of Talḥa.* — To show that an object possesses the highest degree of a quality, the adjective that designates that quality is construed with the genitive plural of the substantive, and being then virtually a substantive need not vary with the gender and number of the object spoken of; as: نَفِيسُ ٱلْجَوَاهِرِ, *the choicest gems* (lit. *the choice of gems);* سَوَابِغُ ٱلنِّعَمِ or سَابِغُ ٱلنِّعَمِ, *the most ample favours.*

Rem. *a.* Compare, in Hebrew, such constructions as קְטֹן בָּנָיו *the youngest of his sons,* קֹדֶשׁ קָדָשִׁים *the holy of holies* (i. e. *the holiest place of all*). See Gesenius' Gr. §. 117, 2.

Rem. *b.* The numeral adjective أَوَّلُ, *first,* being strictly a superlative, is also construed with the genitive; as: أَوَّلُهُمْ, *the first of them;* أَوَّلُ يَوْمٍ, *the first day,* = ٱلْيَوْمُ ٱلْأَوَّلُ; but this construction is not extended in classical Arabic to the other ordinal numbers (vol. I. §. 328), which are nomina agentis from transitive verbs (see §. 109), though later writers not unfrequently use them in this way; as ثَانِىَ مَرَّةٍ, *for the second time,* = ٱلْمَرَّةَ ٱلثَّانِيَةَ.

Rem. *c.* In such phrases as عَزِيزُ كِتَابِكُمْ, *your honoured letter,* the genitive does not designate the whole, of which the ٱلْمُضَافُ is a part, but it is (as in نَهْرُ ٱلْأُرْدُنِّ, *the river Jordan)* merely explicative (see §. 95); so that عَـزِيـزُ كِتَـابِكُمْ = كِتَابُكُمُ ٱلْعَزِيزُ = ٱلْعَزِيزُ ٱلَّذِى هُوَ كِتَابُكُمْ

Part Third. Syntax.

87. The interrogative pronoun أَىُّ, fem. أَيَّةُ (vol. I. §§. 349, 353), is construed with the genitive, definite or indefinite; as: أَىُّ رَجُلٍ, *which man?* أَىُّ ٱلرِّجَالِ, *which of the men?* In the former case the annexation is explicative, in the latter partitive.

88. The genitive of a verbal noun is not unfrequently resolved into a clause consisting of أَنْ or مَا and a finite form of the verb; as: وَقْتَ أَنِ ٱسْتَتَرَ, *at the time he hid himself,* = وَقْتَ ٱسْتِتَارِهِ, *at the time of his hiding himself*;

وَإِنَّمَا سُمِّىَ طَالِبُ ٱلْعِلْمِ مَا تَقُولُ لِكَثْرَةِ مَا يَقُولُونَ فِى ٱلزَّمَانِ ٱلْأَوَّلِ مَا تَقُولُ فِى هٰذِهِ ٱلْمَسْئَلَةِ, *the student of science was named Mā-taḳūlu (what do you say?) for no other reason than that, in the olden time, they used constantly to say, What do you say* (mā taḳūlu) *about this question* (لِكَثْرَةِ قَوْلِهِمْ = لِكَثْرَةِ مَا يَقُولُونَ)? In the same way, a verbal or nominal clause is often found as the ٱلْمُضَافُ إِلَيْهِ or genitive after substantives, especially those denoting time or portions of time. See §. 78.

89. Adjectives, nomina agentis, and nomina patientis, may take after them a restrictive or limitative genitive; as: حَسَنُ ٱلْوَجْهِ, *handsome of face;* طَاهِرُ ٱلْقَلْبِ, *pure of heart;* شَدِيدُ ٱلْحَرَارَةِ, *very warm;* مُسْتَجَابُ ٱلدُّعَآءِ, *one whose prayers are answered;* صَرِيعُ ٱلْكَأْسِ, *smitten down by the wine-cup, intoxicated* (compare הֲלוּמֵי יַיִן, Isaiah 28, 1): صَرِيعُ ٱلْغَوَانِى, *smitten by (enamoured of) the fair sex;* كُلُّ نَفْسٍ ذَآئِقَةُ ٱلْمَوْتِ, *every soul shall taste death;* هٰذَى بَالِغُ ٱلْكَعْبَةِ,

a victim that arrives at the Ká'ba (بَلَغَ is construed with the accusative of the object reached). Compare in Latin *aeger animi, integer vitae scelerisque purus,* &c. This annexation is an improper one (§. 75, rem.), standing in place either of a těmyîz-accusative (§. 44, 5) or an accusative of the object. Hence the genitive, though always defined by the article, exercises no defining influence upon the governing word, any more than the accusative which it represents; and consequently, if we wish to define the governing word, we must prefix to it the article; as: اَلْضَّارِبُ ٱلْمُقِيمُو ٱلصَّلْوةِ, *those who perform the prayer;* رَأْسُ ٱلْجَـانِى, *he who smites the head of the sinner;* مُحَمَّدٌ ٱلْحَسَنُ ٱلْوَجْهِ, *Mohammed, the handsome of face;* اَلْمُبْدِئُكَ اَللَّذِيْ, *he who created thee;* اَللَّذِيْ, *he who rebukes me* (compare הַמַּכֵּהוּ, Isaiah 9, 12).

Rem. *a.* The same construction is usual in Hebrew; Gesenius' Gr. §. 110, 2.

Rem. *b.* Observe, however, that the annexation may in many of these cases be a proper one, either of a partitive or an explicative character. For example, حَسَنُ ٱلْوَجْهِ may mean *the handsome (part) of the face,* or even *the handsome face;* مُسْتَجَابُ ٱلدُّعَآءِ, *that part of the prayer that has been answered;* شَدِيدُ ٱلْحَرَارَةِ, *the intensest portion of the heat* (compare §. 86, with rem. *b,* and §. 95). In this case the article can, of course, never be prefixed to the اَلْمُضَافُ.

90. No word can be interposed between the status

constructus and the genitive, and consequently an adjective that qualifies the former must be placed after the latter; as: كِتَابُ ٱللّٰهِ ٱلْعَزِيزِ, *the glorious book of God;* يَدُهُ ٱلْيُمْنَى, *his right hand.* Exceptions to this rule are very rare, and found almost exclusively in the poets, who sometimes take the liberty of interposing an oath or some other word. For example, in prose: فَلَا تَحْسِبَنَّ أَنَّ ٱللّٰهَ مُخْلِفَ وَعْدَهُ رُسُلِهِ, *do not then think that God will fail to keep his promise to his apostles* (el-Kor'ân, ch. 14, v. 48, according to one reading); وَكَذٰلِكَ زَيَّنَ لِكَثِيرٍ مِنَ ٱلْمُشْرِكِينَ قَتْلَ أَوْلَادَهُمْ شُرَكَآئِهِمْ, *and in like manner the killing of their children by their companions was made to seem good to many of the polytheists* (el-Kor. ch. 6, v. 138, according to one reading): هَلْ أَنْتُمْ تَارِكُو لِي صَاحِبِي, *do you not leave me my companion?* (words of the Prophet, reported by 'Abū 'd-Dardā); تَرْكُ يَوْمًا نَفْسِكَ وَهَوَاهَا سَعْيٌ لَهَا فِى رَدَاهَا, *to let your soul alone one day with its lust is an effort towards its destruction;* إِنَّ ٱلشَّاةَ تَسْمَعُ صَوْتَ وَٱللّٰهِ رَبِّهِ, *the sheep hears the voice, by God, of its master.* Again, in poetry: كَمَا خَطَّ ٱلْكِتَابَ بِكَفِّ يَوْمًا يَهُودِيٍّ يُقَارِبُ أَوْ يُزِيلُ, *as the book was written one day by the hand of a Jew, writing the lines nearer or farther from one another;* فَزَجَجْتُهَا بِمِزَجَّةٍ زَجَّ ٱلْقَلُوصِ أَبِى مَزَادَةَ, *and I stabbed her with a short lance, as 'Abū Mezāda stabs a young camel* (مَزَادَةَ in rhyme for مَزَادَةٍ): وَسِوَاكَ مَانِعُ فَضْلَهُ ٱلْمُحْتَاجِ, *whilst others than you withhold their benefits from the needy;* وَقَانِى كَعْبُ بُجَيْرٍ مُنْقِذٌ لَكَ مِنْ تَعْجِيلِ مَهْلَكَةٍ وَٱلْخُلْدِ فِى سَقَرَ, *agreement with*

The Government of the Noun.

Buǵeir saves thee, Kaʿb, from speedy destruction and from remaining for ever in hell (for وِفَاتِي بُجَيْرٍ يَا كَعْبُ;) وَلَئِنْ حَلَفْتَ عَلَى يَدَيْكَ لَأَحْلِفَنْ بِيَمِينٍ أَصْدَقَ مِنْ يَمِينِكَ مُقْسِمٍ, *and verily, if I swear before thee, I swear with the oath of a swearer that is more truthful than thy oath* (for بِيَمِينٍ مُقْسِمٍ أَصْدَقَ مِنْ يَمِينِكَ). In these examples, with the exception of the last, we find the word interposed to be either an oath, an objective complement of the ٱلْمُضَافُ, an adverbial accusative of time, or a vocative.

Rem. This rule applies equally to the other Shemitic languages. Examples of somewhat similar exceptions in Hebrew are: 2 Sam. 1, 9. אֵין; Ps. 5, 10. כָּל־תִּשָּׂא עָוֺן Hos. 14, 3.; עוֹד נַפְשִׁי בִי אֵין בְּפִיהוּ נְכוֹנָה Ps. 6,6.; אֵין בָּמָיִת זָרֻף 1 Kings, 6, 7. אֶבֶן שְׁלֵמָה; קִדְּמוּ שָׁרִים מְחֹתֲלָה בַּאֲשָׁמָיו Ps. 68, 22. מֶסַע.

91. The relative adjectives ending in ـِيّ (vol. I. §. 249), because standing to some extent in the place of a genitive, admit of a genitive in apposition to them; as: رَأَيْتُ ٱلتَّيْمِيَّ تَيْمَ عَدِيٍّ, *I saw the Teïmi, (namely) of the tribe of) Teïm (bin) ʿAdi*, = رَأَيْتُ ٱلرَّجُلَ مِنْ تَيْمِ تَيْمَ عَدِيٍّ; يَقُولُ عَبْدُ ٱللَّهِ بْنُ ٱلزُّبَيْرِ ٱلْأَسَدِيُّ أَسَدِ خُزَيْمَةَ, *says ʿAbdu 'llāh bin ez-Zebir el-Asedi, of (the tribe of) Ased (bin) Hozeima*.

92. In the proper annexation, if the second noun be indefinite, the first is so too; but if the second be definite, so is the first likewise. For example, بِنْتُ مَلِكٍ is *a daughter of a king, a king's daughter, a princess*, Fr. *une fille de roi*, Germ. *eine Königstochter*; but بِنْتُ ٱلْمَلِكِ

is *the daughter of the king*, *the king's daughter*, Fr. *la fille du roi*, Germ. *die Tochter des Königs* (either his only daughter or that daughter of his who has been already spoken of). — If we wish the first noun to remain indefinite, whilst the second is definite, we must substitute for the annexation the construction with the preposition ل (§ 54, 2, rem. *c*); e. g. بِنْتٌ لِلْمَلِكِ, *a daughter of the king*; مَاتَ لِي أَخٌ, *a brother of mine is dead* (whereas مَاتَ أَخِي would mean *my brother is dead*, that is to say, either *my only brother* or *that one of my brothers of whom we have been speaking*). — There are some nouns, however, of a wide and general signification, that may remain indefinite even when followed by a definite genitive; for instance, بَعْضُ ٱلْفُقَرَآءِ, *something like it*; مِثْلُهُ, نَحْوُهُ, نَظِيرُهُ, *some poor people*; بَعْضُ ٱلْمَقَادِيرِ, *a care*.

Rem. *a*. On the corresponding Hebrew construction, see Gesenius' Gr. §. 109, 1, and §. 113, 2.

Rem. *b*. In such phrases as أَمْرُ آخِرَةٍ وَدُنْيَا, *a matter of this life and the life to come*, the indefinite مُضَافٌ إِلَيْهِ shows that the مُضَافٌ is to be regarded as a single part, *some one matter* &c. In these cases the genitive may even be *virtually definite*, but nevertheless it does not take the article, in order to preserve the governing word from becoming definite; أَمْرُ آخِرَةٍ وَدُنْيَا is in fact equivalent in meaning to أَمْرٌ مِنْ أُمُورِ ٱلْآخِرَةِ وَٱلدُّنْيَا. The same remark applies to those indefinite annexations which supply the place of our compound nouns or adjectives; e. g. قَصْرُ مَلِكٍ,

قَصْرٌ مِنْ قُصُورِ الْمَلِكِ, *a royal castle*, is nearly the same as الْمَلِكِ.

93. Nouns of the forms نَعْلُ, أَنْعَلُ, &c., used as superlatives (see §. 86), are construed as substantives in the singular masculine with the genitive of the word denoting the objects among which the one spoken of is preeminent. The genitive is at times indefinite and explicative, at times definite and partitive. Examples of the indefinite genitive: هُوَ أَفْضَلُ رَجُلٍ, *he is a most excellent man;* هِيَ أَفْضَلُ ٱمْرَأَةٍ, *she is a most excellent woman;* هُمَا أَفْضَلُ رَجُلَيْنِ, *they are two most excellent men;* هُنَّ أَفْضَلُ نِسَاءٍ, *they are most excellent women;* ٱللَّهُ خَيْرُ حَافِظٍ, *God is the best preserver;* كُنْتُمْ خَيْرَ أُمَّةٍ أُخْرِجَتْ لِلنَّاسِ, *ye are the best nation that has been created for mankind;* ٱلْفِقْهُ أَفْضَلُ قَائِدٍ إِلَى ٱلْبِرِّ, *learning is the best guide to piety, and walks in the straightest of paths;* وَأَعْدَلُ قَاصِدٍ, *he described the Jews as being avaricious and envious, two very bad qualities.* Examples of the definite genitive: هِيَ أَفْضَلُ ٱلنِّسَاءِ, *she is the best of the women;* هُمَا أَفْضَلُ ٱلْقَوْمِ, *these two are the two best of the tribe;* أَنْتُمَا أَصْدَقُ ٱلصَّادِقِينَ, *you two are the most truthful of the truthful;* لَتَجِدَنَّهُمْ أَحْرَصَ ٱلنَّاسِ عَلَى ٱلْحَيَوٰةِ ٱلدُّنْيَا, *verily thou wilt find them the greediest of men after this present life;* خَيْرُ ٱلْأُمُورِ أَوْسَاطُهَا, *the best of things are the mediums* (or *means between two extremes*); شَرُّ ٱلنَّاسِ مَنْ

يَذْهَبُ بِدِينِهِ لِدِينِ غَيْرِهِ, *the worst of men is he who changes his religion for that of others;* أَفْضَلُ ٱلْأَوْقَاتِ شَرْخُ ٱلشَّبَابِ وَوَقْتُ ٱلسَّحَرِ, *the best of times are early youth and early morning.* Compare in general §. 86. Here must also be mentioned the indefinite genitive after أَوَّلُ, *first,* and آخِرُ, *last,* these words being (as already remarked in reference to the former, §. 86, rem. a) really superlatives: e. g. أَوَّلُ بَيْتٍ وُضِعَ لِلنَّاسِ, *the first house (temple) that was founded for mankind;* مَسْجِدٌ أُسِّسَ عَلَى ٱلتَّقْوَى مِنْ أَوَّلِ يَوْمٍ, *a mosque founded upon the fear of God from the first day (of its existence);* عَنْ أَبِى عَبَّاسٍ أَنَّهَا آخِرُ آيَةٍ نَزَلَ بِهَا جَبْرِيلُ, *(it is stated) on the authority of Abû Abbâs that this is the last verse (of the Ḳor'ân) that was revealed by Gabriel.* Instead of أَوَّلُ يَوْمٍ it is however very usual to say ٱلْيَوْمُ ٱلْأَوَّلُ. — On the construction of a positive adjective, used substantively, with a definite or indefinite genitive, see §. 78 (at the end) and §. 86, rem. b.

Rem. a. If the genitive be definite, the governing adjective may, according to some grammarians, agree in gender and number with the object or objects spoken of; as: هِيَ فُضْلَى ٱلنِّسَاءِ, *she is the best of the women;* هُمَا أَفْضَلَا ٱلْقَوْمِ, *these two are the two best of the tribe;* هُمْ أَفَاضِلُ ٱلْقَوْمِ or هُمْ أَفْضَلُو ٱلْقَوْمِ, *they are the best of the tribe;* أَحَاسِنُكُمْ أَخْلَاقًا, *the best of you in moral character* (words of the Prophet).

Rem. b. In such constructions as أَوَّلُ يَوْمٍ, أَفْضَلُ رَجُلٍ,

The Government of the Noun.

عَزِيزُ كِتَابِكُمْ, and عَاجِلُ طَعْنَةٍ, شَرُّ خَصْلَتَيْنِ, خَيْرُ أُمَّةٍ, the genitive is explicative (as in مَدِينَةُ بَغْدَادَ §. 95), and not, as might at first sight appear, a substitute for a témyîz-accusative (§. 44, 5). أَفْضَلُ رَجُلًا is not = أَفْضَلُ رَجُلٍ, *most excellent as a man* (très distingué en tant qu'homme); for we cannot say هُمَا طَوِيلًا ٱللِّحْيَةِ, as we say هُمَا أَفْضَلَا ٱلرَّجُلِ, *they are both long of beard*, instead of هُمَا طَوِيلَانِ لِحْيَةً, but, on the contrary, we must say هُمَا أَفْضَلُ رَجُلَيْنِ.

94. The substantive that denotes the material of which anything is made, is put in the genitive, definite or indefinite, after the substantive designating the thing; as: ثَوْبُ حَرِيرٍ, *a silk dress*; صَنَمُ ٱلذَّهَبِ, *the golden image* (see §§. 76, 77, 80 and 92). Frequently, however, — and this is the older construction, — the substantive denoting the material is put in apposition to the object as a determinative of kind (بَيَانٌ), both being either definite or indefinite. For example: ٱلصَّنَمُ ٱلذَّهَبُ, *the golden image* (not ٱلصَّنَمُ ٱلذَّهَبِ); ٱلْكَأْسُ ٱلْفِضَّةُ, *the silver cup*; ٱلصُّلْبَانُ ٱلْخَشَبُ, *the wooden crosses*; عِجْلًا جَسَدًا, *a calf of yellow gold*; إِحْمِلْ إِلَيْهِ دِرْعِي ٱلْحَدِيدَ, *carry to him my iron coat of mail*; وَنَزَعَ مَا كَانَ عَلَيْهِمْ مِنَ ٱلثِّيَابِ ٱلْحَرِيرِ وَأَلْبَسَهُمْ ثِيَابًا مِنَ ٱلشَّعْرِ, *and he stripped off the silken garments they had on, and clothed them in garments of hair*; ٱلْفِرَاءُ ٱلْبُرْطَاسِيُّ, *mantles of Burṭāsi* (i. e. *of fur from the country of the Burṭās*); ٱلثِّيَابُ ٱلْعَتَّابِيُّ, *robes of (the stuff called)* 'A-

'Attâbi (manufactured in ٱلْعَتَابِيَّةُ, one of the quarters of Bagdâd); ٱلْكُسَى ٱلدَّرْجِينِىُّ, cloaks of (the stuff called) ed-Dargini (manufactured in Dargin in North Africa).

Rem. a. Different from the above are such constructions as: رَطْلُ زَيْتٍ, a pound of olive oil; ٱلْبَيْتُ ٱلْحَرَامُ, the sacred house (temple); ٱلْكَعْبَةُ ٱلْحَرَامُ, the holy Ka'ba; ٱلْأَشْهُرُ ٱلْحُرُمُ, the sacred months. In the first of these, زَيْتٌ is not a بَيَانٌ, but a بَدَلٌ or permutative, instead of which we may employ a temyīz- accusative (رَطْلٌ زَيْتًا) or a genitive (رَطْلُ زَيْتٍ); in the others, حَرَامٌ, plur. حُرُمٌ, is an adjective of both genders (originally an infinitive)

Rem. b. Similarly, in Hebrew and Syriac, הַבָּקָר הַנְּחֹשֶׁת, the brazen oxen (2 Kings, 16, 17), ܕܗܒܐ ܕܝܢܪܐ, a golden dinâr. See Gesenius' Gr. §. 108, 2, c, as compared with §. 104, 1.

95. The genitive construction is also often extended in Arabic to things that are identical, the second of which ought strictly to be in apposition to the first. This remark applies:

1. To nicknames in connection with the names of persons; as: سَعِيدٌ ٱلَّذِى هُوَ كُرْزٌ = سَعِيدٌ كُرْزٌ, Said (nicknamed) Wallet.

Rem. Some grammarians admit the apposition سَعِيدٌ كُرْزٌ as correct. In case of either word, or both, being compounds (as أَنْفُ ٱلنَّاقَةِ or عَبْدُ ٱللّٰهِ, camel's nose), the genitive construction is of course impossible, and they must be put in apposition to one another; as: سَعِيدٌ أَنْفُ ٱلنَّاقَةِ or عَبْدُ ٱللّٰهِ كُرْزٌ. Some, however, allow the nickname to be put in the accusative, when the name is in the nominative; in the nominative, when the

3. The Government of the Noun.

name is in the accusative; and in either case, when the name is in the genitive; as: أَغْنِى , (scil.) هٰـذَا سَعِيدٌ أَنْفَ ٱلنَّاقَةِ, *I mean*); مَرَرْتُ بِسَعِيدٍ; (ٱلَّذِى هُوَ) (scil.) رَأَيْتُ سَعِيدًا أَنْفَ ٱلنَّاقَةِ أَنْفُ (أَنْفَ) ٱلنَّاقَةِ.

2. To the names of town, rivers, mountains, &c., when preceded by the words for *town*, *river*, &c.; as: مَدِينَةُ بَغْدَادَ , *the city of Bagdâd* (= ٱلْمَدِينَةُ ٱلَّتِى هِىَ بَغْدَادُ); نَهْرُ ٱلْفُرَاتِ, *the river Euphrates*; طُورُ سِينِينَ , *mount Sinai*.

Rem. Compare in Hebrew נְהַר פְּרָת , *the river Euphrates*, Gesenius' Gr. §. 112, 3; as well as the Latin *fluvius Rheni*, Fr. *la ville de* . . . ., and our own *the city of* . . . .

3. To words, regarded merely as such, and governed by a word signifying *word*, such as كَلِمَةُ or لَفْظُ; e. g. كَلِمَةُ كَانَ, *the word kâna* (see §. 78).

4. To nouns governed by other nouns, when the governing word signifies something to which the object designated by the governed word is similar; as: لُجَيْنُ ٱلْمَآءِ, *the silvery water* (lit. *the silver of the water*), = ٱللُّجَيْنُ ٱلَّذِى هُوَ ٱلْمَآءُ, i. e. ٱلْمَآءُ ٱلَّذِى هُوَ مِثْلُ ٱللُّجَيْنِ. Here the مُضَافٌ إِلَيْهِ is the *primum comparationis*, and the مُضَافٌ the *secundum comparationis*.

5. To adjectives defined by the article in connection with substantives not so defined; as: بَيْتُ ٱلْمُقَدَّسِ, *the Holy Temple* (i. e. *Jerusalem*), = ٱلْبَيْتُ ٱلَّذِى هُوَ ٱلْمُقَدَّسُ; بَابُ ٱلصَّغِيرِ, or, shortly, ٱلْبَيْتُ ٱلْمُقَدَّسُ, *the little*

gate (as a name), — رَبِيعُ ٱلْأَوَّلِ; ٱلْبَابُ ٱلصَّغِيرُ, *the first Rabī*, and رَبِيعُ ٱلْآخِرِ, *the last (second) Rabī* (names of months); عَامُ ٱلْأَوَّلِ, *last year*. In these and similar annexations some grammarians see an إِضَافَةُ ٱلْمَوْصُوفِ إِلَى ٱلصِّفَةِ, or *annexation of the thing described to the descriptive epithet*, i. e. of the substantive to the adjective; but as such an annexation is impossible (see §. 78), those grammarians are correct, who regard the adjective as having been raised to the level of a substantive. Strictly speaking, بَيْتُ ٱلْمُقَدَّسِ means *the house of the holy place* (taking مُقَدَّسٌ, if we like, as the *nomen loci* from قَدَّسَ, *to sanctify*, vol. I. §. 227); رَبِيعُ ٱلْأَوَّلِ, *the Rabī of the first place, first in order;* &c. On the other hand, in صَلٰوةُ ٱلْأُولَى the annexation is an ordinary, proper one (إِضَافَةٌ حَقِيقِيَّةٌ), the word سَاعَةٌ, *hour*, being understood; صَلٰوةُ ٱلْأُولَى = صَلٰوةٌ, i. e. ٱلصَّلٰوةُ فِي ٱلسَّاعَةِ ٱلْأُولَى (see §. 77). Here too the constructions, عَزِيزُ كِتَابِكُمْ, عَاجِلُ هَعْنَهِ, أَفْضَلُ رَجُلٍ, &c., find a place (see §. 78, at the end, §. 86, rem. *b*, and §. 93).

Rem. This sort of annexation is called by the Arabs ٱلْإِضَافَةُ ٱلتَّفْسِيرِيَّةُ or إِضَافَةُ ٱلتَّفْسِيرِ, *the interpretative annexation*, as also ٱلْإِضَافَةُ ٱلْبَيَانِيَّةُ or إِضَافَةُ ٱلْبَيَانِ, *the explicative annexation*. The special sort mentioned in no. 4 is named إِضَافَةُ ٱلتَّشْبِيهِ, *the comparative annexation*.

3. The Numerals.

96. We have already mentioned, in vol. I. §. 319—321, that the cardinal numbers from 3 to 10, when placed in apposition to the things numbered, agree with them in case, and when placed in annexation before them, govern the genitive plural; as: سِتَّةُ رِجَالٍ, *six men*; ثَلْثُنَا, *we three (women)*; أَرْبَعَتُهُمْ, *the four of them* (men). The genitive must, in every possible case, be that of the *broken* plural (vol. I. §. 300, *b*, and §§. 304—305); and if the substantive has a جَمْعُ ٱلْقِلَّةِ as well as a جَمْعُ ٱلْكَثْرَةِ (vol. I. §. 307), the former should be preferred; e. g. ثَلْثَةُ أَفْلُسٍ, *three fels* (a copper coin), not ثَلْثَةُ فُلُوسٍ. — They are very rarely construed with the accusative لِلتَّمْيِيزِ (§. 44, 5); as خَمْسَةً أَثْوَابًا instead of خَمْسَةُ أَثْوَابٍ, *five dresses*.

Rem. See Gesenius' Heb. Gr. §. 118, 1, 2. The construction with the accus., which is so rare in Arabic, is common in Hebrew.

97. اِثْنَانِ, fem. اِثْنَتَانِ or ثِنْتَانِ, is not unfrequently placed, as an adjective, after a noun in the dual, to express the idea of duality more strongly; as: لَا تَتَّخِذُوا إِلَهَيْنِ اثْنَيْنِ, *do not take unto yourselves two gods*; فِيهَا مِنْ كُلٍّ زَوْجَيْنِ اثْنَيْنِ, *bring into it* (the ark) *of every* (species of animals) *a pair* (lit. *two individuals male and female*); وَٱلَّذِى جَعَلَ لَهُ صَلَاحُ ٱلدِّينِ بَدَلًا مِنْ مَكْسِ ٱلْحَاجِّ أَلْفَ دِينَارٍ اثْنَانِ, *what Salaha'd-din has assigned him in lieu of the*

دَارِلِينَ مُنْذُ, *tax levied on the pilgrims is* 2000 *dinārs*; شَهْرَيْنِ ٱثْنَيْنِ, *dwelling (in it) for the last two months;* عَلَى مِيلَيْنِ ٱثْنَيْنِ مِنْهَا, *at a distance of two miles from it.* It is very rarely prefixed to the things numbered, and then requires the genitive singular; as: ٱثْنَتَا حَنْظَلِ, *two colocynth gourds*, = حَبَّتَا حَنْظَلِ (حَبَّةٌ, *grain, berry,* being used, like the Persian دانه, *dāna,* in counting fruit). See vol. I. §. 321, rem. *c*.

98. When the numeral is followed, not by the noun expressing the things numbered, but by a collective designating the whole species or genus, the relation between it and the collective is indicated, not by the simple genitive, but by the preposition مِنْ; as: أَرْبَعَةٌ مِنَ ٱلطَّيْرِ, *four birds,* تِسْعَةٌ مِنَ ٱلرَّهْطِ; أَرْبَعُ طُيُورٍ مِنَ ٱلطَّيْرِ = , *nine of the people,* = تِسْعَةُ أَشْخَاصٍ مِنَ ٱلرَّهْطِ. Sometimes, however, the collective is put in the genitive singular; as: وَكَانَ فِي ٱلْمَدِينَةِ تِسْعَةُ رَهْطٍ, *there were in the city nine persons;* وَهُمْ أَرْبَعَةُ نَفَرٍ, *and they were four in number.*

99. The cardinal numbers from 11 to 99 take, as already mentioned (§. 44, 5, rem. *b*, and vol. I. §. 323, rem. *b*), the objects numbered in the accusative singular; as: ثَلَاثَةَ عَشَرَ رَجُلًا, *thirteen men;* تِسْعَ عَشْرَةَ ٱمْرَأَةً, *nineteen women;* ثَلٰثَةٌ وَسَبْعُونَ رَجُلًا, *seventy-three men;* تِسْعٌ وَتِسْعُونَ نَعْجَةً, *ninety-nine sheep.* They are very rarely followed by the accusative plural; as: وَتَطْعَنَاهُمُ ٱثْنَتَيْ عَشْرَةَ أَسْبَاطًا أُمَمًا,

and we divided them into twelve tribes (or) nations. — As to gender, the *tens* (عِشْرُونَ, &c.) are both masculine and feminine, but the *units* must conform to the gender of the noun denoting the things numbered; as: أَحَدَ عَشَرَ كَوْكَبًا, *eleven stars*; خَمْسٌ وَأَرْبَعُونَ نَاقَةً, *forty-five she-camels*.

Rem. Compare, for the Hebrew, Gesenius' Gr. §. 118, 2, along with the remark.

100. If an adjective be appended to the noun denoting the things numbered, after any numeral between 11 and 99, the adjective may agree either grammatically with the noun, or logically with the cardinal number; as: عِشْرُونَ دِينَارًا نَاصِرِيًّا, *twenty dinars of el-Mèlik en-Nâṣir* (where نَاصِرِيًّا agrees grammatically with دِينَارًا, accus. sing. masc.), or عِشْرُونَ دِينَارًا نَاصِرِيَّةً (where نَاصِرِيَّةً agrees logically with عِشْرُونَ, as representing the broken plural دَنَانِيرُ, which requires an adjective in the sing. fem.).

101. When the object numbered has been already spoken of, the cardinal numbers from 20 to 90 (tens) may be construed, like substantives, with the genitive; as: عِشْرُو زَيْدٍ, *Zeïd's twenty* (camels); ثَلَاثُوكَ, *your thirty* (servants). Compare §. 108.

102. The cardinal numbers from 11 to 19 may also be construed in the same way with the genitive of the possessor (except اِثْنَا عَشَرَ and its fem.). In this case they remain, according to most grammarians, indeclinable, as

خَمْسَ عَشْرَتَكَ, thy fifteen (nom., gen., acc.). According to others, the عَجُزٌ or latter part of the compound is declined; as: خَمْسَةَ عَشْرِكَ, gen. خَمْسَةَ عَشْرَكَ, acc. Others still admit the declinability of the صَدْرٌ or former part of the compound, and put the عَجُزٌ or latter part in the genitive; as: خَمْسَةُ عَشَرِكَ, gen. خَمْسَةَ عَشَرِكَ, acc.

103 The cardinal numbers مِائَةٌ, *a hundred*, and أَلْفٌ, *a thousand*, and their compounds, are construed with the genitive singular of the noun denoting the objects numbered; as: مِائَةُ رَجُلٍ, 100 *men*; مِائَتَا حِمَارٍ, 200 *asses*; ثَلَاثُمِائَةِ كَلْبٍ, 300 *dogs*; أَلْفُ مَدِينَةٍ, 1000 *cities*; أَلْفَا كِتَابٍ, 2000 *books*; أَرْبَعَةُ آلَافِ رَجُلٍ, 4000 *men*; أَحَدَ عَشَرَ أَلْفَ دِينَارٍ, 11,000 *dinars*; ثَلَاثُمِائَةِ أَلْفِ رَجُلٍ, 300,000 *men*.

104. If a sum be composed of several numerals of different kinds, the noun denoting the things numbered falls under the government of the last numeral; as: بَيْنَ الْهِجْرَةِ وَبَيْنَ آدَمَ عَلَى مُقْتَضَى التَّوْرَاةِ الْعِبْرَانِيَّةِ أَرْبَعَةُ آلَافٍ وَسَبْعُ مِائَةٍ وَإِحْدَى وَأَرْبَعُونَ سَنَةً, *between the Hiǵra and Adam, according to the Hebrew Pentateuch, there are* 4741 *years*; بَيْنَ تَبَلْبُلِ الْأَلْسُنِ وَبَيْنَ الْهِجْرَةِ عَلَى اخْتِيَارِ الْمُؤَرِّخِينَ ثَلَاثَةُ آلَافٍ وَثَلَاثُمِائَةٍ وَأَرْبَعُ سِنِينَ, *between the confusion of tongues and the Hiǵra, there are, according to the assumption of the chronologists,* 3304 *years.* The substantive may also, however, be repeated after each

numeral; as: اَلْغَرْبِيَّةُ غِيرَتُهَا أَلْفَا أَلْفِ دِينَارٍ وَمِائَةُ أَلْفِ دِينَارٍ وَأَرْبَعَةٌ وَأَرْبَعُونَ أَلْفَ دِينَارٍ وَثَمَانُونَ دِينَارًا جَيْشِيَّةً, *the revenue of (the province of) el-Garbiya* (in Lower Egypt) *is 2,144,080 military dinars*. In large amounts, consisting of millions, hundreds of thousands and thousands, the word أَلْفٌ must be repeated after each numeral; as: جُمْلَةُ ذٰلِكَ تِسْعَةُ آلَافِ أَلْفٍ وَخَمْسُمِائَةِ أَلْفٍ وَأَرْبَعَةٌ وَثَمَانُونَ أَلْفًا وَمِائَتَانِ وَأَرْبَعَةٌ وَسِتُّونَ دِينَارًا, *the total of this amounts to 9,584,264 dinars*.

105. The higher cardinal numbers; as well as those from 3 to 10 (vol. I. §. 321), may be placed in apposition to the substantive denoting the objects numbered; as: جَذَبَ ٱلشَّبَكَةَ إِلَى ٱلْأَرْضِ إِذْ هِيَ مُمْتَلِئَةٌ حِيتَانًا كِبَارًا مِائَةً وَثَلٰثَةً وَخَمْسِينَ, *he drew the net to land, and lo, it was full of large fishes, a hundred and fifty-three*; كَانَتْ شُعُوبُ أَوْلَادِ نُوحٍ ٱلثَّلٰثَةِ عِنْدَ تَبَلْبُلِ ٱلْأَلْسُنِ ٱثْنَيْنِ وَسَبْعِينَ شَعْبًا. *the nations sprung from the three sons of Noah were, at the time of the confusion of tongues, seventy-two in number* (the substantive denoting the things numbered, شَعْبٌ, is repeated here, because the last numeral requires it in a form different in number and case from شُعُوبٌ).

R e m. See Gesenius' Hebrew Gr. §. 118, 1, 2.

106. As regards the agreement in gender between the cardinal numbers and the nouns denoting the objects numbered, the following rules hold.

1) The numeral agrees in gender with the *singular*

of the substantive denoting the things numbered; as: سَبْعُ
سِنِينَ, *seven years* (sing. سَنَةٌ, fem.), but سَبْعَةُ أَعْوَامٍ, *id.*
(sing. عَامٌ, masc.); ثَلَاثَةُ حَمَّامَاتٍ, *three baths* (sing. حَمَّامٌ,
masc.). This rule holds even when the substantive itself
is suppressed; as: مِنْهُمْ مَا يَمْشِى عَلَى أَرْبَعٍ, *among them are
creatures that walk on four feet* (i. e. عَلَى أَرْبَعِ أَرْجُلٍ, from
رِجْلٌ, fem., *a foot*); يَا عَيْنِ بَكِّى عِنْدَ كُلِّ صَبَاحِ جُودِى
بِأَرْبَعَةٍ عَلَى ٱلْجَرَّاحِ (*O eye of mine, weep every morning*
in rhyme for صَبَاحٍ); *shed copious tears over el-Garrâḥ*
(lit. *weep with the four channels for tears*, بِأَرْبَعَةِ شُؤُونٍ,
from the sing. شَأْنٌ, masc., or *with the four corners of the
eyes*; بِأَرْبَعَةِ جَوَانِبِ ٱلْعَيْنِ, from the sing. جَانِبٌ, masc. *a side*).

Rem. This rule is often disregarded by modern incorrect writers and copyists. See Gesenius' Heb. Gr. §. 95, 1, along with
the note †.

2) The numeral follows the grammatical gender of
the substantive, when the objects numbered are designated
merely by a noun of a vague, general signification; e. g.
ثَلْثُ أَعْيُنٍ, ثَلَثَةُ أَشْخُصٍ, *three persons*, from شَخْصٌ, masc.;
three individuals, from عَيْنٌ, fem. But if another noun be
annexed to this, which determines the real gender of the
objects more precisely, the numeral agrees with the second
noun; as: فَكَانَ مِجَنِّى دُونَ مَنْ كُنْتُ أَتَّقِى ثَلْثَ شُخُوصٍ
كَاعِبَانِ وَمُعْصِرٌ, *and so my shield against those whom I
feared was three persons, two girls and a young woman*

مُعْصِرٌ) and كَاعِبٌ) are used only of women, vol. I. §. 297, rem. *b*; شُخُوصٍ is here employed by the poet, through the exigency of the metre, instead of أَشْخَاصٍ, §. 96; مُعْصِرٌ stands in rhyme for مُعْصِرٌ). Again: هٰذِهِ عَشْرُ فَإِنَّ كِلَابًا أَبْطُنٍ وَأَنْتَ بَرِىءٌ مِنْ قَبَآئِلِهَا ٱلْعَشْرِ, *this* (*tribe of*) *Kilāb has ten branches, but thou hast nought to do with its ten branches* (أَبْطُنٍ is a plural of بَطْنٌ, vol. I. §. 304, rem. *c*, which is masc., but the numeral takes the gender of the feminine substantive قَبِيلَةٌ, which immediately follows in its plural form قَبَآئِلُ); and in the Ḳor'ān, ch. 7, v 160, وَقَطَّعْنَاهُمُ ٱثْنَتَىْ عَشْرَةَ أَسْبَاطًا أُمَمًا, *and we divided them into twelve tribes* (*or*) *nations* (أَسْبَاطٌ is the plural of سِبْطٌ, masc., Heb. שֵׁבֶט, but the numeral agrees with أُمَّةٌ, which follows in the plural form أُمَمٌ). Sometimes, however, the numeral agrees with the real gender of the objects numbered, even when the grammatical gender of the noun used is different; as: ثَلٰثَةُ أَنْفُسٍ, *three persons* (*of the male sex*), where ثَلٰثَةُ is masc., although نَفْسٌ is fem., because نَفْسٌ is here equivalent to رَجُلٌ.

3) If the substantive be suppressed, and its place be taken by an adjective or other word expressive of its quality, the numeral agrees in gender with the understood substantive; e. g. مَنْ جَآءَ بِٱلْحَسَنَةِ فَلَهُ عَشْرُ أَمْثَالِهَا, *he who has done a good thing, shall receive a tenfold recompense for it*, lit. *shall receive ten* (*good things*) *like it* (عَشْرُ is

fem., because مِثْلٌ, plur. أَمْثَالٌ, though masc., is here only an epithet of حَسَنَاتٍ understood, the plur. of حَسَنَةٌ, which is 'fem.).

4) When the numeral is connected with the substantive by the preposition مِنْ (§. 98), it agrees in gender with the substantive; as; أَرْبَعٌ مِنَ ٱلْغَنَمِ, *four sheep* (غَنَمٌ being fem., vol. I. §. 290, 1, c); ثَلْثَةٌ مِنَ ٱلْبَطِّ, *three ducks* (بَطٌّ being masc., vol. I. §. 292, 1). This is the case even when an epithet follows, that fixes the real gender of the objects numbered; as: أَرْبَعٌ مِنَ ٱلْغَنَمِ ذُكُورٌ, *four sheep, males;* ثَلْثَةٌ مِنَ ٱلْبَطِّ إِنَاثٌ, *three ducks, females.* If, however, the epithet be placed between the numeral and the substantive, the numeral must agree in gender with the epithet; as: ثَلْثُ إِنَاثٍ مِنَ ٱلْبَطِّ, أَرْبَعَةُ ذُكُورٍ مِنَ ٱلْغَنَمِ.

5) The numerals as abstract numbers are of the masculine gender; as: ٱلثَّلْثَةُ نِصْفُ ٱلسِّتَّةِ, *three is the half of six.*

6) In the enumeration of several groups of objects of different genders, the following rules hold. — *a)* The numerals from 3 to 5, inclusive, must be repeated before each substantive, and vary in gender accordingly; as: لِي خَمْسَةُ أَعْبُدٍ وَخَمْسُ إِمَآءٍ, *I have five male and five female slaves.* *b)* From 6 to 10, inclusive, they are not repeated, and conform in gender to the nearest substantive: as: لِي ثَمَانِيَةُ أَعْبُدٍ وَإِمَآءٍ, *I have eight male and (eight) female slaves,* or, transposing the words, لِي ثَمَانِي إِمَآءٍ وَأَعْبُدٍ.

The Numerals.

c) The compound numerals, from 11 upwards, take the masculine form, when the following substantives designate rational beings; as: عِنْدِى خَمْسَةَ عَشَرَ عَبْدًا وَجَارِيَةً , *I have fifteen male and (fifteen) female slaves*, or, transposing the words, عِنْدِى خَمْسَةَ عَشَرَ جَارِيَةً وَعَبْدًا. But when the substantives designate irrational objects, the numerals take the gender of the nearest substantive; as: عِنْدِى خَمْسَةَ عَشَرَ جَمَلًا وَنَاقَةً, *I have fifteen male and (fifteen) female camels*, or, transposing the words, عِنْدِى خَمْسَ عَشْرَةَ نَاقَةً وَجَمَلًا. If, however, in the case of irrational objects, a vague, general expression, such as مَا بَيْنَ (§. 61), be interposed between the numeral and the things numbered, the numeral is always of the *feminine* gender; as: عِنْدِى خَمْسَ عَشْرَةَ مَا بَيْنَ جَمَلٍ وَنَاقَةٍ, *I possess fifteen camels, male and female*, or, transposing the words, عِنْدِى خَمْسَ عَشْرَةَ مَا بَيْنَ نَاقَةٍ وَجَمَلٍ.

107. The cardinal numbers become determined or definite in the same cases as substantives; viz.

1) When the numeral is used to express an abstract number, and hence contains the idea of genus; e. g. اَلثَّلْثَةُ نِصْفُ ٱلسِّتَّةِ, *three* (every three) *is the half of six* (every six). The article is here employed لِلْجِنْسِ, *to indicate the genus*.

2) When the objects numbered have already been mentioned, or are supposed to be well known; as: فَرَجَعَ ٱلسَّبْعُونَ بِــفَــرَحٍ, *and the seventy* (disciples) *returned with joy*; وَقَدْ جَاوَزْتُ حَدَّ ٱلْأَرْبَعِينَ, *since I am already past forty*, scil. سَنَةً, *years* (observe ٱلْأَرْبَــعِــيــنَ by poetic license for

اَلْأَرْبَعِينَ). The article is here used لِلْعَهْدِ, *to indicate previous knowledge.*

3) When the numeral is in apposition, as an adjective, to a definite noun; as: اَلرِّجَالُ ٱلْخَمْسَةُ, *the five men* (οἱ ἄνδρες οἱ πέντε, see vol. I. §. 321).

4) When the numerals, from 3 to 10, precede a definite noun in the construct state (see §. 92); as ثَلٰثَةُ ٱلرِّجَالِ, *the three men* (lit. *the triad of the men*). Sometimes, however, the numeral too has the article; as: اَلْخَمْسَةُ ٱلْأَثْوَابِ, *the five dresses;* اَلثَّلٰثَةُ ٱلْأَصْوَاتِ ٱلْمُخْتَارَةِ, *the three selected airs or tunes.* — According to the later and now (but without case-endings) usual construction, the article is dropped before the substantive and appears only prefixed to the numeral; as: اَلثَّلٰثَةُ رِجَالٍ, instead of the older اَلثَّلٰثَةُ ٱلرِّجَالِ or ثَلٰثَةُ ٱلرِّجَالِ. — The same remarks apply to مِائَةٌ and اَلْفٌ, with their derivatives and compounds; e. g. ثَلٰثُمِائَةِ ٱلدِّينَارِ, *the 300 dinars*, but also اَلثَّلٰثُمِائَةِ ٱلدِّينَارِ, and in modern Arabic اَلثَّلٰثُمِائَةِ دِينَارٍ. — Those numerals that take the objects numbered in the accusative singular, must have the article prefixed to them to render them definite; as: اَلتِّسْعُونَ رَجُلًا, *the 90 men;* and in the case of a compound of tens and units, the article must be prefixed to both; as: اَلسَّبْعَةُ وَٱلسَّبْعُونَ جَمَلًا, *the 77 camels.* The compound numbers from 11 to 19, however, according to the best grammarians, prefix the article to the unit alone, without

making any change in the termination; as: اَلثَّلَاثَةَ عَشَرَ جَمَلً, *the thirteen camels.*

R e m. The peculiar construction of the numerals in modern Arabic, alluded to above, is analogous to that employed by the same dialect in such compounds as اَلْمَا وَرْد, *rose-water*, instead of the classical مَآءُ ٱلْوَرْدِ, or اَلْحَصَالْبَان, *frankincense in grains*, instead of حَصَا ٱللُّبَانِ.

108. The ordinal numbers are often construed with the genitive, especially of the month (on the omission of the word for *day*, compare §. 101); as: خَامِسَ عَشَرَهُمْ, *the fifteenth of them*; ثُمَّ سَارَ ٱلسُّلْطَانُ إِلَى عَزَازَ وَنَازَلَهَا ثَالِثَ ذِى ٱلْقَعْدَةِ وَتَسَلَّمَهَا حَادِىَ عَشَرَ ذِى ٱلْحِجَّةِ, *next the sultan proceeded to Azāz, and laid siege to it on the third of Dū'l-Ka'da, and took possession of it by capitulation on the eleventh of Dū'l-Ḥiǵǵa*; وَكَانَ ثَامِنَ عِشْرِى تَمُوزَ, *and it was the twentyeighth of Temūz* (in this example ثَامِنَ is in the construct state before عِشْرِى, lit. *the eighth of the twenties*, and so also in the following ones, in which, however, the modern form عِشْرِينُ, gen. عِشْرِينِ, acc. عِشْرِينَ, is used instead of the classical عِشْرُو, gen. and acc. عِشْرِى; just as in the noun we find سِينِى instead of سِينُو and سِينِى, from سِينُونَ, plur. of سَنَةٌ, *a year*, vol. I. §. 302, rem. d); هُوَ حَادِى عِشْرِينَ تِشْرِى, *it is the twenty-first of Tišri*; فِى ثَالِثِ عِشْرِينِهِ نُودِىَ بِٱلْقَاهِرَةِ, *on the twenty-third of this (month) there was a proclamation made in 'l-Ḳāhira.*

109. An ordinal number is not unfrequently connected with the genitive either *a*) of its own cardinal, or *b*) of the cardinal that is one less than its own.

a) In the former case, the ordinal expresses *indefinitely* one of the individuals designated by the cardinal; as: لَقَدْ كَفَرَ ٱلَّذِينَ قَالُوا إِنَّ ٱللَّهَ ثَالِثُ ثَلْثَةٍ, *verily those are unbelievers who say, God is a third of three (is one of three)*; إِذْ أَخْرَجَهُ ٱلَّذِينَ كَفَرُوا ثَانِيَ ٱثْنَيْنِ, *when those, who were unbelievers, drove him forth a second of two (one of two, along with a single companion)*; خَرَجَ زَيْدٌ سَابِعَ سَبْعَةٍ, *Zeid went out a seventh of seven (with six companions)*. With the numerals from 11 to 19, we may either use the whole ordinal number, or suppress the second part of it, in which case the first part becomes declinable: as: ثَانِيَ عَشَرَ ٱثْنَىْ عَشَرَ or ثَانِىَ ٱثْنَىْ عَشَرَ, *a twelfth of twelve*, fem. ثَانِيَةَ ٱثْنَتَىْ عَشْرَةَ or ثَانِيَةَ ٱثْنَتَىْ عَشْرَةَ.

b) In the latter case, the ordinals from third to ninth are in reality nomina agentis (compare §. 86, rem. *a*) from the verbs ثَلَّثَ, *to make (two) into three*, رَبَّعَ, *to make (three) into four*, &c.; as: هُوَ ثَالِثُ ٱثْنَيْنِ, *he makes a third*, lit. *he makes three of two*. Hence they may also be construed with the accusative; as: هُوَ رَابِعٌ ثَلَاثَةً, *he makes a fourth*, fem. هِىَ رَابِعَةٌ ثَلَاثًا. With the numerals from 11 to 19, we may in like manner say: هُوَ ثَالِثَ عَشَرَ ٱثْنَىْ عَشَرَ, *he makes a thirteenth*; هِىَ رَابِعَةَ عَشْرَةَ ثَلَاثَ عَشْرَةَ, *she makes a fourteenth* (where the cardinal number is in the accusative): though many grammarians wholly disapprove of this construction. With the numerals compounded of units and tens, only the unit is put in the construct state, and the ten is suppressed; as: هُوَ رَابِعُ ثُلْثَةٍ وَعِشْرِينَ, *he makes a twentyfourth;* or, with the accusative, هِيَ رَابِعَةٌ ثَلَاثًا وَعِشْرِينَ, *she makes a twentyfourth.*

Rem. From the tens are formed quadriliteral verbs, the nomina agentis of which may be used in the same way as the ordinal numbers under *b*; e. g. هُوَ مُعَشِّرٌ تِسْعَةَ عَشَرَ, *he makes a twentieth* (lit., if we may be allowed to coin a word, *he twenties nineteen),* from عَشْرَنَ, *to make (nineteen) into twenty.*

110. In stating dates, particularly when reckoning according to the Mohammedan era, the cardinal numbers are employed instead of the ordinal. They are put in the genitive after the word denoting *year,* but agree with it in gender; as: فِي سَنَةِ ثَمَانٍ وَثَمَانِينَ وَثَمَانِي مِائَةٍ لِلْإِسْكَنْدَرِ, *in the year* 888 *of the Alexandrine era;* ثُمَّ دَخَلَتْ سَنَةُ سِتٍّ وَتِسْعِينَ وَثَلَثِمِائَةٍ, *then commenced the year* 396 *(of the Hiġra);* تُوُفِّيَ صلعم ضُحًى يَوْمَ الِاثْنَيْنِ لِثِنْتَيْ عَشْرَةَ لَيْلَةً خَلَتْ مِنْ شَهْرِ رَبِيعِ الْأَوَّلِ سَنَةَ إِحْدَى عَشْرَةَ مِنَ الْهِجْرَةِ. *he* (the Prophet) *died early in the forenoon, on Monday the twelfth* (lit. *twelve nights being passed) of the month of the first Rabī', in the eleventh year of the Hiġra.* But if the years of a life or a reign are meant, the ordinal must be employed: as: فِي السَّنَةِ السَّادِسَةِ مِنْ مُلْكِ الْأَشْرَفِ شَعْبَانَ, *in the sixth year of the reign of el-Ašraf*

Part Third. Syntax.

فِي ٱلسَّنَةِ ٱلثَّانِيَةِ وَٱلْأَرْبَعِينَ مِنْ مُلْكِهِ, *in the for-ty-second year of his reign.* Sâbân;

Rem. Compare, for the Hebrew, such constructions as: בִּשְׁנַת שְׁתַּיִם לְאָחָא, 1 Kings, 15, 25; בִּשְׁנַת עֶשְׂרִים וָשֶׁבַע לְאָסָא, do., 16, 10. See Gesenius' Gr. §. 118, 4.

111. The Arabs have two ways of stating the day of the month. They count either from the first day to the last, as we do, e. g. يَوْمَ عِشْرِينَ مِنْ شَهْرِ رَجَبٍ, *on the twentieth of the month of Règeb;* or they reckon by the *nights* of the month, the civil day being held by them, as well as by the Jews, to commence at sunset. To illustrate this, let us take the month of Règeb, which has thirty days.

1st of Règeb . . . لِأَوَّلِ لَيْلَةٍ مِنْ رَجَبٍ, or

لِلَيْلَةٍ خَلَتْ مِنْ رَجَبٍ, *one night of Règeb being past.**)

2nd . . . . . . لِلَيْلَتَيْنِ خَلَتَا مِنْ رَجَبٍ.

3d . . . . . لِثَلَاثٍ (لِثَلْثِ لَيَالٍ) خَلَوْنَ مِنْ رَجَبٍ; and so on up to the

*) We may also say: غُرَّةَ رَجَبٍ or لِغُرَّةِ رَجَبٍ (from غُرَّةٌ, *the blaze on a horse's forehead, the new moon*). The word مُسْتَهَلّ (from هِلَالٌ, *the new moon*) is likewise frequently used to denote the first of the month, and more rarely اِسْتِهْلَالٌ, إِهْلَالٌ, مِلَّةٌ, and هِلٌّ; e. g. كَانَ ٱبْتِدَآءُ ٱلْوَجَعِ فِي مُسْتَهَلِّ رَبِيعٍ ٱلْأَوَّلِ وَتُوُفِّيَ صلعم فِي ٱلثَّانِي عَشَرَ مِنْهُ, *the disease began on the first of the first Rabî', and he (the Prophet) died on the twelfth of that month.*

The Numerals.

10th . . . . لِعَشْرٍ خَلَوْنَ مِنْ رَجَبٍ.

11th . . . . لِإِحْدَى عَشْرَةَ (لَيْلَةً) خَلَتْ مِنْ رَجَبٍ;
and so on up to the

14th . . . . لِأَرْبَعَ عَشْرَةَ خَلَتْ مِنْ رَجَبٍ.

15th . . . . فِى مُنْتَصَفِ رَجَبٍ or فِى ٱلنِّصْفِ مِنْ رَجَبٍ,
in the middle of Reǵeb.

16th . . لِأَرْبَعَ عَشْرَةَ (لَيْلَةً) بَقِيَتْ مِنْ رَجَبٍ,
fourteen nights remaining of Re-
ǵeb; and so on up to the

20th . . . . لِعَشْرٍ (لِعَشْرِ لَيَالٍ) بَقِينَ مِنْ رَجَبٍ;
and so on up to the

27th . . . . لِثَلَاثٍ بَقِينَ مِنْ رَجَبٍ.

28th . . . . لِلَيْلَتَيْنِ بَقِيَتَا مِنْ رَجَبٍ.

29th . . . . لِلَيْلَةٍ بَقِيَتْ مِنْ رَجَبٍ.

30th . . . لِآخِرِ لَيْلَةٍ مِنْ رَجَبٍ, on the last
night of Reǵeb.*)

Or سَرَارُ or لِيَنْسَلِخُ رَجَبٍ or لِيَسْلَخِ رَجَبٍ. The words
سَرَرُ, سِرَارُ, and more rarely سِرَرُ, are also employed to denote the last
day of the month.

II. The Sentence and its Parts.

A. The Sentence in General.

1. The Parts of the Sentence: the Subject, the Predicate, and their Complements.

112. Every sentence (جُمْلَةٌ, plur. جُمَلٌ, *a sum or total* of words) consists necessarily of two parts, a *subject* and a *predicate*. The latter is called by the native grammarians اَلْمُسْنَدُ, *that which leans upon* or *is supported by (the subject), the attribute;* whilst the former is called اَلْمُسْنَدُ إِلَيْهِ, *that upon which (the predicate) leans or by which it is supported, that to which something is attributed*. The relation between them is known as اَلْإِسْنَادُ, properly *the act of leaning (one thing against another)*, then, as a concrete, *the relation of attribution*.

113. The subject is either a *noun* (substantive or expressed pronoun), or a *pronoun implied in the verb;* the predicate is either a *noun* (substantive or adjective) or a *verb;* e. g. زَيْدٌ عَالِمٌ, *Zeïd is learned;* أَنْتَ شَرِيفٌ, *thou art noble;* اَللّٰهُ هُوَ ٱلْحَقُّ, *God is the truth;* مَاتَ زَيْدٌ, *Zeïd is dead;* مَاتَ, *he is dead* (in which last example the pronoun هُوَ is implied in the verb). — Every sentence that begins with the subject (substantive or pronoun) is called by the Arab grammarians جُمْلَةٌ ٱسْمِيَّةٌ, *a nominal sentence*.

Whether the following predicate be a noun, or a preposition and the word it governs (جَارٌ وَمَجْرُورٌ, *the attracting and the attracted*, §. 115 and vol. I. §. 355), or a verb, is a matter of indifference; زَيْدٌ مَاتَ, *Zeid is dead*, is in their eyes a nominal sentence just as much as زَيْدٌ عَالِمٌ, *Zeid is learned*, or زَيْدٌ فِي ٱلْمَسْجِدِ, *Zeid is in the mosque*. What characterises a nominal sentence, according to them, is the absence of a logical copula expressed by or contained in a finite verb. On the contrary, a sentence of which the predicate is a verb preceding the subject (as مَاتَ زَيْدٌ, *Zeid is dead*), or a sentence consisting of a verb that includes both subject and predicate (as مَاتَ, *he is dead*), is called by them جُمْلَةٌ فِعْلِيَّةٌ, *a verbal sentence*. The subject of a nominal sentence is called ٱلْمُبْتَدَأ, *that with which a beginning is made*, *the inchoative*, and its predicate ٱلْخَبَر, *the enunciative* or *announcement*. The subject of a verbal sentence is called ٱلْفَاعِل, *the agent*, and its predicate ٱلْفِعْل, *the action* or *verb*.

114. The place of the subject both of a nominal and of a verbal sentence may sometimes be supplied by an entire sentence compounded of a verb and one of the particles مَا and أَنْ (called ٱلْحُرُوفُ ٱلْمَصْدَرِيَّةُ, *the particles that supply the place of the masdar* or *nomen verbi*, vol. I. §. 195, rem.); as: أَنْ تَصُومُوا خَيْرٌ لَكُمْ, *it is good for you that you should fast* or *to fast* (صَوْمُكُمْ = أَنْ تَصُومُوا); أَعْجَبَنِي أَنْ خَرَجْتَ, *it pleased me that you went out* or

your going out pleased me (خُرُوجُكَ = أَنْ خَرَجْتَ); وَدُّوا
(عَنَتَكُمْ = مَا عَنِتُّمْ), *they desire your destruction* (مَا عَنِتُّمْ).
Compare §§. 78 and 88.

115. The predicate may be, as mentioned in §. 113, a preposition with its genitive; as: زَيْدٌ فِي ٱلْمَسْجِدِ, *Zeid is in the mosque;* زَيْدٌ عِنْدَكَ, *Zeid is with you or in your house;* نَحْنُ لِلّٰهِ, *we are God's;* أَنَا مِنَ ٱلصَّادِقِينَ, *I am one of those who speak the truth;* عَلَىَّ دَيْنٌ, *I owe some money* (lit. *upon me there is a debt*, see §. 62, 3); لَكَ أَنْ تَفْعَلَهُ, *you may do it* (lit. *it is to thee that thou do it*). When the subject is placed first, these are nominal sentences (§. 113); but when the predicate precedes it, their nature is doubtful, some grammarians holding them to be transposed nominal sentences (in which case عَلَىَّ in عَلَىَّ دَيْنٌ is a خَبَرٌ مُقَدَّمٌ, or *predicate placed in front*, and دَيْنٌ a مُبْتَدَأٌ مُؤَخَّرٌ, or *subject placed behind*), whilst others regard them as being in reality verbal sentences, with the verb suppressed (so that, according to them, عَلَىَّ is equivalent to يَسْتَقِرُّ عَلَىَّ, *there rests upon me*, and دَيْنٌ is the فَاعِلٌ or subject of this suppressed verb). A sentence, of which the predicate is a preposition with a genitive indicating a *place*, is called by the Arabs جُمْلَةٌ ظَرْفِيَّةٌ, *a local sentence* (see vol. I. §. 221, rem. *a*); and if the genitive indicates any other relation but that of place, it is said to be جُمْلَةٌ جَارِيَةٌ مَجْرَى ٱلظَّرْفِيَّةِ, *a sentence that runs the course, or follows the analogy, of a local sentence.* As,

however, the expression ظَرْفٌ is often used in the general sense of جَارٌّ وَمَجْرُورٌ (§. 113), any sentence commencing with a preposition and its genitive as the predicate may be called جُمْلَةٌ ظَرْفِيَّةٌ (see §. 127).

116. When the predicate is a preposition with its genitive, and the subject a sentence compounded of أَنْ and a finite verb (§. 114), the predicate must necessarily be put first; as: لَكَ أَنْ تَفْعَلَهُ, *you may do it*, and not أَنْ تَفْعَلَهُ لَكَ.

117. If a nominal sentence be preceded by an interrogative or negative particle, the predicate is placed before the subject when it agrees with it in number; as: أَقِيَامٌ ٱلرِّجَالُ, *are those men standing?* مَا قَائِمَانِ ٱلرَّجُلَانِ, *those two men are not standing.*

118. In verbal sentences the subject or agent must always follow the predicate or verb; as: مَاتَ عُمَرُ, *'Omar is dead;* مَاتَ عُمَرَ أَبُوهُ, *'Omar's father* (lit. *'Omar, his father*) *is dead* (see §. 120).

119. When the noun (substantive or pronoun) stands first, and the verb second, the former is not a فَاعِلٌ or agent, but a مُبْتَدَأٌ or inchoative, of which the latter is the خَبَرٌ or enunciative, the whole being not a verbal but a nominal sentence (see §. 113). A sentence of this kind, consisting of an inchoative and a complete verbal sentence, the agent of which is contained in the verb itself (§. 113), may be called *compound* (see §. 120, rem.); e. g.

23*

أَنَا قُلْتُ, *I have said*, = هُوَ مَاتَ زَيْدٌ; زَيْدٌ مَاتَ, *Zeid is dead*, where the agent is تُ in قُلْتُ. In such sentences, the pronoun that is contained in the verb takes the place of, and falls back upon, the noun that stands before the compound verbal sentence and constitutes its inchoative. — The difference between a compound nominal sentence, such as زَيْدٌ مَاتَ, and a verbal one, such as مَاتَ زَيْدٌ, is this. In the former, the inchoative is always (tacitly or expressly) contrasted with another inchoative, having not the same predicate but a different or even an opposite one; e. g. زَيْدٌ مَاتَ وَعُمَرُ حَىٌّ, *Zeid is dead and 'Omar is alive*, أَمَّا زَيْدٌ فَمَاتَ وَأَمَّا عُمَرُ فَحَىٌّ; whereas in the latter, in which the logical emphasis rests almost solely upon the verb, such a contrast of two inchoatives is not admissible. Even when the verb is cast into the background by the emphasis falling with specialising or contrasting force upon some one of its complements, the very fact of the emphasis so falling at once sets aside all question of a contrast of the inchoatives; as, for example: إِيَّاكَ نَعْبُدُ وَإِيَّاكَ نَسْتَعِينُ, *thee we worship and to thee we cry for help*; ضَرَبَ زَيْدٌ رَجُلًا وَاحِدًا وَضَرَبَ عُمَرُ رَجُلَيْنِ اثْنَيْنِ, *Zeid struck one man, and 'Omar struck two men.*

120. Those sentences are also compound, which are made up of a noun and a nominal sentence or a verbal sentence, consisting of a verb and a following noun. For example: زَيْدٌ ابْنُهُ حَسَنٌ, *Zeid's son* (lit. *Zeid, his son*) *is handsome;* زَيْدٌ مَاتَ أَبُوهُ, *Zeid's father is dead;* زَيْدٌ

, زَيْدٌ جِىءَ إِلَيْهِ بِكِتَابٍ ,Zèid's brother has been killed; قُتِلَ أَخُوهُ
a letter has been brought to Zèid (lit. Zèid, there has been a coming to him with a letter). In compound sentences of this sort, there is appended to the subject of the nominal or verbal sentence that occupies the place of the خَبَر, a pronominal suffix, which represents, and falls back upon, the noun forming the مُبْتَدَأ. Any such sentence is said by the grammarians to be جُمْلَةٌ ذَاتُ وَجْهَيْنِ, *a sentence with two faces* or *aspects*, because, as a whole, it partakes both of the nominal and the verbal nature.

121. If a sentence consists of a verbal adjective, occupying the first place, and a noun, occupying the second, then the sentence is regarded as a verbal one, the verbal adjective being looked upon as a verb and the noun as its agent; e. g. زَيْدٌ ضَارِبٌ غُلَامُهُ عُمَرَ, *Zèid's slave is beating 'Omar*; جَاءَنِى زَيْدٌ ٱلْحَسَنُ غُلَامُهُ, *the Zèid, whose slave is handsome, came to me.* — The same is necessarily the case, when the verbal adjective is preceded by an interrogative or negative particle, and does *not* agree with the following noun in number; as: أَقَائِمٌ ٱلرِّجَالُ, *are those men standing?* مَا قَائِمٌ ٱلرَّجُلَانِ, *those two men are not standing.* But if the verbal adjective agrees in number with the noun, the sentence may be regarded as either nominal or verbal; for examples see §. 117, where it is also stated that, when a nominal sentence begins with an interrogative or negative particle, and the predicate agrees with the subject in number, the former must be placed first.

122. The Arabic language, like the Hebrew and Syriac, has no *abstract* or *substantive verb* to unite the predicate to the subject of a nominal sentence, for كانَ is not an abstract verb, but, like all other verbs, an attributive, ascribing to the subject the attribute of existence. Consequently its predicate is put, not in the nominative, but in the adverbial accusative (§. 41). The same remark naturally applies to the أَخَوَاتُ كانَ (§. 42).

123. If a definite noun (substantive or pronoun) and an indefinite adjective are placed in juxtaposition, the very fact of the former being defined (no matter in what way) and the latter undefined, shows that the latter is the predicate of the former, and that the two together form a complete nominal sentence; for an adjective which is appended to a noun as a mere descriptive epithet, and forms along with it only one part (either subject or predicate) of a sentence, must be defined according to the nature of the noun. For example: يُوسُفُ مَرِيضٌ, *Joseph (is) sick;* ٱلسُّلْطَانُ مَرِيضٌ, *the sultan (is) sick;* أَبُو يُوسُفَ مَرِيضٌ, *Joseph's father (is) sick;* أَبِي مَرِيضٌ, *my father (is) sick;* هُوَ مَرِيضٌ, *he (is) sick;* هٰذَا مَرِيضٌ, *this man (is) sick;* whereas هٰذَا ٱلْمَرِيضُ would mean either *this (is) the sick man* or *this sick man,* and ٱلسُّلْطَانُ ٱلْمَرِيضُ, *the sick sultan.*

124. When both subject and predicate are defined, the pronoun of the third person is frequently inserted between them (see §. 129), to prevent any possibility of the predicate being regarded as a mere apposition. This is done

even when the subject is a pronoun of the first or second person. For example: اَللّٰهُ هُوَ ٱلْحَىُّ ٱلْقَيُّومُ, *God is the living, the self-subsisting*; اَللّٰهُ هُوَ ٱلْحَيٰوةُ وَٱلْحَقُّ, *God is the life and the truth;* ٱلْغِنٰى هُوَ ٱلْقُنُوعُ, *the (only true) wealth is contentment;* أُولٰئِكَ هُمْ وَقُودُ ٱلنَّارِ, *these are fuel for the fire;* ذٰلِكَ هُوَ ٱلرَّجُلُ, *that man is I;* أَنَا هُوَ ٱلرَّبُّ إِلٰهُكَ, *I am the Lord thy God;* أَنَا هُوَ ٱلطَّرِيقُ وَٱلْحَقُّ وَٱلْحَيٰوةُ, *I am the way and the truth and the life;* مَنْ هُوَ أَنَا, *who am I?* This interposed pronoun is called by the grammarians ضَمِيرُ ٱلْفَصْلِ, *the pronoun of separation*. It is equally common in the other Shemitic languages; see, for example, Gesenius' Heb. Gr. §. 119, 2.

125. In the case of a definite subject in the accusative after إِنَّ, أَنَّ, &c. (§. 36), the ضَمِيرُ ٱلْفَصْلِ is not required, because the predicate is sufficiently marked as such by its remaining in the nominative; as: إِنَّ ٱللّٰهَ ثَالِثُ ثَلٰثَةٍ, *verily God is one of three;* whereas a mere adjective would be in the same case as the subject, viz. the accusative. A pronoun may, however, be inserted, provided it be of the same person as the substantive or pronoun after إِنَّ, &c.; as: إِنَّ ٱلْآخِرَةَ هِىَ دَارُ ٱلْقَرَارِ, *the world to come is the everlasting abode;* إِنَّكَ أَنْتَ ٱلْوَهَّابُ, *thou art the bountiful giver;* إِنِّى أَنَا رَبُّكَ, *I am thy Lord*. Very often the predicate after إِنَّ, &c., is introduced, for the sake of greater distinctness, by the particle لَ (§. 36); as: إِنَّ ٱللّٰهَ لَذُو فَضْلٍ عَلَى ٱلنَّاسِ, *verily God is good towards men;* and

even here the pronoun may be introduced after لَ; as: إِنَّ ٱللَّهَ لَهُوَ ٱلْعَزِيزُ ٱلْحَكِيمُ, *verily God is the mighty, the wise.*

Rem. The noun governed by إِنَّ, &c., is not regarded by the Arab grammarians as a مُبْتَدَأٌ, but as the اِسْمُ إِنَّ, *the noun of 'inna*, &c. See §. 36, rem. *a*.

126. When both the subject and the predicate of a nominal sentence are indefinite, but the former consists of several words, no doubt can arise as to whether they form a complete sentence or only a part of one, because the subject, being cut off by the words annexed to it, cannot possibly form any one portion of a sentence (subject or predicate) in connexion with the noun that is separated from it by these words. For example: قَوْلٌ مَعْرُوفٌ وَمَغْفِرَةٌ خَيْرٌ مِنْ صَدَقَةٍ يَتْبَعُهَا أَذًى, *kind words and forgiveness are better than alms followed by injury;* أَمَةٌ مُؤْمِنَةٌ خَيْرٌ مِنْ مُشْرِكَةٍ وَلَوْ أَعْجَبَتْكُمْ, *a female slave that believes is better than an idolatress, even when she* (the latter) *pleases you* (more).

127. The inchoative or subject of a nominal sentence cannot, according to the Arab grammarians, consist of an indefinite noun*), or one that is not qualified by an adjective

---

*) *Indefinite* is here to be taken in the sense of *not having a genitive after it*, for such a phrase as عَمَلُ بِرٍّ يَزِينُ, *a pious action or good work adorns (a man)*, is quite admissible, and yet the governing noun is indefinite, according to §. 92. The inchoative may, however, be an indefinite or an expression equivalent to an adjective (as: رَجُلٌ مِنَ ٱلْكِرَامِ عِنْدَنَا, *there is a man of the noble with us* = رَجُلٌ كَرِيمٌ, *a noble man*), except in certain cases, of which the following are the most important.

1) When the sentence is of the class called ٱلظَّرْفِيَّةُ (taking this term in its widest sense, §. 115 at the end), and *a*) the predicate is placed first, as: عِنْدَ زَيْدٍ نَمِرَةٌ, *there is a leopard in Zèid's possession;* or *b*) the subject is preceded by an interrogative or negative particle, as: هَلْ إِنْسَانٌ فِي ٱلدَّارِ, *is there any person in the house?* هَلْ فَتًى فِيكُمْ, *is there a man among you?* مَا أَحَدٌ فِي ٱلدَّارِ, *there is no one in the house;* مَا خِلٌّ لَنَا, *we have no friend*.

2) When the subject is preceded by the affirmative لَ; as: لَرَجُلٌ قَائِمٌ, *certainly there is a man standing*.

3) When the subject is a diminutive, because the substantive then includes the idea of the adjective صَغِيرٌ, *small*, or حَقِيرٌ, *contemptible;* as: رُجَيْلٌ عِنْدَنَا, *there is a little man (or a mean fellow) at our house*.

4) When the subject is a noun of a general signification, such as كُلٌّ, *all;* e. g. كُلُّ فَانٍ, كُلٌّ يَمُوتُ, *all perish;* verbal noun, provided that it retains the government of the verb from which it is derived; e. g. رَغْبَةٌ فِي ٱلْخَيْرِ خَيْرٌ, *a desire to do good is a good thing*. In both these cases, however, there is evidently a sort of partial determination.

all die; because كُلّ is here equivalent to كُلُّ ٱلنَّاسِ, *all mankind,* and therefore virtually definite (see §. 82, 1).

5) When the sentence expresses a wish or prayer; as: سَلَامٌ عَلَيْكُمْ, *peace be upon you!*

6) When the subject is a word that contains the conditional meaning of the particle إِنْ, *if,* such as مَنْ (§. 6); e. g. مَنْ يَقُمْ أَقُمْ, *if any one gets up, I will get up.*

7) When the subject is preceded by the وَاوُ ٱلْحَالِ or *wāw* that introduces a circumstantial clause (§. 183), or by the conjunction لَوْلَا, *if not;* as: سَرَيْنَا وَنَجْمٌ قَدْ أَضَاءَ وَمُذْ بَدَا مُحَيَّاكَ أَخْفَى ضَوْءَهُ كُلُّ شَارِقٍ, *we travelled by night, after a star had already shone out, but from the moment thy face appeared, its light obscured every shining star,* لَوْلَا ٱصْطِبَارٌ لَأَرْدَى كُلَّ ذِى مِقَةٍ (شَارِقِ in rhyme for شَارِقٍ) *were it not for patience, every lover would die.*

In all these different sorts of sentences, there can be no doubt that the words form a complete sentence, and not merely a part of one.

Rem. European grammarians have mostly erred in their analysis of the phrase بَلْ سَوَّلَتْ - فَصَبْرٌ جَمِيلٌ in the Ḳor'ān, ch. 12, v. 18, لَكُمْ أَنْفُسُكُمْ أَمْرًا فَصَبْرٌ جَمِيلٌ. This they translate either: *nay, your minds have made a thing seem pleasant unto you (and ye have done it), but patience is becoming* (Lane); or: *mais la patience vaut mieux* (Kasimirski); or: *ergo pati (patientem esse) pulchrum est* (Ewald); according to which translation صَبْرٌ would be an indefinite مُبْتَدَأٌ and جَمِيلٌ its خَبَرٌ. Still worse is it to regard the words as an exhortation: *therefore—becoming patience! (also—geziemende Geduld!* Caspari), which would necessarily be فَصَبْرًا جَمِيلًا (§. 35). The Arab commentators are right in regarding the words either as a compound خَبَرٌ, i. e. فَأَمْرِى صَبْرٌ جَمِيلٌ, *and therefore my business (or duty) is (to show) becoming patience;* or as a compound مُبْتَدَأٌ, i. e. أَمْثَلُ أَجْمَلُ, فَصَبْرٌ جَمِيلٌ أَجْمَلُ, *and therefore (to show) becoming patience is more seemly.* The former of these two views seems to be the preferable one.

128. When both subject and predicate are definite, but the former consists of several words, it is also clear, without the insertion of the ضَمِيرُ ٱلْفَصْلِ, that the words form a complete sentence; as: ٱلدِّينُ عِنْدَ ٱللّٰهِ ٱلْإِسْلَامُ, *the (only true) religion in God's eyes is el-'islām;* مَثَلُ ٱلَّذِينَ يُنْفِقُونَ أَمْوَالَهُمْ فِى سَبِيلِ ٱللّٰهِ كَمَثَلِ حَبَّةٍ أَنْبَتَتْ سَبْعَ سَنَابِلَ, *those who expend their wealth in the path (or cause) of God, are like a grain of corn that produces seven ears.*

129. The ضَمِيرُ ٱلْفَصْلِ is also not rarely omitted in sentences in which both subject and predicate are definite, but the former consists of only one word; as: مُحَمَّدٌ رَسُولُ ٱللّٰهِ, *Mohammed is the apostle of God;* عَلِىٌّ وَلِىُّ ٱللّٰهِ, *'Alī is the friend of God;* ذٰلِكَ ٱلْفَوْزُ ٱلْعَظِيمُ, *this is the great felicity* (el-Ḳor'ān, ch. 9, v. 90, but in v. 73 we read ذٰلِكَ هُوَ ٱلْفَوْزُ ٱلْعَظِيمُ). Here a doubt might at first arise, whether these words form a complete sentence, or merely the compound subject of one; in which case we must only examine whether the words

that follow can be taken as their predicate, without doing violence to sense and grammar, or not.

130. From the ضَمِيرُ ٱلْفَصْلِ, or *pronoun of separation*, must be carefully distinguished the pronoun which is appended to the subject to give it emphasis and contrast it with another subject (ضَمِيرُ ٱلتَّأْكِيدِ أَوِ ٱلتَّوْكِيدِ); as: كَانَ ٱلْمُسْلِمُونَ هُمْ ٱلْجُنْدَ, *this was the reason*; هٰذَا هُوَ ٱلسَّبَبُ, *the Muslims* (and not slaves or mercenaries) *formed the army*. — This pronoun is also frequently appended to a pronominal suffix in any case, to give it emphasis; as: كَانَ رَأْيُهُ هُوَ أَلَّا يَتَنَاوَلَ أَحَدٌ, *you stood up*; قُمْتَ أَنْتَ شَيْئًا, *his opinion was that no one should take anything*: فَأَيْنَ نَصِيبِى أَنَا مِنْ هٰذَا ٱلنَّفَلِ, *where then is my share of this booty?* لِمَنْ هٰذَا ٱلْكِتَابُ لَنَا نَحْنُ, *whose is this book? Ours*; مَا مَنَعَكُمَا أَنْتُمَا مِنْ ذٰلِكَ, *what has prevented you two from doing that?* إِنْ تَرَنِي أَنَا أَقَلَّ مِنْكَ مَالًا وَوَلَدًا, *if you think that I have less wealth and (fewer) children than you*; and more rarely to a noun in the accusative; as: وَجَعَلْنَا ذُرِّيَّتَهُ هُمُ ٱلْبَاقِينَ, *and we made his offspring the survivors*.

Rem. The same usage is found in the other Shemitic languages. See, for example, Gesenius' Heb. Gr. §. 119, 3.

131. If, however, in a nominal sentence, a more precise indication of time and mood be necessary, the Arabs use for this purpose كَانَ or one of its "sisters" (§. 41, 42). The imperfect, يَكُونُ, has in this case the usual meanings

of the imperfect (§. 8); whilst the perfect, كَانَ, admits of four significations; viz. *a)* of the *historical tense* or Greek aorist (§. 1, *a*), in which case it has, according to the Arab grammarians, the sense of صَارَ, *to become; b)* of the actual *perfect* (§. 1, *b*); *c)* of the actual *imperfect*, as it were a shortening of كَانَ يَكُونُ, which also occasionally occurs; and *d)* sometimes, especially in the Ḳor'ân, of the *present*, but only by giving a peculiar turn to its use as a perfect (has become by nature, πέφυκα), as: إِنَّ ٱللَّهَ كَانَ عَلَيْكُمْ رَقِيبًا, *God is watching you* (ch. 4, v. 1). The perfect كَانَ expresses the *present* in particular after the negative particle مَا, and the interrogative particles, such as أَ; e. g. مَا كَانَ حَدِيثًا يُفْتَرَى وَلَٰكِنْ تَصْدِيقَ ٱلَّذِي بَيْنَ يَدَيْهِ, *it* (the Ḳor'ân) *is not a discourse invented* (by Mohammed), *but a confirmation of what* (i. e. *of the sacred writings which) preceded it*: مَا كَانَ لَهُمْ أَنْ يَدْخُلُوهَا إِلَّا خَائِفِينَ, *they cannot enter them* (lit. *it is not to them that they should enter them*) *but with fear*; مَا كَانَ لِنَفْسٍ أَنْ تُؤْمِنَ إِلَّا بِإِذْنِ ٱللَّهِ, *no soul can believe except by the permission of God*; مَا كَانَ هُوَ لِيَضُرَّنَا, *he is not* (the man) *to do us any harm*; مَا كَانَ ٱللَّهُ لِيُضِيعَ إِيمَانَكُمْ, *God is incapable of letting —* lit. *is not* (the one) *to let —* your *belief perish* (i. e. *go without a reward*): أَكَانَ لِلنَّاسِ عَجَبًا أَنْ أَوْحَيْنَا إِلَى رَجُلٍ مِنْهُمْ, *is it a wonder to men that we have made a revelation to one of them?*

132. The subject of a sentence is frequently not specified, either because we do not know it, or do not choose to

mention it. We have, however, the option of expressing ourselves *personally*, by such forms as *one says*, *they say*, *people say*, Germ. *man sagt*, Fr. *on dit*; or *impersonally*, either by means of the passive voice, as *it is said*, Germ. *es wird gesagt*, or the active voice, as *it rains*, Germ. *es regnet*, Fr. *il pleut*. The Arabs too express themselves in both ways (with the restriction stated in §. 133, rem. *b*). If they wish to use the *personal* form, they employ *a*) the third person sing. masc. of the verb along with its own nomen agentis, defined or undefined by the article; as: قَالَ قَآئِلٌ, *one has said*, قَالَ ٱلْقَآئِلُ, *id.* (lit. *he who*, or *every one who*, *was in a position to say*, *has said*); يَقُولُ ٱلْقَآئِلُ, *one says*, *is wont to say* (lit. *every one who is in*, or *gets into*, *a position to say*, *says*). The determination of the singular subject by the article expresses in such cases a distributive totality. *b*) If the undefined subject is one of a number of persons who are known to us, the suffix pronoun of the third person plural is annexed to the nomen agentis to indicate these persons; as: قَالَ قَآئِلُهُمْ, *one of them said*. *c*) If there be several indefinite subjects, the third person plur. masc. of the verb may be used, as: قَالُوا, *they say;* زَعَمُوا, *they think;* but it is more usual to employ the verb in the singular and its nomen agentis, defined or undefined by the article, in the plural; as: مَا سَمِعَ ٱلسَّامِعُونَ قَطُّ شَيْئًا أَحْسَنَ مِنْ ذٰلِكَ, قَالَ قَآئِلُونَ, *some said; no one has ever heard anything more beautiful than this* (lit. *those who can hear have never heard &c.*).

Rem. *a*. Instead of the nomen agentis, defined or undefined,

The Sentence and its Parts. 191

such words as رَجُلٌ, *man*, اِمْرَأَةٌ, *woman*, and the like, are occasionally used with or without the article; as: قَالَ قَائِلٌ = قَالَ رَجُلٌ; يَقُولُ ٱلْقَائِلُ = يَقُولُ ٱلرَّجُلُ; &c. For the nomen agentis with the plural suffix, the word بَعْضٌ, *a part, some one*, is often employed; as: قَالَ قَائِلُهُمْ = قَالَ بَعْضُهُمْ.

Rem. *b*. On the corresponding Hebrew constructions, see Gesenius' Gr. §. 134, 3, along with rem. 1. With rem. *a* compare, in particular, 1. Sam. 9, 9. לִפְנֵי בְיִשְׂרָאֵל כֹּה־אָמַר הָאִישׁ בְּלֶכְתּוֹ לִדְרוֹשׁ אֱלֹהִים.

133. If the *impersonal* form of expression is to be employed, the Arabs use the third person sing. masc. of the passive voice, whether of a transitive or of an intransitive verb; as: كُتِبَ, *it has been written, it is written*; سِيرَ, *there was a travelling, they travelled*; اُخْتُلِفَ, *it has been disputed, there has been a dispute*; ظُمِئَ, *there is thirst felt, they thirst*; أُنْزِلَ عَلَيْهِمْ, *a revelation was made to them*; غُشِيَ عَلَيْهِ, *he fainted* (lit. *there was a covering thrown over him*; comp. הֻגַּד), whence ٱلْمَغْشِيُّ عَلَيْهِ, *the person in a faint*, fem. ٱلْمَغْشِيُّ عَلَيْهَا (in later times incorrectly ٱلْمَغْشِيَّةُ عَلَيْهَا, and, without the preposition, ٱلْمَغْشِيُّ, fem. ٱلْمَغْشِيَّةُ). Verbs thus used are always of the *masculine* gender, which the Arabs frequently employ where we should use the neuter (see Gesenius' Heb. Gr. §. 134, 2). The neuter plural of adjectives and nomina agentis and patientis is, however, always expressed by the feminine plur. san. or the plur. fract. (see Gesenius' Heb. Gr. §. 105, 3, *b*) as: ٱلْحَسَنَاتُ, *beau-*

tiful things (not اَلْحِسَانُ, which means *handsome persons*); اَلطَّيِّبَاتُ, *good things* (not اَلطَّيِّبُونَ, which means *good men*); اَلْمَوْجُودَاتُ, *existing things*; اَلْوَاجِبَاتُ, *necessary things*; اَلْمُمْكِنَاتُ, *possible things*; اَلشَّدَآئِدُ, *difficult things, calamities*; اَلْبَوَاعِثُ, *exciting causes* (from بَاعِثٌ); اَلْمَوَانِعُ, *hindrances* (from مَانِعٌ).

Rem. *a*. The passive of directly transitive verbs may be used either personally or impersonally; as: كُتِبَ, *it (a book or letter) was written*, and *the act of writing was performed*. In the former case, the direct object or accusative of the active voice becomes the subject of the passive (قَآئِمٌ مَقَامَ ٱلْفَاعِلِ); in the latter, according to the Arab grammarians, the subject is the nomen actionis of the verb itself, as اُخْتُلِفَ, *there is a dispute*, = اُخْتُلِفَ ٱخْتِلَافٌ, *a disputing is disputed*; so that, according to their view, the impersonal passive becomes really personal. If a passive that is, according to our ideas, impersonal, governs an object by means of a preposition (as غُشِيَ عَلَيْهِ), this object becomes virtually the subject of the passive voice, just as it was virtually the object of the active, and consequently if the nomen actionis be expressed along with it, it must be put in the accusative; as: سِيرَ إِلَيْهِ سَيْرًا (not سَيْرٌ), from the active سَارَ إِلَيْهِ سَيْرًا, *he journeyed to him (a journeying)*. In either case, — whether the passive be personal or impersonal, — it is مَا لَمْ يُسَمَّ فَاعِلُهُ, *a verb of which the agent*, i. e. the acting person, *is not named*, not even by means of a preposition, as with us (for the subject of the passive voice is, as we have said above, merely the اَلْمَفْعُولُ بِهِ,

or object of the active voice,*) converted into the subject, and so نَائِبٌ مَنَابَ ٱلْفَاعِلِ or قَائِمٌ مَقَامَ ٱلْفَاعِلِ, *supplying the place of the agent*). If the agent is to be named, the active voice must be used. — Since the Arab uses many verbs as directly transitive, which in our idiom are only indirectly so, their passives may of course be employed in both of the above ways; e. g. جِيَ means not only *ventum est* (impers.), but also *ventum est ad eum* (pers.). In the former case, only the third person sing.' masc. is used, جِيَ بِشَيْءٍ, *a thing was brought*, imperf. يُجَاءُ; in the latter, all the numbers and persons are employed, sing. 3. p. m. جِيَ, f. جِيئَتْ, 2. p. m. جِئْتَ, &c., as جِيَ بِشَيْءٍ, *a thing was brought to him* (act. جَاءَ بِشَيْءٍ, *he brought him something*).

Rem. *b*. Our impersonal actives indicating natural phenomena, such as *it snows, it rains*, &c., are always expressed by the Arabs personally. They say either ثَلَجَ ٱلثَّلْجُ, *the snow snows*, مَطَرَ ٱلْمَطَرُ, *the rain rains*, or ثَلَجَتِ ٱلسَّمَاءُ, *the sky snows*, مَطَرَتِ ٱلسَّمَاءُ, *the sky rains*. In the latter of these two forms of expression the substantive ٱلسَّمَاءُ is sometimes suppressed, leaving only the verb in the third person sing. fem., مَطَرَتْ, ثَلَجَتْ.

Rem. *c*. In the case of words like يَجُوزُ, *it is allowed*, يَجِبُ, *it is necessary*, &c., followed by أَنْ with the subjunctive, the subject naturally is the following clause, and therefore the verb does not come under the head of impersonal.

*) The ٱلْمَفْعُولُ بِهِ, or *object*, may be either صَرِيحٌ, *pure*, i. e. the accusative, or غَيْرُ صَرِيحٍ, *impure*, i. e. a preposition with the genitive (جَارٌّ وَمَجْرُورٌ).

134. The complements of the subject and predicate are annexed to them either by *subordination* (the accusative or a preposition with the genitive) or *coordination* (apposition).

135. When the pronominal suffixes are attached to a substantive in the accusative, governed by a verb, or to one in the genitive, governed by a preposition annexed to a verb, they may refer to the agent of the verb, and consequently have a *reflexive* meaning, for which the Arabic, as well as the other Shemitic languages, has no distinct pronominal form; as: أَنْفَقَ مَالَهُ, *he has spent his (own) fortune;* قَالُوا لِإِخْوَانِهِمْ, *they said to their (own) brothers.* But a suffix attached to the verb itself, or to the preposition annexed to the verb, cannot have a reflexive meaning; to give it such, the word نَفْسٌ, *soul,* or عَيْنٌ, *eye, essence,* (and in later Arabic رُوحٌ, *spirit,* ذَاتٌ, *substance, essence,* or حَالٌ, *state,*) must be interposed; as: قَتَلَ نَفْسَهُ, *he killed himself;* عَزِّ بِهِ نَفْسَكَ, *console thyself therewith;* أَهْلَكْتُ رُوحِي, *I have destroyed myself;* except in the case of the *verba cordis* (§. 24), when the pronominal suffix is the first object and the second object is either a noun or a whole sentence; as: خَالَهُ مُصَابًا, *he imagined himself struck;* رَآهُ يَعْصِرُ خَمْرًا, *he saw himself* (in a dream, it appeared to him as if he were) *pressing out wine.*

Rem. Compare the use, in Heb. and Aram., of נֶפֶשׁ, נַפְשָׁא; in post-biblical Hebrew, of עֶצֶם or גֶּרֶם, *bone,* and גּוּף, *body;* and in Ethiopic, of ርእስ: (reʾes) *head.*

136. The complements that are coordinated with, or

placed in apposition to, the subject or predicate, are called by the Arab grammarians اَلتَّوَابِعُ, *sequentia*, *followers* or *appositives* (sing. تَابِعٌ), and the word to which they are placed in apposition is called اَلْمَتْبُوعُ, *that which is followed* (by some word in apposition). They are generally connected with a noun, more rarely with a verb. — With the noun is thus united the *adjective*, which, like all other words in apposition, follows the noun, and agrees with it in respect of determination or indetermination, as well as of gender, number, and case (see Gesenius' Heb. Gr. §. 110, 1, and §. 109, 2); e. g. اَلرَّجُلِ ٱلْكَرِيمِ, رَجُلٌ كَرِيمٌ, *a noble man*; *of the noble man*; زَيْدًا ٱلْكَرِيمَ, *the noble Zeid* (acc.); كِتَابُهُ ٱلْعَزِيزُ, *his glorious book*; قَاعِدَةٌ مُرَبَّعَةٌ, *a square pedestal*; كُنُوزًا كَثِيرَةً, *great treasures* (acc.). A noun may have two or more adjectives connected with it; as: اَلْكَوْكَبُ ٱلنَّيِّرُ ٱلْأَحْمَرُ, *the bright red star*. Sometimes a substantive is used adjectively; as: جَارِيَةٌ بِكْرٌ, *a young woman (who is) a virgin* (נַעֲרָה בְתוּלָה); مَسَاجِدُ عِدَّةٌ, *a number of mosques*; تَشْتَمِلُ عَلَى خَيْلٍ وَرِجَالٍ عِدَّةٍ, *it contains a number of horses and men*; وَذَاكَ مِنْهُ خُلُقٌ عَادَةٌ, *and this is a usual custom of his*; وَأَنْتُمْ مَعْشَرُ زَيْدٍ عَلَى مِائَةٍ, *and ye are a band of more than a hundred*. Compare, in Hebrew, אֲנָשִׁים פ̄, Num. 9, 20, אֲנָשִׁים ס̄, Nehem. 2, 12; and in Syriac, ܓܲܢ̈ܐ ܣܲܓܼ̈ܝܼܐܹܐ, *many gardens*, ܒܢ̈ܝܵܐ ܘܒܢ̈ܵܬܼܵܐ ܣܲܓܼ̈ܝܼܐܹܐ, *many sons and daughters*. — As regards the demonstrative pronouns, which are looked upon by the Arabs as substantives (vol. I. §. 190, 4, and §. 338), either they may be placed in apposition to the substantive, or the substantive to them; as: هٰذَا ٱلْمَلِكُ, *this king*, lit. *this (person), the king*; زَيْدٌ هٰذَا, *Zeid, this (person)*, i. e. *this Zeid* or *Zeid here*. In both cases the apposition is a qualificative one, whence the first word in each is called by the Arabs ٱلْمَوْصُوفُ, *that which is described*, and the second, ٱلصِّفَةُ, *the description* or *descriptive epithet*. As the demonstrative pronoun is by its nature definite, the noun in apposition to it must of course be definite likewise. If it be defined by the article, the demonstrative usually precedes, as مَتْبُوعٌ, though it sometimes follows, as تَابِعٌ; e. g. هٰذَا ٱلرَّجُلُ, *this man*, rarely ٱلرَّجُلُ هٰذَا. But if the substantive be definite by its own nature (as a proper name or a mere word, §. 78), or defined by having a genitive after it, the demonstrative always follows; as: زَيْدٌ هٰذَا, *this Zeid* (see above)*); هٰذِهِ إِذَنْ أَنَّ ٱلنَّحْوَ ٱلْمَشْهُورُ, *this (word) 'idan*; هٰذِهِ بِمَعْنَى مَعَ, *it is well known in grammar that this 'ilâ has the meaning of maa*; هٰؤُلَاءِ عِبَادِي, *these my servants* or *these servants of mine*; هٰذَا وَقْتِنَا إِلَى, *to this age of ours*; كِتَابُهُ هٰذَا ٱلْجَلِيلُ, *this famous book of his*.

*) If the proper name has the article, هٰذَا may also precede, because it is to a certain extent a common noun defined by the article; as: ٱلْحٰرِثُ هٰذَا or هٰذَا ٱلْحٰرِثُ, *this el-Hârit*.

On the other hand, in such a phrase as هٰذِهِ نَاقَةُ ٱللّٰهِ لَكُمْ آيَةً, the words نَاقَةُ ٱللّٰهِ are the predicate (خَبَرٌ) of هٰذِهِ, and لَكُمْ آيَةً is a circumstantial accusative, *this is the she-camel of God as a sign unto you.*

137. كُلٌّ, جَمِيعٌ, and more rarely عَامَّةٌ, *totality,* are often placed after the definite noun which they might govern in the genitive (§. 82, 1, 2), in which case a pronominal suffix is appended to them, referring to that noun; as: ٱلنَّاسُ جَمِيعُهُمْ or ٱلنَّاسُ كُلُّهُمْ, *all men* (also ٱلنَّاسُ جَمِيعًا §. 82, 2); ٱلْقَبِيلَةُ جَمِيعُهَا or ٱلْقَبِيلَةُ كُلُّهَا, *the whole tribe;* ٱلْجَيْشُ عَامَّتُهُ, *the whole army.* A peculiar use of كُلٌّ as an appositive, is exemplified by the phrases: هُوَ ٱلْعَالِمُ كُلُّ ٱلْعَالِمِ, *he is a real hero;* هُوَ ٱلشُّجَاعُ كُلُّ ٱلشُّجَاعِ, *he is a thorough scholar.* If the noun be indefinite, this construction is inadmissible, for the pronominal suffix, being by nature definite, can not refer to any other than a definite noun. There is, however, one exception, namely, when the indefinite noun indicates a *precise period of time;* e. g. شَهْرٌ كُلُّهُ, *a whole month;* سَنَةٌ كُلُّهَا, *a whole year.* Words of a vague signification, such as وَقْتٌ, *time,* مُدَّةٌ, *a space of time,* &c., cannot be thus construed. — After كُلٌّ and its suffix we often find a second apposition, agreeing with the preceding substantive in gender, number and case, namely, the adjective أَجْمَعُ, fem. جَمْعَاءُ, plur. masc. أَجْمَعُونَ, fem. جُمَعُ (the dual masc. أَجْمَعَانِ, and fem. جَمْعَاوَانِ, are not admitted by the great majority of grammarians); as:

نَسَجَدَ ٱلْمَلٰئِكَةُ كُلُّهُمْ أَجْمَعُونَ, *and the angels all (without exception) prostrated themselves.* Sometimes this word is used without كُلٌّ, as لَأُغْوِيَنَّهُمْ أَجْمَعِينَ, *verily I will lead them all astray;* إِذَنْ ظَلِلْتُ ٱلدَّهْرَ أَبْكِى أَجْمَعَا, *in that case I would pass all my time in weeping* (أَجْمَعَا in rhyme for أَجْمَعَ).

Rem. To أَجْمَعُ are sometimes appended other synonymous words, which form their feminine sing. and masculine and feminine plur. in the same way; viz. أَكْتَعُ, أَبْصَعُ, and أَبْتَعُ. The usual sequence of these synonyms is exemplified in the phrase جَآءَ ٱلْجَيْشُ كُلُّهُ أَجْمَعُ أَكْتَعُ أَبْصَعُ أَبْتَعُ, *the entire army came.* They are scarcely ever used singly and without كُلٌّ.

138. Like كُلٌّ and its synonyms are used كِلَا, fem. كِلْتَا, *both* (§. 83), and نِصْفٌ, *a half.* They follow the nouns to which they refer, and take the appropriate pronominal suffix; as: إِنَّ ٱلْمُعَلِّمَ وَٱلطَّبِيبَ كِلَيْهِمَا, *the teacher and physician, both of them;* ٱلْجَيْشُ نِصْفُهُ, *half the army.*

139. نَفْسٌ, *soul,* and عَيْنٌ, *eye, essence (of a thing),* are often employed in the sense of *ipse, self* (compare §. 135). They are then not seldom prefixed to a noun, which they govern in the genitive; as: عَيْنُ ٱلْكَوْكَبِ, *the star itself;* رَأَيْتُ نَفْسَهُ, *I have seen himself;* إِزَالَةُ ٱلْجَهْلِ عَنْ نَفْسِهِ, *the removing of ignorance from himself* (compare the Hebrew use of עֶצֶם, and also of עֶרֶם in 2 Kings 9, 13, provided this passage be not corrupt); but more

generally they are used, like كُلّ, as appositives to a definite noun, and are followed by the appropriate pronominal suffix; as: جَآءَ زَيْدٌ نَفْسُهُ, *Zeid himself came;* جَآءَتْ زَيْنَبُ نَفْسُهَا, *Zeineb herself came;* رَأَيْتُ عَمْرًا نَفْسَهُ, *I saw Amr himself.* If the noun be in the dual or plural, the plural forms أَنْفُس and أَعْيُن must be employed; as: رَأَيْتُ ٱلْأَمِيرَيْنِ أَنْفُسَهُمَا, *I saw the two emirs themselves;* مَرَرْتُ بِٱلْهِنْدَيْنِ أَنْفُسِهِمَا, *I passed by the two Hinds themselves;* قَتَلَهُ ٱلْوُزَرَآءُ أَنْفُسُهُمْ, *the vizirs themselves killed him.* They are also often connected with the nouns to which they refer by means of the preposition بِ; as: جَآءَ بِنَفْسِهِ, *he came in person;* ٱلْهَوَانُ بِعَيْنِهِ, *degradation itself, utter degradation;* وَٱلْآنَ يَخْتَارُونَ بِأَنْفُسِهِمْ, *and now they are choosing in person.* Occasionally, too, عَيْنٌ is appended in the form of an adverbial accusative, or by means of the preposition بِ, but without any suffix; as: هُوَ هُوَ عَيْنًا (بِعَيْنٍ), *he is the very person.* — When نَفْسٌ and عَيْنٌ are in apposition to a pronominal suffix in the accusative or genitive, a *pronomen separationis* may be interposed; as: مَرَرْتُ بِكَ أَنْتَ نَفْسِكَ or مَرَرْتُ بِكَ نَفْسِكَ, *I passed by you yourself;* رَأَيْتُكَ أَنْتَ نَفْسَكَ or رَأَيْتُكَ نَفْسَكَ or رَأَيْتُكَ إِيَّاكَ نَفْسَكَ, *I saw you yourself;* but if the pronominal suffix represent the agent, as in the verb, the insertion of this pronoun is a matter of necessity; as: قُمْتَ أَنْتَ نَفْسَكَ, *you yourself stood up;* قُومُوا أَنْتُمْ أَنْفُسَكُمْ, *stand up yourselves.*

Rem. *a.* The words كِلَانِ, &c., أَجْمَعُ, عَامَّةٌ, جَمِيعٌ, كُلُّ and كِلْتَانِ, نِصْفُ, نَفْسُ and عَيْنُ, form one division of that class of appositives, اَلتَّوَابِعُ, which the grammarians name اَلتَّأْكِيدُ (or اَلتَّوْكِيدُ), *the strengthening or corroboration*, and اَلْمُؤَكِّدُ, *the corroborative*, because they strengthen the idea of totality or of self, already contained in the اَلْمَتْبُوعُ, by the addition of their own. This class of appositives is designated by the special name of اَلتَّوْكِيدُ ٱلْمَعْنَوِيُّ, *the corroboration in meaning*, to distinguish them from the اَلتَّوْكِيدُ ٱللَّفْظِيُّ, or *verbal corroboration*, which consists in the emphatic repetition of the word itself; as in the verse: فَأَيْنَ إِلَى أَيْنَ ٱلنَّجَاةُ بِبَغْلَتِي أَتَاكَ أَتَاكَ ٱللَّاحِقُونَ ٱخْبِسِ ٱخْبِسِ, *whither, whither can I escape with my mule? The pursuers are come up, come up to you; halt! halt!* ٱخْبِسِ in rhyme for ٱخْبِسْ). So also in answers: نَعَمْ نَعَمْ, *yes, yes*; لَا لَا, *no, no*. If a word is governed by a preposition or other particle, both must be repeated; as: مَرَرْتُ بِكَ بِكَ, *I passed by you—you*; إِنَّ زَيْدًا إِنَّ زَيْدًا قَائِمٌ, *Zeid — Zeid is standing up*.

Rem. *b.* Besides the اَلتَّوْكِيدُ, the Arab grammarians acknowledge three other classes of تَوَابِعُ; viz. اَلنَّعْتُ or اَلصِّفَةُ, *the description or descriptive word, qualificative, adjective*; اَلْبَدَلُ, *the substitution or permutative*; and عَطْفُ ٱلْبَيَانِ, *the explanatory apposition*.—1) The اَلنَّعْتُ or اَلصِّفَةُ may refer to the اَلْمَتْبُوعُ either directly (in which case it is a simple adjective), as: جَآءَنِي رَجُلٌ حَسَنٌ, *there came to me a handsome man*; or indirectly, in virtue of a following word that is connected with it, as: جَآءَنِي رَجُلٌ حَسَنٌ أَخُوهُ, *there came to me a man whose brother is handsome*. In this latter case the adjective belongs, as a prefixed predicate, to the following noun, which is its subject, and the two together form a صِفَة, or qualificative clause, of the preceding substantive, with which the adjective agrees in *case* by attraction; as: رَأَيْتُ رَجُلًا حَسَنًا أَخُوهُ, *I saw a man whose brother is handsome*; مَرَرْتُ بِرَجُلٍ كَرِيمٍ أَبُوهُ, *I passed by a man whose father is noble*; مَرَرْتُ بِرَجُلٍ حَسَنَةٍ أُمُّهُ, *I passed by a man whose mother is handsome*. If the following noun be in the dual or plural, the adjective is still left in the singular; as: مَرَرْتُ بِآمْرَأَتَيْنِ حَسَنٍ أَبَوَاهُمَا, *I passed by two women whose parents are handsome*; رَأَيْتُ رِجَالًا حَسَنًا آبَاؤُهُمْ, *I saw some men whose fathers are handsome*. If the preceding noun be defined in any way, the adjective takes the article; as: رَأَيْتُ زَيْدًا ٱلْحَسَنَ وَجْهُهُ, *I saw Zeid, whose face is handsome*; حَكَى أَبُو ٱلْفُتُوحِ ٱلْعِجْلِيُّ ٱلْمُتَقَدِّمُ ذِكْرُهُ, *Abū 'l-Futūḥ el-Iglī, who has been mentioned before, narrates*; ٱلْمُلُوكُ ٱلْمُتَقَدِّمُ ذِكْرُهُمْ, *the kings who have been mentioned before*; فَوَيْلٌ لِلْقَاسِيَةِ قُلُوبُهُمْ, *woe to those whose hearts are hard!* The Arab grammarians assume that every adjective contains a pronominal agent within itself, when no other agent is expressed, and they therefore call the adjective شِبْهُ ٱلْفِعْلِ, *that which is like the verb*. Consequently رَجُلٌ حَسَنٌ is with them = رَجُلٌ حَسَنٌ (هُوَ) = رَجُلٌ حَسَنٌ هُوَ, but رَجُلٌ حَسَنٍ أَخُوهُ; where another agent is expressed, is = رَجُلٌ حَسَنٌ أَخُوهُ; and so with the rest: مَرَرْتُ بِرَجُلٍ حَسَنَتْ أُمُّهُ = مَرَرْتُ بِرَجُلٍ حَسَنَةٍ أُمُّهُ; رَأَيْتُ رِجَالًا حَسَنٌ آبَاؤُهُمْ = رَأَيْتُ رِجَالًا حَسَنًا آبَاؤُهُمْ; رَأَيْتُ زَيْدًا ٱلَّذِى حَسَنٌ وَجْهُهُ = رَأَيْتُ زَيْدًا ٱلْحَسَنَ وَجْهُهُ

&c. In such cases the seemingly nominal sentence is in reality a verbal sentence, serving as صِفَة to the preceding substantive. On the other hand, if the substantive precedes the adjective, as in جَآءَنِى رَجُلٌ أَبُوهُ حَسَنٌ, the second substantive and the adjective that follows it form together a really nominal sentence, of which the substantive is the مُبْتَدَأ and the adjective the خَبَر; and consequently both must remain, under all circumstances, in the nominative, and the adjective must agree regularly with the substantive; as:

2) The مَرَرْتُ بِرَجُلٍ أُمُّهُ حَسَنَةٌ, رَأَيْتُ رَجُلًا أَخُوهُ حَسَنٌ.

اَلْبَدَلُ, or *permutative*, is of four kinds. a) بَدَلُ ٱلْكُلِّ مِنَ ٱلْكُلِّ, *the substitution of the whole for the whole*; as: جَآءَنِى عُمَرُ أَخُوكَ, *Omar, your brother, came to me*; جَآءَنِى ٱلْقَوْمُ كُلُّ, *the whole people came to me*; جَآءَنِى قَوْمُ ٱلْمَدِينَةِ كُبَرَآؤُهُمْ وَضُعَفَآؤُهُمْ, *the people of the city came to me, great and small*. b) بَدَلُ ٱلْبَعْضِ مِنَ ٱلْكُلِّ, *the substitution of the part for the whole*; as: جَآءَنِى ٱلْقَوْمُ بَعْضُهُمْ, *some of the people came to me*; أَكَلْتُ ٱلرَّغِيفَ ثُلْثَهُ, *I ate a third of the loaf*. c) بَدَلُ ٱلْإِشْتِمَالِ, *the comprehensive substitution*, i. e. the permutative which indicates a quality or circumstance possessed by or included in the preceding substantive; as: أَعْجَبَنِى زَيْدٌ عِلْمُهُ, *Zeid's learning filled me with surprise*; وَذَكَرَتْ تَفَقُّدَ بَرْدَ مَآئِهَا, *and she called to mind the coldness of the water of Taktud*, lit. *Taktud, the coldness of its water*; يَسْأَلُونَكَ عَنِ ٱلشَّهْرِ ٱلْحَرَامِ قِتَالٍ فِيهِ, *they will question thee about fighting in the sacred month*, lit. *about the sacred month, (about) fighting in it. d)* The fourth case is where the permutative is wholly different from the word for which it is substituted (اَلْبَدَلُ الْمُبَايِنُ لِلْمُبْدَلِ). It is of two sorts: α) بَدَلُ الْإِضْرَابِ, *the permutative of retraction* (from أَضْرَبَ, *to turn away from*), or بَدَلُ الْبَدَآءَ, *the substitution of something else one would like to state for the original statement*; as, for instance, when one says أَكَلْتُ خُبْزًا, *I ate bread*, but then, preferring to state that he had eaten meat, adds the word لَحْمًا (أَكَلْتُ خُبْزًا لَحْمًا). Here, to use the words of the grammarians, يُقْصَدُ الْمَتْبُوعُ كَمَا يُقْصَدُ التَّابِعُ, *the metbû' is designed as well as the tâbi'*; and this is what distinguishes it from β) بَدَلُ الْغَلَطِ, *the permutative of error*, or بَدَلُ النِّسْيَانِ, *the permutative of forgetfulness*, in which the الْمَتْبُوعُ is uttered merely by mistake, and the correct word immediately substituted for it; as when one says: مَرَرْتُ بِكَلْبٍ فَرَسٍ, *I passed by a dog, (I mean to say) a horse*. The بَدَلُ الْإِضْرَابِ is equivalent to the use of the particle بَلْ (أَكَلْتُ خُبْزًا بَلْ لَحْمًا). — 3) The عَطْفُ الْبَيَانِ or *explicative apposition*, which is the asyndetic connection of a substantive with a preceding substantive, which it more nearly defines; as: جَآءَنِى أَخُوكَ زَيْدٌ أَقْسَمَ بِاللّٰهِ, *your brother Zeid came to me*, أَبُو حَفْصٍ عُمَرُ, *'Abû Hafṣ 'Omar swore by God* in rhyme for عُمَرُ). This apposition is equivalent to the use of وَهُوَ, وَهِيَ, &c. (e.g. جَآءَنِى أَخُوكَ وَهُوَ زَيْدٌ), and, being asyndetic, is opposed to the عَطْفُ النَّسَقِ, or *connection of sequence*, which takes place by means of connective particles, such as وَ, فَ, ثُمَّ, حَتَّى, أَمْ, and أَوْ.

Rem. *c*. The word to which a مُؤَكِّدٌ is annexed is called by the grammarians اَلْمُؤَكَّدُ, *that which is strengthened or corroborated;* that which is followed by a صِفَةٌ or نَعْتٌ, اَلْمَنْعُوتُ or اَلْمَوْصُوفُ, *the qualified or described;* that which has a بَدَلٌ after it, اَلْمُبْدَلُ مِنْهُ, *that for which something is substituted;* and that to which an عَطْفُ ٱلْبَيَانِ is appended, اَلْمَعْطُوفُ عَلَيْهِ, *the word to which an explanatory word is attached by means of a virtual conjunction.*

Rem. *d.* In sentences like تَقَاتَلُوا بَعْضُهُمْ لِبَعْضٍ, *they fought with one another,* the words بَعْضُهُمْ لِبَعْضٍ are a permutative of the agent هُمْ, contained in the verb تَقَاتَلُوا, and serve to strengthen the idea of reciprocity belonging to that verbal form. The لَامٌ in لِبَعْضٍ, لِتَقْوِيَةِ ٱلْعَامِلِ which supplies the place of the accusative, is dependent upon قَاتَلُوا, *they fought with,* contained in تَقَاتَلُوا.

140. One finite verb may also be put in apposition to another. In this case either *a)* the first is the preparative act, introductory to the second; as: قَامَ سَجَدَ لَهُ, *he arose (and) prostrated himself before him:* فَأَرْسَلَ أَعْلَمَ بِذٰلِكَ أَبَاهُ, *then he sent (and) informed his father of this;* or *b)* the second modifies the first; as: سَجَدَ أَطَالَ, *he continued long prostrate;* غَنَّى أَحْسَنَ, *he sang well.* In both cases the older and more elegant form of expression is to insert the conjunction فَ; as: سَجَدَ فَأَطَالَ, قَامَ فَسَجَدَ لَهُ. If the first of the two verbs be a perfect, the second must be so likewise; for the imperfect would be a حَالٌ مُقَدَّرٌ (see §. 8, *d, e),* and, as such, would virtually stand in the accusative;

as: اَرْسَلَ يُعْلِمُ, *misit nuntiaturus, he sent to inform*. If both verbs are in the imperfect, the second may either be an apposition or a خَالٌ مُقَدَّرٌ; as: يُرْسِلُ يُعْلِمُ, *he sends (and) informs*, or *mittit nuntiaturus, he sends to inform*.

Rem. The later Arabic construction, without the conjunction, is very common in Syriac (e. g. ܐܣܬܡܪ̈ܗ, *he sent (and) seized him*), and also occurs in Hebrew. See Gesenius' Gr. §. 139, 3, *b*.

2. Concord in Gender and Number between the Parts of a Sentence.

141. In verbal sentences, in which (according to §. 118) the predicate (verb) must always precede the subject (agent), the following rules hold regarding their agreement in gender and number.

142. 1) If the subject be a singular substantive, that is feminine by signification (vol. I. §. 290, 1), two constructions are possible. *a*) If it immediately follows the verb, the verb must be put in the fem. sing.; as: قَالَتِ امْرَأَةُ الْعَزِيزِ, *the wife of 'l-'Aziz said*. But *b*) if it be separated from the verb by one or more words, the verb may stand in the sing. masc., although the fem. is preferable; as: إِنْ امْرَأَ غَرَّهُ مِنْكُنَّ وَاحِدَةٌ, *a man, whom one of you* (women) *has deceived*.

2) If the subject be a singular substantive, that is fe-

minine merely by form (vol. I. §. 290, 2), the preceding verb may be put either in the masculine or feminine, whether the subject immediately follows it or not. In the following examples it is masculine: فَيَنْظُرُونَ كَيْفَ كَانَ عَاقِبَةُ ٱلَّذِينَ مِنْ قَبْلِهِمْ, *and they see what was the end of those who preceded them;* لِئَلَّا يَكُونَ لِلنَّاسِ عَلَيْكُمْ حُجَّةٌ, *that the people may not have any pretext against you.*

3) If the feminine subject be separated from the verb by the particle إِلَّا, the verb is put in the masculine; as: مَا زَكَا إِلَّا فَتَاةُ ٱبْنِ ٱلْعَلَاءِ, *no one was innocent except the maidservant of 'Ibnu 'l-'Alā* (i. e. مَا زَكَا أَحَدٌ). The feminine is, however, admissible, especially in poetry; for instance, in the above example, زَكَتْ.

4) The verbs نِعْمَ and بِئْسَ (vol. I. §. 183) take the masculine form in preference to the feminine, even when the subject is feminine by signification; as: نِعْمَ ٱلْمَرْأَةُ زَيْنَبُ, *Zeïneb is an excellent woman!*

143. If the subject be a plur. sanus masc., or a plur. fractus denoting persons of the male sex, the preceding verb is usually put in the sing. masc., particularly when one or more words are interposed between it and the subject; as: جَاءَ ذَاتَ يَوْمٍ رِجَالٌ مِنْ مَكَّةَ قَالَ ٱلْمُؤْمِنُونَ, *the believers said; there came one day (some) men from Mekka;* كَمَا أَنُؤْمِنُ آمَنَ ٱلسُّفَهَاءُ, *shall we believe as fools have believed?*

Rem. بَنُونَ, *sons* (pl of ٱبْنٌ), and other similar words (vol. I. §. 302, 5; and rem. d), are exceptions, being treated as plurales fracti (see §. 144), and therefore admitting the verb in the fem. sing. This remark applies, however, to بَنُونَ only when it is used to denote a *family* or *tribe* (compare §. 147); as: قَالَتْ بَنُو إِسْرَآئِيلَ, *the Bĕnū 'Isrā'īl (children of Israel) said.*

144. If the subject be a pluralis fractus, no matter whether derived from a masc. or a fem. sing., the preceding verb may be either masc. or fem.; as: ثُمَّ قَسَتْ قُلُوبُكُمْ مِنْ بَعْدِ ذٰلِكَ, *then, after this, your hearts became hard* (from قَلْبٌ, masc.); نَقَدْ كُذِّبَتْ رُسُلٌ مِنْ قَبْلِكَ, *(other) apostles have been accused of falsehood before you* (from رَسُولٌ, masc.); مَتَى كَانَ ٱلْخِيَامُ بِذِى طُلُوحٍ, *when the tents are (set up) at Dū Tolūḥ* (from خَيْمَةٌ, fem.).

Rem. The remark made in §. 142, 3, regarding the particle إِلَّا, applies here too. An example of the fem. is: وَمَا بَقِيَتْ ٱلضُّلُوعُ ٱلْجَرَاشِعُ, *and nothing remained but the low rugged ridges of hills* (from ضِلَعٌ, fem.), where a prose writer would have said شَىْءٌ, scil. وَمَا بَقِىَ.

145. If the subject be a collective, like قَوْمٌ, *people*, or a noun designating a whole class of animals, like غَنَمٌ, *sheep*, or طَيْرٌ, *birds* (vol. I. §. 290, 1, e, and §. 292, 1), the preceding verb may be put in the fem. sing.; as: قَالَتِ ٱلْيَهُودُ لَيْسَتِ ٱلنَّصَارَى عَلَى شَىْءٍ, *the Jews say, the Christians stand upon nothing* (have no foundation for their belief); إِنِّى أَرَانِى أَحْمِلُ فَوْقَ رَأْسِى خُبْزًا تَأْكُلُ ٱلطَّيْرُ مِنْهُ, *I saw myself (in a dream) carrying upon my head (some) bread, of which the birds were eating.*

146. If the subject be a feminine noun in the plural number, whether plur. sanus or plur. fractus, the preceding verb may be put either in the masc. or fem. sing.; unless the plur. sanus refers to persons of the female sex, in which case the fem. is decidedly to be preferred. Examples: فَأَصَابَهُمْ سَيِّئَاتُ مَا عَمِلُوا, *the evil consequences of what they did, came upon them*; قَالَ نِسْوَةٌ فِى ٱلْمَدِينَةِ, (*some*) *women in the city said;* فَبَكَى بَنَاتِى شَجْوَهُنَّ, *and my daughters lamented their misery*. Such instances as إِذَا جَآءَكُمُ ٱلْمُؤْمِنَاتُ, *when believing women come unto you,* are comparatively rare.

147. The names of the Arab tribes, which are mostly of the feminine gender, take a preceding verb in the fem. sing. (see §. 143, rem.); but a following verb may be put in the plur. masc., because such names have the sense of collectives. For example: تَجَمَّعَتْ عُقَيْلٌ وَقُشَيْرٌ وَتَشَاكَوْا مَا يَلْحَقُهُمْ مِنْ سَيْفِ ٱلدَّوْلَةِ, (*the tribes of*) *'Okail and Kosheir assembled and complained to one another of what was done to them by Seifu 'd-daula*.

148. In general, when once the subject has been mentioned, any following verb must agree with it strictly in gender and number; as: خَرَجَ عَلَيْهِ ٱلصَّيَّادُونَ فَٱنْهَزَمَ مِنْهُمْ فَأَمَّا وَهُوَ فِى ٱلسَّهْلِ فَلَمْ يُدْرِكُوهُ, *the hunters came out against him and he fled from them, and, whilst he continued on level ground, they did not overtake him* (خَرَجَ sing., but يُدْرِكُوهُ plur.); كَانَ فِيهِ قُبَّةٌ تُعْرَفُ بِقُبَّةِ ٱلْهَوَآءِ, *there was*

upon it a cupola, known by (the name of) the cupola of the air (وَبِمَغَارَةِ ٱلْخَضِرِ) كَانَ masc., but تُعْرَفُ fem.); ٱلزُّوَّارُ أَسْبَابَهُمْ وَيَصْعَدُونَ مِيلَيْنِ إِلَى أَعْلَى ٱلْجَبَلِ, *and the pilgrims leave their baggage at the cave of el-Ḥiḍr, and ascend two miles to the top of the mountain* (يَتْرُكُ sing., but يَصْعَدُونَ plur., because ٱلزُّوَّارُ is a plur. fract. denoting rational beings); لِلّٰهِ مَلَائِكَةٌ يَتَعَاقَبُونَ فِيكُمْ, *God has angels who watch over you in turn* (يَتَعَاقَبُونَ plur., for the same reason as in the last example); فَجَالَ ٱلصِّوَارُ وَٱتَّقَيْنَ بِقَرْهَبٍ, *and the herd wheeled and guarded (their rear) with an old buck* (ٱتَّقَيْنَ fem., because, with the exception of the single buck, the rest of the herd were does); فَأَبْرَزَ مِنْهُ رِقَاعًا قَدْ كُتِبْنَ بِٱلْوَانِ ٱلْأَصْبَاغِ, *and he took out of it scraps of paper written with (ink of) various colours* (where كُتِبَتْ might also be used). — If irrational or inanimate objects are spoken of (for example, in fables) as persons, the plur. fractus may be followed by the verb in the plur. masc.; as: كِلَابٌ مَرَّةً أَصَابُوا جِلْدَ سَبُعٍ, *once on a time (some) dogs found the skin of a beast of prey;* وَقَالُوا لِجُلُودِهِمْ لِمَ شَهِدْتُمْ عَلَيْنَا قَالُوا أَنْطَقَنَا ٱللّٰهُ, *and they shall say to their skins* (members), *Why have ye borne witness against us? They shall answer, God has made us speak.*

149. If the subject be a substantive in the dual number, the preceding verb must be put in the singular, but must agree with the subject in gender. Examples: وَدَخَلَ مَعَهُ ٱلسِّجْنَ فَتَيَانِ, *and two young men went into*

the prison along with him; لَمَّا تَنَازَعَنِى ٱلرَّجُلَانِ, after the two men disputed with one another about me; وَسُمِّرَتْ يَدَاهُ وَعَضُدَاهُ وَرِجْلَاهُ, and his hands and arms and feet were pierced with nails; لَوْ كَانَ بَذْرٌ حَاضِرًا وَٱبْنُ حَمَلٍ مَا نُقِشَتْ كَفَّاكِ, had Bèdr been present and 'Ibn Ḥamèl, thy hands would not have been branded (حَمَلْ in rhyme for حَمَلٍ); لَا رَقَأَتْ عَيْنَاهُ مِنْ طُولِ ٱلْبُكَآءِ, may his eyes never cease from constant weeping; خُذْ مِنْ شَارِبِكَ حَتَّى تَبْدُوَ شَفَتَاكَ وَمِنْ ثَوْبِكَ حَتَّى تَبْدُوَ عَقِبَاكَ, cut your moustache till your lips can be seen, and your dress till your heels can be seen (compare, in Hebrew, Micah 4, 11. וְחָזֶה בְצִיּוֹן עֵינֵינוּ; see Gesenius' Gr. §. 143, 5). — A following verb must, of course, agree strictly with the preceding subject in gender and number; as: إِنْ هَمَّتْ طَآئِفَتَانِ مِنْكُمْ أَنْ تَفْشَلَا, when two troops among you were on the point of behaving with cowardice. But if it be a collective, designating rational beings, the masc. plur. is admissible; as: وَإِنْ طَآئِفَتَانِ مِنَ ٱلْمُؤْمِنِينَ ٱقْتَتَلُوا فَأَصْلِحُوا بَيْنَهُمَا, and if two parties of believers fight with one another, make peace between them.

Rem. a. Sometimes, however, a preceding verb is found in actual agreement with a following subject in the dual or plural, or even in virtual agreement with a singular collective; as: وَقَدْ أَسْلَمَاهُ مُبْعَدٌ وَحَمِيمٌ, after both far and near (after every one) had abandoned him (حَمِيمٌ in rhyme for حَمِيمُ); ٱحْمَرَّتَا عَيْنَاهُ, his eyes were red; رَأَيْنَ ٱلْغَوَانِى ٱلشَّيْبَ لَاحَ بِعَارِضِى يَلُومُونَنِى فِى ٱشْتِرَآءِ, the women saw the white hairs that glittered in my whiskers;

اَلنَّخِيلِ أَهْلِي, *my family abuse me for the purchase of the palm-trees;* نَصَرُوكَ قَوْمِي فَاعْتَزَزْتَ بِنَصْرِهِمْ, *my people aided you, and you became powerful through their aid.* The phrase أَكَلُونِي ٱلْبَرَاغِيثُ, *the fleas have devoured me,* is generally cited by the native grammarians to exemplify this construction.

Rem. *b.* With reference to Hebrew, compare with the above sections Gesenius' Gr. §. 143 (especially 1 and 3) and §. 144 (esp. *a* and *d*).

150. If the preceding verb has several subjects, it may be put in the plural, as: جِئْنَا أَنَا وَأَنْتَ, *you and I are come;* or it may agree in number and gender with the nearest subject, as: وَيَسْنِدُ هَرُونُ وَبَنُوهُ أَيْدِيَهُمْ عَلَى رَأْسِهِ, *and Aaron and his sons shall lay their hands upon his head;* تَكَلَّمَتْ مَرْيَمُ وَهَرُونُ فِي مُوسَى, *Miriam and Aaron spoke about Moses.* — If the subjects precede, and are either three or more singulars, or a singular and a dual, the verb is put in the plural; if they are merely two singulars, in the dual; as: اَلْبَطْنُ وَٱلرِّجْلَانِ تَخَاصَمُوا, *the belly and the two feet disputed with one another;* اَلْبَرْدُ وَٱلْحَرُّ تَخَاصَمَا, *the cold and the heat disputed with one another;* وَٱلنَّجْمُ وَٱلشَّجَرُ يَسْجُدَانِ, *and the plants and trees worshipped* (not ٱلشَّجَرُ ... يَسْجُدُونَ, because ٱلنَّجْمُ and ٱلشَّجَرُ are not individuals but species); وَحُمِلَتِ ٱلْأَرْضُ وَٱلْجِبَالُ فَدُكَّتَا دَكَّةً وَاحِدَةً, *and (when) the earth and the mountains shall be lifted up and dashed in pieces at one stroke* (not دُكِّنَ or دُكَّتْ, ٱلْجِبَالُ being a plur. fract.). If the subjects be of different genders, the verb is usually put in the mas-

culine, as in the first of the above examples, or in: اَلْكَسَلُ
وَكَثْرَةُ ٱلنَّوْمِ يُبْعِدَانِ مِنَ ٱللّٰهِ وَيُورِثَانِ ٱلْفَقْرَ, *indolence and excess of sleep remove us far from God and make us heirs of (reduce us to) poverty.*

Rem. Compare Gesenius' Heb. Gr. §. 145, 2.

151. The verb frequently agrees in respect of gender, not with the grammatical subject, but with its complement (the genitive annexed to it), which is the logical subject; e. g. يَوْمَ تَجِدُ كُلُّ نَفْسٍ مَا عَمِلَتْ مِنْ خَيْرٍ مُحْضَرًا, *on the day (when) every soul shall find the good it has done present* (along with itself before God); اِسْتَرْخَتْ جَمِيعُ أَعْضَائِي, *all my limbs were relaxed;* تَفْتَدِي مِنْهُ بَعْضُهَا بِبَعْضٍ, *some of them ransom themselves from him with others* (by giving up others to him); إِذَا بَعْضُ ٱلسِّنِينَ تَعَرَّقَتْنَا, *when some years shall have gnawed at us;* كُنْتُمْ خَيْرَ أُمَّةٍ أُخْرِجَتْ لِلنَّاسِ, *ye are the best people that has been brought forth (created) for mankind.* As the above examples show, this agreement of the verb with the logical subject most frequently takes place when the grammatical subject expresses a subordinate idea, like كُلُّ, جَمِيعٌ, بَعْضٌ and غَيْرٌ (see §. 82).

Rem. Compare Gesenius' Heb. Gr. §. 145, 1.

152. What has been said regarding the concord of gender and number in a verbal sentence, is nearly all applicable to a nominal sentence

1) When the predicate follows the subject, they must agree strictly in gender and number; unless the subject be

a plur. fractus, in which case the predicate may also be put in the fem. sing., as: تَعْمَى ٱلْقُلُوبُ وَٱلْعُيُونُ نَاظِرَةٌ, *the hearts are blind, whilst the eyes are seeing* (see §. 148). This latter remark applies also to the names of the Arab tribes (see §. 147); as: وَبَنُو عَبْسٍ يَوْمَئِذٍ نَازِلَةٌ فِى بَنِى عَامِرِ بْنِ صَعْصَعَةَ, *and the Benû Abs were at that time dwelling among the Benû ʿĀmir bin Saʿṣaʿa*.

2) When the predicate precedes the subject, as happens in negative and interrogative sentences, then *a)* if the sentence be nominal, the predicate and subject must agree in number (see §. 117); but *b)* if the sentence be verbal, the predicate is put in the singular (see §. 121).

3) If the subject be a collective, the predicate may be put in the plural; as: كُلٌّ لَهُ قَانِتُونَ, *all are obeying him*. Similarly, when a verb is placed after a collective subject, as: وَلَكِنَّ أَكْثَرَ ٱلنَّاسِ لَا يَشْكُرُونَ, *but the greatest part of mankind are thankless*; فَرِيقٌ مِنْهُمْ يَخْشَوْنَ ٱلنَّاسَ, *a part of them are afraid of men* (see §. 148).

4) The predicate frequently agrees in gender, not with the grammatical subject, but with its complement, which is the logical subject; as: كُلُّ نَفْسٍ ذَائِقَةُ ٱلْمَوْتِ, *every soul shall taste of death*; أَتَى ٱلْفَوَاحِشُ عِنْدَهُمْ مَعْرُوفَةٌ, *the committing of crimes is held laudable by them* (see §. 151).

5) If the subject of a nominal sentence be a personal or demonstrative pronoun, and the predicate a feminine substantive or a plur. fractus,*) then the former is generally

---

*) For the plur. fract., even when derived from a masc. sing., agrees with adjectives, personal or demonstrative pronouns, and verbs, in the fem. sing.

put in the fem. sing., even when the preceding substantive, to which it refers, is of the masc. gender; as: إِنَّ هٰذِهِ تَذْكِرَةٌ, *this is an admonition* (Germ. *dies ist eine Erinnerung*, Fr. *ceci est un avertissement*); تِلْكَ حُدُودُ ٱللّٰهِ, *such are God's ordinances* (Germ. *dies sind Gottes Regeln*, Fr. *ce sont-là les règles de Dieu*); تِلْكَ آيَاتُ ٱللّٰهِ نَتْلُوهَا عَلَيْكَ, *such are God's signs, which we repeat to thee.*

B. The Different Kinds of Sentences.

1. Negative and Prohibitive Sentences.

153. The negative particles may, as in the Indo-european languages, deny any part of the sentence — the predicate, the subject (e. g. لَا نَافِيَةُ ٱلْجِنْسِ, §. 39), the object, the *ḥâl* or circumstantial expression, &c.

154. The negative particle sometimes immediately precedes that part of the sentence which it denies, at other times is separated from it by some other part; e. g. لَا يُكْرِمُ ٱلسَّخِىُّ ٱلْبَخِيلَ, *the liberal man does not respect the niggardly;* مَا هٰذَا بَشَرًا, *this is no human being* (see §. 42, rem. c); مَا قَالَ هٰذَا, *he has not said this.*

155. The predicate of a simple declarative verbal sentence, which is neither optative nor asseverative (§. 1, *e* and *f*), may, when denied by لَا, be put either in the imperfect or the perfect. *a*) When put in the *imperfect*, it may be

rendered into English by the present, the future, or, when connected with preceding past tenses, by the Latin imperfect (§§. 8, 9); as: لَا يُكْرِمُ ٱلسَّخِىُّ ٱلْبَخِيلَ, *the liberal man does not respect* (or *will not respect*, or, under certain circumstances, *did not respect*, non honorabat) *the niggardly.*
b) The *perfect* can properly be used only *a*) when لَا is repeated twice or oftener in clauses connected by وَ, in which case it may be translated by the perfect or the past (§. 1, *a* and *b*), as: لَا صَدَّقَ وَلَا صَلَّى, *he has neither believed nor prayed*, or *he neither believed nor prayed*; or *β*) when لَا is connected by وَ with a preceding negative, such as مَا, لَمْ, or لَمَّا, and merely carries on the negation of something past (see §. 1, *c*, rem. *b*, and §. 160).

156. The particle لَنْ — a contraction of لَا أَنْ —, which is construed with the subjunctive of the imperfect (§. 15, 1), is a very strong negation of the future, *not at all*, *never*; *e. g.* فَإِنْ لَمْ تَفْعَلُوا وَلَنْ تَفْعَلُوا فَٱتَّقُوا ٱلنَّارَ, *if ye do not do it — and ye will never do it — then dread the fire (of hell).*

Rem. On لَمْ and لَمَّا see §. 12 and §. 18.

157. The particle مَا, when joined to the perfect, denies the past; when joined to the imperfect, the present (see §. 8, rem. *b*).

158. The particle إِنْ is often found with negative force in verbal as well as in nominal sentences (see §. 42, rem. *c*), and that before both the perfect and the indicative of the imperfect. For example: وَإِنِ ٱلْكَافِرُونَ إِلَّا فِي غُرُورٍ

the unbelievers are in utter blindness (lit. *are not except in blindness*); أَيَا ٱللّٰهُ إِنْ أَفْعَلُ هٰذَا ٱلْفَعَالَ, *O God! I will not commit this action*; وَلَئِنْ زَالَتَا إِنْ أَمْسَكَهُمَا مِنْ أَحَدٍ مِنْ بَعْدِهِ, *and if they* (heaven and earth) *should fail, no one could support them after him* (if he, i. e. God, should withdraw his support); إِنْ أَجْرِيَ إِلَّا عَلَى ٱلَّذِى فَطَرَنِى, *it is for him alone to reward me, who has created me*; ثُمَّ جَآءُوكَ يَحْلِفُونَ بِٱللّٰهِ إِنْ أَرَدْنَا إِلَّا إِحْسَانًا, *then they will come unto thee swearing by God (and saying), We intended to do nothing but good*. In the elevated prose style, as well as in poetry, the negative مَا is often prefixed to this إِنْ; e. g. وَمَا إِنْ يَتَجَّمُ لَهَا عَنَآءٌ, *but her pains were (all) of no avail*; مَا إِنْ يَمَسُّ ٱلْأَرْضَ إِلَّا مَنْكِبٌ مِنْهُ, *only one shoulder of his touches the ground*; مَا إِنْ رَأَيْتَ لَهُمْ فِى ٱلنَّاسِ أَمْثَالَا, *thou hast never seen (any) like them among men* (أَمْثَالَا in rhyme for أَمْثَالً).

Rem. This إِنْ (called by the grammarians إِنِ ٱلنَّافِيَةِ, *the negative 'in*) is not to be confounded with the conditional particle of the same sound (إِنِ ٱلشَّرْطِيَّةِ, *the conditional 'in*); for 1) it admits of a nominal sentence after it; 2) it does not govern the jussive; 3) it lets the perfect retain its past signification; 4) its predicate is sometimes put in the accusative, like that of مَا (§. 42, rem. c); and 5) it is joined, as a corroborative, to مَا. It seems rather to be connected with the Hebrew negative אַיִן, אֵין, and occurs itself in that language in the form אִם.

159. The negative verb لَيْسَ (vol. I. §. 182) is used
a) as equivalent sometimes to كَانَ ٱلتَّامَّةُ (§. 41), e. g.

Negative and Prohibitive Sentences.

لَيْسَ لِصَحِيحِ ٱلْعَقْلِ وَٱلْبَدَنِ عُذْرٌ فِي تَرْكِ ٱلتَّعَلُّمِ, *for him who is healthy in mind and body, there is no excuse for neglecting the acquisition of knowledge;* at other times to (§. 41), e. g. لَيْسَ بِعَالِمٍ or لَيْسَ عَالِمًا, كَانَ ٱلنَّاقِصَةُ, *he is not learned.* But it is also employed *b)* as an indeclinable negative particle, stronger than لَا, to deny some part of the sentence to which it is prefixed; e. g. لَيْسَ لِهٰذَا خُلِقْتَ وَلَا بِهٰذَا أُمِرْتَ, *thou wast not created for this, nor bidden to do this;* لَيْسَ كُلُّ مَا فَاتَ يُدْرَكُ, *nothing that has escaped us can be overtaken* (an opportunity once lost never recurs); إِنَّمَا يَجْرِى ٱلْفَتَى لَيْسَ ٱلْجَمَلْ, *it is only the man that makes a return, not the camel* (ٱلْجَمَلْ in rhyme for ٱلْجَمَلُ); أَلَيْسَ قَدْ نَوَيْتَ أَنْ تُعْتِقَنِى, *have you not formed the intention of setting me free?* In connection with an imperfect, it expresses a strongly denied present or future; as: لَسْتُ أَقْصِدُ ٱلْحَرْبَ بَلْ جِئْتُ لِأَهْدِمَ ٱلْكَعْبَةَ, *I do not intend to make war (upon you), but I am come to destroy the Ka'ba;* لَسْتَ تَنَالُ ٱلْعِزَّ حَتَّى تُذِلَّهَا, *you will never attain greatness till you humble it (your spirit);* فَلَيْسَ تُدْخَلُ بَعْدَ ٱلْجَنَّةِ ٱلنَّارُ, *for the fire (of hell) is never entered after (one has been a dweller in) Paradise;* لَيْسَ تُرْجَى لِفَآئِدَهْ, *no good is hoped of thee* (لِفَآئِدَهْ in rhyme for لِفَآئِدَةٍ). It may even be governed by كَانَ, so as to express the negative imperfect of that verb; as: كَانَ ٱلنَّبِىُّ صلعم لَيْسَ بِٱلطَّوِيلِ وَلَا بِٱلْقَصِيرِ, *the Prophet was neither of high nor low stature.*

160. When to a clause containing one of the negative particles مَا, لَمْ, لَمَّا or لَنْ, or the negative verb لَيْسَ, there is appended, by means of the conjunction وَ, another dependent clause, then, in place of repeating the particular negative of the former clause, the general negative لَا is used, because the special kind of negation has already been sufficiently made known. For example: لَنْ تُغْنِيَ عَنْهُمْ أَمْوَالُهُمْ وَلَا أَوْلَادُهُمْ مِنَ ٱللّٰهِ شَيْئًا, *neither their goods nor their children shall avail them aught against God;* رَأَى أَنَّ ذٰلِكَ ٱلْبَدَنَ لَمْ يُخْلَقْ لَهُ عَبَثًا وَلَا قُرِنَ بِهِ لِأَمْرٍ بَاطِلٍ, *he saw that this body was not created for him in jest, nor connected with him for any vain purpose;* لَمْ يَبْقَ عَلَيْهِ مُشْكِلٌ فِي ٱلشَّرْعِ إِلَّا تَبَيَّنَ وَلَا مُغْلَقٌ إِلَّا ٱنْفَتَحَ وَلَا غَامِضٌ إِلَّا ٱتَّضَحَ, *there remained for him no difficulty in the (divine) law that did not become clear, and nothing sealed up that was not opened, and nothing obscure that was not made plain;* لَسْتُ أَعْنِى بِٱلْقَلْبِ قَلْبَ ٱلْجِسْمِ وَلَا ٱلرُّوحَ ٱلَّذِى فِى تَجْوِيفِهِ, *I understand by the (term) heart neither the corporeal heart nor the spirit that dwells in its cavity.* If, however, the second clause be conceived as independent of the first, and the connection be merely an external one, the particular negative is repeated; as: هَلْ هُوَ أَمْرٌ لَمْ يَزَلْ مَوْجُودًا فِيمَا سَلَفَ وَلَمْ يَسْبِقْهُ ٱلْعَدَمُ بِوَجْهٍ مِنَ ٱلْوُجُوهِ, *is it a thing which has never ceased existing during the past, and which a period of non-existence has never in any way preceded?*

Rem. *a.* When غَيْر requires to be repeated, its place is sup-

plied by لا, which is followed by the genitive governed by غَيْر;
as: فَنَحَرَهَا غَيْرَ مُحْتَبَسَةٍ وَلَا مُعَقَّلَةٍ, *and he slaughtered them without their being either shut up or bound;* هُوَ غَيْرُ غَرِيبٍ وَلَا عَجِيبٍ,
this is neither strange nor wonderful. See §. 82, 4, rem. a.

Rem. b. لا is sometimes repeated emphatically after a preceding negative, and requires to be rendered in English by *even*; as:
وَلَا أَرَى أَنْ خَرَجَ مِنْهُمْ وَلَا وَاحِدٌ, *but I do not see that there has come out even a single one of them.*

161. In oaths and asseverations لا is followed by the perfect with the signification of our future (see §. 1, c); as:
وَٱللّٰهِ لَا عَصَيْتُ رَبِّي, *by God, I will not disobey my Lord;* وَٱللّٰهِ لَا فَتَحْتُ هٰذَا ٱلْبَابَ, *by God, I will not open this door;* وَحَيٰوةِ فِرْعَوْنَ لَا خَرَجْتُمْ مِنْ هٰهُنَا, *by the life of Pharaoh, ye shall not quit this place;* لَا عَتَبْتُ عَلَيْهِ بَقِيَّةَ عُمْرِي, *I will never reproach him (again) during the remainder of my life.* In blessings and curses it is followed by the perfect as an optative (see §. 1, f); as: لَا رَأَيْتَ شَرًّا, *may you never see (suffer) evil!* لَا كَانَ, *may he not be (may he perish)!*

162. When verbs signifying to forbid, fear, and the like, are followed by أَنْ with the subjunctive, the negative لا is sometimes inserted after أَنْ لَا or أَلَّا) without affecting the meaning (see §. 15, 1); as: مَا مَنَعَكَ أَلَّا تَسْجُدَ, *what prevented you from worshipping (him)?* مَا مَنَعَكَ إِذْ, رَأَيْتَهُمْ ضَلُّوا أَنْ لَا تَتَّبِعَنِي, *what hindered thee from following me, since thou sawest that they have gone astray?*

وَإِنْ خِفْتُمْ أَلَّا تُقْسِطُوا فِي ٱلْيَتَامَى, *and if ye are afraid of being unjust towards the orphans* (but if we read تُقْسِطُوا, لَا is no longer redundant: *if ye are afraid of not being just &c.*).

163. The prohibitive لَا governs either the jussive or the energetic. See §. 17, 2, §. 19, 2, and §. 20.

2. Interrogative Sentences.

164. The Arabic language ignores the difference between the direct and the indirect question, in so far as regards the arrangement of the words and the mood of the verb. Every interrogative clause, even when dependent upon a preceding one, takes the direct form.

165. A question is sometimes indicated merely by the tone of the voice, and that both when it stands alone, and when it is connected with a second question by أَمْ or أَوْ; as: فَقَالُوا تَخْشَى عَلَيْنَا مِنْ نَفْسِكَ شَيْئًا, *and they said, Dost thou fear any evil to us from thyself?* رَمْيُ ٱلْجِمَارِ رَاكِبًا, أَنْفَلُ أَمْ رَاجِلًا, *is it better to cast the stones* (one of the ceremonies of the pilgrimage to Mekka) *riding or on foot?* لَا أَدْرِي هُوَ مِنْ رُحْتُ أَوْ مِنْ أَرَحْتُ, *I do not know whether it comes from* roḥtu *or from* 'araḥtu. In general, however, a question is introduced by one or other of the interrogative particles mentioned in vol. I. §§. 361, 362.

166. The simplest interrogative particle is أَ, which is also prefixed to the word إِنْ, and to the conjunctions وَ

and نَ ; as: اَنُؤْمِنُ كَمَا آمَنَ ٱلسُّفَهَآءُ, *shall we believe as fools have believed?* اَئِنَّكَ لَأَنْتَ يُوسُفُ, *art thou really Joseph?* فَقَالَ أَبُو بَكْرٍ أَوَكُلُّكُمْ رَأْيُهُ عَلَى هٰذَا, *and 'Abū Bekr said, Are you all of this opinion?* اَنَسَمِعْتَنِى أَقُولُ إِلَّا خَيْرًا, *have you then heard me saying aught but good?* If another clause be connected by أَمْ with the one beginning with أَ (in this case called هَمْزَةُ ٱلتَّسْوِيَةِ, *the hemza of equalisation*), there arises a disjunctive or alternative question; as: أَزَيْدٌ عِنْدَنَا أَمْ عُمَرُ, *(is it) Zeid or 'Omar?* سَوَآءٌ عَلَيْنَا أَجَزِعْنَا أَمْ صَبَرْنَا, *it is all the same to us, whether we bear (our torments) impatiently or with patience;* سَوَآءٌ عَلَيْهِمْ أَأَنْذَرْتَهُمْ أَمْ لَمْ تُنْذِرْهُمْ, *it is all one to them, whether thou hast warned them or not;* وَمِنَ ٱلْعَجَآئِبِ عُجْبُ مَنْ هُوَ جَاهِلٌ أَهْوَ ٱلسَّعِيدُ أَمِ ٱلشَّقِىُّ أَمْ كَيْفَ يَخْتِمُ عُمْرَهُ, *one of the strange things is the self-conceit of him who does not know whether he will be saved or damned, or how his life will end.* Instead of أَمْ we may use أَوْ; as: اِخْتِلَافُهُمْ فِى نَعِيمِ ٱلْجَنَّةِ أَهْوَ مِنْ جِنْسِ نَعِيمِ ٱلدُّنْيَا أَوْ غَيْرِهِ, *their difference of opinion in regard to the delights of Paradise, whether they are of the same kind as the delights of the world, or of a different kind.*

167. The interrogative particle هَلْ introduces questions of a more lively sort; as: هَلْ تَحْفَظِينَ مِنْ أَبِى يُوسُفَ ٱلْفِقْهِ شَيْئًا, *do you recollect any of 'Abū Yūsuf's sayings* (lit. *do you recollect anything from 'Abū Yūsuf) regarding*

222   Part Third. Syntax.

jurisprudence? — On the elliptical expression هَلْ لَكَ فِي كَذَا, see §. 54, 2, rem. *e*. When followed by a clause commencing with أَنْ, the preposition فِي may be omitted; as: هَلْ لَكَ أَنْ تَنَامَ, *do you wish to go to sleep?*

168. The compound negative particle أَلَا, *nonne*, is often used to draw close attention to the certainty of the following assertion, and hence admits of being rendered into English by *truly, verily, certainly* (compare in Hebrew הֲלֹא = הִנֵּה, Gesenius' Gr. §. 150, 2), in which case it is frequently followed, as a farther asseverative, by إِنَّ; e. g. أَلَا لَا تَنَالُ ٱلْعِلْمَ إِلَّا بِسِتَّةٍ, *certainly you will never attain learning except through six things* (lit. *is it not so? you will not &c.*); أَلَا إِنَّ ٱلْحَدَاثَةَ لَا تَدُومُ, *verily youth does not last for ever;* أَلَا إِنَّهُمْ هُمُ ٱلسُّفَهَاءُ, *verily these are the fools;* أَلَا أَيُّهَا ذَا ٱلنَّابِحُ ٱلسَّيِّدَ إِنِّي عَلَى نَأْيِهَا مُسْتَبْسِلٌ مِنْ وَرَائِهَا, *O thou that barkest at (revilest) the Bĕnŭ 's-Sid, I am ready to fight to the death in their defence, though they are far away.* It is also used as a corroborative before the optative perfect (§. 1, *f*), the imperative, jussive, and energetic; as: أَلَا تَبَّعَ ٱللّٰهُ وَجْهَكَ, *may God disfigure thy face!* — The synonymous particle أَمَا is used in the same way as أَلَا; e. g. أَمَا وَٱللّٰهِ لَوْ تَعَدَّيْتَهَا قَتَلْتُكَ, *verily, by God, had you transgressed it, I would have put you to death;* أَمَا إِنَّهُ لَا خَيْرَ بِخَيْرٍ بَعْدَهُ ٱلنَّارُ, *verily there is no good in prosperity that is followed by the fire* (*of hell*); أَمَا وَٱلرَّاقِصَاتِ بِذَاتِ عِرْقٍ وَمَنْ صَلَّى بِنُعْمَانِ ٱلْأَرَاكِ

لَقَدْ أَضْمَرْتُ حُبَّكِ فِي فُؤَادِي, *by those who are dancing at Dāt 'Irḳ, and who pray at Naʿmān abounding in 'arāk-trees. (I swear that) I have treasured up love for thee in my heart.*

169. لَوْمَا, لَوْلَا, هَلَّا, أَلَّا, and لَوْمَا, (called by the grammarians حُرُوفُ ٱلتَّحْضِيضِ وَٱلتَّعْرِيضِ, *the particles of incitement and reproof*), are used before the imperfect to incite one to perform an act, and before the perfect to rebuke the neglect of it; as: أَلَّا تُصَنِّفُ كِتَابًا فِي ٱلزُّهْدِ, *why do you not write a book upon asceticism?* equivalent to *write one, pray*; but: أَلَّا صَنَّفْتَ كِتَابًا فِي ٱلزُّهْدِ, *why have you not written a book upon asceticism?* هَلَّا أَعْلَمْتَنِي, *why did you not inform me of it?* يَقُولُ ٱلَّذِينَ كَفَرُوا لَوْلَا أُنْزِلَ عَلَيْهِ آيَةٌ مِنْ رَبِّهِ, *those who do not believe, say, Why has no sign from his Lord been sent down to him?* لَوْلَا يُكَلِّمُنَا ٱللَّهُ أَوْ تَأْتِينَا آيَةٌ, *why does not God speak to us or a sign come to us?* لَوْمَا تَأْتِينَا بِٱلْمَلَٰئِكَةِ إِنْ كُنْتَ مِنَ ٱلصَّادِقِينَ, *why dost thou not bring the angels to us, if thou art (one) of those who speak the truth?* In later times the simple مَا is so used; e. g. مَا تَقُومُ, *dost thou not stand up?* or *thou dost not stand up!* equivalent to *pray, stand up.*

170. The interrogative pronouns مَنْ, *who?* and مَا, *what?* may stand in any one of the three cases, nominative, genitive, or accusative; as: مَنْ أَنْتَ, *who art thou?* بِنْتُ مَنْ أَنْتِ, *whose daughter art thou?* مَنْ قَتَلْتَ, *whom hast thou slain?* Even when they ought, strictly speaking, to

follow another word in the genitive, they may be put first in the nominative absolute, and their proper place supplied by a pronoun that falls back upon them (عَآئِدٌ or رَاجِعٌ); as: قُلْ مَنْ بِيَدِهِ مَلَكُوتُ كُلِّ شَىْءٍ (instead of مَنْ بِيَدِ), *Say, In whose hand is the kingdom over everything?* But no such pronoun can be used, unless مَنْ and مَا precede in the nominative absolute. — To render the interrogation more lively, the demonstrative pronoun ذَا is appended (like the Heb. זֶה) to the interrogatives مَنْ and مَا, even when the subject of the interrogative clause is introduced by the relative pronoun اَلَّذِى; as: مَا ذَا تَقُولُ or مَا ذَا الَّذِى تَقُولُ, *what is it (that) you say?* مَنْ ذَا أَمَرَ or مَنْ ذَا الَّذِى أَمَرَ, *who is it that has given orders?* لِمَا ذَا وَلَّيْتَ بَعْدَ مَجِيئِكَ إِلَى هُهُنَا, (pron. *limā dā*), *why do you run away after your coming hither?* — The pronouns مَنْ and مَا are always used substantively, but can neither govern a genitive nor be followed by another substantive in apposition to them in any case (nom., gen., or acc.); مَنْ فَارِسٌ, مَنْ فَتًى, *do not mean* τίς ἀνήρ; *quisnam vir? quis eques (est ille quem vides)?* but *quis (est) vir? quis (est) eques?* مَنْ *being the subject and the following word the predicate. E. g.* إِذَا ٱلْقَوْمُ قَالُوا مَنْ فَتًى خِلْتُ أَنِّى عُنِيتُ, *when the tribe ask, Who is a man? I think that I am meant;* لَوْ كَانَ فِى ٱلْآلِفِ مِنَّا وَاحِدٌ فَدَعَوْا مَنْ فَارِسٌ خَالَهُمْ إِيَّاهُ يَعْنُونَا يَعْنُونَا, *were there one of us among a thousand, and they cried out, Who is a horseman? he would think that it was he they meant*

Interrogative Sentences.

in rhyme for مَنْ إِلٰهٌ غَيْرُ ٱللّٰهِ يَأْتِيكُمْ بِضِيَآءٍ, lit. (يَعْنُونَ); who (is) a god, different from the (true) God, (that) can give you light? the words يَأْتِيكُمْ بِضِيَآءٍ forming a relative clause in connection with the indefinite substantive إِلٰهٌ (see §. 172). Even such a case as is represented by the words مَنْ زَيْدٍ, مَنْ زَيْدًا, in no way violates our rule. One person says رَأَيْتُ زَيْدًا, I have seen Zèid; another, repeating the exact words of the former speaker (ٱلْحِكَايَةُ), asks: مَنْ زَيْدًا, who is (the person you meant, when you said "ra'èitu Zèidan", by the word) „Zeidan"? Similarly, in the genitive, مَرَرْتُ بِزَيْدٍ, I passed by Zèid, مَنْ زَيْدٍ. In general, however, the حِكَايَةٌ (imitation, citation or quoting of the exact words of a speaker) is neglected, and the questioner asks مَنْ زَيْدٌ, who is Zèid? in the nominative. This حِكَايَةٌ is allowed only when the word quoted is a proper name, and مَنْ is not preceded by any connective particle, such as وَ. We can only say وَمَنْ زَيْدٌ, and who is Zèid? مَنْ غُلَامُ زَيْدٍ, who is the slave of Zèid? — As an interrogative, مَنْ is construed with the masculine singular of a verb, but occasionally admits of the feminine, when the predicate is a person of the female sex; as: مَنْ كَانَتْ أُمَّكَ, who was thy mother? — If inquiry be made regarding the nature, qualities, social position, &c., of a person, مَا is used as the predicate, and not مَنْ; e. g. وَقُلْنَا لَهُ مَا أَنْتَ, and we said to him, What art thou? مَا رَبُّ ٱلْعَالَمِينَ, what is the Lord of created things? أَخْبِرِينِى عَنْ قَوْلِكَ وَلَمَّا رَأَتْ رَكْبَ ٱلنُّمَيْرِيِّ أَعْرَضَتْ وَكُنَّ مِنْ أَنْ

يَلْقَيْنَهُ حَذِرَاتٍ)* مَا كُنْتُمْ قَالَ كُنْتُ عَلَى حِمَارٍ هَزِيلٍ وَمَعِي صَاحِبٌ لِي عَلَى أَتَانٍ مِثْلِهِ, *tell me about your verse:* "*And after she descried the cavalcade of the Numèiri, she turned aside, and they were on their guard against meeting him*", — *what were you? He said, I was upon a lean he-ass, and along with me was a companion of mine upon a she-ass like it.*

Rem. On the shortening of مَا into مَ, see vol. I. §. 351, rem.

171. Regarding the interrogative pronoun أَيُّ, of which we have spoken before (§. 87), there are here two remarks to be made. 1) أَيُّ is used, not only instead of the fem. أَيَّةُ, but also instead of the plur. أَيُّونَ; as: مِنْ أَيِّ قَبِيلَةٍ أَنْتَ, *of what tribe art thou?* مِنْ أَيِّ ٱلنَّاسِ أَنْتَ, *of what people art thou?* 2) A nominal sentence with a nominal predicate, of which the subject (ٱلْمُبْتَدَأُ) is أَيُّ with a pronominal suffix, may, as a whole, without any change of case, supply the place of an accusative to a verb or of a genitive after a preposition; as: ثُمَّ لَنَنْزِعَنَّ مِنْ كُلِّ شِيعَةٍ أَيُّهُمْ أَشَدُّ عَلَى ٱلرَّحْمَنِ عُتِيًّا, *then will we draw forth from every sect those who have been most violent in rebellious pride towards the Merciful;* مَضَغَهَا لِيَنْظُرَ أَيُّهَا أَصْلَبُ, *he bit them with his teeth in order to see which of them was the hardest;* إِذَا مَا لَقِيتَ بَنِى مَالِكٍ فَسَلِّمْ عَلَى أَيِّهِمْ أَفْضَلُ, *when you meet the Benū Mālik, salute him who is most excellent*

*) in حَذِرَاتٍ and مِنْ أَنْ, by poetic license for مِنْ أَنَّ rhyme for حَذِرَاتِ.

amongst them. In such cases, however, أَيٌّ may be put alone, without any suffix, in the accusative or genitive, the vacant place of the subject in the nominal clause being supplied by the pronoun of the third person. In the former case أَيٌّ is treated as an interrogative, in the latter as a relative pronoun.

Rem. أَيٌّ also serves to express astonishment, in which case it is always put in the masc. sing., and the noun which it governs in the genitive is undefined. If the preceding noun, to which أَيٌّ refers, be indefinite, then أَيٌّ agrees with it in case; as: جِئْتَنِى بِرَجُلٍ أَىِّ رَجُلٍ, *you have brought me a man, (and) what a man!* = *what a man you have brought me!* But if the preceding noun be definite, أَيٌّ is always put in the circumstantial accusative or *ḥāl*; as: جَآءَنِى زَيْدٌ أَىَّ رَجُلٍ, *Zeid came to me, (and) what a man (he is)!* The reason of this is, that the interrogative and exclamatory أَيٌّ, being by its very nature always indefinite, can never be in concord with a definite substantive. — The substantive that constitutes the object of wonder may be understood, when it is virtually contained in the verb, and أَيٌّ must then be put in whatever case that substantive would have stood, had it been expressed; as: إِنْتَكَوْا أَىَّ نِكَايَةٍ, *how they have been tormented!* i. e. نِكَايَةً أَىَّ نِكَايَةٍ.

3. Relative Sentences.

172. There are in Arabic, as well as in the other Shemitic languages, two sorts of relative sentences; namely 1) *indefinite*, i. e. such as are annexed to an immediately preceding indefinite substantive, without the aid of a conjunctive noun (vol. I. p. 219); and 2) *definite*, i. e. such as are introduced by a conjunctive noun, whether substantive or adjective, which is definite by its very nature. A sentence of the former kind is called صِفَةٌ, *a descriptive* or *qualificative sentence;* of the latter kind, صِلَةٌ, *a conjunctive sentence;* and the conjunctive noun itself is called اَلْاِسْمُ ٱلْمَوْصُولُ or simply اَلْمَوْصُولُ. Examples of the *first* kind: مَرَرْتُ بِرَجُلٍ يَنَامُ, *I passed by a man who was sleeping;* أَوَّلُ بَيْتٍ وُضِعَ لِلنَّاسِ, *the first temple that was founded for mankind;* آيَاتٌ مُحْكَمَاتٌ هُنَّ أُمُّ ٱلْكِتَابِ, *firmly constructed* (i. e. *unambiguous*) *verses, which form the chief portion* (lit. *are the mother*) *of the Scriptures;* يَوْمٌ لَا بَيْعٌ فِيهِ وَلَا خُلَّةٌ وَلَا شَفَاعَةٌ, *a day on which neither traffic, nor friendship, nor intercession shall be of any avail* (compare Gesenius' Heb. Gr. §. 121, 3). Examples of the *second* kind: مَنْ فَعَلَ ذٰلِكَ, *he who did* or *has done this;* اَلْمَلِكُ ٱلَّذِى يَعْدِلُ, *the king who is just.* — Sometimes, however, a noun defined by the article is followed by a qualificative sentence, when that noun indicates, not a particular individual (animate or inanimate), but any individual bearing the name; e. g. مَا يَنْبَغِى لِلرَّجُلِ يُشْبِهُكَ, *what becomes the man who is like you;* كَمَثَلِ ٱلْحِمَارِ يَحْمِلُ أَسْفَارًا, *like the ass that carries books;* كَالْجَمْرِ يُوضَعُ فِى ٱلرَّمَادِ, *like the coal that is put among the ashes.* In such phrases as نِعْمَ ٱلرَّأْىُ رَأَيْتَ, *what an excellent resolution you have adopted!* the substantive ٱلرَّأْىُ is the first nominative after the verb of praise, and the clause رَأَيْتَ the second nominative, standing for مَا رَأَيْتَ; so that the expression is equivalent to نِعْمَ ٱلرَّأْىُ رَأْيُكَ.

Rem. *a.* The Arabs, like the other Shemites, have no relative pronoun which they can employ when the antecedent to the relative clause is indefinite. Further, it should be observed that أَىُّ and ٱلَّذِى are always definite, whether the latter be used substantively or adjectively, whilst مَنْ and مَا, which can only be used substantively, are either definite or indefinite; e. g. مَنْ جَآءَ, *he who comes* or *one who comes;* مَا لِى, *that which I have* or *something which I have.* When employed indefinitely, مَنْ and مَا are not regarded by the Arabs as conjunctive nouns, but as indeclinable substantives (equivalent in meaning to شَخْصٌ, *a person,* and شَىْءٌ, *a thing*), to which the words that we regard as the complement of the relative pronoun, are annexed as a qualificative clause, which is virtually in the same case. We even find, though very rarely, a single adjective so annexed to مَنْ or مَا, and actually agreeing with them in case. When thus used, مَنْ and مَا are said to be مَوْصُوفَةٌ.

Rem. *b.* The pronoun in the qualificative clause, which falls back upon the antecedent (اَلْعَائِدُ or اَلرَّاجِعُ), ought, strictly speaking, to be of the third person, even when the subject of the qualified substantive is a pronoun of the first or second person. In practice, however, the one is usually brought into agreement with the other; as: إِنَّا لَقَوْمٌ مَا, إِنَّكُمْ قَوْمٌ تَجْهَلُونَ, *ye are people who are foolish;* نَرَى ٱلْقَتْلَ سُبَّةً, *verily we are people who count it no disgrace to be slain;* إِنِّى ٱمْرُؤٌ تَجِدُ ٱلرِّجَالَ عَدَاوَتِى, *verily I am a man whose hostility (brave) men find (to be terrible).*

173. The qualificative sentence necessarily contains a pronoun (اَلرَّاجِعُ or اَلْعَائِدُ), referring to the qualified noun and connecting it with the qualificative sentence. This pronoun is either contained in the verb of the qualificative sentence, as its nominative, e. g. رَجُلٌ جَآءَ, *a man who came;* or, in case of its being a nominal sentence, is expressed by a separate pronoun, e. g. رَجُلٌ هُوَ صَدِيقِى, *a man who is my friend;* or, lastly, appears as a suffix in the genitive or accusative, e. g. مَرَرْتُ بِرَجُلٍ أَبُوهُ نَائِمٌ, *I passed by a man whose father was asleep;* زَوَّجْتُ ٱبْنِى بِٱمْرَأَةٍ كَانَ عَمْرٌو يُحِبُّهَا, *I married my son to a woman with whom 'Amr was in love.* The suffix is, however, not unfrequently suppressed, when the sense clearly indicates the connection between the qualified noun and the qualificative clause; as: فَمَا أَدْرِى أَغَيَّرَهُمْ ثَنَآءٌ وَطُولُ ٱلْعَهْدِ أَمْ مَالٌ أَصَابُوا, *and I do not know whether distance and length of time have altered them, or wealth which they have won* (أَصَابُوهُ for أَصَابُوا); ضَرَبْتُهُ ضَرْبَةً خَرَّ كَٱلْمَيِّتِ, *I struck him a blow at which he fell like dead* (خَرَّ بِهَا for خَرَّ).

174. The conjunctive noun اَلَّذِى may be used either substantively or adjectively. In the former case, it includes the idea of a person or thing, that is to say, it is equivalent to the substantive مَنْ and مَا, when they are definite (مَوْصُولَةٌ), *he who, that which*. In the latter case, it agrees, like any other adjective, with its antecedent, which is always a definite substantive, in gender, number and *case*, and thus markedly differs from the relative pronouns of the Indogermanic languages; as: عِنْدَ ٱلرَّجُلَيْنِ ٱللَّذَيْنِ جَآءَا, *in the possession of the two men who are come*; رَأَيْتُ ٱلرَّجُلَيْنِ ٱللَّذَيْنِ هُمَا بَخِيلَانِ, *I saw the two men who are niggardly*.

175. As the case in which the conjunctive nouns stand, is altogether independent of the conjunctive clause, they cannot express the syntactical relations of our relative pronouns. If they stand (as is always the case with مَنْ, مَا, and أَىُّ, and frequently with اَلَّذِى) as substantives at the beginning of an independent sentence, they form its subject or inchoative (مُبْتَدَأٌ), and are consequently in the nominative; and the same is the case with اَلَّذِى, when it is annexed as an adjective to any such subject in the nominative. In every other case, they stand, it is true, at the commencement of the conjunctive sentence, but are in whatever case the preceding governing word requires, be it noun, verb, or particle; that is to say, they are in that case which, according to our idiom, pertains to the demonstrative pronoun implied in them, or to the substantive antece-

dent to which they refer. The syntactical place of our relative pronoun is supplied by a pronoun in the conjunctive sentence, which falls back upon the conjunctive noun and agrees with it in gender and number. This pronoun is called by the grammarians اَلضَّمِيرُ ٱلْعَآئِدُ (ٱلرَّاجِعُ) or) إِلَى ٱلْمَوْصُولِ, *the pronoun that returns to the conjunctive noun*, or simply اَلرَّاجِعُ or اَلْعَآئِدُ.

1) If this pronoun stand, as the subject, in the nominative case, it is represented, in a *verbal* sentence, by the personal pronoun implied in the verb; e. g. أُحِبُّ مَنْ يَعْدِلُ, *I love him who is just*; مِنْهُمْ مَنْ يَسْتَمِعُونَ إِلَيْكَ, *among them are some who will hearken to thee*; يَا نَكُنْ مِثْلَ مَنْ, ذِئْبُ يَضْطَحِبَانِ, *(if so,) we shall be like those, O wolf, who are comrades*; أَخَافُ مِنَ ٱلْمَلِكِ ٱلَّذِى يَظْلِمُ ٱلنَّاسَ, *I am afraid of the king who oppresses mankind*. But in a *nominal* sentence, it is expressed by a separate pronoun; e. g. مَنْ هُوَ بَرٌّ, *he who is pious*; مِمَّا هُوَ ضَلَالٌ, *of that which is error*; عُدْتُ ٱلشَّيْخَ ٱلَّذِى هُوَ مَرِيضٌ, *I have visited the old man who is sick*. In nominal sentences of which the predicate is an adverb, or a preposition with its genitive, depending upon the idea of *being* understood, the virtually existing subject of the substantive verb suffices to connect the clauses, without any separate pronoun being expressed; as: مَرَرْتُ بِمَنْ ثَمَّ, *I passed by him who is there* or *those who are there*; لَهُ مَا فِى ٱلسَّمَٰوَاتِ وَٱلْأَرْضِ وَمَنْ عِنْدَهُ لَا يَسْتَكْبِرُونَ عَنْ عِبَادَتِهِ, *to him belongs what is in heaven*

and upon earth, and those who dwell with him are not too proud to serve him; إِنَّ أَوَّلَ بَيْتٍ وُضِعَ لِلنَّاسِ لَلَّذِى بِبَكَّةَ, *verily the first temple that was founded for mankind is that which is at Bèkka (Mèkka).* The عَائِدٌ may also be omitted in a nominal sentence of more than the usual very limited length; as: جَآءَ ٱلَّذِى ضَارِبٌ زَيْدًا, *he who beats Zèid, is come;* هُوَ ٱلَّذِى فِى ٱلسَّمَآءِ إِلٰهٌ وَفِى ٱلْأَرْضِ إِلٰهٌ, *he it is who is a God in heaven and a God upon earth;* مَا أَنَا بِٱلَّذِى قَآئِلٌ لَكَ سُوءَ, *I am not he who speaks evil of you;* but this omission is rare in very short nominal sentences; e. g. جَآءَ ٱلَّذِى قَآئِمٌ, *he who stands, is come;* مَنْ يُعْنَ بِٱلْحَمْدِ لَا يَنْطِقُ بِمَا سَفِهَ, *he who strives hard after praise, does not speak what is foolish.*

2) If the عَائِدٌ be an objective complement in the accusative, it is appended as a suffix to the verb; e. g. ٱلسَّارِقُ ٱلَّذِى قَتَلَهُ ٱبْنِى, *he whom I have seen;* مَنْ رَأَيْتُهُ, *the thief whom my son killed.* The suffix is, however, not unfrequently omitted; as: ٱلْمَالُ ٱلَّذِى تَشْتَهِى أَنْفُسُنَا, *the wealth which our souls desire* (تَشْتَهِى for تَشْتَهِيهِ); ٱلْكِتَابُ ٱلَّذِى أَنْزَلَ ٱللّٰهُ, *the book which God has sent down or revealed* (أَنْزَلَ for أَنْزَلَهُ).

3) A pronominal suffix also supplies the place of our relative, when it stands in the genitive, dative, &c., or is governed by a preposition; as: ٱلطَّبِيبُ ٱلَّذِى ٱبْنُهُ عِنْدِى, *the physician whose son is at my house;* مَنْ لَهُ مَالٌ كَثِيرٌ,

he who has great possessions; مَا تَدْعُوهُمْ إِلَيْهِ, *that to which you summon them.* Should the suffix, however, be preceded by the same preposition as the preceding conjunctive noun, the suffix and its preposition may be omitted; as: أَنَا عِنْدَ مَنْ أَنْتَ, *I am at the house of the same person as you* (أَنْتَ); مَرَرْتُ بِٱلَّذِي مَرَّ سُلَيْمٰنُ (أَنْتَ عِنْدَهُ); *I passed by the same person as Sulaimān did* (مَرَّ) for مَرَّ بِهِ). But this is not allowed when the preposition is used before the suffix in a different meaning from that which it has before the conjunctive noun, nor when the preceding verb is a different one; as: زَهِدْتُ فِي ٱلَّذِي رَغِبْتَ فِيهِ, *I have had no longing after that which you desired* (not فِي ٱلَّذِي رَغِبْتَ).

Rem. The عَائِدٌ after ٱلَّذِي originally was, and, strictly speaking, ought to be, a pronoun of the third person, even when the preceding subject is a pronoun of the first or second person; as: نَحْنُ ٱلَّذِينَ أَضْجَرُوا إِصْبَاحًا, *it is we who were up early.* More usually, however, the عَائِدٌ is brought into agreement with the word to which it refers (compare §. 172 rem. *b*); as; أَنَا ٱلَّذِي سَمَّتْنِي أُمِّي حَيْدَرَة, *I am he whom his* (lit. *my*) *mother named Haidara* (*Lion*);(*) أَلَسْتَ ٱلْعَبْدَ ٱلْأَسْوَدَ ٱلَّذِي كُنْتَ تُرَاعِينَا بِمَوْضِعِ كَذَا, *are you not the negro slave, who used to attend upon us in such and such a place?*

(*) سَمَّتْنِي by poetic license for سَمَّتْنِي, and حَيْدَرَةَ in rhyme for حَيْدَرَةَ.

4. Copulative Sentences.

176. We have already spoken of the difference between the copulative particles وَ and فَ in Vol. I. §. 366. To what has been there said, the following remarks may be added. — *a)* If to the subject implied in any form of the finite verb, there be added another subject, the former must be repeated in the shape of a separate personal pronoun; as: حَضَرْتُ أَنَا وَيَعْقُوبُ, *I and Ya'ḳūb were present;* أَتَى هُوَ وَأَصْحَابُهُ, *he and his companions came;* اِذْهَبْ أَنْتَ وَرَبَّكَ, *Go, thou and thy master.* — *b)* If a substantive be connected by وَ with the pronominal suffix of a verb, the suffix may be repeated in the shape of a separate pronoun, but not necessarily; as: أَجْنِبْنِى وَبَنِىَّ, *remove me and my sons;* أَجْلَاهُ وَقَوْمَهُ, *he removed him and his people to another country.* But if a pronoun is to be connected by وَ with a substantive or pronoun in the accusative, it must be suffixed either to the repeated verb or to the particle إِيَّا (Vol. I. §. 188); as: قَتَلَهُ وَإِيَّاهَا or قَتَلَهُ وَقَتَلَهَا, *he killed him and her.* — *c)* If with a pronominal suffix in the genitive there be connected a substantive in the same case, the former must be repeated as a separate pronoun; as: اِتِّفَاقُهُ هُوَ وَأَخِيهِ, *his and his brother's agreement.* — *d)* The form of expression given under *a* may be varied by repeating the verb after وَ, but even then it is customary to employ the separate pronoun; as: حَضَرْتُ أَنَا وَحَضَرَ يَعْقُوبُ, *I and Ya'ḳūb were present.* The verb may be repeated in the same way, when a substantive object is annexed to a pronominal object (see above, b); as: قَتَلْتُهُ وَقَتَلْتُ مَنْ كَانَ مَعَهُ مِنْ أَهْلِهِ, *I killed him and those of his family who were with him*, or قَتَلْتُهُ وَمَنْ كَانَ الخ. — *e*) If a substantive be connected by وَ with the pronominal suffix of a preposition, the preposition must be repeated; as: لِي وَلِأَخِيهِ, *to me and his brother*. This rule is sometimes violated in poetry, but very rarely in prose; as: فَقَدْ خَابَ مَنْ يَصْلَى بِهَا وَسَعِيرِهَا, *and lost is he who is scorched in it* (war) *and its flame*. — *f*) If a genitive belongs alike to two or more nouns, it is, in classical Arabic, attached to the first of them, and represented after the other by a pronominal suffix; as: بَنُو ٱلْمَلِكِ وَبَنَاتُهُ, *the king's sons and daughters*. But in later times, and even occasionally in ancient poetry, this rule is neglected, the genitive being annexed to the last substantive, and the preceding ones put in the construct state (see §. 78, rem.); as: مُوسَى يَذْكُرُ أَوْلَادَ وَأَحْفَادَ آدَمَ, *Moses mentions by name the sons and grandsons of Adam*, instead of أَوْلَادَ آدَمَ وَأَحْفَادَهُ. — *g*) The negative particle لَا, when it follows وَ, supplies the place of a preceding negative sentence (see §. 160); as: لَمْ يَبْقَ أَبِي وَلَا أُمِّي, *neither my father nor my mother remains alive*. Sometimes لَا is prefixed even to the first substantive, notwithstanding the negative that precedes the whole sentence; as: مَا وَقَعَ بَيْنَنَا لَا قِتَالٌ وَلَا كَلَامٌ, *there has been neither combat nor dispute between us*.

177. When two verbs, connected by وَ and referring

Copulative Sentences.

to the same subject, precede that subject, one of them (in general the second) agrees with it in gender and number, whilst the other is put in the singular masculine; as: بَغَى وَٱعْتَدَيَا عَبْدَاكَ, *your two servants acted insolently and with violence;* يُحْسِنَانِ وَيُسِىءُ ٱبْنَاكَ, *your two sons do good and evil.* This involved form of expression occurs, however, but rarely in classical Arabic, in which we usually find: يُحْسِنُ ٱبْنَاكَ وَيُسِيئَانِ, بَغَى عَبْدَاكَ وَٱعْتَدَيَا.

R e m. This and the following sections, as far as §. 180, furnish examples of what the Arab grammarians call ٱلتَّنَازُعُ فِي ٱلْعَمَلِ, *the conflict in regard to government.*

178. Sometimes a noun belongs to two verbs as the subject of the one and the objective complement of the other. *a)* When this is the case, if the verb to which it is the complement be placed first, the noun is expressed only as the subject of the second verb, and the first verb is left without any complement; as: ضَرَبْتُ وَضَرَبَنِى زَيْدٌ, *I struck (Zeid) and Zeid struck me.* Some Arab grammarians, however, allow the first verb a pronominal complement; as: ضَرَبْتُهُ وَضَرَبَنِى زَيْدٌ. *b)* If the verb, of which the noun is the subject, be placed first, the second verb takes a pronominal complement, and the first verb agrees with the noun according to the rules laid down in §. 141 .etc.; as: ضَرَبَنِى وَضَرَبْتُهُمَا ٱلزَّيْدَانِ, *the two Zeids struck me and I struck them.* The omission of the pronominal complement is rare; as: ضَرَبَنِى وَضَرَبْتُ ٱلزَّيْدَانِ. The noun may also be made the complement of the second verb, and the first

verb, which has now no subject expressed, must agree with the noun in gender and number; as: ضَرَبَانِي وَضَرَبْتُ ٱلزَّيْدَيْنِ, *the two (Zeids) struck me, and I struck the two Zeids*; ضَرَبُونِي وَضَرَبْتُ ٱلزَّيْدِينَ, *they (the Zeids) struck me, and I struck the Zeids*. — All these involved forms of expression occur but seldom in classical Arabic, the usual and regular construction being: ضَرَبَنِي ٱلزَّيْدَانِ وَضَرَبْتُهُمَا, ضَرَبْتُ زَيْدًا وَضَرَبَنِي, ضَرَبْتُ ٱلزَّيْدَيْنِ وَضَرَبَانِي, ضَرَبَنِي ٱلزَّيْدُونَ وَضَرَبْتُهُمْ, ضَرَبْتُ ٱلزَّيْدِينَ وَضَرَبُونِي.

179. In the case of a verb that must be connected with both a subject and a predicate (such as كَانَ or صَارَ), if the predicate be common to two propositions, it is expressed only once, being either entirely omitted the second time or having its place supplied by إِيَّا and a pronominal suffix. For example, we may express *I was sick and Zeid was sick* by كُنْتُ مَرِيضًا وَكَانَ زَيْدٌ, or كُنْتُ وَكَانَ زَيْدٌ مَرِيضًا, or lastly كُنْتُ مَرِيضًا وَكَانَ زَيْدٌ إِيَّاهُ, the first of the three forms being preferred. These involved forms of expression likewise occur but rarely in classical Arabic, the ordinary construction being كُنْتُ مَرِيضًا وَكَانَ زَيْدٌ مَرِيضًا or وَكَانَ زَيْدٌ إِيَّاهُ.

180. Almost the same thing takes place after the verb ظَنَّ, *to think, suppose*, حَسِبَ, *to reckon, think*, etc., which take for their objective complement a clause consisting of a subject and a predicate (§. 24), as: ظَنَنْتُ زَيْدًا عَالِمًا, *I thought Zeid learned*. The predicate of the clause, that

serves as complement to the فِعْلُ ٱلْقَلْبِ, may belong to two different propositions, and consequently refer to two different subjects; whilst the noun, that is the subject of the فِعْلُ ٱلْقَلْبِ in the one proposition, may in the other be the subject of the clause which is dependent upon the فِعْلُ ٱلْقَلْبِ. When this is the case, we may, in accordance with §. 179, translate such a phrase as *Zeid thought me learned and I thought him learned*, by ظَنَّنِى وَظَنَنْتُ زَيْدًا عَالِمًا, or ظَنَّنِى وَظَنَنْتُ زَيْدًا, or lastly ظَنَّنِى إِيَّاهُ وَظَنَنْتُ زَيْدًا عَالِمًا عَالِمًا إِيَّاهُ. The first of these modes of expression is the commonest, but all three are rare, the natural and usual construction being ظَنَّنِى زَيْدٌ عَالِمًا وَظَنَنْتُهُ إِيَّاهُ. — If the subjects differ in gender or number, the predicate must be repeated; as: أَظُنُّ وَيَظُنَّانِى أَخَا زَيْدًا وَعَمْرًا أَخَوَيْنِ, *I think Zeid and 'Amr two brothers (of mine), and they think me a brother (of theirs).*

181. If two verbs are dependent upon another verb, which is preceded by a negative particle, the second of the dependent verbs usually takes the negative لَا along with the conjunction وَ; as: مَا أَمْكَنَنِى أَنْ أَعْمَلَ شَيْئًا وَلَا أَقْطَعَ أَمْرًا, *it was not possible for me to do anything or to conclude anything.* Here لَا is equivalent to a repetition of the words مَا أَمْكَنَنِى أَنْ in the former part of the sentence.

182. The Arabs, as well as the other Shemites, often connect single verbs and entire sentences with one another merely by means of the particles وَ and فَ, where we should

employ particles of a more definite meaning to indicate the precise relation between them. They use وَ, for example, where we would prefer a disjunctive or adversative particle; as: اَللّٰهُ يَعْلَمُ وَأَنْتُمْ لَا تَعْلَمُونَ, *God knows, but ye do not know*. In such cases, however, وَ has in reality only a copulative force; the adversative relation lies in the nature of the two clauses themselves. — The Arabs also use وَ and فَ with a separate verb in some cases in which we avail ourselves of a subordinate modifying expression; e. g. رَكَعَ فَأَطَالَ, *he bowed down and made long (his bowing down)*, equivalent to *he bowed down for a long time*, instead of أَطَالَ ٱلرُّكُوعَ, as we may also say (see §. 140).

183. The particle وَ in Arabic, like its equivalents in the other Shemitic languages, often serves to connect two clauses, the second of which describes the state or condition either of the subject or one of the complements of the first clause, or else of a new subject. This takes place in such a way that:

1) The clause descriptive of the state is nominal; as: اِنْقَرَضَ فِي وَقْتِهِ, قَامَ زَيْدٌ وَهُوَ بَاكٍ, *Zèid rose up weeping*; قَرْنَانِ مِنَ ٱلنَّاسِ وَهُوَ حَىٌّ, *two generations of men passed away in his time, whilst he still lived*; كَذَبْتُمْ وَأَنْتُمْ تَعْلَمُونَ, *ye lied, knowing (that ye did so), ye lied willingly*, in which example the nominal circumstantial clause has a finite verb for its predicate; ذَهَبَ زَيْدٌ وَعَمْرٌو بَاقٍ, *Zèid went away, whilst 'Amr remained*, where the circumstantial clause has a distinct subject; ذَهَبَ زَيْدٌ وَعَمْرٌو يَشْتَغِلُ, *Zèid went away,*

whilst 'Amr was busy, in which case the circumstantial clause has a distinct subject and a finite verb for its predicate.

Rem. We rarely find a nominal clause merely appended to the preceding proposition, without وَ, and even without a pronoun; as: مَرَرْتُ بِٱلْبُرِّ قَفِيزٌ بِدِرْهَمٍ, *I passed by the wheat, (whilst) a bushel (of it was selling) for a dirhem* (قَفِيزٌ for قَفِيزٌ مِنْهُ).

2) The clause descriptive of the state is verbal and affirmative, the verb being in the Imperfect, preceded by وَقَدْ; as: لِمَ تُؤْذُونَنِى وَقَدْ تَعْلَمُونَ أَنِّى رَسُولُ ٱللّٰهِ إِلَيْكُمْ, *why do ye insult me, knowing as ye do, that I am the apostle of God unto you?* If the particle قَدْ be not employed, وَ must also be dropped, so that the circumstantial Imperfect is outwardly unconnected with the previous proposition; as: جَاءَ زَيْدٌ يَضْحَكُ, *Zeid came laughing* (see §. 8, *e*).

3) The clause descriptive of the state is verbal and negative, the verb being in the Imperfect, preceded by وَلَمْ; as: قَالَ أُوحِىَ إِلَىَّ وَلَمْ يُوحَ إِلَيْهِ شَىْءٌ, *he has said, Something has been revealed to me, whilst nothing has been revealed to him*. In this case وَ may be dropped; as: فَٱنْقَلَبُوا بِنِعْمَةٍ مِنَ ٱللّٰهِ وَفَضْلٍ لَمْ يَمْسَسْهُمْ سُوءٌ, *and so they returned, (laden) with favours and benefits from on high, without any evil having touched them*. Where the negation is expressed by لَا, the particle وَ is rarely used; e. g. لَوْ أَنَّ قَوْمًا لِٱرْتِفَاعِ قَبِيلَةٍ دَخَلُوا ٱلسَّمَاءَ دَخَلْتُهَا لَا أُحْجَبُ, *if any persons entered heaven because of distinction of tribe, I would enter it without being hindered*.

4) The clause descriptive of the state is verbal and affirmative, the verb being in the Perfect, preceded by وَقَدْ; as: هٰذَا غِنَآؤُهَا وَقَدْ أَسَنَّتْ, *such is her singing, now that she has grown old.* Sometimes قَدْ is omitted, and, more rarely, either وَ or قَدْ alone; as: جَآءُوكُمْ حَصِرَتْ صُدُورُهُمْ أَنْ يُقَاتِلُوكُمْ, *they are come unto you, their hearts being reluctant to fight against you;* اَلَّذِينَ قَالُوا لِإِخْوَانِهِمْ وَقَعَدُوا لَوْ أَطَاعُونَا مَا قُتِلُوا, *those who, having remained (at home), say of their brethren* (who went out to battle), *If they had taken our advice, they would not have been killed;* مَا كَانَ يَنْفَعُنِى مَقَالُ نِسَآئِهِمْ وَقُتِلَتْ دُونَ رِجَالِهَا لَا تَبْعَدِ, *what can it boot me that their women say, O do not perish! when I am already slain fighting for their husbands?* رَأَيْنَاهُ قَدْ تَغَيَّرَ لِيَزِيدِ وَكَانَ عَلَى جُنْدِهِ, *we saw him enraged against Zeid, who was in command of his army.*

Rem. The وَ that introduces such circumstantial clauses, is called by the Arab grammarians, وَاوُ ٱلْحَالِ, *the wāw that expresses the state, condition* or *circumstance.*

5. Adversative, Restrictive and Exceptive Sentences.

184. The principal adversative particles in Arabic are لٰكِنْ or لٰكِنَّ and بَلْ.

1) لٰكِنْ or لٰكِنَّ, which is often preceded by وَ, is opposed in particular to a preceding negative proposition or a prohibition; as: لَا تَضْرِبْ زَيْدًا وَلٰكِنْ عَمْرًا, *do not beat*

Adversative, Restrictive and Exceptive Sentences.

مَا ظَلَمُونَا وَلٰكِن كَانُوا أَنْفُسَهُم يَظْلِمُون, *Zeid, but Amr; they did not injure us, but they injured themselves;* فَلَا صَدَّقَ وَلَا صَلَّى وَلٰكِن كَذَّبَ وَتَوَلَّى, *he neither believed nor prayed, but accused (the apostle) of imposture and turned away;* يَلُومُونِى فِى حُبِّ لَيْلَى عَوَاذِلِى وَلٰكِنِّى مِن حُبِّهَا لَعَمِيدُ, *my reproachers blame me for loving Leila, but I am deeply smitten with love for her* (عَمِيدُ in rhyme for عَمِيدُ). When introducing a nominal clause, لٰكِنَّ requires the subject to be put in the accusative (see §. 36), whereas لٰكِن leaves it in the nominative; as: لٰكِنِ ٱلظَّالِمُونَ ٱلْيَوْمَ فِى ضَلَالٍ مُبِينٍ, *but the ungodly are today in manifest error.*

2) بَل is opposed either to a preceding affirmative or negative proposition, a command or a prohibition; as: مَا قَامَ زَيْدٌ بَل عَمْرٌو, *Zeid got up — not so, it was Amr;* مَا قَامَ زَيْدٌ بَل عَمْرٌو, *Zeid did not get up, on the contrary, it was Amr;* مَا نَرَى لَكُم عَلَيْنَا مِن فَضْلٍ بَل نَظُنُّكُم كَاذِبِينَ, *we do not see that you are in any way superior to us — on the contrary, we think you liars;* قَالُوا قُلُوبُنَا غُلْفٌ بَل لَعَنَهُمُ ٱللّٰهُ بِكُفْرِهِم, *they say, Our hearts are uncircumsized — that is not it, but God hath cursed them for their unbelief;* خَلَعُوا عَنْهُ خِلْعَتَهُ بَل وَثَوْبَ ٱلْحَيٰوةِ, *they stripped him of his dress, and not only that, but also of the garment of life.*

185. The particle إِنَّمَا is one of the most important in the language as a حَرْفُ حَصْرٍ, or *particle of limitation* or *restriction*. It stands at the beginning of a proposition, whilst the word or portion of the proposition which is affected by

it, is always placed for emphasis' sake at the end (compare §. 36, rem. b)); as: اِنَّمَا نَحْنُ مُسْتَهْزِئُونَ, *we are only making fools (of you)*; اِنَّمَا تَلِدِينَ فِى كُلِّ عُمْرِكِ وَاحِدًا أَوِ اثْنَتَيْنِ, *you give birth in your whole life to only one or two;* اِنَّمَا أَخْشَى سَيْلَ تَلْعَتِى, *I fear the overflow only of my own streamlet.*

186. The exceptive particle that chiefly requires to be noticed in this place, is إِلَّا, a compound of إِنْ, *if*, and لَا, *not*. The rules for the construction of the exception (اَلْاِسْتِثْنَاءُ) are as follows. *a*) When the thing excepted (اَلْمُسْتَثْنَى) is placed *after* the general term (اَلْمُسْتَثْنَى مِنْهُ, *that from which the exception is made*), and the proposition containing that term is affirmative, the exception must be put in the accusative; e. g. قَامَ ٱلْقَوْمُ إِلَّا زَيْدًا, *the people stood up, with the exception of Zeid*: مَرَرْتُ بِٱلْقَوْمِ إِلَّا زَيْدًا, *I passed by the people, excepting Zeid.* — *b*) When the thing excepted is placed *after* the general term, and the proposition containing that term is negative, the exception may be put either in the accusative, or in the same case with the general term (as a بَدَلٌ or *permutative*), the latter construction being preferred; e. g. مَا جَآءَنِى أَحَدٌ إِلَّا زَيْدٌ, or إِلَّا زَيْدًا, *no one came to me but Zeid;* مَا مَرَرْتُ بِأَحَدٍ إِلَّا زَيْدٍ, or إِلَّا زَيْدًا, *I passed by no one but Zeid;* unless it should happen that the thing excepted is wholly different in kind from the general term, in which case the preference is given to the accusative; as: مَا جَآءَنِى أَحَدٌ إِلَّا حِمَارًا, or إِلَّا حِمَارٌ.

Adversative, Restrictive and Exceptive Sentences.

no one (i. e. *person*) *came to me but an ass*. If, however, the general term, from which the exception is made, is not expressed, the thing excepted is put in whatever case the general term would have beenin, had it been expressed (ﺁﻹِﺳْﺘِﺜْﻨَﺂءُ ٱﻟْﻤُﻔَﺮَّغُ, *the empty exception*); e. g. مَا جَآءَنِى إِلَّا زَيْدٌ (not زَيْدًا), *no one came to me but Zeid*; مَا مَرَرْتُ إِلَّا بِزَيْدٍ, *I passed by no one but Zeid*; لَمْ يَضْرِبْ إِلَّا زَيْدًا, *he did not beat any one but Zeid*; for had the general term been expressed, we should have said, مَا مَرَرْتُ بِأَحَدٍ, مَا جَآءَ أَحَدٌ, and لَمْ يَضْرِبْ أَحَدًا. — *c*) When the thing excepted is placed *before* the general term, it is invariably put in the accusative, if the proposition containing the general term is affirmative; as: قَامَ إِلَّا زَيْدًا ٱلْقَوْمُ, *the people stood up, excepting Zeid*; but if that proposition be negative, the thing excepted may be put either in the accusative or in the nominative, though the former is the usual construction; e. g. مَا لِى إِلَّا آلَ أَحْمَدَ شِيعَةً, *I have no helpers but the family of 'Ahmed*; مَا لِى إِلَّا أَخُوكَ نَاصِرٌ, *I have no helper but your brother*, where أَخَاكَ would be better.

R e m. *a*. The verbal clauses مَا خَلَا, *what is free from*, and مَا عَدَا, *what goes beyond*, are often used in the sense of *except*, and govern the accusative; e. g. فَأَنْزَلُوهُمْ مَا خَلَا عَبَّاسًا, *and they made them alight, excepting 'Abbas*; أَلَا كُلُّ شَىْءٍ مَا خَلَا ٱللّٰهَ بَاطِلٌ, *verily, everything, excepting God, is vanity* (بَاطِلُ in rhyme for بَاطِلٌ); ذُقْتُ أَنْوَاعَ ٱلْحَلْوَآءِ مَا عَدَا ٱلْخَبِيصَ, *I have tasted all kinds of sweetmeats, except the ḥabīs*. When مَا is dropped, as is frequently the case, they may be construed with the genitive, though this is disputed with regard to عَدَد; e. g. خَلَا ٱللّٰهِ لَا أَرْجُو سِوَاكَ, *saving God, I have no hope but in thee*; لَبِسْتُ ٱلْمَلَابِسَ ٱلْفَاخِرَةَ خَلَا ٱلسَّوَادِ, *I have worn all sorts of splendid garments, except the black*; أَبَحْنَا حَيَّهُمْ قَتْلًا وَأَسْرًا عَدَا ٱلشَّمْطَآءَ وَٱلطِّفْلِ ٱلصَّغِيرِ, *we gave up their tribe to slaughter and bondage, except the old woman and the young child.* — Like خَلَا is construed حَاشَى or حَاشَا; (rarely حَاشِ and حَشَى), which is seldom preceded by مَا; as: أَحْسَنْتُ إِلَى ٱلْأَكَابِرِ وَٱلْأَصَاغِرِ حَاشَى ٱلْبَرَامِكَةِ, *I have benefited the high and low, with the exception of the family of Barmek*; أُسَامَةُ أَحَبُّ ٱلنَّاسِ إِلَيَّ مَا حَاشَ فَاطِمَةَ, *'Usāma is the dearest of mankind to me, excepting Fātima* (words of the Prophet).

Rem. b. لَا سِيَّمَا, *especially, above all* (see Vol. I. §. 364, 6), may be construed either with the nominative or the genitive; as: وَهِيَ كَنِيسَةٌ تُعَظِّمُهَا ٱلنَّصَارَى غَايَةَ ٱلتَّعْظِيمِ وَلَا سِيَّمَا مُلُوكُ ٱلْفِرَنْجِ, *this is a church which the Christians hold in very great reverence, but especially the kings of the Europeans*; وَلَا سِيَّمَا يَوْمٌ بِدَارَةِ جُلْجُلِ, *but especially a day in the valley of Gulgul* (جُلْجُلِ in rhyme for جُلْجُلٍ). The word سِيّ is the accusative of the noun سِيّ, *an equal* (see §. 39), and, if the construction with the genitive be adopted, مَا is regarded as redundant (compare §. 57, rem. f). Later writers incorrectly use سِيَّمَا, without لَا; as: هٰذَا مَعَ مَزِيدِ إِحْسَانِهِ سِيَّمَا إِلَيْهِ سِيَّمَا فِي زَمَنِ ٱلْفَلَآءِ, *this (he did), notwithstanding his excessive kindness to him, especially in time of dearth.*

6. Conditional and Hypothetical Sentences.

187. To what we have said above (§§. 4—6, §. 13, and §. 17), regarding the use of certain moods and tenses in the protasis and apodosis of conditional and hypothetical clauses, we must here add a few words on the use of the particle ف at the commencement of a conditional apodosis. — This particle is used to separate the protasis and apodosis of a conditional sentence, when the conditional particle of the protasis either cannot exercise any influence upon the apodosis, or is not wanted to do so. This is the case:

1) When the apodosis is a nominal clause; as: إِنْ قُلْتَ هٰذَا فَأَنْتَ مِنَ ٱلْكَافِرِينَ. *if thou sayest this, thou art one of the unbelievers.*

2) When the apodosis is a verbal clause, but the verb is a defective one, such as لَيْسَ, *he is not*, عَسَى, *perhaps he is*, and the like; e. g. مَنْ لَمْ يَكُنْ تَعْظِيمُهُ بَعْدَ أَلْفِ مَرَّةٍ كَتَعْظِيمِهِ فِي أَوَّلِ مَرَّةٍ فَلَيْسَ بِأَهْلِ ٱلْعِلْمِ, *he whose reverence (for his teacher) is not the same after (seeing him) a thousand times as after (seeing him) for the first time, is not worthy of science.*

3) When the apodosis is a verbal clause, expressing a desire, wish, command, or prohibition; as: إِنْ كُنْتُمْ تُحِبُّونَ ٱللّٰهَ فَٱتَّبِعُونِى, *if ye fear God, follow me;* مَنْ شَآءَ أَنْ يَخْتَرِىَ آمَالَهُ جَمَلًا فَلْيَتَّخِذْ لَيْلَهُ فِى ذَرِيهَا جَمَلًا, *whoever*

wishes to attain all his desires, let him make use of his nights, as of a camel, to overtake them.

4) When the apodosis is a verbal clause, preceded by one of the affirmative particles سَ, سَوْفَ, قَدْ and إِنَّ, or one of the negative particles مَا and لَنْ; as: إِنْ يَسْرِقْ فَقَدْ سَرَقَ أَخٌ لَهُ مِنْ قَبْلُ, *if he steals, (what wonder is it? for) a brother of his has stolen before him;* إِنْ كُنْتُمْ فِي رَيْبٍ مِنَ ٱلْبَعْثِ فَإِنَّا خَلَقْنَاكُمْ, *if ye are in doubt about the resurrection, (bethink yourselves that) it is we who have created you;* إِنْ تَسْتَغْفِرْ لَهُمْ فَلَنْ يَغْفِرَ ٱللَّهُ لَهُمْ, *if thou askest forgiveness for them, (know that) God will not forgive them.*

5) When the perfect tense in the apodosis is intended to retain the signification of the perfect (see §. 6, *c*).

188. The conditional particle is constantly omitted at the beginning of an alternative sentence; as: أَنَا ٱلْمَلِكُ شِئْتُمْ أَوْ أَبَيْتُمْ, *I am king, whether you like it or not* (instead of the fuller: غَرِيبًا كَانَ أَوْ قَرِيبًا, سَوَاءٌ أَشِئْتُمْ أَوْ أَبَيْتُمْ, *no matter* etc.); *whether he be a stranger or a kinsman.* If both parts of the sentence are dependent upon the same verb, it is placed between them; as: غَنِيًّا كَانَ أَوْ فَقِيرًا, *whether he be rich or poor*; صَبَاحًا جَاءَ أَمْ مَسَاءً, *whether he comes in the morning or in the evening* (more fully: سَوَاءٌ أَصَبَاحًا جَاءَ أَمْ مَسَاءً, *no matter whether* etc.).

189. The particle لَوْ (Heb. לוּ), which forms hypothetical clauses, and the particle إِنْ (Heb. אִם) differ from one another

Conditional and Hypothetical Sentences.

in this, that the latter simply indicates a condition, whilst the former implies that what is supposed, either does not take place or is not likely to do so; as: إِنْ تَدْعُوهُمْ لَا يَسْمَعُوا دُعَاءَكُمْ وَلَوْ سَمِعُوا مَا ٱسْتَجَابُوا, *if you call them, they do not hear your call; and even if they did hear it, they would not give ear to it.*

Rem. a. After the verb وَدَّ, *to love, wish, like,* لَوْ is often used instead of أَنْ (compare لَوْ, *utinam, O si*); as: يَوَدُّ أَحَدُهُمْ لَوْ يُعَمَّرُ أَلْفَ سَنَةٍ, *one of them would fain live a thousand years;* وَدُّوا لَوْ يُضِلُّونَكُمْ, *they would fain lead you astray.*

Rem. b. Before nominal clauses لَوْ أَنَّ is used instead of لَوْ; as: لَوْ أَنَّ ٱلنَّاسَ سَمِعُوا, *if the people had listened;* يَوَدُّ لَوْ أَنَّ بَيْنَهَا وَبَيْنَهُ أَمَدًا بَعِيدًا, *he would be glad if there were a long interval between it* (the thing that he has done) *and him.*

190. The particle لَ is prefixed to the apodosis of hypothetical sentences, like فَ to that of conditional sentences; as: لَوْ كَانَ ٱلنَّاسُ كُلُّهُمْ عَبِيدِى لَأَعْتَقْتُهُمْ, *if all mankind were my slaves, I would set them free.* The employment of this particle is, however, unlike that of فَ, quite arbitrary; and it is only in the case of a very long protasis that it is never omitted, in order thereby to mark the apodosis more distinctly (compare the German *so*). The same remark applies to لَ before a negative apodosis of this sort, introduced by مَا; but it is never prefixed to لَمْ, in order to avoid the cacophony produced by the repetition of the letter *l.*

PART FOURTH.
Prosody.

I. The Form of Arabic Poetry.
A. The Rhyme.

191. Poetry (اَلـشِّعْرُ) always takes, during the classical period, — that is to say, from the earliest times down to the fall of the 'Umaiyade dynasty (A. H. 132, A. D. 749—50), — the form of short poems, rarely exceeding the length of a hundred and twenty verses. Such poems are called *kaṣīdas*, قَصِيدَةٌ, collect. قَصِيدٌ, plur. قَصَآئِدُ; whereas a mere fragment, consisting of only a few verses, is termed قِطْعَةٌ, plur. قِطَعٌ, also مُقَطَّعَاتٌ. A poem, the special object of which is the eulogy of an individual or a tribe, is named مَدِيحٌ, plur. مَدَائِحُ; a satire, هِجَآءٌ or أُهْجِيَّةٌ, plur. أَهَاجِيُّ; an elegy, رِثَآءٌ or مَرْثِيَةٌ, plur. مَرَاثٍ: and a poem in the metre *rajez* (see §. 204), أُرْجُوزَةٌ, plur. أَرَاجِيزُ. Verses set to music are termed أُغْنِيَّةٌ, plur. أَغَانِيُّ.

192. Each verse, بَيْتٌ (lit. *tent, house*), plur. أَبْيَاتٌ, consists of two hemistichs, termed مِصْرَعٌ or مِصْرَاعٌ (*one half*

of a *folding-door*), plur. مَصَارِيعُ and مَصَارِعُ, or شَطْرُ (*a half*), pl. شُطُورُ and أَشْطُرُ. The first of these hemistichs is called ٱلصَّدْرُ (*the breast*), and the second ٱلْعَجُزُ (*the rump*).

193. The rhyme, ٱلْقَافِيَةُ, plur. ٱلْقَوَافِي, labours under peculiar restrictions, for, according to ancient rule, the two hemistichs of the first verse of a kaṣîda must rhyme with one another, and the same rhyme must be repeated at the end of every verse through the whole poem. — The rhyme may be of two sorts, مُقَيَّدَةٌ and مُطْلَقَةٌ. It is called مُقَيَّدَةٌ or *fettered*, when the verse ends with a consonant, and مُطْلَقَةٌ or *loose*, when it ends with a vowel.

194. The essential part of the rhyme is the letter called ٱلرَّوِيُّ, which remains the same throughout the entire poem, and, as it were, binds the verses together, so as to form one whole (رَوَى, *to bind fast*). Hence a kaṣîda, of which the *rawi* is the letter *l* is called قَصِيدَةٌ لَامِيَّةٌ; *r*, رَائِيَّةٌ; *t*, تَائِيَّةٌ; and so on.

Rem. The letters ا, و and ي cannot be employed as *rawi*, when they are *a*) long vowels, e. g. غَزَا, تَتْلُوا, كِتَابِي; *b*) inflexions of the feminine singular, the dual and the plural of verbs, e. g. تَقْتُلِي, اُقْتُلُوا, يَقْتُلَا (unless they form a diphthong with a preceding fétha, e. g. رَمَوْا, اِرْضَى); *c*) inflexions of the dual and plural of nouns: and *d*) the final letters of the pronouns هُوَ, هِيَ and هَا. The same remark applies to the tenwîn, and to the letter ن of the second energetic form of verbs; as also to the letter ه, when it is not radical, as in رَحْمَهْ for رَحْمَةٌ, كِتَابِيَهْ for كِتَابِيَ (pausal form for كِتَابِهْ for كِتَابِي).

The ه of the pronouns هِ and هَا may, however, be used as *rawi*, if preceded by a long vowel, e. g. عَصَاهُ, عَصَاهَا.

195. The loose kāfiya (see §. 193) terminates in what is called أَلصِّلَةُ, *the annex* or *appendix* to the *rawi*, which may be either a long vowel (i. e. اَ—, ىَ—, or وَ—). or the letter ه, preceded by one of the short vowels (هَ —, هِ —, هُ —).

Rem. *a*. We say „a *long* vowel", because the final vowel of a verse is regarded as being followed by the homogeneous letter of prolongation, whether this latter be written or not. The vowel-letter ا is invariably expressed, but و and ى are frequently omitted, even where they are always written in prose; e. g. وَيَدِى for وَيَدِ, *and my hand*, صَنَعْ for صَنَعُوا or صَنَعُو, *they made*.

Rem. *b*. If the letter ه has a long vowel after it, as in the suffix pronouns هَا, ه (=هِى), ه (=هُو), the letter of prolongation, ا, و or ى, is called أَلْخُرُوج, *that which goes beyond (the ṣila)*; as in نَعْلِلُهُ مَوْكِبِهَا, تَعْصِهِ (=تَعْصِهِى), نَعْلِلُهُو).

Rem. *c*. Both *ṣila* and *ḥorūǧ* must accompany the *rawi*, without the slightest change, through the whole poem.

196. The *rawi* may also be preceded by one or two letters, which form, to a greater or less extent, a necessary portion of the kāfiya (whether loose or fettered). These are named by the grammarians أَلتَّأْسِيسُ, أَلدَّخِيلُ, and أَلرِّدْفُ.

1) أَلتَّأْسِيسُ, or *the foundation*, is the name given to the ا of prolongation, preceding the *rawi*, and separated

The Rhyme.

from it by a consonant, which is called the دَخِيلٌ or *stranger*. The former is invariable, the latter variable; but the vowel that separates the *daḫil* from the *rawi* ought, strictly speaking, to remain unchanged. For example, in a verse ending with the word نَامِرٌ, the ر is the *rawi*, the long vowel ا the *ta'sīs*, and the م the *daḫil*, whilst the vowel that separates this last from the *rawi* is *i*; but the next verse may terminate with the word اَلدَّوَائِرُ, where the *daḫil* is ى, though the other parts of the *kāfiya* remain unchanged. The same holds when the *kāfiya* is loose, instead of fettered, as in عَامِرٍ and اَلْوَائِرِ (where the *daḫil* is in the one case م, and in the other ت), or بَاطِلَةٌ and رَوَاجِلَةٌ.

2) The رِدْفٌ, or *what rides behind*, is the technical name given to one of the letters of prolongation, ا, ى or و, when it immediately precedes the *rawi*; as in the words طَرُوبٌ, تَرِيحٌ, رِجَامُهَا, اَلسَّلَامُ, تُهَالَةٌ, جَنَاحَانِ. The long vowel *ā* remains invariable, but the poet may use *ī* and *ū* indifferently; تَرِيحٌ is regarded as rhyming with جَمُوحٌ, مَشِيبٌ with سُوقَهُ, طَرُوبٌ with بَرِيقُهُ.

Rem. *a*. Strictly speaking, the *rawi* and the *ta'sīs* should form parts of the same word, but an exception is allowed in the case of the separate pronoun هُمَا, and of a pronominal suffix preceded by a preposition, as لَنَا, لِيَا (for لِي or لِي).

Rem. *b*. When the *kāfiya* is unaccompanied by either a *ta'sīs* or a *ridf*, it is said to be مُجَرَّدٌ, *naked* or *bare*; otherwise, it is either مُرْدَفَةٌ or مُؤَسَّسَةٌ.

197. The vowels that accompany the ḳâfiya are also designated by peculiar names.

1) The *mağrâ*, اَلْمَجْرَى, is the vowel that follows the *rawi* in the loose ḳâfiya; e. g. *â* in سَارَا (for سَارَ), *i* in بَعْضٍ, *u* in سَلَكُوا or اَلْقَلْبُ. It is, strictly speaking, invariable.

2) The *nafâd*, اَلنَّفَاذ, is the vowel between the letter ه, as *ṣila*, and the *ḥorûğ* (see §. 195, rem. *b*); e. g. fetḥa in مَـوْكِبُهَـا, kèsra in تَعْصِهِ (= تَعْصِهى), and ḍamma in نَعَلِلُهُ (=نَعَلِلُهُو). It is, of course, invariable.

3) The *taugîh*, اَلتَّوْجِيهُ, is the vowel that immediately precedes the *rawi* in a قَـافِيَةٌ مُجَـرَّدَةٌ, e. g. fetḥa in نَجَبَرْ (for نَجَبَرَ), and kèsra in أَيْرْ (for أَيْرٌ), or separates it from the *daḫîl* in a قَـافِيَـةٌ مَـوَّسَّسَةٌ (see §. 196, rem. *b*), e. g. kèsra in نَامِرْ (for نَامِرٌ) or وَالرَّواتِرْ. The latter is, however, more frequently distinguished by the special name of اَلْإِشْبَاعُ. The *'išbâ'* ought, strictly speaking, to be invariable; whereas, in the *taugîh*, the vowels ḍamma and kèsra may interchange, as in أَيْرُّ, for أَيْرٌ, and صُبْرُ, for صُبْرٌ (compare the case of و and ى as *ridf*, §. 196. 2).

Rem. The *taugîh* is absolutely necessary in a fettered ḳâfiya, unless it be مُرْدَفَةٌ (as مُطَاعْ, تَرِيحْ, اَلْلَّيْلْ); but it is not necessary in a loose ḳâfiya, as اَلْعُمْرُ, قَدْرٍ.

4) The *rass*, اَلرَّسُّ, is the vowel which accompanies the

letter preceding the *ta'sìs* (see §. 196, 1). It can, of course, be none but fetha.

5) The *ḥaḏw*, اَلْحَذْوُ, is the vowel that accompanies the letter preceding the *ridf* (see §. 196, 2). It is either fetha, kèsra or ḍamma, according as the *ridf* is ا, ى or و; but the vowel fetha before و or ى (َـوْ , َـى) is also included under this name.

198. The last two *quiescent* (سَاكِين) letters of a verse form, according to the preceding sections, the limits between which is comprised the rhyme. Hence the Arab grammarians divide the rhyme into five kinds, according to the number of *moving* (مُتَحَرِّك) letters that come between these two;[*)] viz. مُتَرَادِفٌ, مُتَوَاتِرٌ, مُتَدَارِكٌ, مُتَرَاكِبٌ, and مُتَكَاوِسٌ.

1) The مُتَرَادِفٌ is where there is *no* moving letter between the two quiescents, — in other words, a fettered kafiya, in which the *rawi* is preceded by a *ridf*; as: جَنَاحَانْ, يَخُولْ قَرِيحْ ٱللَّيْلْ لَوْنَيْنْ. It is of comparatively rare occurrence.

2) The مُتَوَاتِرٌ is where *one* moving letter intervenes between the quiescents; as: ظُلْمْ (= ظُلْمِي), سِحْرْ (= سِحْرُو), ظُنُونْ (= ظُنُونِي), جَمِيلْ (= جَمِيلُو), شَيْبَانَا.

---

*) The student should bear in mind that the grammarians designate the vowels by the term حَرَكَات, *motions* (sing. حَرَكَةٌ); whence a consonant, that is followed by a vowel, is said to be مُتَحَرِّك or *in motion*, and one that has no following vowel, to be سَاكِين, *at rest*, *inert* or *quiescent*. Hence too the *ǵèzm* is often called سُكُونْ.

3) The مُتَدَارِك is where there are *two* moving letters between the two quiescents; as: (اَلْمُبَاسِلُو=) اَلْمُبَاسِيلُ, اَلْمُلْتَهِبْ, قَدْ ظَلَمَ, (هَيْكَلِى=) هَيْكَلِ, يَزُورَهَا.

4) The مُتَرَاكِبْ is where there are *three* moving letters between the quiescents; as: (وَضَمِى=) عَلَى وَضَمٍ, وَلَا تَرَنَا, قَدْ حُسِدُوا.

5) The مُتَكَاوِسٌ is where there are no less than *four* moving letters between the two quiescents, as in the half-verse: قَدْ جَبَرَ ٱلَّذِينَ ٱلْإِلَٰهُ نَجَبَرْ, *God has healed the true religion, and it has become whole.* This sort of rhyme is of rare occurrence.

199. A violation of any of the rules laid down in sections 194—197, is regarded as a fault (عَيْبٌ). Of these faults the grammarians reckon five; viz. ٱلْإِقْوَآءُ, ٱلسِّنَادُ, ٱلتَّتْمِيمُ or ٱلتَّضْمِينُ, ٱلْإِيطَآءُ, and ٱلْإِكْفَآءُ.

1) The *sinâd*, ٱلسِّنَادُ, consists in a certain change of the vowels called ٱلتَّوْجِيهُ, ٱلْإِشْبَاعُ, and ٱلْحَذْوُ. *a*) In the *taujîh*, kèsra and ḍamma may freely interchange, but the use of fetḥa to rhyme with either is a sinâd (see §. 197, 3). 'Imru'u 'l-Ḳais, for example, commits this fault in rhyming تَرّ (for تَرُّ) with أَبِرُّ and صُبْرُ. *b*) In the *'iśbâ*, the same fault is exemplified by rhyming جَانِبُ with يَتَجَانَبُ, or ٱلتَّدَافُعُ with فَٱلْقَوَارِعُ. *c*) In the *ḥaḏw*, *i* may interchange with *u* (see §. 196, 2), and *ai* with *au* (e. g. تَوِيبِى may rhyme with بِرَيْبٍ); but to rhyme خُمُوشَا with عَيْشَا or تُرَيْشَا is a sinâd. In the case of the *taujîh* and *'iśbâ*,

The Rhyme.

this fault is but a trifling one, and not seldom committed even by the best poets.

Rem. The name of اَلسِّنَاد is also applied to cases in which a word having a *ridf* or *ta'sîs* before the *rawî*, is rhymed with one that has not; e. g. تَوْسِيعِ and تَغْضِيعِ, خَمْسِى and تَوْسِى, تَسْلِيمِى and اَلْعَالَمِ.

2) The *'ikwâ*, اَلْإِقْوَآءُ, is the name given to a change of the vowel called اَلْمَجْرَى (see §. 197, 1); e. g. مُزَوَّدٍ and اَلْأَسْوَدُ, or تَجُورُ and نَزُورِ. Though this fault is considered a serious one, the older poets not unfrequently allow themselves the interchange of kèsra and ḍamma (compare §. 196, 2, and §. 197, 3). If, however, the *rawî* is followed by the letter ه as *sila* (§. 195), any alteration of the *maǵrâ* is exceedingly rare; to rhyme دُونَهَا with ظُنُونَهَا, or اِنْتِقَامُهُ with أُسَامَهُ, is condemned by all the native critics.

3) The *'ikfâ*, اَلْإِكْفَآءُ, is the substitution of some cognate letter for the *rawî*; as when one rhymes اَللَّيْلُ with اَلْعُنَّذَا and أَنْقَيْنَ, or عَيْنٍ, or صُدْغٍ with صُقْعٍ, or سَطَا with وَسَطَا. This is a very grave fault, and carefully avoided by all good poets.

Rem. Many good authorities call this change اَلْإِقْوَآءُ, and apply the term اَلْإِكْفَآءُ to the alteration of the *maǵrâ* (see no. 2).

4) The *'îṭâ*, اَلْإِيطَآءُ, is the repetition of the same word in rhyme in the course of a kaṣîda. However, not to impose too great a restriction on the poet, this repetition is held to be allowable, provided there be some slight shade of difference in meaning, even if it be only to the extent of the word having the article in the one place and not in the

other. Many authorities, too, permit the repetition in the same sense, provided at least seven verses intervene.

5) Each verse of a poem ought to be independent in construction and sense (مُفْرَدٌ). That two or more verses should be so connected with one another, is regarded as a fault, and technically named *taḍmīn*, اَلتَّضْمِيــنْ, or *tètmīm*, اَلتَّتْمِيمُ. It is not, however, a serious defect, unless the one verse be wholly destitute of meaning, if separated from the other; as when ĕn-Nābiġa says:

ثُمَّ وَرَدُوا ٱلْمِيَاهَ عَلَى تَمِيمٍ   وَهُمْ أَصْحَابُ يَوْمِ عُكَاظَ إِنِّى

They water their herds at the wells in spite of Tĕmīm, and they are the victors on the day of 'Okáẓ; verily I — which is unintelligible, because the *ḫabar* of إِنّ is unknown, till we hear or read the next verse:

شَهِدْتُ لَهُمْ مَوَاطِنَ صَالِحَاتٍ   أُثِيبُنْهُمْ بِوُدِّ ٱلصَّدْرِ مِنِّى

have seen them fight many a good fight, (for which) I reward them with my heart's whole love.

B. The Metres.

200. Every verse in Arabic poetry consists of a certain number of *feet*, called individually تَفْعِيلٌ, plur. تَفَاعِيلُ, but as constituent parts of a verse, جُزْءٌ *(a part)*, plur. أَجْزَاءٌ. A certain collocation of feet constitutes a *metre*, بَحْرٌ *(a sea)*, plur. أَبْحُرٌ. To *scan* a verse is expressed by the word قَطَعَ *(to cut into pieces)*, infin. تَقْطِيعٌ.

201. The metres are ordinarily reckoned to be *sixteen* in number, and are exemplified in the following composition,

made up partly of verses, either taken from the poets or written for the occasion, and partly of sentences from the Ḳor'ān.

أَبْحُرُ ٱلشِّعْرِ وَهِىَ سِتَّةَ عَشَرَ بَحْرًا،

ٱلْبَحْرُ ٱلْأَوَّلُ ٱلطَّوِيلُ ،

طَوِيلٌ مَدَى ٱلْهِجْرَانِ مَنْ كُنْتُ أَهْوَاهُ   أَذَابَ فُؤَادِى وَٱلتَّصَبُّرُ أَفْنَاهُ
فَعُولُنْ مَفَاعِيلُنْ فَعُولُنْ   وَلَا تَقْتُلُوا ٱلنَّفْسَ ٱلَّتِى حَرَّمَ
مَفَاعِيلُنْ   ٱللَّـٰهُ ،،

ٱلْبَحْرُ ٱلثَّانِى ٱلْمَدِيدُ ،

فَاعِلَاتُنْ فَاعِلُنْ فَاعِلَاتُنْ   يَا لَبَكْرٍ ٱنْشِرُوا لِى كُلَيْبَا ،،

ٱلْبَحْرُ ٱلثَّالِثُ ٱلْبَسِيطُ ،

يَنْبَسِطُ فِى أَمَلِى أَنِّى أُدَاهِنُهُمْ   خَوْفًا مِنَ ٱلْجَوْرِ لَمَّا أَنْ أُعَايِنُهُمْ
مُسْتَفْعِلُنْ فَاعِلُنْ مُسْتَفْعِلُنْ فَعِلُنْ   فَأَصْبَحُوا لَا يُرَى إِلَّا مَسَاكِنُهُمْ ،،

ٱلْبَحْرُ ٱلرَّابِعُ ٱلْكَامِلُ ،

يَا كَامِلًا سَلِّمْ وَقُلْ تَعْظِيمًا   لِلْمُجْتَبَى خَيْرِ ٱلْوَرَى تَسْلِيمًا
مُتَفَاعِلُنْ مُتَفَاعِلُنْ مُتَفَاعِلُنْ   صَلُّوا عَلَيْهِ وَسَلِّمُوا تَسْلِيمَا ،،

ٱلْبَحْرُ ٱلْخَامِسُ ٱلْوَافِرُ ،

أُوَايِرُ كَيْدَ شِعْرِى فِى مَزِيدٍ   عَلَى رَغْمِ ٱلْأَعَادِى وَٱلْحَسُودِ
مَفَاعَلَتُنْ مَفَاعَلَتُنْ فَعُولُنْ   أَلَا بُعْدًا لِعَادٍ قَوْمِ هُودِ ،،

اَلْبَحْرُ ٱلسَّادِسُ ٱلْهَزَجُ ،

هَزَجْتُمْ يَا مُنَى ٱلنَّفْسِ   عَنِ ٱلْأَوْطَانِ بِٱلْأُنْسِ
مَـفَـاعِيلُنْ مَفَاعِيلُنْ   كَأَنْ لَمْ تَغْنَ بِٱلْأَمْسِ ،،

اَلْبَحْرُ ٱلسَّابِعُ ٱلرَّجَزُ ،

اَلرَّجَزُ ٱلْمَوْزُونُ إِذْ تُجَزَّءُوا   أَجْزَآءَهُ بَيْنَ ٱلْوَرَى لَا تُنْكَرُ
مُسْتَفْعِلُنْ مُسْتَفْعِلُنْ مُسْتَفْعِلُنْ   يَا أَيُّهَا ٱلَّذِينَ آمَنُوا ٱصْبِرُوا ،،

اَلْبَحْرُ ٱلثَّامِنُ ٱلرَّمَلُ ،

رَمَلٌ أُكْرِمْ بِهِ مِن رَمَلِ   لَذَّ لِلْمُكْتَفِى وَٱلْمُجْتَلِى
فَاعِلَاتُنْ فَاعِلَاتُنْ فَاعِلُنْ   وَٱلَّذِى أَطْمَعُ أَنْ يُغْفِرَ لِى ،،

اَلْبَحْرُ ٱلتَّاسِعُ ٱلسَّرِيعُ ،

سَرِيعٌ بَحْرٌ قَدْ سَدَاهُ ٱلْحَكِيمُ   كَرَّرْ عَلَى سَمْعِى بِهِ يَا نَدِيمْ
مُسْتَفْعِلُنْ مُسْتَفْعِلُنْ فَاعِلُنْ   ذٰلِكَ تَقْدِيرُ ٱلْعَزِيزِ ٱلْعَلِيمِ ،،

اَلْبَحْرُ ٱلْعَاشِرُ ٱلْمُنْسَرِحُ ،

مُنْسَرِحُ ٱلشِّعْرِ صَاغَهُ ٱلْأَوَّلُ   مِمَّنْ تَرَاهُمْ عَنِ ٱلْهُدَى نَكَلُوا
مُسْتَفْعِلُنْ فَاعِلَاتُ مُسْتَفْعِلُنْ   بَدَا لَهُمْ سَيِّئَاتُ مَا عَمِلُوا ،،

اَلْبَحْرُ ٱلْحَادِى عَشَرَ ٱلْخَفِيفُ ،

خَفَّ لَمَّا أَرَدْتُ أَشْدُو ٱلْخَفِيفَا   لَذَّ فِى مَسْمَعِى فَكَانَ طَرِيفَا
فَاعِلَاتُنْ مُسْتَفْعِلُنْ فَاعِلَاتُنْ   إِنَّ كَيْدَ ٱلشَّيْطَانِ كَانَ ضَعِيفَا ،،

اَلْبَحْرُ ٱلثَّانِى عَشَرَ ٱلْمُضَارِعُ ،

مَفَاعِلُنْ فَاعِلَاتُنْ   أَيَا مُحْىِّ ٱلْبِلَادِ ،،

The Metres.

اَلْبَحْرُ الثَّالِثُ عَشَرَ اَلْمُقْتَضَبُ ،
اِقْتَضِبْهُ حِينَ صَبَا فَنَّ مَعْشَرِ اَلْأُدَبَا
فَاعِلَاتُ مُفْتَعِلُنْ مَالُهُ وَمَا كَسَبَا ،،

اَلْبَحْرُ الرَّابِعُ عَشَرَ اَلْمُجْتَثُّ ،
مُجْتَثُّ شِعْرِيَ اَلْقَى فِي اَلْقَلْبِ مِنِّيَ عِشْقًا
مُسْتَفْعِلُنْ فَاعِلَاتُنْ وَاَللهُ خَيْرٌ وَأَبْقَى ،،

اَلْبَحْرُ اَلْخَامِسُ عَشَرَ اَلْمُتَدَارِكُ ،
فَاعِلُنْ فَاعِلُنْ فَاعِلُنْ فَاعِلُنْ جَآءَنَا عَامِرٌ سَالِمًا غَانِمًا ،،

اَلْبَحْرُ اَلسَّادِسُ عَشَرَ اَلْمُتَقَارِبُ ،
تَقَارَبَ مَوْعِدُ جَمْعِ اَلْعُصَاةِ فَيَا أَيُّهَا اَلنَّاسُ أَدُّوا اَلصَّلَاةَ
فَعُولُنْ فَعُولُنْ فَعُولُنْ فَعُولُ أَقِيمُوا اَلصَّلٰوةَ وَآتُوا اَلزَّكٰوةَ ،،

202. Instead, however, of following the system and arrangement here laid down, we prefer to adopt that of Ewald*), and to treat of the metres in the following order: 1. اَلرَّجَزُ, 2. اَلسَّرِيعُ, 3. اَلْكَامِلُ, 4. اَلْوَافِرُ, 5. اَلْهَزَجُ, 6. اَلْمُتَقَارِبُ, 7. اَلطَّوِيلُ, 8. اَلْمُضَارِعُ, 9. اَلْمُتَدَارِكُ, 10. اَلْبَسِيطُ, 11. اَلْمُنْسَرِحُ, 12. اَلْخَفِيفُ, 13. اَلرَّمَلُ, 14. اَلْمَدِيدُ, 15. اَلْمُقْتَضَبُ, and 16. اَلْمُجْتَثُّ. Among these, if we leave the *rajez* out of account, the favourites with the old poets are the *ṭawîl*, *kâmil*, *wâfir*, *besîṭ*, *mutekârib* and *sarî'*.

*) See his work entitled: *De Metris Carminum Arabicorum Libri Duo*, Braunschweig, 1825; and the second volume of his *Grammatica Critica Linguae Arabicae*, p. 323.

203. The *iambic* metres are four in number, namely, the *ragĕz*, *sari'*, *kâmil*, and *wâfir*.

204. The most common varieties of the *ragĕz* (اَلرَّجَزُ, *the trembling*) are the dimeter and the trimeter, both of which may be cataleclic. The trimeter is the more usual. The basis is the diiamb (⏑ – ⏑ –), which may be varied in one or two places by the substitution of the third epitrite (– – ⏑ –), the choriamb (– ⏑ ⏑ –), and, more rarely, the fourth paeonian (⏑ ⏑ ⏑ –). — The older poets almost always use this metre as مَشْطُورٌ, that is to say, each hemistich (شَطْرٌ) forms, as it were, an independent verse and rhymes with the preceding one. The moderns, on the contrary, not unfrequently follow the rule of the other metres in rhyming only the second hemistich of each verse.

Trimeter acatalectic: ᷎ – ⏑ – | ᷎ – ⏑ – | ᷎ – ⏑ –
 ᷎ ⏑ ⏑ – | ᷎ ⏑ ⏑ – | ᷎ ⏑ ⏑ –

„ catalectic: ᷎ – ⏑ – | ᷎ – ⏑ – | ᷎ – –
 ᷎ ⏑ ⏑ – | ᷎ ⏑ ⏑ – | ᷎ – –

Dimeter acatalectic: ᷎ – ⏑ – | ᷎ – ⏑ –
 ᷎ ⏑ ⏑ – | ᷎ ⏑ ⏑ –

„ catalectic: ᷎ – ⏑ – | ᷎ – –
 ᷎ ⏑ ⏑ – | ᷎ – –

205. The *sari'* (اَلسَّرِيعُ, *the swift*) admits in its first and second feet the same variations as the ragĕz. Its normal form is:

᷎ – ⏑ – | ᷎ – ⏑ – | – ⏑ – ‖ ᷎ – ⏑ – | ᷎ – ⏑ – | – ⏑ –
᷎ ⏑ ⏑ – | ᷎ ⏑ ⏑ – | ‖ ᷎ ⏑ ⏑ – | ᷎ ⏑ ⏑ – |

but a spondee (– –) is frequently substituted for the amphimacer (– ⏑ –) at the end of the second hemistich. The use of the final anapaest (⏑ ⏑ –) in either hemistich, but more especially in the second, is very rare. A few later poets have taken the liberty of adding a syllable to the second hemistich, so that the last foot of the verse becomes – ⏑ – –.

206. The *kāmil* (اَلْكَامِل, *the perfect*) is either dimeter or trimeter. The normal form of the trimeter is:

≅ – ⏑ – | ≅ – ⏑ – | ≅ – ⏑ – ‖ ≅ – ⏑ – | ≅ – ⏑ – | ≅ – ⏑ –

but we frequently find it catalectic:

≅ – ⏑ – | ≅ – ⏑ – | ≅ – ⏑ – ‖ ≅ – ⏑ – | ≅ – ⏑ – | ≅ – –

The omission of another syllable, so as to convert the last foot of the verse into a spondee (– –), is more rare, though sometimes even both hemistichs are shortened in this way.

≅ – ⏑ – | ≅ – ⏑ – | ≅ – ⏑ – ‖ ≅ – ⏑ – | ≅ – ⏑ – | – –
„ | „ | ⏑ – –   ‖ „ | „ | ≅ –

The normal form of the dimeter is:

≅ – ⏑ – | ≅ – ⏑ – ‖ ≅ – ⏑ – | ≅ – ⏑ –

It is sometimes used as catalectic (≅ – – for ≅ – ⏑ – in the last foot of the second hemistich), but far more usually the verse is lengthened by the addition of a syllable:

≅ – ⏑ – | ≅ – ⏑ – ‖ ≅ – ⏑ – | ≅ – ⏑ – | –

in which case it is said to be مُرَفَّل, *possessed of a train*.

207. The basis of the *wāfir* (اَلْوَافِر, *the exuberant*) is the same as that of the kāmil, but with the order of the component parts reversed (⏑ – ≅ –). It is either trimeter or dimeter, but the latter is comparatively rare. The trimeter is always shortened by one syllable in each hemistich, so as to become:

$$\smile - \overline{-} - \mid \smile - \overline{-} - \mid \smile - - \parallel \smile - \overline{-} - \mid \smile - \overline{-} - \mid \smile - -$$

The dimeter has the form:

$$\smile - \overline{-} - \mid \smile - \overline{-} - \parallel \smile - \overline{-} - \mid \smile - - -$$

for the last foot of which there may be substituted $\smile - - -$, but these two forms are not used indiscriminately in the same poem.

208. Of *antispastic* metres there is only one, namely the *hazèj* (اَلْهَزَج, *the trilling*), which consists in a single repetition of the antispast ($\smile - - \smile$), varied by the first epitrite ($\smile - - -$). It may be either catalectic or acatalectic.

Acatalectic: $\smile - - \overline{-} \mid \smile - - \overline{-} \parallel \smile - - \overline{-} \mid \smile - - -$

Catalectic: $\smile - - \overline{-} \mid \smile - - \overline{-} \parallel \smile - - \overline{-} \mid \smile - -$

209. The *amphibrachic* metres are three in number, *mutèkârib*, *tawîl*, and *mudârî*.

210. The basis of the *mutèkârib* (اَلْمُتَقَارِب, *the tripping*, lit. *taking short steps*) is the simple amphibrachys ($\smile - \smile$), for which may be substituted the antibacchius ($\smile - -$). The latter is indeed almost invariably employed as the penultimate foot of the hemistich. One great peculiarity of this metre is, that the first hemistich may be either acatalectic or catalectic, independently of the second. If, however, the first be acatalectic and the second catalectic, then the last syllable of the first halfverse must be short, and must coincide with the end of a word. Of this metre no form but the tetrameter is in common use.

Acatalectic:
$$\smile - \overline{-} \mid \smile - \overline{-} \mid \smile - \overline{-} \mid \smile - \overline{-} \parallel \smile - \overline{-} \mid \smile - \overline{-} \mid \smile - \overline{-} \mid \smile - -$$

Catalectic:
$$\smile - \overline{-} \mid \smile - \overline{-} \mid \smile - \overline{-} \mid \smile - \overline{-} \parallel \smile - \overline{-} \mid \smile - \overline{-} \mid \smile - \overline{-} \mid \smile -$$

The Metres.

A rarer form reduces the last foot of the second hemistich to a single long syllable, in which case the preceding foot must be an antibacchius:

⏑–⏒ | ⏑–⏒ | ⏑–⏒ | ⏑–⏒ ‖ ⏑–⏒ | ⏑–⏒ | ⏑–– | –

211. The *ṭawîl* (اَلطَّوِيلُ, *the long*) is one of the finest, as well as the most common, of the Arab metres. It is formed by the single repetition of an amphibrachys and a diiamb (⏑–⏑ | ⏑–⏑–), for the former of which may be substituted the antibacchius (⏑––), and for the latter the first epitrite (⏑–––). The epitrite is restricted to the first place in each halfverse, where it is, however, far more usual than the diiamb. The verse may be either acatalectic or catalectic. If the latter, then the last syllable of the penultimate foot should be short (⏑–⏑).

Acatalectic:

⏑–⏒ | ⏑–⏒– | ⏑–⏒ | ⏑––– ‖ ⏑–⏒ | ⏑–⏒– | ⏑–⏒ | ⏑–––

Catalectic:

⏑–⏒ | ⏑–⏒– | ⏑–⏒ | ⏑––– ‖ ⏑–⏒ | ⏑–⏒– | ⏑–⏑ | ⏑––

In the acatalectic verse, the last foot is also sometimes changed into an epitrite:

⏑–⏒ | ⏑–⏒– | ⏑–⏒ | ⏑––– ‖ ⏑–⏒ | ⏑–⏒– | ⏑–⏒ | ⏑–––

212. The *muḍâriʿ* (اَلْمُضَارِعُ, *the similar*) is one of the rarest metres, and not employed by any early poet. Each halfverse consists of an amphibrachys and a diiamb, with a single syllable appended, and the two generally rhyme with each other, as in the *ragèz*. For the amphibrachys (⏑–⏑) may be substituted the antibacchius (⏑––), and for the diiamb (⏑–⏑–) the third epitrite (–––⏑), but both changes must not take place together. Consequently the entire verse is:

⏑–⏒ | –⏑–⏑ | – ‖ ⏑–⏒ | –⏑–⏑ | –

213. The *anapaestic* metres are likewise four in number, namely, the *mutedârik*, *bèsit*, *munsariḥ*, and *muḳtaḍab*.

214. The *mutedârik* (اَلْمُتَدَارِك, *the continuous*) is one of the rarer and later metres. The basis is an anapaest (⏑⏑-), which is convertible into an amphimacer (-⏑-) or a spondee (--). It is generally either trimeter or tetrameter, the former having occasionally an extra syllable in the second hemistich, so as to make it مُرَفَّل (see §. 206).

Trimeter: ⏑⏑- | ⏑⏑- | ⏑⏑- ‖ ⏑⏑- | ⏑⏑- | ⏑⏑-

Tetrameter:

⏑⏑- | ⏑⏑- | ⏑⏑- | ⏑⏑- ‖ ⏑⏑- | ⏑⏑- | ⏑⏑- | ⏑⏑-

215. The *bèsit* (اَلْبَسِيط, *the outspread*), on the contrary, is a favourite metre with the older poets. Its base consists of a diiamb and an anapaest (⏑-⏑- | ⏑⏑-), which may be repeated so as to yield either a trimeter or a tetrameter verse. In either case, the diiamb may be converted into a third epitrite (--⏑-), and occasionally into a choriamb (-⏑⏑-), or even a fourth paeonian (⏑⏑⏑-), though these changes are very rare indeed in the second place. The anapaest may be changed in the first place into an amphimacer (-⏑-), but either remains unaltered in the second, or becomes a spondee. Hence arise the following forms of the tetrameter.

⏑-⏑- | -⏑- | -⏑-- | -⏑- ‖ ⏑-⏑- | -⏑- | -⏑-- | --⏑-

The trimeter may be either acatalectic or catalectic, more usually the latter. If the loss of a syllable be extended, as is commonly the case, to both hemistichs, the last foot in each is an antibacchius (⏑ – –).

Acatalectic: – ⏑ ⏑ – | – ⏑ – – | ⏑ – – – ‖ – ⏑ ⏑ – | – ⏑ – – | ⏑ – – –

Catalectic: – ⏑ ⏑ – | – – – | ⏑ – – – ‖ – ⏑ ⏑ – | – – – | ⏑ – – –

or: – ⏑ ⏑ – | – – – | – – – ‖ – ⏑ ⏑ – | – – – | – – –

216. The *munsariḥ* (اَلْمُنْسَرِحْ, *the flowing*) has the same base as the *besiṭ*, but the first anapaest is reduced to a single long syllable. It scarcely occurs in any form but the tetrameter.

– ⏑ ⏑ – | – – | – ⏑ – – | ⏑ – – ‖ – ⏑ ⏑ – | – – | – ⏑ – – | ⏑ – –

R e m. This verse may also be scanned as follows:

– ⏑ ⏑ – | – ⏑ – – | ⏑ – – – ‖ – ⏑ ⏑ – | – ⏑ – – | ⏑ – – –

217. The *muḳtaḍab* (اَلْمُقْتَضَبْ, *the lopped* or *curtailed*) is an exceedingly rare metre, the normal form of which appears to be

– ⏑ ⏑ – | ⏑ – – | ⏑ – – | – ⏑ ⏑ – | ⏑ – – | ⏑ – –

It is said that the iambus may be transferred to the first place, thus giving the form

⏑ – – | – ⏑ ⏑ – | ⏑ – – | ⏑ – – | – ⏑ ⏑ – | ⏑ – –

218. The *ionic* metres are also four in number, namely, the *ramèl*, *mèdīd*, *hafīf*, and *mujtell*.

219. The *ramèl* (اَلرَّمَلْ, *the running*) has for its base an ionicus a minore (⏑ ⏑ – –). It may be either dimeter or trimeter. The trimeter is almost invariably catalectic in the first hemistich, and generally so in the second; the dimeter very commonly in the second. For the ionic a minore may be substituted the second epitrite (– ⏑ – –), and, though very

rarely, the ditrochee (–⌣–⌣), or the third paeonian (⌣–⌣⌣), in which case the next foot must begin with a long syllable.

Dimeter: –⌣– – | –⌣– – ‖ –⌣– – | $\genfrac{}{}{0pt}{}{-\smile--}{\smile\smile}$

Trimeter acatalectic: –⌣– – | –⌣– – | –⌣– – ‖ –⌣– – | –⌣– – | –⌣– –

„ catalectic: –⌣– – | –⌣– – | –⌣– | –⌣– – | –⌣– – | $\genfrac{}{}{0pt}{}{-\smile--}{\smile\smile}$

Rem. *a.* The tetrameter catalectic is a late innovation, in which the second epitrite has entirely usurped the place of the ionic.

–⌣– – | –⌣– – | –⌣– – | –⌣– | –⌣– – | –⌣– – | –⌣– – | –⌣–

Rem. *b.* In this metre the later poets occasionally rhyme the single hemistichs, as in the ragéz.

220. The *medíd* (ٱلْمَدِيدُ, *the extended*) has for its base two ionics, separated by an anapaest. Either ionic, but more especially the second, may be converted into a second epitrite; the anapaest into an amphimacer.

–⌣– – | –⌣– | –⌣– – ‖ –⌣– – | –⌣– | –⌣– –

The second hemistich is sometimes catalectic, whilst the first remains complete; but usually both are catalectic, in which case the last foot is almost invariably an anapaest (⌣⌣–), passing at the end of the verse into a spondee.

–⌣– – | –⌣– | $\genfrac{}{}{0pt}{}{-\smile--}{\smile\smile-}$ ‖ –⌣– – | –⌣– | –⌣–

–⌣– – | –⌣– | –⌣– ‖ –⌣– – | –⌣– | ⸗⸗

Rem. *a.* A very rare variety shortens the first hemistich and leaves the second complete:

–⌣– – | –⌣– | –⌣– ‖ –⌣– – | –⌣– | –⌣– –

Rem. *b.* A still rarer species consists in a repetition of the entire base, each hemistich rhyming, as in the ragéz. The last foot is usually an anapaest.

–⌣– – | –⌣– | –⌣– – | –⌣– ‖ –⌣– – | –⌣– | –⌣– – | –⌣–

221. The *hafíf* (ٱلْخَفِيفُ, *the light* or *nimble*) is one of

the more usual metres. Its base is an ionic a minore and a diiamb (⏑⏑--|-⏑⏑-). The former may be varied by the second epitrite (-⏑--), and more rarely by the ditrochee (-⏑-⏑) or third paeonian (⏑⏑-⏑); the latter by the third epitrite (--⏑-), and occasionally the ionic a majore (--⏑⏑) or diiamb (⏑-⏑-). The second hemistich is sometimes catalectic, in which case the last foot is by preference an antibacchius (⏑--).

-⏑--|-⏑⏑-‖-⏑--|-⏑⏑-

A far more usual form, however, is the trimeter, which is generally acatalectic, though we now and then find it defective in both hemistichs, or in the second only. In the acatalectic verse, a molossus (---) may be substituted for the last anapaest.

Acatalectic: -⏑--|-⏑⏑-|-⏑--‖-⏑--|⏑⏑--|-⏑⏑-

Catalectic: -⏑--|-⏑--|-⏑⏑-‖-⏑--|-⏑⏑-|-⏑-

222. The *mujtell* (اَلْمُجْتَثّ, *the docked* or *amputated*) has the same base as the ḥafîf, but with the order of the component parts reversed, namely ⏑-⏑-|⏑-⏑--. The changes which the feet may respectively undergo, are also the same as in the ḥafîf. It is used only as dimeter acatalectic.

-⏑--|-⏑⏑-‖-⏑⏑-|-⏑--

II. The Forms of the Words in Pause and in Rhyme.

223. We must next treat of the forms that the final syllables of words assume at the end of a verse; and as these are often identical with those which they take at the end of a sentence in ordinary prose, or of a clause in rhymed prose (ٱلسَّجَعُ or ٱلتَّنْجِيمُ), we shall handle the whole subject briefly in the following sections.

224. As a general rule, all final short vowels, both of the noun and verb, are dropped in prose; e. g. جَآءَ زَيْدْ, instead of زَيْدٌ; مَرَرْتُ بِزَيْدْ, instead of بِزَيْدٍ; ضَرَبْتُ ٱلرَّجُلْ, for ٱلرَّجُلَ; رَأَيْتُهْ, for رَأَيْتُهُ; مَرَرْتُ بِهْ, for بِهِ. But in poetry it constantly happens that the vowel is retained as long, the tenwîn of the noun disappearing at the same time; e. g. وَفِيهِمْ شُبَّتِ ٱلنَّارُ, *whilst fire is kindled among them;* فِى زَمَنٍ مَحْلِى, *in times of sterility*, for مَحْلٍ. In this case, the final vowel fetḥa is invariably accompanied by an elif; e. g. كِرَاعَ قَوْمٍ يُحْسِنُونَ ٱلضَّرْبَا, *as a people strike, who can strike well*, for ٱلضَّرْبَ; إِيَّاهَا يَعْنُونَا, *him they mean*, for يَعْنُونَ.

    Rem. It is also allowable to double the final consonant after the elision of the vowel, as: أَحْمَرُّ أَحْمَرْ, for أَحْمَرُ; ٱلْجَمَلِّ ٱلْجَمَلْ, for ٱلْجَمَلِ, provided always that the penult letter has a vowel, and that the final letter is neither elif with hemza (as ٱلْخَطَأَ) nor elif maksûra (ٱلْعَصَا, ٱلْفَتَى).

225. The accusative termination ا ـً generally becomes ا ـ, both in prose and poetry, though it occasionally disappears, like the short ـً, as أَضْبَعَ كَثِيبْ, *he was deeply grieved*, for كَثِيبًا (i. e. كَثِيبَا). The termination ـً نْ or ا ـً in the Energetic of verbs, and in the particle إِذَنْ or إِذًا, is also changed into *à*.

226. The feminine terminations ةً, ةٍ, and ةٌ, become ةْ. The same remark naturally applies to ةَ and ةِ, whether masculine or feminine; e. g. حَمْزَةَ, for حَمْزَةُ (name of a man). In rhyme, the ة may also be changed into ت, and the final vowel retained as long; e. g. وَأَهْلُكَ بِاللِّوَى فَالْحُلَّتِي, *whilst your family are at el-Liwa and el-Hilla*, for فَالْحُلَّةِ.

227. Nouns ending in ىً simply drop the tenwin; e. g. فَتًى becomes فَتَى or فَتَا. Those ending in ٍ drop the tenwin, and either resume the third radical or not, at pleasure; قَاضٍ, for example, may become either تَقَاضِي or قَاضْ, either بِقَاضٍ or بِقَاضِي, جَوَارٍ (plur. of جَارِيَةٌ *a girl*) either جَوَارِي or جَوَارْ, مَعَانٍ (plur. of مَعْنًى *meaning*) either مَعَانِي or مَعَانْ. The accusative singular merely loses the tenwin, e. g. قَاضِيًا (and not قَاضِي) for قَاضِيًا; the accusative of the broken plural drops the final vowel in prose, but may retain it as long in poetry, e. g. مَوَالِي for مَوَالِيَ (accus. of مَوْلًى, *a client*), in rhyme also مَوَالِيَا.

Rem. If a word ending in ٍ has lost another radical besides

the final ‍و or ی, the only pausal form admissible in the nominative and genitive is that which ends in the long vowel; e. g. مُرٍ, participle active IV. of رَأَى, *to see*, can become only مُرِي, never مُرْ.

228. The long vowels ‍ا َـ , ی َـ , ی ِـ , and ‍و ُـ , usually remain unchanged; as قَتَلَ, غَزَا, حُبْلَى, يَرْمِي, يَغْزُو. In nouns derived from radicals third ‍و or ی, the omission of final ی ِـ is allowed in the nominative and genitive, as اَلْقَاضِ, اَلتَّنَادِ, اَلْمُتَعَالِ, for اَلْقَاضِي, اَلتَّنَادِي, اَلْمُتَعَالِي; the accusative, however, admits only the form اَلْقَاضِيَ, etc.

Rem. *a*. The interrogative pronoun مَا, when governed in the genitive by another word, is shortened in pronunciation, and often in writing, to مَ, especially when used interrogatively. In pause, if governed by a noun, it takes the هَآءَ اَلْوَقْفِ (see §. 300), as مِثْلُ مَهْ, اِقْتِضَآءَ مَهْ; but if governed by a preposition, it may also drop its final vowel, as عَمَّهْ, بِمَهْ or بِمْ or لِمَهْ, لِمْ or حَتَّامَهْ or حَتَّامْ.

Rem. *b*. The genitive and accusative suffixes of the first personal pronoun, ی ِـ and نِي, have several pausal forms, namely, in prose نِيَهْ or يِي, يَهْ َـ or ی ِـ (see §. 300), and in poetry also يَا َـ , نِيَا; besides which, the long vowel may be altogether omitted, as فَأْتُفُونْ, أَكْرَمَنْ, for بَالْ, فَأْتُقُونِي, أَكْرَمَنِي, بَالِي.

Rem. *c*. In rhyme the long vowels ی ِـ and ‍و ُـ are often expressed merely by kèsra and damma, as يَدِ for يَدِي, صَنَعْ for صَنَعُو or صَنَعُوا. This is done for the purpose of preserving the uniformity of the حَاشِيَةُ or *fringe* (i. e. the succession of rhyming syllables) throughout a poem.

229. When the penult letter of a word has no vowel, the vowel of the final letter may be transferred to it in pause; as بَكْرٌ, اَلنَّقْرُ, بِبِكْرٍ, اِضْرِبْهُ, ضَرَبْتْهُ for (بَـكْرٌ), ضَرَبْتَهُ, اِضْرِبَهُ, (بِبَكَرٍ), (اَلنَّقَرُ). With regard to the vowel fetḥa, however, the grammarians are not agreed, some allowing the transference in all cases, e. g. اَلْبَكْرَ for اَلْبَكَرَ; others limiting it to the case in which the final consonant is élif with ḥemza, as اَلْخَبَأْ for اَلْخَبَأَ or اَلْخَبْءَ. This transference is technically called اَلنَّقْلُ.

Rem. The نَقْلْ is forbidden when it would give rise to a form that has no example in the language. For instance, there is no substantive of the form فِعْلْ, and therefore we must not say in pause اَلْعِلْمُ (اَلْعِلِمُ). Some grammarians, nevertheless, allow this form when the third radical is élif with ḥemza, as (اَلرَّدْءُ) اَلرِّدْءَ, whilst others recommend the change of the damma into késra, pronouncing اَلرِّدِئُ or اَلرَّدْءُ instead of اَلرَّدْءُ or اَلرِّدْءَ.

230. Indeclinable words, ending in a vowel, take in their pausal form a final ه, technically called the هَآءُ اَلسَّكْتِ or اَلْوَقْفِ, *the hā of pause* or *of silence*; e. g. كَيْفَهْ, ثَمَّهْ, for كَيْفَ, ثَمَّ. The same letter is added to verbal forms in which both the first and third radicals have disappeared; as قِهْ for قِ (imperat. of وَقَى), لَمْ يَفِهْ for لَمْ يَفِ (jussive of وَفَى); also رَهْ for رَ, and لَمْ يَرَهْ for لَمْ يَرَ, imperat. and jussive of رَأَى. It may also be appended to those in which only the third radical is dropped; as اِرْمِهْ for اِرْمِ (imperat. of رَمَى), لَمْ يَغْزُهْ for لَمْ يَغْزُ (jussive of غَزَا), اِقْتَدِهْ

for اِنْتَدِ (imperat. VIII. of قَدَ). We likewise find it added to مَ, the shorter form of the interrogative pronoun مَا (see §. 228, rem. *a*); and to ـِيَ and نِيَ, the older forms of the genitive and accusative suffixes ـِي and نِي (see §. 228, rem. *b*).

Rem. *a*. The هَآءُ ٱلْوَقْفِ is never added either to nouns, or to the perfect of verbs, or to adverbs ending in *u* (see Vol. I. §. 363), with the single exception, it is said, of مِنْ عَلُهْ for مِنْ عَلُ. The Arabs do not say مِنْ بَعْدُهْ, لَا رَجُلَهْ, يَا رَجُلُهْ, تَتْلَهْ.

Rem. *b*. The ordinary pausal forms of أَنَا and هُوَ are أَنَا and هُوْ, but we also find أَنَهْ (see Vol. I. §. 89, 1, rem. *b*.) and هُوَهْ. — هٰؤُلَاءِ and هٰهُنَاهْ are likewise used instead of the common هٰؤُلَاءِ and هٰهُنَا.

III. Poetic Licenses.

231. The Arab poets allow themselves a certain latitude, both as to the forms of words and the construction of sentences. We shall here confine ourselves chiefly to the illustration of some of the principal licenses which fall under the former of these two heads.

232. The poet may find himself obliged, by the exigencies of metre or rhyme (ضَرُورَةُ ٱلشِّعْرِ, *poetical necessity*), to make some slight change either in the *consonants* of a word, or in its *vowels*.

Poetic Licenses. 275

233. Under the former of these divisions we include *a*) the various affections of the letter ا, *b*) irregularities in the use of the tèsdîd, *c*) the employment of ancient uncontracted forms instead of the more modern contracted ones, and *d*) the suppression of the letter ن in certain nominal and verbal forms.

a. Affections of the letter Élif.

234. Élif with hèmza (أ) may be affected in several different ways.

1. It may be totally absorbed by a preceding vowel, like the ألِفُ ٱلْوَصْلِ (vol. I. §. 19); e. g. أَلَا أَبْلِغْ, *convey the news*, for أَلَا أَبْلِغْ, imperat. IV. of بَلَغَ; وَأَبْشِرْ, *and rejoice*, for وَأَبْشِرْ, imperat. IV. of بَشَرَ; مُجِيرُ أُمِّ عَامِرٍ, *he who gave shelter to 'Umm Ámir* (a name for the hyaena), for مُجِيرُ أُمِّ; هَلْ رَأَيْتَ, *hast thou seen?* for هَلْ رَأَيْتَ; ذُو ٱلشَّنَانِ, *one who hates*, for ٱلشَّنَآنِ (ٱلشَّنْآنِ); إِنْ تُنْصِفُونَا يَالَ مَرْوَانَ نَقْتَرِبْ, *if ye do us justice, O family of Marwán, we will draw near (to you)*, for أَآلَ (يَا آلَ); فِي رُوَيْسِهَا, *on their heads*, for رُؤَيْسِهَا; مَسَاتِي, *my hurt*, for مَسَآتِي from سَآءَ.

2. When preceded by a vowelless consonant, the vowel of the أ may be transferred to that consonant, as in the case of مِنْ and مَنْ, when followed by the article (Vol. I. §. 20, 4), يَرَى for يَرْأَى (Vol. I. p. 140), and the like. Examples: لَوَ أَنْ, *if that*, for لَوْ أَنْ; مِنَ آجْلِكَ, *on thy account*, for مِنْ أَجْلِكَ; عَنَ آجْبُلِهَا, *from her hills*,

35*

مِـنْ أَنْ يَـلْقِيَنَهُ ;عَـنْ أَجْلِهَا for, *from meeting him*, for إِنْ أَغْزُ زُبَيْدًا ;مِنْ أَنْ, *if I make a raid upon Zubèid;* نِزَارُ أُولُو ٱلسَّدَادِ, *the upright Nizar* (pron. *Nizārū-nū-lus*), يَا دَارَا أَمْسَى دَارِسًا رَسْمُهَا ;أُولُو for, *O house, whose site has become desolate!* (pron. *dā-rā-nam*), for أَمْسَى : مِنْ آلِ أَبِي مُوسَى, *of the family of Abū Mūsā*, for أَأَالِ); مِنْ آلِ) فَقُلْ إِذَا, لِلْمُنَاوِى ٱلنَّارِى ٱلْآنَ ٱلْأَذَى, *say then to the enemy who now aims at doing mischief* (pron. *nāwī lāna*, see Vol. I. §. 20, 2), for بَيْنَ ٱلزَّوْجِ وَٱلْمَرْءِ, (أَلْأَانَ) ٱلْآنَ, *between husband and wife*, for ٱلْمَرْأَةِ.

Rem. In this case, the ﺁ is sometimes assimilated to a preceding و or ى; e. g. فَلَمْ يُغْنِ ٱلْبُكَاءُ عَلَيْكَ شَيًّا, *but to weep over thee was of no avail*, for شَيْئًا.

3. ﺁ, preceded by a vowel, may also be converted into the letter of prolongation that is homogeneous with that vowel; e. g. فَلَمْ يَجِدْ عِنْدَهُ ٱلنَّصْرَ ٱلَّذِى سَالَ, *but he did not find with him the help that he demanded*, for سَأَلَ; أَطَعْتُهُمْ وَأَنَا عَلَى فَازِ, *I obeyed them, though I was in haste*, for وَأَنَا. This is most frequent when ﺁ is the third radical of a word, in which case the word virtually becomes third و or ى (compare Vol. I. §. 132, rem. *a*). For example, in verbs, لَا هَنَاكِ, *may it do thee no good!* for هَنَاَكِ; وَأَبْطَا, *and it delayed*, for أَبْطَأَ; أَنْبَاكَ, *who told thee?* for أَنْبَأَكَ; أُدَارِى, for أُدَارِئُ, III. of دَرَأَ; تُرْجِعِ, for تُرْجِئُ, IV. of رَجَأَ; and in nouns, ظَمَا, *thirst*, رَشَا, *a fawn*, أَجَا, *the name of a mountain*, for ظَمَأَ, رَشَأَ, أَجَأَ; قَارٍ, *a reader*, for قَارِئٌ, participle of نَرَأَ.

Poetic Licenses.

4. Élif with hèmza and ǵèzm (ْ) is constantly changed by the poets into the letter that is homogeneous with the preceding vowel; e. g. اَلْقَالْ, *the omen* (for اَلْفَأْل), rhyming with اَقْفَالْ (plur. of تُفْعَلْ); اَلرَّاسِ, *of the head* (for اَلرَّأْسِ), rhyming with اَلنَّاسِ; اَلرُّودِ, *of the tender* (for اَلرُّؤْدِ), rhyming with اَلسُّودِ (plur. of اَسْوَدْ); ذِيبْ, *a wolf*, (for ذِئْبْ), rhyming with رَبِيبْ.

235. Élif mèmdûda (see Vol. I. §. 23, rem. *a*) is not unfrequently changed into élif maksûra; e. g. اَلسَّمَا, for اَلسَّمَآء, *the sky*; بَلَا, for بَلَآءً, *a misfortune*; تَفْرَى or تَفْرَى, *desert, desolate*, for تَفْرَآءَ, fem. of اَتْفَرُ; اَشَا, for اَشَآءَ, *I wish*, 1. pers. sing. Imperf. Indic. of شَآءَ.

236. The élifu 'l-waṣl (vol. I. §. 19, rem. *e*) is often retained in poetry, where it would naturally be elided in prose; e. g. كَمَنْ اِقْتَادَ; وَاَصْبِرِى, *be patient*, for وَاصْبِرِى; كَمَنِ اقْتَادَ, *like one who leads*, for فِى اَلْبَذْلِ وَاَلْاِمْتِنَاعِ, *in bestowing and withholding*, for وَاَلْاِمْتِنَاعِ; وَاَنْتَ لِشَاتِنَا اِبْنُ رَبِيبْ, *and thou wast a fosterchild of our sheep*, for لِشَاتِنَا ابْنُ; اِذَا جَاوَزَ اَلْاِثْنَيْنِ سِرّْ, *when a secret goes beyond two*, for الْاِثْنَيْنِ.

b) Irregularities in the use of the Tèśdîd.

237. The necessary tèśdîd is occasionally dropped; e. g. اَيْهُمَا, for اَيُّهُمَا, *which of them*; فَلَوْ اَنَكَ, *if that thou*, for اَنَّكَ; اَيُهَا اَلسَّائِلُ عَنْهُمْ وَعَنِى, *O thou that askest after them and after me!* for وَعَنِّى.

Part Fourth. Prosody.

238. Sometimes too the tešdīd is introduced where it would be inadmissible in prose, through a false application of the pausal form mentioned in §. 224, rem.; e. g. يُحِبُّ ٱلْخُلُقَ ٱلْأَضْخَمَّا, for ٱلْكَلْكَلِّ, *the breast*; مِنَ ٱلْكَلْكَلِّ, *he likes a stout figure*, for ٱلْأَضْخَمَا, acc. sing. of أَضْخَمُ; فِي مِرْوَدِهَا, *on her bodkin* (for applying *kohl* to the eyes), for مِرْوَدِهَا; فِي ٱلطِّوَلِّ, *in the tether*, for ٱلطِّوَلِ.

c. Uncontracted Forms for contracted ones.

239. These are most common in the case of radicals in which the second and third letters are identical (vol. I §. 119), and occur in both the verb and the noun; e. g. وَإِنْ, وَإِنْ لَمْ تَقْتُلِيهِ فَأَلْمِمِي, *though they be stingy*, for ضَنُّوا; ضَنِنُوا, *and if thou dost not (actually) kill him, yet come near it*, for فَأَلِمِّي; وَيُذْمَمْ, *and he is blamed*, poetic form in rhyme for وَيُذْمَمْ; وَلَا يُبْرَمُ ٱلْأَمْرُ ٱلَّذِى هُوَ حَالِلٌ, and that for يُذَمُّ; وَلَا يُحْلَلُ ٱلْأَمْرُ ٱلَّذِى هُوَ مُبْرَمٌ, *what he loosens cannot be bound fast, and what he binds fast cannot be loosened*, for حَالٌّ and يُحَلُّ; ٱلْحَمْدُ لِلّٰهِ ٱلْعَلِيِّ ٱلْأَجْلَلِ, *praise belongs to God, the exalted, the glorious*, for ٱلْأَجَلِّ. Compare, in Hebrew, אָפֵפוּנִי, סְבָבוּנִי, and similar forms.

240. The poets also use the uncontracted forms of nouns derived from radicals third و and ى, instead of the contracted (see Vol. I. §. 167, II. 2); e. g. مَوَالِىْ كَكِبَاشِ ٱلْعُرِيسِ نُجَّاحْ, *freedmen as fat as rams of the kind called üs*, for مَوَالٍ; لَا بَارَكَ ٱللّٰهُ فِي ٱلْغَوَانِى, غَيْرَ مَاضِى, *not past*, for مَاضٍ; مَوَالٍ;

كَجَوَارٍ يَاْعَبْنَ *may God not bless the women!* for فِى ٱلْغَوَانِى : فِى ٱلْعَذْرَآءِ, *like girls sporting in the mead.*

R e m. It sometimes happens that the usual accusative form is incorrectly transferred to the genitive; e. g. تَعَالَى وَلَوْ كَانَ عَبْدُ ٱللَّهِ مَوْلًى هَجَوْتُهُ وَلَكِنْ عَبْدَ ٱللَّهِ مَوْلَى مَوَالِيَا, *were 'Abdu'llāh a freedman, I would lampoon him, but 'Abdu 'llāh is merely a freedman's freedman,* for مَوْلَى مَوَالٍ.

d. Suppression of the letter ن in certain Nominal and Verbal Forms.

241. This is a license of which the poets but rarely avail themselves, but it occasionally occurs in the dual and plural of nouns, and in the jussive and energetic of verbs; e. g. هُمَا خُطَّتَا إِمَّا إِسَارٌ وَمِنَّةٌ وَإِمَّا دَمٌ, *these are the alternatives, either captivity and quarter, or bloodshed,* for أَبَنِى كُلَيْبٍ إِنَّ عَمَّىَّ ٱللَّذَا تَقَتَلَا ٱلْمُلُوكَ وَفَكَّكَا ٱلْأَغْلَالَا; خُطَّتَانِ, *ye Benū Kulēib, 't was my two uncles who slew kings and burst asunder the yokes (of captives),* for ٱللَّذَانِ; هُمَا كَنَفَا ٱلْأَرْضِ ٱللَّذَا لَوْ تَزَعْزَعَا, *these are the two pillars of the earth, which, if they are shaken,* for إِنَّ ٱلَّذِى; ٱلَّذَيْنِ; حَانَتْ بِفَلْجٍ دِمَاؤُهُمْ, *those whose blood was shed unavenged at Felj,* for لَا تُهِينِ ٱلْفَقِيرَ عَلَّكَ أَنْ تَرْكَعَ يَوْمًا; ٱلَّذِينَ; وَٱلدَّهْرُ قَدْ رَفَعَهْ, *despise not the poor, for perhaps you may one day be cast down, when Fortune has lifted him up,* for تُهِينَنْ إِنْ طَرَقَتْ, إِضْرِبْ عَنْكَ ٱلْهُمُومَ, *drive away sad thoughts from thee, if they come by night,* for اِضْرِبَنْ;

280   Part Fourth. Prosody.

and more frequently نَكُنْ, تَكُنْ, نَكُ, تَكُ, يَكُ, for يَكُنْ, تَكُنْ, نَكُنْ, jussive of كَانَ.

Rem. a. The same elision of ن occurs in the particle لٰكِنْ, *but*; e. g. وَلٰكِ أَسْقِينِى, *but give me to drink*.

Rem. b. On the contrary, some poets have even dared to add the energetic ن to the perfect and participle of the verb; e. g. دَامَنْ سَعْدُكِ إِنْ رَحِمْتِ مُتَيَّمَا, *may thy good fortune last, if thou hast compassion upon one enslaved (by love)*, for دَامَ; أَقَاتِلَنْ أَحْضِرِ, *will he say, Bring in the witnesses?* for أَقَاتِلْ ٱلشُّهُودَا.

242. Other letters, and even whole syllables, are sometimes dropped under the pressure of metrical necessity. For example, *a*) at the *beginning* of a word: لَآنَ for ٱلْآنَ (compare §. 234, 2), as in the halfverse: فَبُحْ لَآنَ مِنْهَا بِٱلَّذِى أَنْتَ بَآئِحُ, *so now disclose in regard to her what thou mayest disclose*; لَآبِ for لِأَبِ, as: لَآبِ ٱبْنُ عَمِّكَ لَا أَفْضَلْتَ فِى حَسَبٍ عَنِّى, *what a man thy cousin is! thou dost not surpass me in noble qualities* (compare §. 54, 2, rem *e*); لَاهُمَّ إِنْ كُنْتَ قَبِلْتَ حَجَّتِى, *O God! if thou hast accepted my pilgrimage* (حَجَّتِى rare pausal form for حَجَّتِى); اِتَّقُوا for تَقُوا, imperat. VIII. of وَقَى, as: تَقُوهُ أَيُّهَا ٱلْفِتْيَانُ, *fear him* (God), *O young men!* *b*) In the *middle* of a word: اِسْطَاعَ (X. of طوع), imperf. يَسْطِيعُ, for يَسْتَطِيعُ, as: وَلَوْ أَنِّى أَسْطِيعُ يَوْمَ حِمَامِهِ اِسْتَطَاعَ لَقَاتَلْتُ عَنْهُ, *and had I been able, on the day of his death, I would have fought in his defence*. *c*) At the *end* of a word: مِنَ ٱلْمَالِ for مِلْمَالِ (also written مِنْ مَالِ)

(see vol. I. §. 358, rem. c), as: فَمَا أَبْقَتِ ٱلْأَيَّامُ مِلْمَالٍ عِنْدَنَا, *Fate has left* (lit. *the days have left*) *no wealth in our possession*; عَلَى ٱلرِّزْقِ (or عَلَ مَآءَ), for عَلَى ٱلْمَآءِ; مِنْ ٱلرِّزْقِ, for مِرْ-*rizķi*; and even عَلَى ٱلنَّبِي, *'an-nabi*, for عَلَى ٱلنَّبِيّ; عَنْ فُلٍ for عَنْ فُلَانٍ (owing to the vocative form بِيَا فُلُ, §. 38, 1, rem. c, 3).

R e m. The following are specimens of even still more violent abbreviations: ٱلْمَنَا for ٱلْمَنَازِلُ, as in the halfverse of Lebîd: دَرَسَ ٱلْمَنَا بِمُتَالِعٍ فَأَبَانِ, *the dwellings are desolate at Mutâli' and 'Abân;* and also for ٱلْمَنَايَا (plur. of ٱلْمَنِيَّةُ), as in: تُرِيكَ ٱلْمَنَا بِرُؤُوسِ ٱلْأَسَلِ, — *will let you see death at the points of the spears*; ٱلسَّبَا for ٱلسَّبَائِبُ (plur. of سَبِيبَةٌ), used by Alķama in the line: مُقَدَّمٌ يَسَبَا ٱلْكَتَّانِ مَلْثُومٌ, *having its mouth covered and enwrapped with strips of linen*; ٱلْحُبَا for ٱلْحُبَاحِبُ, as in the words of 'Ibn Dureid: أُورَى بِهَا نَارَ ٱلْحُبَا, *he strikes out of them small sparks of fire;* ٱلْحَمَا, used by el-Aġġāġ for ٱلْحَمَامُ, in the halfverse: تَوَاطِنًا مَكَّةَ مِنْ وُرْقِ ٱلْحَمَا, *the slate-coloured doves that inhabit Mekka;* ٱلْعِنَا for ٱلْعِنَانُ, in the words: حَتَّى إِذَا أَعْيَيْتُ, أَطْلَقْتُ ٱلْعِنَا, *till, when I was exhausted, I slackened the reins*; and even رَآ for رَحِمٌ, *the womb* (see el-Makkarî, tom. I. p. ٤٣٠, l. 11, and tom. II. p. ٢٠٠, l. 8), and مَرْ for مَرْحَبًا, according to one rendering of the line: فَلَمْ يُقِمْ إِلَّا بِمِقْدَارِ أَنْ قُلْتُ لَهُ أَهْلًا وَسَهْلًا وَمَرْ, *but he stopped only for the space of time that I could say, Welcome* (others think that وَمَرْ is here nothing more than the usual pausal form of وَمَرَّ, *and passed on*).

243. Under the second of the two heads mentioned in

§. 232, namely, poetic licenses in regard to the *vowels* of a word, we include *a*) the lengthening of a short vowel in the middle of a word; *b*) the shortening of a long vowel; *c*) the suppression of a short vowel; *d*) the addition of a final vowel to certain verbal and pronominal forms, and to some particles; and *e*) the irregular use of the tenwin and other case-endings in the noun.

a) The lengthening of a short vowel in the middle of a word.

244. This is technically called اَلْإِشْبَاعُ, *filling full* or *saturation*, and is not uncommon with the vowels *a* and *i*, rarer in regard to *u*. Examples: يَنْبَاعُ, for يَنْبَعُ, in the halfverse of 'Antara: يَنْبَاعُ مِنْ ذِفْرَى غَضُوبٍ جَسْرَةٍ, *flows from behind the ears of a fierce, bulky she-camel;* اَلْكَلْكَالُ, for اَلْكَلْكَلُ, in the words: قُلْتُ وَقَدْ خَرَّتْ عَلَى اَلْكَلْكَالِ, *I said, after she had fallen upon her breast;* مُنْتَزَاحٍ, for مُنْتَزَحٍ, in the hemistich: وَمِنْ ذَمِّ اَلرِّجَالِ بِمُنْتَزَاحٍ, *and (art thou) far removed (i. e. quite free) from the blame of men?* عَامُودٌ, for عَمُودٌ, in the halfverse: فِيهِ مِنَ اَلذَّهَبِ اَلْإِبْرِيزِ عَامُودٌ, *in it there is a pillar of purest gold;* اَلصَّيَارِيفُ and اَلدَّرَاهِيمُ, for اَلصَّيَارِفُ and اَلدَّرَاهِمُ, in the hemistich: نَفْيَ اَلدَّرَاهِيمِ تَنْقَادُ اَلصَّيَارِيفِ, *as the money-changers scatter the dirhems, whilst selecting (those that are of full weight);* أَنْظُورُ, for أَنْظُرُ, in the words: مِنْ حَيْثُمَا سَلَكُوا أَدْنُو فَأَنْظُورُ, *I draw near to whatever place they go and look (at them).*

b) The shortening of a long vowel.

245. This may take place either in the middle or at the end of a word. Examples in the middle of a word: قَتَمْ, for قَتَامْ, as in the words: فِى قَتَمِهِ, *in its dust or its darkness;* عَوَاوِرْ, plur. of عُوَّارْ, *a mote in the eye*, مَقَاصِرْ, plur. of مَقْصُورَةْ, *a cell or chamber*, for مَقَاصِيرْ, عَوَاوِيرْ, and the like; هَذَا (⏑ ‒), instead of هٰذَا (‒ ‒), as in the halfverse: إِلَى كَمْ هَذَا ٱلْهِجْرَانْ فِى كُلِّ لَيْلَةٍ, *how long shall this estrangement last every night?* ٱللَّهُ (⏑ ‒), for ٱللَّهُ (‒ ‒), as in the hemistich: أَلَا لَا بَارَكَ ٱللَّهُ فِى سُهَيْلِ, *may God not bless Suhèil!* and, with double license, كَتَنْ, for كَتَّانْ, in the words: بَيْنَ ٱلْحَرِيرِ وَبَيْنَ ٱلْكَتَنْ, *partly silk and partly linen.* Examples at the end of a word: ٱلنَّوَاحْ, for ٱلنَّوَاحِى, as in the hemistich: كَنَوَاحْ رِيشِ حَمَامَةٍ نَجْدِيَّةٍ, *like the tips of the feathers of a dove of Nejd;* ٱلْأَيْدْ, for ٱلْأَيْدِى, as in the words: دَوَامِى ٱلْأَيْدْ, *with their fore-feet bleeding;* ٱلنَّاسْ, for ٱلنَّاسِى, as in the words: عَنِ ٱلنَّاسِ أَبْرَادًا وَأَثْوَابًا, *from one who forgets robes and garments.* The 1. pers. plur. of the Perfect, قَتَلْنَا (⏑ ‒ ‒), is also sometimes shortened into قَتَلْنَ (⏑ ‒ ‒), but the élif is usually retained in writing, in order to distinguish it from the 3. pers. plur. fem.

c) The suppression of a short vowel.

246. This license is of most frequent occurrence in the case of the very few nouns of the form فَعِلْ (becoming

فِعْلٌ), and of verbs of the forms فَعِلَ and فَعُلَ (becoming فَعَلَ, see vol. I. §. 183, rem. b); e. g. كَمَا ٱسْتَنْوَنَصَتْ خَيْلٌ بِكَتِيبَتِهَا ٱلْإِبْلَا, *as horses scatter camels by their charge* (for ٱلْإِبِلِ); وَإِنْ أَهْجُهُ يَضْجَرْ كَمَا ضَجِرَ بَازِلٌ مِنَ ٱلْإِبْلِ دَبِرَتْ صَفْحَتَاهُ وَكَاهِلُهْ, *and if I lampoon him, he cries out, like a two year old camel whose sides and withers are galled* (for ضَجِرَ, ٱلْإِبِلِ, and دَبِرَتْ). Rarer instances are exemplified by رَجْلٌ, for رَجُلٌ, as in the halfverse: فَقَدْ كَانَ رَجْلًا وَكُنْتُمْ رِجَالَا, *for he was a man, and ye are men;* and ٱلْكَبْرُ, for ٱلْكُبَرُ (plur. of ٱلْكُبْرَى), in the words: هِيَ ٱلْأَنْفُسُ ٱلْكَبْرُ ٱلَّتِي *these are the great souls which.* — The suffix pronoun of the 1. pers. sing., ـِي, may be suppressed in rhyme, as بَالْ, for بَالِي, *my heart,* in the first verse of et-Tantarāni's ḳaṣīda, which rhymes with زَالْ, for زَالَ, *has passed away.*

Rem. The poets also take the contrary liberty of adding a supplementary vowel in the nominal form فِعْلٌ, using, for example, إِطِلٌ, for إِطْلٌ, *flank,* and جِلِدٌ, for جِلْدٌ, *skin.*

d) The addition of a final short vowel to certain verbal forms and to some particles.

247. The vowel *kèsr* is frequently added in the rhyme to the 3. p. sing. fem. of the Perfect, the 2. p. sing. masc. of the Imperative, and those persons of the Jussive that end in a consonant. E. g. أَنَاخُوا ٱلْمَطَايَا قَدْ أَمِلَّتْ وَكَلَّتِ, *they made the camels lie down, that were tired and weary* (for

Poetic Licenses.

كَلَّتْ); وَتَجَلَّدِ أَسًى تَهْلِكْ لَا يَقُولُونَ, *they say, Do not die of grief, but bear it like a man* (for تَجَلَّدْ); وَإِنْ يَأْتِكَ ٱلْأَعْدَاءُ بِٱلْجَهْدِ أَجْهَدِ, *and if the foe come upon thee, I will do my very best* (for أَجْهَدْ).

Rem. The vowel preceding the final consonant may have been originally long, and only shortened because of its being in a shut syllable, but it is, nevertheless, not restored after the addition of this késra. For example: غَزَتِ (for غَزَاتِ, 3. p. sing. fem. Perf. of غَزَا, vol. I. §. 166, rem.) becomes غَزَتِ, not غَزَاتِ; طِرْ (for طِيرْ, 2. p. sing. masc. Imperat. of طَارَ, vol. I. §. 152) becomes طِرِ, not طِيرِي; أَنَمْ (for أَنَامْ, 1. p. sing. Jussive of نَامَ, vol. I. §. 151) becomes أَنَمِ, not أَنَامِ.

248. The same license is allowable in the case of particles that end in a consonant, particularly such as are monosyllabic; e. g. وَكَأَنْ قَدِ بِرِحَالِنَا تَزَلْ لَمَّا, *they* (the camels) *have not yet moved off with our saddles, but it is as good as done* (namely, وَكَأَنْ قَدْ زَالَتْ, *but it is as if they had already moved off*); وَكَمِ ٱلنَّوَى ذَا أَنْفُسِنَاكُمْ أَحْبَابَ, *beloved of our souls, how long will this absence continue? how long?*

Rem. The reader may here be reminded that, instead of the ordinary pronominal forms هُمْ, أَنْتُمْ, and كُمْ, and the verbal form فَعَلْتُمْ, the poets constantly make use of the archaic أَنْتُمُ, هُمُ, كُمُ and فَعَلْتُمُ. The final vowel is in these cases more usually long than short.*) When هُمْ is changed into هِمْ, either هِمُ or هِمِ may be used.

---

*) The quantity of the singular suffix هُ is also doubtful.

e) The irregular use of the tênwīn and other case-endings in the noun.

249. The poets constantly use the triptote inflection of a noun, when the diptote inflection alone is admissible in prose. This remark applies equally to the singular and the broken plural. Examples of the singular: تَضَوَّعَ مِسْكًا بَطْنُ نَعْمَانٍ إِنْ مَشَتْ بِهِ زَيْنَبُ فِي نِسْوَةٍ عَطِرَاتٍ, *the vale of Naʿmān is scented with musk, if Zeineb walks in it amid (her) perfumed attendants* (for زَيْنَبُ); قَالُوا يَزُورُكَ أَحْمَدُ وَتَزُورُهُ, *they say, 'Ahmed visits you and you visit him* (for أَحْمَدَ); يَسْقِيهِمْ ذُو مِرَّةٍ أَحْوَرُ, *a smart black-eyed (page) hands them wine* (for أَحْوَرَ); قَدْ قَالَ شَاعِرُ كِنْدَةٍ فِيمَا مَضَى, *the poet of (the tribe of) Kinda has said in olden time* (for كِنْدَةَ); تَقُولُ سَلِ ٱلْمَعْرُوفَ يَحْيَى بْنَ أَكْثَمِ, *you say, Ask largesse of Yaḥyā bin Ekṯem* (for أَكْثَمَ); وَنَبَّهْتُ عُثْمَانًا لِدَفْعِ خُطُوبِهِ, *and I warned ʿOthmān to repel the dangers that threatened him* (for عُثْمَانَ); وَنَسِيتَ أَنَّ ٱللَّهَ أَخْرَجَ آدَمًا, *and thou forgettest that God turned Adam out of it* (for آدَمَ). Examples of the broken plural: إِلَّا وَهُمْ شُرَكَاءٌ فِي دِمَائِهِمْ, *but they are companions in (shedding) their blood* (for شُرَكَاءَ); عَجَائِزًا مِثْلَ ٱلْأَفَاعِي خَمْسًا, *old women, like vipers, five in number* (for عَجَائِزَ).

250. On the contrary, the tênwīn is sometimes suppressed in cases where it could not be dispensed with in prose; e. g. فَمَا كَانَ حِصْنٌ وَلَا حَابِسٌ يَفُوتَانِ مِرْدَاسَ فِي مَجْمَعِ, *neither Ḥiṣn nor Ḥābis surpassed Mirdās in any assembly* (for

Poetic Licenses.

(مِرْدَاسًا ;) عَمْرُو ٱلَّذِى هَشَمَ ٱلثَّرِيدَ لِقَوْمِهِ, *Amr, who broke up (bread to make) soup for his people* (for عَمْرُو ٱلَّذِى, but there is another reading, عَمْـرُو ٱلْعُلَى هَشَمَ, *the noble 'Amr broke up*); فَأَلْفَيْتُهُ غَيْرَ مُسْتَعْتِبٍ وَلَا ذَاكِرِ ٱللّٰهَ إِلَّا قَلِيلًا, *and I found him not seeking (the Lord's) favour, and seldom thinking upon God* (for ذَاكِرٍ); وَحَىُّ مُحَارِبِ ٱلْأَبْطَالِ قِدْمَا, *and the tribe of Moḥârib, heroes of old* (for مُحَارِبٍ); كَسِنَّوْرٍ مَغْلُوبٍ يَصُولُ عَلَى ٱلْكَلْبِ, *like an overmatched cat that springs at the dog* (for كَسِنَّوْرٍ); عَلَى جِسْمٍ مُصْفَرٍّ مِنَ ٱلتِّبْرِ أَمْلَسِ, *upon a yellow body, smoother than gold* (for جِسْمٍ, and أَمْلَسِ in rhyme for أَمْلَسَ, instead of أَمْلَسَ, § 249).

251. The genitive plural in ـِينَ is sometimes changed in the rhyme into ـِينِ; e. g. وَقَدْ جَاوَزْتُ حَدَّ ٱلْأَرْبَعِينِ, *seeing that I have already passed the limit of forty years* (for ٱلْأَرْبَعِينَ); لَا بَارَكَ ٱللّٰهُ فِى بِضْعٍ وَسِتِّينِ, *may God not bless sixty and odd years!* (for وَسِتِّينَ); وَأَنْكَرْنَا زَعَانِفَ آخَرِينِ, *and we ignore the offscourings of other tribes* (for آخَرِينَ).

Rem. Still more rarely is the dual inflected by means of the final vowel *feth*, instead of the usual change of انِ into ـَيْنِ; e. g. أَعْرِفُ مِنْهَا ٱلْأَنْفَ وَٱلْعَيْنَانَا وَمَنْخِرَيْنِ أَشْبَهَا ظَبْيَانَا, *I recognize her nose and eyes, and nostrils that resemble gazelles'* (for ظَبْيَيْنِ and ٱلْعَيْنَيْنِ).

252. In verbs and nouns derived from radicals of which the third consonant is و or ى, the poets not unfrequently use the Indicative form of the Imperfect instead of the Subjunctive or Jussive, and the nominative case instead

of the accusative. Examples of the verb: أَبَى ٱللّٰهُ أَنْ أَسْمُوَ بِأُمٍّ
وَلَا أَبٍ, *God has not willed that I should be of noble descent either on the mother's or the father's side* (for أَسْمُوَ);
فَآلَيْتُ لَا أَرْثِى لَهَا مِنْ كَلَالَةٍ وَلَا مِنْ حَفًى حَتَّى تُلَاقِى مُحَمَّدَا,
and I swear, I will not show pity for weariness or footsoreness of hers, until she encounters Mohammed (for تُلَاقِىَ);
إِذَا غَرَّ أَنْ يُنْسِىَ ٱلْفَتَى فِيهِ أَوْ يَضْحَى, *when to spend an evening or a forenoon in it, fills one with vain delight* (for
أَلَمْ يَأْتِيكَ وَٱلْأَنْبَآءُ تَنْمِى بِمَا لَاقَتْ ;(إِذَا غَرَّ ٱلْفَتَى أَنْ يُنْسِىَ فِيهِ
لَبُونُ بَنِى زِيَادِ, *did he not bring you word—for news travels fast—of what has befallen the milch-camel of the Benū Ziyād* (for يَأْتِيكَ)? هَجَوْتَ زَبَّانَ ثُمَّ جِئْتَ مُعْتَذِرًا مِنْ هَجْوِ
زَبَّانَ لَمْ تَهْجُ وَلَمْ تَدَعْ, *you lampooned Zabbān, and then you came making excuses for having lampooned Zabbān,—(so that) you neither lampooned him nor let it alone* (for تَهْجُ);(عُوجِى عَلَيْنَا يُحَيِّيكِ ٱبْنُ عَنَّابِ, *turn aside to us, (and) 'Ibn 'Annab will salute you*, i. e. *receive you with honour* (for يُحَيِّيكِ);كَأَنْ لَمْ تَرَى قَبْلِى أَسِيرًا يَمَانِيَا, *as if you never saw a Yemenite prisoner before me* (for تَرَ);
مَا أَنْسَ لَا أَنْسَاهُ آخِرَ عِيشَتِى, *whatever I forget, I shall not forget him to the end of my life* (for أَنْسَهُ). Examples of the noun: وَمَنْ أَرَادَ ٱلتَّأَسِّى فِى مُصِيبَتِهِ, *and whoever seeks for consolation in his misfortunes* (for ٱلتَّأَسِّىَ);وَجَدْتُ
مَعَالِيكَ أَصْلًا لِشِعْرِى, *I found thy noble qualities a subject for my poetry* (for مَعَالِيَكَ);تَرَكْنَ رَاعِيهِنَّ مِثْلَ ٱلشَّنِّ,
they have left their shepherd like an old (useless) waterskin

Poetic Licenses.

كَأَنَّ أَيْدِيهُنَّ فِي ٱلْقَاعِ ٱلْقَرِقْ, *as if their forefeet were on level ground* (for أَيْدِيَهُنَّ; رَاعِيَهُنَّ) وَلَوْ كَانَ طَاوِى ٱلْخَشَا خَاتِعَا, *and if he had been hungry and famished* (for طَاوِىَ).

253. The poets occasionally use pausal forms (see §. 223—230) out of pause. For example, رَضِى, for رَضِىَ, in the verse: بِشُرُورٍ سَيِّدِى أَخْدُمُهُ إِنْ رَضِى بِى وَبِسَمْعِى وَٱلْبَصَرْ *with joy, my lord, will I wait upon him, if he be contented with me, and with my hearing and sight* (i. e. *most willingly and cheerfully*); سَلْعَنْ, for سَلْعَنَ, in the halfverse: فَسَلْعَنْ عُبَيْدُ ٱللَّهِ ثُمَّ أَبَى بَكْرُ, *'Obeidu 'l-lāh ran quickly, and thereupon Bekr held back*; هُوْ, for هُوَ, in the halfverse: فَلَا هُوَ مِنَ ٱلدُّنْيَا مُضِيعٌ نَصِيبَهْ, *and so he does not lose his share of (the pleasures of) this world.*

———————

INDEX.

I. Arabic Words, Technical Terms, etc.

ا

اِ, interj., I. 369; II. 39.*)
اِ, interrog., I. 361; II. 131; 166.
آ, interj., I. 369; II. 39.
اَبّ, I. 315, 1, rem. *a*; II. 38, rem. *b*; 81.
اَبَتَ, II. 38, rem. *b*.
اَبْتَغَ, II. 137, rem.
اَبْحَرُ ٱلشِّعْرِ, II. 201.
اَبَدًا, I. 364.
اَبْصَعُ, II. 137, rem.
اِبْنٌ, I. 19, 4; 21, 2; 302, 5; 315, 1, rem. *b*; II. 38, 1, rem. *e*; 81.
اِبْتَغَى, I. 19, 4; II. 81.
اِبْنُمٌ, I. 19, 4; 308, rem.

اَبْنِيَةُ ٱلْمُبَالَغَةِ, I. 232, rem. *c*.
اَتَى, I. 175, rem.
اِثْنَتَانِ, اِثْنَانِ, I. 19, 4; II. 97.
اَجَرَّ, I. 139.
اَجَلْ, I. 362.
اَجْمَعُ, II. 137.
اَحَدٌ, I. 295, rem. *b*; II. 49, 6, rem. *b*.
اَخٌ, I. 315, 1, rem. *a*; II. 81.
اِخْبَارٌ, II. 35, 1.
اُخْتُ ٱلْفَتْحَةِ, I. 7.
اُخْتُ ٱلضَّمَّةِ, I. 7.
اُخْتُ ٱلْكَسْرَةِ, I. 7.
اَلْاِخْتِصَاصُ, II. 35, 2, *c*.
اَخَذَ, I. 137; 138; 139.

*) The *Roman* numerals indicate the *volume*, the *Arabic* numerals the *section*.

آخَر, I. 295, rem. b; 309, 2, c.	اِسْمُ ٱلْعَدَدِ, I. 190, 3.
آخِر, II. 93.	„ ٱلْفَاعِلِ, I. 192, 2; 229; 230.
أَخَوَاتُ إِنَّ, II. 36, rem. a.	„ ٱلْفِعْلِ, I. 192, 1; 195 and foll.
„ كَانَ, II. 6, c; 42; 122.	„ ٱلْكَثْرَةِ, I. 194, 2; 247.
أَدَاةُ ٱلتَّعْرِيفِ, I. 345.	„ ٱلْكَيْفِيَّةِ, I. 194, 5; 268.
إِذْ, conj., I. 367.	„ ٱلْمُبَالَغَةِ, I. 233.
إِذْ, interj., I. 368, rem. e.	„ ٱلْمَرَّةِ, I. 193, 1; 219.
إِذَا, conj., I. 367; II. 5.	مَصْدَر, II. 27, 2, rem. a, note.
إِذَا مَا, II. 5, rem. a.	ٱلِٱسْمُ ٱلْمُصَغَّرِ, I. 194, 6; 269.
إِذَا ٱلْمُفَاجَأَةِ أَوِ ٱلْفُجَائِيَّةِ L. 368, rem. e.	ٱلْمُضْمَرُ, I. 190, 6.
إِذَنْ, إِذًا, I. 362; II. 15, 7; 225.	اِسْمُ ٱلْمَفْعُولِ, I. 192, 2; 229; 230.
أُرْجُوزَةٌ, II. 191.	„ ٱلْمَكَانِ وَٱلزَّمَانِ, I. 193, 3; 221—227.
أَزَرَ, I. 139.	ٱلِٱسْمُ ٱلْمَنْسُوبُ, I. 194, 4; 249—267.
اِسْتٌ, I. 19, 4.	ٱلْمَوْصُولُ, II. 172.
ٱلِٱسْتِثْنَاءُ, II. 186.	اِسْمُ ٱلنَّوْعِ, I. 193, 2; 220.
„ ٱلْمُفَرَّغُ, II. 186.	„ ٱلْوَحْدَةِ, I. 194, 1; 246.
اِسْتَفْعَلَ, I. 35; 60—65.	„ ٱلْوِعَاءِ, I. 194, 3; 248.
أَسْفَرَ, II. 42.	ٱلْإِسْنَادُ, II. 112.
اِسْمٌ, I. 19, 4.	ٱلْإِشْبَاعُ, II. 197, 3; 199, 1; 244.
ٱلْإِسْمُ, I. 190.	إِشْمَامُ ٱلضَّمِّ, I. 154, rem.
اِسْمُ ٱلْإِشَارَةِ, I. 190, 4.	أَصْبَحَ, II. 6, c; 42.
„ ٱللّٰهِ, I. 193, 4; 228.	أَصْوَاتٌ, L. 368.
„ أَنَّ, II. 36, rem. a.	آضَ, II. 42.
„ ٱلتَّفْضِيلِ, I. 234—5.	أَفْعَى, II. 42.
„ ٱلظَّرْفِ, I. 193, 3; 221, rem. a.	

أَنْعَالُ ٱلتَّعَجُّبِ، I. 194.	ٱلْإِضَافَةُ، II. 75.
" ، II. 24، rem. b.	إِضَافَةُ ٱلْبَيَانِ، II. 95، 5، rem.
ٱلْأَنْعَالُ غَيْرُ ٱلْمُتَعَدِّيَةِ، I. 75.	ٱلْإِضَافَةُ ٱلْبَيَانِيَّةُ، II. 76؛ 95، 5، rem.
أَنْعَالُ ٱلْقَلْبِ، II. 24، b؛ 25؛ 180.	" ٱلتَّبْعِيضِيَّةُ، II. 76.
ٱلْأَنْعَالُ ٱللَّازِمَةُ، I. 75.	إِضَافَةُ ٱلتَّشْبِيهِ، II. 95، 5، rem.
ٱلْمُتَعَدِّيَةُ، I. 75؛ II. 23، rem. a.	إِضَافَةُ ٱلتَّفْسِيرِ وَٱلْبَيَانِ، II. 62، 1؛ 95، 5، rem.
ٱلْأَنْعَالُ ٱلْمُتَعَدِّيَةُ بِأَنْفُسِهَا، II. 23، rem. a.	ٱلْإِضَافَةُ ٱلتَّفْسِيرِيَّةُ، II. 95، 5، rem.
" " بِغَيْرِهَا، II. 23، rem. a.	ٱلْحَقِيقِيَّةُ، II. 30، 1؛ 75، rem. a؛ 95، 5.
أَنْعَالُ ٱلْمَدْحِ وَٱلذَّمِّ، I. 183.	ٱلْإِضَافَةُ غَيْرُ ٱلْحَقِيقِيَّةِ، II. 30، 1؛ 75، rem. a.
" ٱلْيَقِينِ وَٱلشَّكِّ، II. 24، b؛ 25.	" غَيْرُ ٱلْمَحْضَةِ، II. 75، rem. a.
أَفْعَلَ، I. 35؛ 44؛ 45.	ٱللَّفْظِيَّةُ، II. 75، rem. a.
أَفْعَلُ، I. 231؛ 232؛ 234؛ 295، 2؛ 296؛ 309، 2، c؛ II. 31.	ٱلْمَحْضَةُ، II. 75، rem. a.
أَفْعَلُ ٱلتَّفْضِيلِ، I. 234.	ٱلْمَعْنَوِيَّةُ، II. 75، rem. a.
ٱفْعَلَّ، I. 35؛ 58؛ 59.	إِضَافَةُ ٱلْمَوْصُوفِ إِلَى ٱلصِّفَةِ، II. 95، 5.
ٱفْعَلَلَّ، I. 68؛ 72.	ٱلْإِغْرَاءُ، II. 35، 2، b.
ٱفْعَنْلَلَ، I. 68؛ 71.	أُغْنِيَةٌ، II. 191.
ٱفْعَنْلَى، I. 35؛ 66.	آقِّ، أَقِّ، أَقِّ، I. 368.
ٱلْإِنْوَاءُ، II. 199، 2.	ٱفْتَعَلَ، I. 35؛ 54—57.
ٱكْتَنَعَ، II. 137، rem.	ٱنْفَعَالَ، I. 35؛ 58؛ 59.
ٱلْإِكْفَاءُ، II. 199، 3.	
أَكَلَ، I. 137؛ 138.	
أَلْ، I. 19؛ 21، 3، 4؛ 345.	
أَلَّا، I. 362؛ 369؛ II. 169.	

أَ, interrog., I. 362; II. 169.
أَلَّا conj., I. 367; II. 11; 15, 1, a.
إِلَّا, I. 367; II. 42, rem. c; 156.
اَلْآتِي, I. 347.
اَلْحْ, II. 52, 3.
اَلَّذِي, I. 347; II. 172, rem. a; 174 and foll.
اَلْأَلِف, II. 103; 107, 1.
أَلِفُ ٱلْقَطْعِ, I. 19, rem. c.
اَلْأَلِفُ وَٱللَّامُ, I. 345.
لِلْجِنْسِ „ , II. 107, 1.
لِلْعَهْدِ „ , II. 107, 2.
اَلْأَلِفُ ٱلْمَقْصُورَةُ, I. 7, rem. b; 23, rem. a.
ٱلْمَمْدُودَةُ „ , I. 7, rem. b; 23, rem. a.
أَلِفُ ٱلْوَصْلِ, I. 19, rem. c.
أَلَكَ, I. 140.
اَللّٰهُ, II. 38, 1, rem. d.
اَللّٰهُمَّ, II. 38, 1, rem. d, note.
إِلَى, I. 358; II. 29, rem. a; 52; 61; 67, rem. a.
إِلَيْكَ عَنِّي, II. 52, 3.
إِلَيْكَهَا, II. 35, rem.
أُمْ, I. 362; II. 165; 166; 188.

أُمّ, I. 305, rem. c; II. 38, rem. b; 81.
أَمَّا, I. 362; II. 168.
أَمَّا, I. 367.
إِمَّا, I. 367; II. 19, 4.
أَمَامَ, I. 359.
أُمِّتَ, II. 38, rem. b.
أَمَرَ, I. 137; 138.
اِمْرُؤٌ, I. 19, 4; 308, rem.
اِمْرَأَةٌ, I. 19, 4; 305, rem. c.
أَمْسِ, I. 364, rem. a.
أَمْسَى, II. 6; 42.
أَنْ, I. 367; II. 11; 15, 1, a; 16; 88; 114; 116; 162.
أَنْ لَا, I. 367; II. 11; 15, 1, a.
أَنِ ٱلنَّاصِبَة, II. 15, 1, b.
إِنْ, I. 367; II. 6; 13; 17, 3; 127, 6; 159.
إِنِ ٱلشَّرْطِيَّة, II. 158, rem.
ٱلْمُخَفَّفَة „ , II. 15, 1, b.
ٱلنَّافِيَة „ , II. 42, rem. c.; 158.
أَنَّ, I. 367; II. 15, 1, b; 36; 125.
إِنَّ, I. 362; II. 36; 125; 168; 187, 1.
أَنَا, I. 23, rem. d.
أَنَّا, I. 89, 1, rem. b; II. 230, rem. b.

اُنَاسٌ, L 305, rem. e.	اِي, adv., L 362.
اَنْتُمْ, L 20, 4; 89, 1, rem. c; II. 248, rem.	اِي, interj., L 368; II. 38.
	اِي, L 362.
اِنْشَآءٌ, II. 35, L	اَيٌّ, اَيَّةٌ, L 349; 353; II. 6; 87; 171; 172, rem. a.
اِنْفَعَلَ, I. 35; 51—53.	
اِنْفَكَّ, II. 42.	اَيًا, L 368; II. 38.
اِنَّمَا, L 362; II. 185.	اِيَّا, L 158; 159; II. 31, rem.; 176; 179.
اَنَّى, L 362; II. 6.	
آهَ, آهَا, آهِ, اَهِ, L 368.	الْاِيطَآءُ, II. 199, 1.
اُهْجِيَّةٌ, II. 191.	اَيَّانَ, II. 6.
اَوْ, I. 20, 3; 367; II. 6; 15, 6; 165; 166; 188.	اَيَّانَ مَا, II. 6.
	اَيْمَا, L 350; 353, rem. b; II. 6.
اَوَاهُ, L 368.	اَيْمَنْ, I. 350; II. 6.
اَوَّلُ, L 295, rem. b; II. 86, rem. b; 93.	اَيْنَ, L 19, 1, rem. a.
اُولَآءِ, L 340.	اَيْنَ, I. 362; II. 6.
اُولُو, L 302, rem. c; 340, rem. b.	اَيْنَمَا, L 362; II. 6.
اُولَى, L 340.	اَيُّهَا, L 368; II. 38, 2.
اَوَّةٌ, L 368.	اَيْهَاتِ, L 368.

ب

بِ, I. 184; 356; II. 57; 65; 139.	بِ لِلتَّعْلِيلِ, II. 57, rem. d.
بِ لِلْاِسْتِعَانَةِ, II. 57, rem. d.	لِلثَّمَنِ, " , " "
لِلْاِلْصَاقِ, " , " "	لِلْقَسَمِ, " , " "
لِلتَّعْدِيَةِ, " , " "	لِلْمُصَاحَبَةِ, " , " "
لِلتَّعْرِيضِ, " , " "	لِلْمُلَابَسَةِ, " , " "

بِسْمِ ٱللّٰهِ, I. 21, L.	بَآءُ ٱلتَّفْدِيَةِ, II. 57, rem. b.
ٱلْبَسِيطُ, II. 215.	ٱلثَّمَنِ ,, ,, ,,
بَعْدَ, I. 359; II. 67, 3.	بَاتَ, II. 6; 42.
بَعْدُ, I. 363.	بِئْسَ, I. 183.
بَعْضُ, II. 82, 3; 132, rem. a.	بَخْرٌ, II. 200.
بِغَيْرِ, II. 57, rem. a.	بَجَحَ, I. 368.
بَلْ, I. 362; II. 85; 184, 2.	ٱلْبَدَلُ, II. 94, rem. a; 139, rem. b; 186.
بِلَا, II. 57, rem. a.	
بَلَى, I. 362.	بَدَلُ ٱلْاِشْتِمَالِ, II. 139, rem. b.
بِنَآءٌ, II. 35, rem.	ٱلْإِضْرَابُ ,, ,, ,, ,,
بِنَآءٌ عَلَى, II. 62, 6.	ٱلْبَعْضِ مِنَ ٱلْكُلِّ ,, ,, ,, ,,
بَنُونَ بَنُو, I. 302, 5; II. 143, rem.	ٱلْغَلَطِ ,, ,, ,, ,,
بَيَانٌ, II. 94.	ٱلْكُلِّ مِنَ ٱلْكُلِّ ,, ,, ,, ,,
بَيْتٌ, II. 192.	ٱلْبَدَلُ ٱلْمُبَايِنُ لِلْمُبْدَلِ ,, ,, ,, ,,
بَيْنَ, I. 359; II. 61.	بَدَلُ ٱلنِّسْيَانِ ,, ,, ,, ,,
بَيْنَا, I. 362; II. 61, rem. a.	بِدُونِ, II. 57, rem. a; 63, 6.
بَيْنَمَا, II. 61, rem. a.	بَرِحَ, II. 42.

ت

ٱلتَّأْسِيسُ, II. 196, L.	تَ, I. 356; II. 65.
ٱلتَّأْكِيدُ, II. 139, rem. a.	رتِ, I. 175, rem.
ٱلتَّقْسِيمُ, II. 199, 5.	تَا, I. 340.
ٱلتَّجَدُّدُ, II. 69, note.	تَابِعٌ, II. 136.

Index. 297

تَحْتَ, I. 359; II. 67, 2.
تَحْتُ, I. 363.
اَلتَّحْذِير, II. 35, 2, b.
اَلتَّرْخِيم, II. 39, 1, rem. c.
اَلتَّسْجِيع, II. 223.
اَلتَّشْدِيد, I. 11 and foll.
اَلتَّصْغِير, I. 194, 6; 269 and foll.
تَصْغِيرُ التَّرْخِيم, I. 253.
اَلتَّضْمِين, II. 199, 5.
تَفَاعَل, I. 35; 49; 50.
تَفَعَّل, I. 35; 46—49.
تَفَعْلَل, I. 68; 70.
تَفْعِيل, II. 200.

اَلتَّقْطِيع, II. 200.
تِلْكَ, I. 343.
ثُمَّ, I. 20, 4.
اَلتَّمْيِيز, II. 44, 5, rem. a.
اَلتَّنَازُعُ فِي ٱلْعَمَل, II. 177, rem.
اَلتَّنْوِين, I. 8.
اَلتَّوَابِع, II. 136; 139, rem. a, b.
اَلتَّوْجِيه, II. 197, 3; 199, 1.
اَلتَّوْكِيد, II. 139, rem. a.
اَللَّفْظِيّ, " " "
ٱلْمَعْنَوِي, " " "
تِي, I. 340.

ث

ثُمَّتَ, ثُمَّ, I. 367.
ثَلَثَةٌ, ثَلٰثُ, I. 6, rem. a; 318, rem. a.
ثَمَّةَ, ثَمَّ, I. 362.
ثَنَا, I. 23, rem. d.
ثِنْتَانِ, I. 318, and rem. b.

ج

جَارٌّ وَمَجْرُورٌ, II. 113; 115.
جِدًّا, I. 364.
جَزْم, II. 200.
جَزْمَة, جَزْم, I. 2.
V. II.

جَمْعُ ٱلْجَمْع, I. 305, rem. c.
اَلْجَمْعُ ٱلسَّالِم, I. 300, a.
ٱلصَّحِيح, " " "
جَمْعُ ٱلْقِلَّة, I. 307; II. 96.

38

298 Index.

جَمْعُ ٱلْكَثْرَةِ, L. 307; II. 96.
ٱلْجَمْعُ ٱلْمُكَسَّرُ, L. 300, b.
جُمْلَةٌ, II. 112.
جُمْلَةٌ ٱسْمِيَّةٌ, II. 113.
جُمْلَةٌ جَارِيَةٌ مَجْرَى ٱلظَّرْفِيَّةِ, II. 115.

جُمْلَةٌ حَالِيَّةٌ, II. 31.
„ ظَرْفِيَّةٌ, II. 115; 127, 1.
„ فِعْلِيَّةٌ, II. 113.
جَمِيعٌ, II. 52, 2; 137.
جَمِيعًا, L. 364.

ح

ح, L. 23, rem. d.
حَاشَ, II. 156, rem. a.
حَاشَا, حَاشَى, II. 156, rem. a.
ٱلْحَالُ, II. 3, b and c; 8, d and e; 21, rem. b; 135.
ٱلْحَالُ ٱلْمُقَارِنُ, II. 73.
„ ٱلْمُقَدَّرُ, II. 73; 140.
حَبَّةٌ, II. 97.
حَتَّى, L. 358; II. 5, rem. b; 11; 15, 3, 4; 53.
ٱلْحُدُوثُ, II. 69, note.
ٱلْحَدُّ, II. 197, 5; 199, 1.
حَرْفُ ٱسْتِثْنَاءٍ, L. 367, 5.
ٱلتَّنْبِيهِ „ , L. 344.
تَرْتِيبٍ „ , L. 366, 2.
تَعْلِيلٍ „ , L. 367, 9.
حَضَرَ „ , II. 185.

حَرْفُ شَرْطٍ, L. 367.
„ عَطْفٍ, L. 366, 1, 2.
„ ٱلنُّدْبَةِ, II. 38, 3.
حَرَكَةٌ, II. 198, note.
ٱلْحُرُوفُ, L. 354.
حُرُوفُ ٱلْإِضَافَةِ, L. 355.
„ ٱلتَّخْصِيصِ وَٱلْتَعْرِيضِ, II. 169.
„ ٱلْجَرِّ, L. 355.
ٱلْحُرُوفُ ٱلْجَوَازِ, L. 355.
حُرُوفُ ٱلْخَفْضِ, L. 355.
„ ٱلشَّرْطِ, L. 365.
ٱلْحُرُوفُ ٱلشَّمْسِيَّةُ, L. 14, 1, rem.
حُرُوفُ ٱلْعَطْفِ, L. 365.
ٱلْحُرُوفُ ٱلْقَمَرِيَّةُ, L. 14, 1, rem.
حُرُوفُ ٱلْمَدِّ, L. 6.

Index.

اَلحُروفُ ٱلمَصدَرِيَّةُ, ll. 114.
حُروفُ ٱلمُنَادَاةِ, ll. 38.
ٱلنِّدَآءِ ,, ll 38.
حَسِبَ, L. 92. rem.
حَشَى, ll. 156, rem. a.
ٱلحِكَايَةُ, ll. 170.
حَمْ, L. 315, rem. a.
حَوَّلَ, L. 359.
حَى, interj., L. 368.
حَى, verb, L. 179, rem. b.
حَيْثُ, L. 363; ll. 6.
حَيْثُمَا, L. 363; ll. 6.

حِين, L. 364.
حَىَّ هَلَا, L. 368.
حَيِىَ, L. 179, rem. b.
خَارِجًا, L. 364.
ٱلخَبَرُ, ll. 113; 119; 120.
خَبَرُ أَنَّ, ll. 36, rem. a.
خَبَرٌ مُقَدَّم, ll. 115.
ٱلخُروج, ll. 195, rem. b.
خِطَاب, ll. 38, l.
ٱلخَفض, L. 355.
ٱلخَفيف, ll. 221.
خَلَا, ll. 156, rem. a.

د

دَاخِلًا, L. 364.
اَلدَّخِيل, ll. 196, L.
دُون, L. 359; ll. 63.

دُونَكَ, ll. 35, rem.; 63, 2, 6, rem.
دُوَيْن, ll. 63, 7, rem.

ذ

إِذًا, l. 340; ll. 38, 2; 170.
ذَاتُ, L. 340, rem. b; 347, rem. e.
ذَاتٌ, ll. 135.
ذَاكَ, L. 342.

ذٰلِكَ, L. 343.
ذُو, l. 302, 5; 315, rem. a; 340,
 rem. b; 347, rem. e; ll. 81.
ذِى, L. 340.

ر

اَلرَّاجِعُ, ll. 170; 172, rem. b;
 173; 175.

رَأَى, L. 140; 175, rem.; 176;
 ll. 230.

38*

Index.

رَبّ, II. 84.
رَبَّتْ, II. 84, rem. a.
رَبَّتَمَا, II. 84, rem. a.
رُبَّمَا, I. 364; II. 84, rem. b, c.
رُبَّةَ, رُبَّهَا, II. 84.
رِثَآء, II. 191.
اَلرَّجَزُ, II. 204.
رَح, I. 23, rem. d.
اَلرَّدْفُ, II. 196, 2.

اَلرَّشّ, II. 197, 4.
رِضَة, I. 23, rem. d.
اَلرَّقْمُ الْهِنْدِيّ, I. 32.
اَلرَّمَلُ, II. 219.
رُوح, II. 135.
اَلرَّوِيّ, II. 194 and foll.
رُوَيْدَ, II. 35, rem.
رَيْثَمَا, رَيْثُ, I. 364.

ز

زَالَ, II. 42.

س

سَ, I. 361, 2; II. 8, c; 197, 4.
سَائِرٌ, II. 82, 2, rem.
سَأَلَ, I. 140.
سَاكِنٌ, II. 198.
اَلسَّجْعُ, II. 223.
اَلسَّرِيعُ, II. 205.

اَلسُّكُونُ, I. 9; II. 198, note.
اَلسِّنَادُ, II. 199, 1.
سَوْفَ, I. 364; II. 8, c; 157, 4.
سَوَآء, II. 82, 5.
سِوَى, II. 82, 5.
سِيمَا, I. 364; II. 186, rem. b.

ش

شِبْهُ الْجُمَلِ, I. 290, 1, e; 292, 1; 306, rem.
" , II. 139, rem. b.
اَلشِّدَّةُ, I. 11.

شَطْرٌ, II. 192.
اَلشِّعْرُ, II. 191.
شِمَالًا, I. 364.

Index.

ص

صَاحٍ, ll. 39, 1, rem. c.
صَاحِبٌ, ll. 51.
صَارَ, ll. 6; 42; 131.
اَلصَّدْرُ, ll. 192.

اَلصِّفَةُ, I. 190, 2; ll. 136; 139, rem. b; 172.
اَلصِّلَةُ, I. 18; ll. 172; 195.
صلعم, I. 23, rem. d.
صَةٌ, I. 368.

ض

ضَرُورَةُ ٱلشِّعْرِ, ll. 232.
ضَمٌّ, ضَمَّةٌ, I. 4.
اَلضَّمِيرُ, I. 190, 6.
ضَمِيرُ ٱلشَّأْنِ, I. 367, 6.

اَلضَّمِيرُ ٱلْعَائِدُ (ٱلرَّاجِعُ)
    إِلَى ٱلْمَوْصُولِ, ll. 175.
    ضَمِيرُ ٱلْفَصْلِ, ll. 124; 125; 128—130.
    اَلْقِصَّةِ ,, I. 367, 6.

ط

اَلطَّوِيلُ, ll. 211.

ظ

اَلظَّرْفُ, ll. 44, 2, rem. c; 115.
ظَلَّ, ll. 6; 42.

ع

عَادَ, ll. 42.
عَامَّةٌ, ll. 137.
اَلْعَائِدُ, ll. 170; 172, rem. b; 175.

اَلْعَجُزُ, ll. 192.
عَدَا, ll. 186, rem. a.
عَسَى, ll. 187, 2.

Index

عَطْفُ ٱلْبَيَانِ, II. 139, rem. b.
ٱلنَّسَقِ   "   "   "
عَلَّ, I. 364, rem. b; II. 36, rem. d.
عَلَى, I. 359, rem. a; 359; II. 62.
عَلَى لِلْاِسْتِعْلَاءِ, II. 62, L
عَلَى بِهِ, II. 62, rem. a.
عَلَيْكَ, II. 35, rem.; II. 62, rem. a.
عَمْ, I. 23, rem. d.

عَنْ, L 358; II. 50.
عِنْدَ, I. 359; II. 59.
عِنْدَكَ, II. 35, rem.; 59, rem. a.
عِوَضٌ, L 363.
عِوَضَ, L 359.
عَيْنٌ, II. 135; 139.
عَيْنُ ٱلْفِعْلِ, I. 35, rem. b.
غُيُوبُ ٱلشِّعْرِ, II. 199.

غ

غَدٌ, II. 82, 1, rem. a.
غَدًا, I. 364.
غُشِيَ عَلَيْهِ, II. 62, 1.

غَيْرٌ, L 363.
غَيْرُ, II. 63, 5; 82, 4; 160, rem. a.
غَيْرُ مُنْصَرِفٍ, L 308.

ف

فِي, L 89, rem. a; 138; 366, 2; II. 1, f; 6, c; 15, 4; 17, 1, 3; 65; 85; 176; 182; 187.
فَاءُ ٱلْفِعْلِ, L 35, rem. b.
فَاعَلَ, I. 35; 42; 43.
ٱلْفَاعِلُ, II. 113; 119.
فَتًى, II. 42.
نَتْحَةُ فَمْ, L 4.

فَمْ, I. 23, rem. d.
فَضْلًا عَنْ, II. 50, 4.
فَعَالِ, I. 99, rem. c; 309, 3, h.
فِعَالٌ, I. 233; II. 33.
فُعَالٌ, L 309, 2, c.
فَعَالٌ, L 297.
فُعَالٌ, L 233, rem. c.
فُعَالَى, L 335.

نَعَالَةٌ, I. 233, rem. b.
نُعَالَةٌ, I. 258.
نَعَلَ, I. 35; 37.
نَعُلَ, I. 35; 38.
نَعِلَ, I. 35; 39—41.
نَعِلٌ, II. 33.
نَعُلٌ, I. 337.
اَلْفِعْلُ الْأَجْوَفُ, I. 149.
اَلْأَصَمُّ ,, , I. 119.
اَلْمُضَاعَفُ ,, , I. 119.
نُعْلٌ, نَعْلٌ, I. 336.
نَعَلٌ, I. 309, 3, h.
نَعْلَاءُ, I. 296.
نَعْلَانِ, I. 295, 1; 309, 2, d.
نُعْلَانِ, I. 295, rem. a; 309, 2, d.
فِعْلَةٌ, I. 295.
نُعْلَةٌ, I. 256.
نَعْلَةٌ, I. 233, rem. c.
نَعَلْتُمْ, I. 20, 4; 186, 2; II. 248, rem.
نَعْلَلَ, I. 67—69.

نَعْلَى, I. 295, 1.
نُعْلَى, I. 295, 2.
نَعُولٌ, I. 231; 232, rem. b, c; 297; II. 33.
نَعُّولٌ, I. 233, rem. c
نَعُولَةٌ, I. 297, 1.
نَعِيلٌ, I. 231; 232, rem. b; 297, 2; 336; II. 33.
نُعَيْلٌ, I. 233, rem. c.
نُعَيْلَةٌ, I. 297, 2.
نَقَطَ, I. 362.
فَلْ, II. 17, 1.
فُلْ, II. 38, 1, rem. c.
فَمْ, I. 305, rem. e; 315, 1, rem. a.
فُو, I. 315, 1, rem. a.
فَوْقَ, I. 359; II. 67, 2.
تَوْقَ, I. 363.
فِى, I. 358; II. 27, 2, rem. d; 44, 2, rem. a; 56; 77.
فِى لِلظَّرْفِيَّةِ, II. 56, rem. a.

ق

قَآئِمٌ مَقَامَ ٱلْفَاعِلِ, II. 133, rem. a.
ٱلْفِعْلِ ,, ,, ,, ,,
قَابِلٌ, II. 82, 1, rem. a.

اَلْقَافِيَةُ, II. 193.
قَافِيَةٌ مُؤَسَّسَةٌ, II. 196, rem. b.
مُجَرَّدَةٌ ,, ,, ,,

Index.

قَابِيَةٌ مُرْدَفَةٌ, II. 196, rem. b.
مُطْلَقَةٌ ,, II. 193.
مُقَيَّدَةٌ ,, ,, ,,
قَالَ, II. 54, 4.
قَبَلَ, I. 359; II. 67, 3.
قِبَلُ, I. 363.
قَبِلَ, II. 67, 6.

قَدْ, I. 362; II. 2; 3, b; 36; 187, 4.
قُدَّامَ, L. 359.
قَدْرُ, II. 82, 6, rem.
قَصِيدَةٌ, II. 191.
قَطُّ, I. 362.
قِطْعَةٌ, II. 191.
قَلِيلًا, L. 364.

ك

ك, L. 356, rem. c; II. 44, 6; 66.
كَ لِلتَّشْبِيهِ, II. 66, rem. c.
كَآئِنٍ, II. 44, 5, rem. b.
ٱلْكَامِلُ, II. 206.
كَأْنْ, L. 367, 4.
كَأَنَّ, L. 367, 6; II. 36; 57.
كَانَ, L. 151, rem.; I. 3, c; 6, c; 9; II. 71, rem. a; 74; 122; 131.
كَانَ ٱلتَّامَّةُ, II. 42, rem. b; 159.
كَانَ قَدْ, II. 3, d.
كَانَ ٱلنَّاقِصَةُ, II. 159.
كَأَيِّ, II. 44, 5, rem. b.
كَثِيرًا, L. 364.
كَذَا, II. 44, 5, rem. b.
كَسْرَةٌ ,كَسْرُ, I. 4.

كُلُّ, II. 82, L.
كَلَّا, I. 362, 18.
كِلْتَانِ ,كِلَانِ, II. 83; 138.
كِلٌّ, II. 137.
كُلْمَا, II. 6.
كَمْ, L. 351; II. 44, 5, rem. b.
كُمْ ,كُمْ, L. 20, 4; II. 248, rem.
كَمَا, II. 44, 6.
كَمِثْلِ, II. 66, rem. b.
ٱلْكِنَايَةُ, L. 190, 6.
كَيْ, I. 367; II. 11; 15, 2.
كَيْفَ, L. 364; II. 6.
كَيْفَمَا, II. 6.
كَيْلَا, I. 367; II. 11; 15, 2.

ل

َل, adv., I. 21, 3, b; 361; II. 19, 1, 3; 36; 125; 190.

َل, prep., I. 356, rem. b; II. 54, 4, rem. b.

لِ, conj., II. 11; 15, 2; 17, I.

لِ, prep., I. 21, 3, a; 356; II. 27, 2, rem. d; 29; 31; 33; 34; 39, rem. b; 54; 77.

لِ لِلْآخْتِصَاصِ, II. 54, 2, rem. a.

لِ لِلْاِسْتِغَاثَةِ, II. 54, 4, rem. b.

لِ لِلتَّعَجُّبِ, II. 54, 4, rem. b.

لِ لِلتَّعْدِيَةِ, II. 54, 1, rem. b.

لِ لِلْعِلَّةِ أَوِ التَّعْلِيلِ, II. 54, 3, rem.

لِ لِلْمِلْكِ, II. 54, 2, rem. a.

لَا, I. 362; II. 1, c, and rem. b; 1, f; 5, rem. b; 15, 7; 17, 2; 82, 4, rem. a and b; 155; 160—63; 176, g.

لَا الْحَاجِزِيَّةُ, II. 42, rem. c.

لَا لِنَفْيِ الْجِنْسِ أَوْ نَايَبَةُ الْجِنْسِ, II. 39, and rem. a.

لَاتَ, I. 152, rem. b; II. 42, rem. c.

لَا سِيَّمَا, I. 364; II. 156, rem. b.

لَا غَيْرُ, I. 363.

آلَاءِ, II. 241, rem. a.

لِئَلَّا, I. 367, 4; II. 15, 2.

اَللَّامُ, I. 345.

اَللَّامُ لِتَقْوِيَةِ الْعَامِلِ, II. 29.

لَامُ التَّعْرِيفِ, I. 345.

لَامُ الْفِعْلِ, I. 35, rem. b.

لِأَنْ, I. 367, 4; II. 15, 2.

لِأَنَّ, I. 367, 4; II. 36.

لَئِنْ, I. 367, 5.

لَدَى, لَدُنْ, I. 358; II. 60.

لَعَلَّ, I. 361, rem. b; II. 36, rem. d.

لَكِنْ, لٰكِنَّ, I. 367, 10; II. 36; 184, 1.

لِكَيْ, I. 367, 9; II. 11; 15, 2.

لِكَيْلَا, II. 11; 15, 2.

لِلَّهِ دَرُّهُ, II. 54, 2, rem. e.

لَمْ, I. 362; II. 12; 18.

لَمَّا, adv., I. 362; II. 12; 18.

لَمَّا, conj., I. 367.

لَنْ, I. 362; II. 11; 15, 1, a; 156; 187, 4.

306   Index.

لَوْ, I. 20, 3; 367; II. 4; 189, and rem. a.

لَوْ أَنْ, II. 4; 189, rem. b.

لَوْلَا, I. 367; II. 1; 167; 169.

لَوْلَمْ, I. 367.

لَوْمَا, I. 367; II. 169.

لَيْتَ, I. 364, rem. b; II. 36, rem. d.

لَيْسَ, I. 182; II. 42; 159; 187, 2.

لَيْلَا, I. 364.

لَيْمُنُ اللّٰهِ, I. 19, rem. a.

م

مْ, I. 351, rem.; II. 170, rem.; 228, rem. a.

مَا, adv., I. 362; II. 8, rem. b; 131; 157; 158; 169; 187, 4.

مَا, pron.; I. 184; 348; II. 6; 49, 7; 88; 114; 170; 172, rem. a.

مَا الْحَارِيَّةُ, II. 42, rem. c.

مَا الدَّيْمُومَةِ, I. 367; II. 7; 18; 42.

مَا الزَّائِدَةُ, II. 66, rem. a.

مَا الْكَائَّةُ, II. 36, rem. c. and d.

مَا بَيْنَ, II. 61.

مَا حَاشَى, II. 186, rem. a.

مَا خَلَا, II. 186, rem. a.

مَا عَدَا, II. 186, rem. a.

مَا لَمْ, II. 7.

مَا لَمْ يُسَمَّ فَاعِلُهُ, II. 133, rem. a.

مَآء, I. 305, rem. c.

مِائَةُ, II. 103; 107, 4.

الْمَاضِى, II. 1.

الْمُبْتَدَأُ, II. 113; 119; 120; 171.

مُبْتَدَأ مُؤَخَّر, II. 115.

الْمُبْدَلُ, II. 139, rem. c.

مُتَمَامًا, II. 6.

الْمَتْبُوعُ, II. 136; 139, rem. a.

مُتَحَوِّلٌ, II. 198.

الْمُتَدَارَكُ, II. 198, 3; 214.

الْمُتَرَادِفٌ, II. 198, 1.

الْمُتَرَاكِبٌ, II. 198, 4.

الْمُتَعَجَّبُ مِنْهُ, II. 54, 4, rem. b.

الْمُتَقَارِبٌ, II. 209.

الْمُتَكَاوِسٌ, II. 198, 5.

الْمُتَوَاتِرٌ, II. 198, 2.

مَتَى, I. 362; II. 6.

مِثْلٌ, II. 82, 6.

مَجَّانًا, I. 364.

الْمُجْتَثُّ, II. 222.

Index.

اَلْمَجْرَى, II. 197, 1; 199, 2.
مَدّ ,مَدَّةٌ, I. 22.
مَدِيْم, II. 191.
اَلْمَدِيْد, II. 220.
مُذْ, I. 20, 4; 358; II. 64.
مُذَكَّر, I. 289.
مُرَكَّب مَزْجِى, I. 264; 309, rem. b.
مَرْثِيَّة, II. 191.
مُرْتَجَل, II. 206; 214.
اَلْمُسْتَثْنَى, II. 186.
مِنْهُ „ „ „ „
اَلْمُسْتَغَاث, II. 54, 4, rem. b.
بِهِ „ „ „ „
اَلْمُسْنَد, II. 112.
إِلَيْهِ „ „ „ „
مَشْطُور, II. 204.
اَلْمُصَدَّر, I. 195, rem.; II. 26.
مِضْرَع ,مِضْرَاع, II. 192.
اَلْمُضَارِع, I. 95, rem. a; II. 30, 1; 75, rem. a; 212.
اَلْمُضَارِع اَلْمَجْزُوم, II. 12.
اَلْمَرْفُوع „ II. 8.
اَلْمَنْصُوب „ II. 11; 15, b.
اَلْمُضَاف, II. 30, 1, rem. a; 75.
إِلَيْهِ „ „ „ „

مَطَّة, I. 22.
مَعَ, I. 20, 4; 359; II. 58.
مَعًا, I. 364.
اَلْمَعْطُوف عَلَيْهِ, II. 139, rem. c.
مَعْنَى إِنَّ, II. 6.
اَلشَّرْطِ „ „ „ „
مِفْعَال, I. 233, rem. c; 297, 3; II. 33.
مَفْعَل, I. 300, 2, c; 333.
مِفْعَل, I. 233, rem. c; 297, 3.
اَلْمَفْعُول بِهِ, II. 133, rem. a.
اَلصَّرِيح „ „ „ „ note.
غَيْرُ الصَّرِيح „ „ „ „ „
فِيهِ „, II. 44, 2, rem. c.
لَهُ أَوْ لِأَجْلِهِ, II. 44, 4, rem. a.
اَلْأَوَّل „, II. 24, rem. a.
اَلثَّانِى „ „ „ „
اَلْمُطْلَق „, II. 26; 35, 1; 68.
مِفْعِيل, I. 233, rem. c; 297, 3.
اَلْمُغْتَصَب, II. 217.
مُقَطَّعَات, II. 191.
مَلِك, I. 140.
مَن, I. 20, 4; 348; 352; II. 6; 27, rem. d; 170; 172, rem. a.
مِن, I. 20, 4; 358, rem. b and c; II. 49; 64, rem. b; 77; 106, 1.

مِن لِلْاٰبْتِدَآءِ, II. 49, 2, rem.	مِن قَبْلِ, II. 67, 6.
مِن لِلْبَيَانِ أَوْ لِلتَّبْيِينِ, II. 49, 7, rem.	مِن لَدُنْ, II. 67, 5.
مِن لِلتَّبْعِيضِ, II. 49, 6, rem. c.	اَلْمُنَادَى, II. 38.
مِن لِلتَّغْلِيلِ, II. 49, 3, rem. a.	مُنْذُ, I. 358; II. 64.
مِن أَجْلِ, II. 49, 3, rem. b.	اَلْمُنْسَرِحُ, II. 216.
مِن أَحَدٍ, II. 49, 6, rem. b.	مُنْصَرِفٌ, I. 308.
مِن بَعْدِ, II. 67, 3.	اَلْمَنْعُوتُ, II. 139, rem. c.
مِن بَيْنِ, II. 67, 1.	مَنَّة, L 352.
مِن تَحْتِ, II. 67, 2.	مَنُو, L 352.
مِن دُونِ, II. 63.	مَهْ, L 368; II. 225, rem. a.
مِن عَلَى, II. 67, 4.	مَهْمَا, II. 6.
مِن عِنْدِ, II. 67, 5.	اَلْمَوْصُوفُ, L 190, 1; II. 136; 139, rem. c.
مِنْ غَيْرِ, II. 57, rem. a.	اَلْمَوْصُولُ, II. 172.
مِن فَوْقِ, II. 67, 2.	„ الاِسْمِيّ, I. 190, 5.
مِن قَبْلِ, II. 67, 3.	اَلْمُؤَكِّدُ, II. 139, rem. a and c.
	مُؤَنَّثٌ, L 259.

ن

ن, II. 241.	نَحْوَ, II. 55.
نَآئِبُ مَنَابَ ٱلْفَاعِلِ, II. 133, rem. a.	نِسَآءٌ, I. 305, rem. e.
نَاسٌ, L 305, rem. e.	اَلتِّسْبَةُ, L 194, 4; 249.
نَبْرَةٌ, I. 15.	نَصْبُ ٱلْمَدْحِ وَٱلذَّمِّ, II. 35, 2, c.
نَحْوَ, II. 82, 7.	نِصْفٌ, II. 135.

Index. 309

اَلنَّعْتُ, II. 139, rem. b.
نَعَمْ, L 362.
نِعْمَ, L 183.
اَلنَّقَاذُ, II. 197, 2.
نَفْسٌ, II. 135; 139.

اَلنَّقْلُ, II. 229.
نَمَسَ, I. 113.
نَهَارًا, I. 364.
نِى, L 20, 2; II. 225, rem. b.

ه

هَا, L 344; 368, and rem. c.
هَآءُ ٱلسَّكْتِ, II. 230.
هَآءُ ٱلْوَقْفِ, II. 225, rem. a; 230.
هَاذَاكَ, L 344.
هَاكَ, I. 368, rem. c; II. 35, rem.
هَاؤُلَآءِ, L 344.
مِجَآءِ, II. 191.
هَـٰذَا, L 311; II. 39, 1, rem. d.
هَـٰذِى, هَـٰذِهِ, L 314.
اَلْهَزْجُ, II. 208.
هَلْ, I. 362; II. 167.
هَلْ لَكَ, II. 54, 2, rem. c; 167.
هَلَا, I. 368.

هَلَّا, L 362; II. 169.
هَلُمَّ, L 368, rem. c.
هَمْزَةٌ, هَمْزٌ, L 15.
هَمْزَةُ ٱلتَّسْوِيَةِ, II. 166.
هُمْ, هِمْ, L 20, 4; 89, 1, rem. c;
    II. 248, rem.
هَنْ, L 315, rem. a.
هُنَا, L 362.
هُوَ, I. 89, 1, rem. a; II. 230, rem. b.
هُؤُلَآءِ, L 344.
هِىَ, I. 89, 1, rem. a.
هَيْتَ, L 368.
هَيْهَاتَ, I. 368.

و

وَ, conj., L 89, 1, rem. a; 139; 366;
    II. 8, e; 15, 5, 7; 17, 1; 30, 1,

rem. b; 37; 39, 4; 61; 85;
    176; 182—183.

310 Index.

وَ, prep., I. 356; II. 65.
وَا, I. 368; II. 39, 3.
اَلْوَرَايِرُ, II. 207.
وَإِنْ, I. 367, 5.
وَاهًا, I. 368.
وَاوُ ٱلْجَمْعِ „ II. 15, 5.
ٱلْحَالِ „ II. 127, 7; 183, rem.
رُبَّ „ II. 85.
ٱلْمُصَاحَبَةِ „ II. 37.
ٱلْمَعِيَّةِ „ II. 15, 5; 37.
وُجِدَ, II. 42, rem. b.
وَجَحَ, I. 23, rem. d.
وَحْدَ, I. 364.
وَدَعَ, I. 144.
وَذَرَ, I. 144.
وَرَآءَ, I. 359.

وَزَعَ, I. 144.
وَسَطَ, I. 359.
وَسِعَ, I. 144.
وَصْلَةَ ,وَصْلٌ, I. 18.
وَضَعَ, I. 144.
وَطِئَ, I. 144.
وَقَدْ, II. 3, b; 183, 4.
وَقَعَ, I. 144.
وَلَّ, II. 17, L.
وَلَا, II. 160, rem. b; 181.
وَلَكِنْ ,وَلَكِنَّ, II. 36; 181, L.
وَهَبَ, I. 144.
وَنَى, I. 368.
وَنْجُ, I. 368, rem. b.
وَيْلٌ, I. 368, rem. b.

ى

ى, I. 20, 2; II. 38, 1, rem. b; 228, rem. b.
يَا, II. 30, 1, c; 38, 1; 54, 1, rem. b.
يَا أَيُّهَا, I. 368; II. 38, 2.
يَا رَبِّ, II. 84, rem. c.

يَكَ, I. 151, rem.; II. 211.
يَكُونُ قَدْ, II. 10.
يَمِينًا, I. 364.
ٱلْيَوْمَ, I. 345; 364.
يَوْمًا, I. 364.

II. Index of English and Latin technical terms (including some Arabic, expressed in the Roman character), grammatical forms, constructions, etc.

Abbreviation, mark of, I. 23, rem. d.

Accent, I. 28—31.

Accusative — after a transitive verb, II. 23; after verbs in the passive voice, II. 25; double, after causatives and the اِفْعَالُ ٱلْقَلْبِ, II. 24; cognate, after verbs transitive and intransitive, II. 26; depending on a verb that is understood, II. 35; after كَانَ, أَنَّ, إِنَّ, II. 36; after لٰكِنَّ, لِأَنَّ, لَعَلَّ, عَلَّ or لَيْتَ and, II. 36, rem. d; after رُبَّ, II. 37; after لَا نَافِيَةُ ٱلْجِنْسِ, II. 39; after كَانَ and cognate verbs, II. 41 and 42; after لَا ٱلْحِجَازِيَّةُ and مَا ٱلْحِجَازِيَّةُ, II. 42, rem. c; after إِنْ ٱلنَّافِيَةُ and لَاتَ, II. 42, rem. c; adverbial, II. 41; instead of a preposition with the genitive, II. 67, rem. c; of the nomina agentis and patientis, or participles, after كَانَ, II. 74; after numerals, II. 99.

Adjectives — verbal, I. 229—245; intensive, I. 232—233; comparative, I. 234—235; superlative, I. 234—235; 'relative, I. 249—267; distributive, I. 333; multiplicative, I. 334; verbal, construed with the accus. and with لِ, II. 33—34; of the form أَفْعَلُ, construed with إِلَى, II. 34, rem. a; verbal, construed with the genitive, II. 86; relative, construed with the genitive, II. 91.

Adverbs — numeral, I. 331—332; inseparable, I. 361; separable, 362—364.

Agent, II. 113.
Alphabet, I. 1.
Apposition, II. 94; 136 and foll.
Article, I. 19, 1; 21, 3; 345.
Bĕsit, II. 215.
Clause, circumstantial, II. 72—73; as a genitive after a substantive, II. 58.
Concord in gender and number, II. 141 and foll.
Conjunctions, inseparable, I. 366; separable, I. 367.
Consonants, final, how affected by the *waṣl*, I. 20, 1.
Ḍamm, damma, I. 4.
Dates, II. 110—111.
Day of the month, II. 111.
Declension of undefined nouns, I. 308; of defined nouns, I. 313—316.
Degrees of comparison, I. 234—5.
Diminutives — in the verb, I. 184, rem. *d*; in the noun, I. 269—284.
Diphthongs, how affected by the *waṣl*, I. 20, 3.
Doubling of a consonant, how marked, I. 11.
Dual number in nouns, I. 299.

Elif productionis omitted in writing, I. 6, rem. *a*; élif omitted in writing, I. 19, rem. *a*, and 21; élif conjunctionis, I. 19, rem. *d*. and *e*; élif separationis, I. 19, rem. *e*; élif maksūra, I. 7, rem. *b*, and 23, rem. *a*; élif mémduda, I. 7, rem. *b*, and 23, rem. *a*.
Energetic, its use, II. 11; after ﺝ, II. 19, 1; in commands and prohibitions, II. 19, 2; in the apodosis of correlative conditional clauses, II. 19, 3; after إِمَّا, II. 19, 4.
Enuntiative, II. 113.
Féth, fétha, I. 4.
Figures, arithmetical, I. 32.
Forms of praise, salutation, etc., II. 35.
Fractions, I. 336.
Future-perfect, how expressed, II. 10.
Genders, I. 81; gender of nouns, I. 289; fem., I. 290; masc. or fem., I. 292; formation of the fem., I. 293 – 297.
Genitive, II. 76—79; 92; 95; supplying the place of an adjective, II. 80; after كُلّ, II. 82, 1; after

Index.

جَمِيع, II. 82, 2; after بَعْض,
II. 82, 3; after غَيْر, II. 82, 4;
after لَا, II. 82, 4, rem. *a*; after
سِوَى, II. 82, 5; after مِثْل, II.
82, 6; after وَ, فَ and بَلْ, II.
85; after أَيْ, II. 87; of limitation, after adjectives, II. 89;
genitive plural after numerals,
II. 96; genitive singular after
مِائَة and أَلْف, II. 103.

Gézm, gézma, I. 9.
Halíf, II. 221.
Hazég, II. 208.
Hèmz, hèmza, I. 15.
Imperative, I. 98; in the first of
two correlative conditional clauses, II. 13; negative, how expressed, II. 20; negative, expressed
by the jussive, II. 17, 2, and 20.
Imperfect, formation of the, I. 91—
93; indicative, I. 95; subjunctive, I. 95; jussive, I. 95; energetic,
I. 97; passive, I. 100; subjunctive
or potential, how expressed, II. 4;
significations of the imperfect,
II. 8; as a حَال, may be translated by our infinitive or participle, II. 8, *d* and *e*; preceded
V. II.

by كَان, expresses the Latin
and Greek imperfect, II. 9; preceded by يَكُونُ قَدْ or يَكُونُ
expresses the future-perfect,
II. 10.

Inchoative, II. 113; 127.
Infinitive, I. 60.
Interjections, I. 368.
Interrogations, II. 164 and foll.
Jussive, after لَم and لَمَّا = the
perfect, II. 12; after إِنْ = the
perfect, II. 13; in two correlative conditional clauses = the
perfect, II. 13; after لِ, II. 17, 1;
after لَا in prohibitions, II. 17, 2;
in correlative conditional clauses, II. 17, 3; after لَم and لَمَّا,
II. 18.

Kāmil, II. 206.
Kèsr, kèsra, I. 4.
Letters of the alphabet, I. 1; order
in North Africa, I. 1, rem. *b*;
pronunciation, I. 2; letters of
prolongation, I. 6; solar letters,
I. 14, rem.; lunar letters, I. 14,
rem.; numerical value of the
letters, I. 32; weak letters, I.
53, rem., and 127.

40

Licenses, poetic, II. 231 and foll.
Ligatures, L 1, rem. c.
Literae productionis, L 6.
Médd, médda, I. 22.
Médīd, II. 220.
Metres, II. 200 and foll.; iambic, II. 203; antispastic, II. 208; amphibrachic, II. 209; anapaestic, II. 213; ionic, II. 218.
Moods, L 18.
Mudāri, II. 212.
Muḡtétt, II. 222.
Mukţadab, II. 217.
Munsariḥ, II. 216.
Mutédārik, II. 214.
Mutékārib, II. 210.
Nebra, L 15.
Nomina actionis, L 195—218; vicis, L 219; speciei, L 220; loci et temporis, L 221—227; instrumenti, L 228; agentis et patientis, L 229—245; unitatis, L 246; abundantiae vel multitudinis, L 247; vasis, L 248; relativa, L 249—267; nomina verbi, their government, II. 27—29; nomina agentis, their construction, II. 30; nomina patientis, followed by an accusative, II. 32; nomina verbi, agentis et patientis, II. 68.

Noun, L 190; primitive, L 191; derivative, L 191; abstract nouns of quality, L 268; triptote, L 308; diptote, L 308; declinable, L 308; indeclinable, L 308; diptote, L 309; indeclinable, L 309, 3, h, and rem. b; defined in various ways, L 313.
Numbers, L 81; 298.
Numerals, cardinal, L 318—327; gender of the cardinal numbers, L 319; ordinal, L 328; construction of, II. 96—111; arrangement in compound numbers, II. 104; agreement of, II. 106; ordinal, with the genitive, II. 108—109.
Nunation, L 8.
Participles, L 80.
Particles, L 354; negative, II. 153 and foll.
Perfect—passive, L 100; contracted form of, L 163, rem. b; its significations, II. 1; equivalent to the past, II. 1, a; to the perfect, II. 1, b; used to indicate the absolute certainty of a future

act, II. 1, *e*; equivalent to the optative, II. 1, *f*; preceded by قَدْ, its significations, II. 2, and 3, *b*; preceded by كَانَ or كَانَ قَدْ = pluperfect, II. 3, *c* and *d*; equivalent to imperfect or pluperfect subjunctive or potential, II. 4; after إِذَا, takes the meaning of the imperfect, II. 5; after إِنْ, takes a future sense, II. 6, *a*, unless كَانَ be interposed, II. 6, *b*; its use in correlative conditional clauses, II. 6, *b*; after مَا آلَّذِي يَمُومَهُ, takes the signification of the imperfect, II. 7; expressed by the jussive after لَمْ and لَمَّا, II. 12.

Persons, L. 81.

Pluperfect, how expressed, II. 3; subjunctive or potential, how expressed, II. 4.

Plural number, L. 300; secondary plurals, L. 305, rem. *c*; anomalous do., L. 305, rem. *e*; plurals of abundance, and of paucity, I. 307.

Pluralis sanus, L. 301; pl. sanus masc., when formed, L. 302; pl. sanus fem., when formed, L. 303; pl. fractus of triliterals, L. 304; of quadriliterals, etc., L. 305; pl. fractus, how declined, L. 308; pl. sanus, how declined, L. 308.

Prose, rhymed, II. 223.

Pause, forms of words in, II. 223 and foll.

Predicate, II. 112; 115 and foll.

Prepositions, L. 355; II. 46—67; inseparable, L. 356; separable, L. 357—359; ل after a nomen actionis, II. 29; ل after a nomen agentis, II. 31; ellipsis of, II. 67, rem. *b*.

Pronouns — personal, separate, L. 89, 1; suffixed, expressing the nom., L. 89, 2; prefixed, expressing the nom., L. 89, 3; suffixed, expressing the accus., L. 185, expressing the genit., L. 317; personal, compound, L. 188 — 189; demonstratives L. 340—344; relative, L. 346—350; interrogative, L. 351—353; reflexive, II. 135.

Ragez, II. 204.

Ramel, II. 219.

Rhyme, II. 191 and foll.; forms of words in rhyme, II. 223 and foll.

Root, secondary, derived from verbs of which the first radical is a weak letter, L. 139, rem.; 148, rem. b.

San', II. 205.

Sentence — nominal, II. 113; verbal, II. 113; compound, II. 119, 120; relative, II. 172; copulative, II. 176 and foll.; adversative, II. 184; restrictive, II. 185; exceptive, II. 186; conditional, II. 187 — 189; hypothetical, II. 189.

Sila, L. 18.

States or Tenses of the verb, L. 77.

Subject, II. 112 and foll.

Subjunctive of the imperfect after أَنْ, لَنْ, كَيْ, etc., II. 11; after أَنْ, II. 15, 1, a; after لِ, لِأَنْ, كَيْ, II. 15, 2; after حَتَّى, II. 15, 3, a; after فَ, II. 15, 4; after وَ, II. 15, 5; after أَوْ, II. 15, 6; after إِذَنْ or إِذًا, II. 15, 7.

Sukûn, L. 9; II. 198, note.

Superlatives construed with a genitive, II. 93.

Syllable, open, L. 24; shut, L. 25.

Tawil, II. 211.

Tènwìn, L. 8.

Tèsdìd, L. 11; necessary, L. 13; euphonic, L. 14.

Verbs — triliteral, L. 33; various forms of, L. 35; first or ground form, L. 36—38; second, L. 39—41; third, L. 42—43; fourth, L. 44—45; fifth, L. 46—48; sixth, L. 49, 50; seventh, L. 51—53; eighth, L. 54—57; ninth and eleventh, L. 58—59; tenth, L. 60—65; twelfth, thirteenth, fourteenth and fifteenth forms, L. 66. — Quadriliteral, their formation, L. 67; first form, L. 69; derived forms, L. 70 — 72. — States or Tenses, L. 77; moods, L. 78; numbers, L. 81; persons, l. 81; 89, 2 and 3; distinction of gender in the persons, L. 81. — Weak, L. 82; 126—129; strong, L. 82—83; of which the second and third radicals are identical, L. 119—125; of which one radical is ا, l. 130—140; of which the first radical is و or ى, L. 142—148; of which the second radical is و or ى, l. 149—163; 184, rem. b; of which the third radical is و or ى, L. 161 — 170; doubly weak, L. 171—181; negative substantive verb, L. 182; verbs of praise and blame, L. 183; of wonder, L. 184; substantive verb, II. 122; impersonal form of expression, II. 132—133.

Vocative, expressed by the nom., II. 38, 1, *a*, and 2, 3; by the accus., II. 38, 1, *b*, and 3.

Voices, active, L. 73; passive, L. 74.

Vowels, long, L. 3; short, L. 4; their pronunciation. L. 5 — 7; final, how affected by the *waṣl*, l. 20, 1, 2.

Wāfir, II. 207.

Waṣl, waṣla, L. 18.

ADDITIONS AND CORRECTIONS.

Vol. I.

To §. 1. add the following remark.

Rem. d. Those letters which are identical in form, and distinguished from one another in writing only by the aid of the small dots usually called *diacritical points* (نُقْطَةٌ, plur. نُقَطٌ), are divided by the grammarians into اَلْحُرُوفُ ٱلْمُهْمَلَةُ, the *loose* or *free*, i. e. unpointed, letters, and اَلْحُرُوفُ ٱلْمُعْجَمَةُ, the *bolted* or *fastened*, i. e. pointed, letters. To the former class belong ط, ص, س, ر, ذ, ح and ع; to the latter خ, ز, ذ, ش, ض, ظ and غ. The letters ب, ت, ث and ى are generally distinguished as follows.

ب is called اَلْبَآءُ ٱلْمُوَحَّدَةُ, the ب *with one point* (ب);
ت „ „ اَلتَّآءُ ٱلْمُثَنَّاةُ مِنْ فَوْقِهَا, the ب *with two points above* (ت);
ى „ „ اَلْيَآءُ ٱلْمُثَنَّاةُ مِنْ تَحْتِهَا, the ب *with two points below* (ي);
ث „ „ اَلثَّآءُ ٱلْمُثَلَّثَةُ, the ب *with three points* (ث).

The unpointed letters are sometimes still farther distinguished from the pointed ones by various contrivances, such as writing the letter in a smaller size below the line, placing a point below, or an angular mark above it, and the like; so that we find in carefully written manuscripts ص, ض; س, ش; ر, ز; ذ, د; ح, خ; ع, غ; etc. Also هٜ or هۭ by way of distinction from ة.

Additions and Corrections. 319

§. 2. Under the letter ا (p. 4), delete the word *mobile*, and to the Hebrew examples add יֹאכַל. — Under the letter ه (p. 6), instead of أهل, *ahl*, write أَهْلَكَ, *'ahlaka*.

§. 6. Rem. *a*. On p. 9, l. 7, there is a misprint of ثَلُثَة for ثَلُثَة. — The long vowel *i* is in a very few instances written defectively at the end of a word; e. g. حُذَيْفَة, الْحَافِ *el-Ḥāfi*, الْعَاصِ *el-'Âṣi*, الْيَمَانِى *el-Yemâni*, بْنُ الْيَمَانِ *bnu 'l-Yemâni*, for الْحَافِي, الْعَاصِى, الْيَمَانِى. — To this section add:

Rem. *b*. The letter ه, preceded by damma, is used by the Arabs of North Africa and Spain to indicate a final *o* in foreign words; e. g. قَارْلُه, *Carlo*; دُون بِطْرُه, *Don Pedro*; وَادِى آرُه, *the river Guadiaro*.

Rem. *c*. The sound of ا inclines, in later times and in certain localities, from *â* to *ê*, just as that of fètḥa does from *a* to *e* (see §. 4, 1, and §. 5, 2). This change is called الْإِمَالَة, *el-'imâla*, the inflection of the sound of *a* and *â* towards that of *i* and *î*. The Maġribi Arabs actually pronounce *â* in many cases as *i*. Hence رِكَاب *rikâb*, لِكِن *lâkin*, بَاب *bâb*, لِسَان *lisân*, are sounded *rikêb*, *lekin*, *bîb*, *lisîn*; and, conversely, the Spanish names *Beja*, *Jaen*, *Caniles*, *Lebrilla*, are written بَاجَه, جَيَّان, تَنَالَش, لَبْرَالَه.

§. 8, rem. *b*. The و of عَمْرُو and عَمْرٍو is often neglected in old manuscripts.

§. 10. Add the following:

Rem. In many manuscripts a ǧezma is placed even over the letters of prolongation ا, و and ى; e. g. سِيمَ, صَبُورْ, قَالْ.

§. 11, rem. *d*. In the oldest and most carefully written manuscripts, the form of the tesdîd is ش. Its opposite is حف, i. e. خف (from

مُخَفَّف, *lightened, single*), e. g. سِرًّا وَعَلَانِيَةً, *secretly and openly.*

§. 11, rem. e. ـٓ is used occasionally for ـٔ as well as ـٕ.

§. 14, 1. After اَللَّيْل add: "or, in African and Spanish manuscripts, اَلَّيْل."

§. 17, 2 (p. 16, line 15). Write خَطِئَة for خَطِيئَة.

§. 20, 4. What is here said of the preposition مَعَ is not quite accurate. The classical form is مَعَ, with final fetha, abbreviated in later times into مَعْ; but the fetha is always retained in the waṣl, and hence we read مَعَ اَبْنِهِ, مَعَ اَلرَّجُلِ, and not مَعِ ابْنِهِ.

§. 21, 2. Delete the words "or mother", and the example عِيسَى بْنُ مَرْيَمَ, *Jesus the son of Mary."*

§. 21, 4. We also find ٱلْآنَ ٱلْمَآءُ (el-Korʾān, X. 52), and the like.

§. 22. In the oldest and best manuscripts the form of the medda is ـــــ (i. e. مدّ). Its opposite is ـــــ (i. e. قَصْر, *shortening*), though this is but rarely written.

§. 23, rem. b. For "not unfrequently" write "occasionally".

§. 23, rem. c. A medda is also written over the final vowels of the pronominal forms أَنْتُمْ, كُمْ, هُ or هُ, هِمْ or هُمْ, and the verbal termination تُمْ, when they are used as long in poetry.

§. 23, rem. d. Add the following abbreviations: تَعَ for تَعَالَى, *may He (God) be exalted!* for اِلَى آخِرِهَا or اِلَى آخِرِهِ اَلخ, *to the end of it, i. e. etc.*; م م, written over two words that have been erroneously transposed in a manuscript, for مُؤَخَّر, *to be placed last*, and مُقَدَّم, *to be placed first.* — On the margin of Mss. we often find words with the letters خ

Additions and Corrections.

ں and صح over them. The first of these indicates a variant, and stands for نُسْخَةٌ, *a copy*, *another manuscript*; the second means that a word has been indistinctly written in the text, and is repeated more clearly on the margin (بَيَانٌ, *explanation*); the third implies that the marginal reading, and not that of the text, is, in the writer's opinion, the correct one (صَحَّ, *it is correct*, or تَصْحِيحٌ, *correction, emendation*). Written over a word in the text, صح stands for صَحَّ, and denotes that the word is correct, though there may be something peculiar in its form or vocalization.

§. 26. Add to the examples: أَفْلَاطُونُ, Πλάτων, *Plato*.

§. 45, rem. c. Compare the Hebrew הֵימִין, *to go to the right* (يَمِنَ, يَمِينٌ), and הִשְׂמְאִיל, *to go to the left* (شِمَال, شَأْمَل). — To the general remarks add at the end:

These, however, are treated in Arabic as quadriliterals, imperf. مُهَيْمِنٌ, مُهَرَاقٌ or مُهْرَاقٌ, nom. patient. يُهَيْمِنُ, يُهْرِيقُ or يُهَرِيقُ.

§. 50. Additional examples: تَخَادَعَ, *to pretend to be deceived*; تَمَارَضَ, *to pretend to be sick*.

§. 53. General Rem. The original vowel *a* is sometimes retained in Hebrew, under the influence of an initial guttural; as נַעֲשֶׂה, נֶחֱזֶה.

§. 59. Additional examples: اِرْمَدَّ, *to be ash-coloured*, *to be gloomy*; اِرْفَضَّ, *to flow freely* (of tears); اِرْقَدَّ, *to make great haste*; اِشْعَانَّ, *to be dishevelled* (of hair).

§. 65. Additional example: اِسْتَقْضَى, *to appoint as kâdi or magistrate* (قَاضٍ).

§. 89. 1, rem. b. For "often" read "almost always."

§. 91, rem. After the word يَبْلُغُ insert as additional examples: يَقْعُدُ, *to sit*; يَطْعُنُ, *to thrust, stab*, طَعَنَ.

§. 120. A very few of the verba med. rad. gemin. remain uncon-

Additions and Corrections.

tracted; at least the Kâmûs specifies such forms as رَكَكَتِ ٱلسَّمَآءُ, *a small thick rain fell*; ضَبِبَتِ ٱلْأَرْضُ, *the spot abounded with lizards*; لَحِحَتِ ٱلْعَيْنُ, *the eye is sore*.

§. 120, rem. *a*, 1. Add to the examples, رَدَدْتَ for رَدَدْتُ.

§. 133. The rule requires some alteration. Read:

In the same way, ا passes into وُ or ىِ, when it is pronounced with damma or kèsra, and preceded by fètha, or with fètha, and preceded by damma or kèsra; and into ىِ, when it is pronounced with kèsra, and preceded by damma.

Examples of the last part of the rule are: سُئِلَ, *he is asked*, for سُأِلَ, perf. pass. of سَأَلَ, *to ask*; لُوئِمَ, *peace is made (between them)*, for لُؤِمَ, perf. pass. III. of لَأَمَ, *to join together*.

§. 139, rem. For تَخَذَ read تَخِذَ, with kèsra.

§. 140. After the words "سَأَلَ for سَالَ" add: "2. p. sing. m. سِلْتَ."

§. 154. Some of the Arabs contracted قُولَ and بُيِعَ into قُولَ and بُوعَ, instead of قِيلَ and بِيعَ.

§. 160. Additional example: غَيِدَ, *to be soft and flexible*, يَفْيَدُ.

§. 163. General Remarks. The Arabs sometimes contract into نَامْ, just as in Hebrew קָם for קָאֵם; e. g. هَاعْ لَاعْ, for هَائِعْ لَائِعْ, *feeble*, هَارْ, for هَائِرْ, *timid*.

§. 167, 2, c. For تَرْمِي read تَرْمِ, with gèzm.

§. 170 (p. 90, line 2). Read "though مَرْضِيٌّ is far more common."

§. 175. rem. Compare the Syriac imperative ܐܺܙܶܠ.

§. 186, 3. The same thing happens to the 2. p. sing. fem.; e. g. تُشَوِّقِينِي, *thou makest me long*, for تُشَوِّقِينِينِي.

Additions and Corrections.

§. 186, 5. Read: "(which is far more usual)."

§. 198, rem. *a*. Additional example: نَظَرَ, *to see, look at*, نَظَرْ.

§. 199. Delete the words "رَنْعَةٌ and."

§. 220. Read: "It is often placed." Additional examples: جِلْسَةٌ, مِشْيَةٌ, رِكْبَةٌ, *one's manner of sitting, riding, walking*.

§. 224. The nouns of time and place derived from verba tert. rad. و et ى violate the rule laid down in §. 221, for they always take *fetha* in the second syllable, whatever be the vowel of the imperfect.

§. 226. Delete the words "et ى". Add the remark:

This is the usual form in Ethiopic from all verbs; as: ምሥራቅ: *misrâk* = مَشْرِقٌ, *the east*; ምዕራብ: *miʿrâb* = مَغْرِبٌ, *the west*; ምርዓይ: *mirʿây* = مَرْعًى, *pasture ground*.

§. 228. The examples مِقْوَدٌ and مِزْوَدَةٌ show that this form of noun, when derived from verba med. rad. و et ى, does not undergo contraction.

§. 228, rem. *a*. Additional example: مُنْصُلٌ, *a sword*. These words may also take *fetha* in the second syllable; as: مُنْصَلٌ, مُنْتَحَلٌ.

§. 230. After "مَكْتُوبٌ, *written*", add "*a letter*."

§. 231. The nomen patientis, not only of the first, but also of the derived conjugations, is occasionally used in the sense of the nomen actionis; e. g. بَذَلَ مَجْهُودَهُ, *he exerted himself to the utmost, did his best* (= جَهْدَهُ); إِلَى ٱللهِ ٱلْمُشْتَكَى وَٱلْمُعَوَّلُ, *to God complaint is made and (in him) trust is placed*.

§. 233, rem. *b*. Read: جَمَاعَةٌ لِلْكُتُبِ.

§. 235. Read: "(el-Korʾân II. 69)."

§. 254, rem. *c*. There is a third adjective of this kind, namely تَهَامٍ (with the art. ٱلتَّهَامِى), fem. تَهَامِيَةٌ, from تَهَامَةٌ, *Tihâma*.

§. 255, rem. a. Additional example: جَزِيرِيّ, *belonging to Alge-ziras*, اَلْجَزِيرَة, *in Spain* (to distinguish it from جَزَرِيّ, *belonging to Mesopotamia*).

§. 259, rem. From حَرُورَآء is formed حَرُورِيّ. — With بَهْرَانِيّ from بَهْرَآء, and صَنْعَانِيّ from اَلصَّنْعَآء, compare the Hebrew forms שִׁילֹנִי, from שִׁילֹה, and גִּילֹנִי, from גִּילֹה.

§. 269, rem. c. This view is confirmed, as regards the Hebrew words, by the modern pronunciation of North Africa, where, for example, قُفَيْفَة, the diminutive of قُفَّة, *a basket*, is pronounced *k'fîfè* or *g'fîfè*, — in post-biblical Hebrew קוּפָּה and קְפִיפָה.

§. 274, rem. c. بَحْر, *the sea, a lake*, makes بُحَيْرَة.

§. 291. Add: شَاة, *a sheep*, شُوَيْهَة. — For مُدَيْع and تُوَيْض read مُدَيِّع and تُوَيِّض.

§. 293. Read سُوَيْك for سُوَيْك.

§. 294, rem. Add: دُخَان, *smoke*, دُوَيْخِن.

§. 291. Read مُوَيْسَى, *razor*, instead of مُوسَى.

§. 292, 3. After فُلْك, *ship*, add: قِدْر (gen. fem.), *pot*. — For *intestines*, read: مِعًى, *an intestine*.

§. 295, rem. b. For *last* read *other*.

§. 302, rem. a. After "plur. sanus" add "masc."

§. 303, 6, rem. Add: إِسْنَاد, *a chain of authorities*, أَسَانِيد. Alter no. 10 as follows: All diminutives (except those specified in §. 302, 1), even when masculine.

§. 304. VI. 1. Add: دَلْو, *a bucket*, دُلَيّ or دِلِيّ (for دُلُوِيّ).

§. 304. VI. 2. Add: عَصَا (for عَصَوّ), *a staff*, عُصَيّ or عِصِيّ (for عُصُوِيّ).

Additions and Corrections.

§. 304. XIII. 2 (p. 172, last line). Read: نُفْلٌ, *a lock*.

§. 304. XVI. 2 (p. 175, last line). Read غَارِبٌ for غَارِبٌ.

§. 304. XVIII. 2. Add: أَخٌ (for أَخَوٌ), *a brother*, إِخْوَانٌ. — After no. 5, add:

6. ظَلِيمٌ: قَضْبَانٌ (rare): as قَضِيبٌ, *a twig or rod*, صِبْيَانٌ (for صَبِيوٌ), *a boy*, ظِلْمَانٌ; صَبِيٌّ, *a male ostrich*.

In the remark delete the words أَخٌ and صَبِيٌّ.

305. II. (p. 186, l. 2). After أَكَالِيلُ add: أُرْجُوزَةٌ, *a poem in the metre rağéz*, أَرَاجِيزُ: أُمْنِيَّةٌ (for أُمْنُوِيَةٌ), *a wish*, أَمَانِيٌّ. — Rem. *b*. Add: إِيوَانٌ, *a portico*, أَزَاوِينُ (as if from a sing. إِوَانٌ); and after أَتُّونٌ insert "(by assimilation for أَتْنُونٌ)".

§. 305. III. 1. After اُسْتَاذٌ insert "(Pers.)"; and after تِلْمِيذٌ, "(Heb. תַּלְמִיד)".

§. 305, rem. *c* After the words "by adding اتٌ —ٌ;" insert: "or changing ةٌ —َ into اتٌ —َ", and add the examples: شَرَابٌ, *a drink*, pl. أَشْرِبَةٌ, pl. pl. أَشْرِبَاتٌ; عَطَاءٌ, *a gift, pay*, pl. أَعْطِيَةٌ, pl. pl. أَعْطِيَاتٌ.

§. 306. Delete the words "ٱلْعُثْمَانِيَّةُ, *the whole race of Othman*."

§. 308 (p. 192, l. 9). Read نُوحٌ.

§. 308. General Remarks. On p. 195, l. 21, I have said that "the absolute form ־ֵ, ־ַ, is difficult to account for". It bears, however, exactly the same relation to ־ִין, ־ִי, ־ָן, וּן, that the verbal form יִקְטְלוּן to תִּמְכִי, מֵיכִי, קָטְלָן does to קָטְלִין (see p. 53), or יִקְטְלָן, תִּמְכָן (see p. 54).

§. 309, 2, *c*. Add أَوَّلُ, the plur. fract. of أَوَّلُ, *first*, and of its fem. أُولَى: and also جُمَعُ, the plur. of جُمْعَاءُ, fem. of أَجْمَعُ, *all* (see vol. II. §. 137).

§. 318, rem. a. ثَمَانِيَةٌ is also written defectively ثَمَنِيَةٌ.

§. 322. In these compound numbers some of the Arabs pronounce عَشْرَةٌ instead of عَشَرَةٌ.

§. 323, rem. a. ثَمَانُونَ is also written defectively ثَمَنُونَ.

§. 328, rem. a. Read أَوَّلُ instead of أُوَّلُ in both places.

§. 342 (p. 216, last line). Delete the *médda* over أُولَاكَ.

§. 343, rem. a. Read: "تِلْكَ is a contraction for تِيلِكَ."

§. 347, rem. a. Read: "The other forms, which are not in such constant use, generally retain" etc.

§. 351, rem. See vol. II. §. 229.

§. 358. The preposition عَلَى should be transferred from §. 359 to its proper place in this section, after حَتَّى. — In rem. b, after the words "1. pers.", add "sing.", and delete the examples عَنَّا, مِنَّا and لَدُنَّا.

§. 362, 12. Correct this article as follows:

بَلْ, *nay, on the contrary.* — بَلَى, a particle used in replying to a negative statement or question, when the speaker wishes to affirm the contrary; as: لَمْ يَقُمْ زَيْدٌ, *Zeid did not stand up,* بَلَى, *but (I say) he did* (scil. قَدْ قَامَ); أَلَمْ يَقُمْ زَيْدٌ, *did Z. not stand up?* بَلَى, *he did.*

§. 362, 14. Delete the form ثَمَّتَ.

§. 362, 25. Add: "This particle is used in replying affirmatively to a preceding statement or question, whether expressed in positive or negative terms; as: قَامَ زَيْدٌ, *Zeid stood up,* نَعَمْ, *yes (he did);* أَلَمْ يَقُمْ زَيْدٌ, *did Z. not stand up?* نَعَمْ, *he did not.*"

§. 367, 5. Read: "أَوْ .... أَوْ, or وَإِمَّا .... إِمَّا, *either .... or*".

§. 368, rem. a. After the words "the ending ‍َ—" insert "(sometimes written ى—)." — Rem. d. For يَأْبَنُ write يَأْبِنُ, and for "generally" substitute "often."

Additions and Corrections.

Page 213, last line. Read "(2. m. مَلِلْتَ)."

Page 253, last line. Read أُنْدُرونَانِ.

Page 257, line 9. After مُقَاضَاةٌ add تِقَآءٌ.

Vol. II.

§. 19, 4. Write اِهْبِطُوا.

§. 38, 2. Write يَاأَيَّهَا.

§. 39. To the examples add: دَوَابُّ ٱلْمَآءِ ٱلَّتِى لَا رِئَاتِ لَهَا, *the aquatic animals, which have no lungs*.

§. 44, 5. rem. b. After كَذَى add "(also written in Mss. كَذَى)."

§. 83, rem. b. Add: "We also occasionally find in Mss. the form كِيَى instead of كِلَّا."

§. 157, 4. Write "and إِنْ."

§. 229, rem. *a* and *b*. Write "(see §. 230)."

www.ingramcontent.com/pod-product-compliance
Lightning Source LLC
Chambersburg PA
CBHW031849220426
43663CB00006B/547